I0820521

THE LAST KINGS OF HOLLYWOOD

ALSO BY PAUL FISCHER

A Kim Jong-Il Production: The Extraordinary True Story of a Kidnapped Filmmaker, His Star Actress, and a Young Dictator's Rise to Power

The Man Who Invented Motion Pictures: A True Tale of Obsession, Murder, and the Movies

THE LAST KINGS OF HOLLYWOOD

. . . . .

COPPOLA · LUCAS · SPIELBERG
AND THE BATTLE FOR THE SOUL OF
AMERICAN CINEMA

PAUL FISCHER

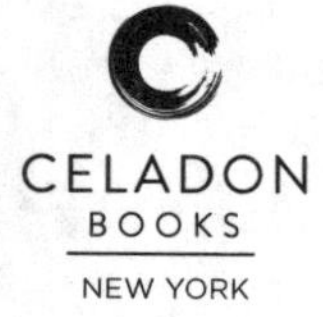

CELADON
BOOKS
NEW YORK

For Crosby

For information, address Celadon Books, a division of
Macmillan Publishers, 120 Broadway, New York, NY 10271.
EU Representative: Macmillan Publishers Ireland Ltd.,
1st Floor, The Liffey Trust Centre, 117–126 Sheriff Street
Upper, Dublin 1, D01 YC43.

www.celadonbooks.com

Designed by Michelle McMillian

Library of Congress Cataloging-in-Publication Data

Names: Fischer, Paul (Documentary film producer), author.
Title: The last kings of Hollywood : Coppola, Lucas, Spielberg—and the battle for the soul of American cinema / Paul Fischer.
Description: First edition. | New York : Celadon Books, 2026. | Includes bibliographical references and index.
Identifiers: LCCN 2025030207 | ISBN 9781250878724 (hardcover) | ISBN 9781250878762 (ebook)
Subjects: LCSH: Coppola, Francis Ford, 1939– | Lucas, George, 1944– | Spielberg, Steven, 1946– | Motion picture producers and directors—United States—Biography | LCGFT: Biographies
Classification: LCC PN1998.3.C69 F57 2026 | DDC 791.4302/33092 [B]—dc23/eng/20250804
LC record available at https://lccn.loc.gov/2025030207

First Edition: 2026

10 9 8 7 6 5 4 3

I am sitting on an airplane with the hors d'oeuvres plate on the folding table in front of me. Crab legs, cocktail sauce, mayonnaise, lettuce leaf, macadamia nuts, lemon wedge, parsley, a fork, paper napkin and a glass of water with ice cubes, all lit from the side window like a little still life. Francis is next to me. George Lucas is leaning over the seat in front of him. Steve Spielberg is across the aisle. Between them they hold the top three film grosses of all time. *Jaws* is number one. George just said that *Star Wars* will be number one at 7:05 next Saturday night. *Godfather* is number three. Between them, their films have grossed over a billion dollars. Steve calls them the billion boys. They are talking about the depression they felt after a big success.

—Eleanor Coppola, *Notes: On the Making of "Apocalypse Now"*

CONTENTS

PART THREE: COMPANY MEN

AUTHOR'S NOTE

This is a work of nonfiction.

Any passage presented between quotation marks is a direct quote from an interview, written account, diary, letter, transcript, or contemporary document. Quotes taken from conversations and interviews conducted by the author are tagged in the present tense. Quotes taken from primary and secondary sources are tagged in the past tense. If words are eliminated from the beginning, middle, or end of a single sentence, their absence is marked by an ellipsis; if a sentence or several sentences are omitted, the absence is marked by an ellipsis inside brackets. In all instances, I have endeavored to preserve the meaning of the quotation, as well as its voice and spirit. The sources for all quotations are recorded in the back of the book, along with the sources for any particular dates or details I have judged—if not arbitrarily, then more by instinct than by system—to necessitate "showing my work."

Whenever accounts of a particular incident differed in the memories of its various participants, I have endeavored to corroborate one or the other through third-party statements, documentation, or other evidence. None of the people interviewed for this book were given control over which of their words would appear in the text, or how they would appear.

Any errors herein are mine alone.

CELADON BOOKS

PRESENTS

THE LAST KINGS OF HOLLYWOOD

WRITTEN BY

PAUL FISCHER

EDITED BY

RYAN DOHERTY

EDITORIAL ASSISTANT

FAITH TOMLIN

MANAGING EDITORS

MORGAN MITCHELL

EMILY WALTERS

ART DIRECTOR

ERIN CAHILL

JACKET DESIGN

ALEX CAMLIN

INTERIOR DESIGN

MICHELLE McMILLIAN

COPY EDITOR

MARY BETH CONSTANT

PROOFREADERS

MARY LOUISE MOONEY

STEVEN ROMAN

INDEXER

LISA KLEINHOLZ

PRODUCTION MANAGER

VINCENT STANLEY

PRODUCTION EDITOR

RYAN T. JENKINS

MARKETING & PUBLICITY

SUSIE BRUSTIN
RACHEL CHOU
ALEX CRUZ-JIMENEZ
GREGG FLEISCHMAN
CHRISTINE MYKITYSHYN
JAIME NOVEN
EMILY RADELL
REBECCA RITCHEY
YELIZAVETA ROGULINA

AUDIOBOOK DIRECTOR

STEVE WAGNER

AGENTS FOR MR. FISCHER

JENNY HEWSON
MACKENZIE BRADY WATSON

FOREIGN RIGHTS FOR MR. FISCHER

PREMA RAJ
LILY EVANS

INTRODUCTION

Hollywood's biggest year ever turned out to be the same year it lost its head. It works out that way, sometimes. A screenwriter will tell you the best ending is the one that has a beginning sown into it. Or, in this case, the best beginning is the one that carries its own ending within it.

The Hollywood studio system had been the greatest, and most American, of American achievements. A dream factory built in a single generation by a resourceful melting pot of immigrants, making magic for the masses, generating global goodwill.

The eight major studios—20th Century Fox, Columbia, Metro-Goldwyn-Mayer, Paramount, RKO, United Artists, Universal, Warner Bros.—reported record profits in 1947. The studios had directors, stars, and crew under binding long-term agreements. They decided what films were made and how. They owned the cinemas. Even World War II had been good for them; every picture sold out and played three, four, six months. Jack Warner, the loudest and most vulgar of the brothers, boasted that those early decades were like "manufacturing money." Men like Jack had the last word and they prioritized the bottom line.

Those men grew arrogant. Greedy. Oligarchies are the death of innovation.

Studio workers went on strike for better conditions, and their bosses hired strikebreakers and violent security—and lost. Movie star Olivia de Havilland took Warner to court for the right to break her seven-year contract, and Jack tried to blackball her—and failed. Other stars followed her lead and broke for freedom. In October 1947, Warner appeared in Congress as a "friendly" witness to the House Committee on Un-American Activities, along with MGM head Louis B. Mayer and B-movie actor and FBI informant Ronald Reagan, and a month later, Warner and Mayer put their names to a joint statement from the Hollywood moguls, blacklisting the writers and directors, collectively known as the Hollywood Ten, HUAC had held in contempt for refusing to collaborate. Intended as a show of power, it marked the start of a decade of paranoia, division, and recrimination in the film industry. Six months later, the Supreme Court ruled that studios could no longer own their cinemas, separating the making of motion pictures from their exhibition. By the end of that year, 1948, the studios' profits had been cut in half.

Television came into American living rooms. European countries imposed quotas and levies on American pictures to protect their own national film industries. The studio system, whereby a handful of big studios controlled the entire pipeline of screen entertainment, was dead—torn down, in less than two years, by the cruelty and hubris of the men who had made it.

"What's that saying?" asked Jack's son, Junior, many years later. "Power corrupts, absolute power corrupts absolutely. I always think of my father when I hear that. He was the man who fights to get up the trail to the mountaintop and when he gets there rolls rocks down the trail to keep other people from joining him."

Jack Warner, who would be the last of the original moguls still standing, sat at the top of his mountain and rolled the boulders down.

He heard the wind of change and figured he could fight it. In the valley below, his fiefdom crumbled.

"An era ended," wrote critic Charles Champlin, "a marvellous era; a new day commenced, darkly."

Part One

THE OUTSIDERS

· 1 ·

TWENTY YEARS LATER

George Lucas walked through the gates of Warner Bros. the exact same day Jack Warner walked out—at least, that's how George liked to tell it. After twenty years of steady decline, Warner had just sold the place to upstart Canadian businessmen. George drove in through the gates of the lot in the morning and Jack left out of them in the afternoon. One event didn't cause the other, but they weren't, in the great scheme of things, unrelated. By late July 1967, the studios were on their last legs. Kids like George Lucas were a Hail Mary pass: a desperate, last-gasp attempt to do something about it.

George, a brand-new graduate of the University of Southern California's cinema department, had just turned twenty-three. He was short and skinny and jug-eared, and hid much of his face behind square eyeglasses and a tight, scrupulously shaped black beard. He wore simple clothes in plain, often dark colors. He was handsome in a preppy, boyish kind of way, and though shy, he was vocally sure of his ideas, if not socially confident in himself. His taste tilted to the artsy. He loved the serious documentaries produced by the National Film Board of Canada, for instance, and the experimental films popular on the underground circuit, films he thought of as "abstract mood poems." He had started working with a camera in his late teens, shooting high-speed car races around his Northern California hometown of Modesto, and had lately been gaining experience cutting propaganda films for the US government. He wanted to make films that moved an audience without the need for story or character. Friends described him as having "the temperament of an artist who works alone in an attic." He was not, in other words, the kind of film student who longed to work at Warner Bros., the historical home of Humphrey Bogart and James Cagney, of gangsters and musicals and the Looney Tunes.

The truth was, he'd won a contest. The Sam Warner Scholarship. Warner Bros. gave it every year to a film student of distinction, and it granted the winner a six-month work-experience contract at the studio. George and his friend and film school classmate Walter Murch had been the two finalists. When they'd met in the hallway before their final interviews, Murch—a rangy, brainy kid from New York—was playing with a pair of mewling kittens, and he asked George if he'd adopt one. Winning the scholarship wasn't all-consuming to Walter. The same couldn't be said about his friend. "Look," George said, eyeing the animals, "one of us is going to get this—and the other one isn't. Whoever does get it, turns around and helps the other if something good comes along."

They shook on it. George won the scholarship, and took home one of the cats. Walter took a position doing odd jobs for Encyclopaedia Britannica Educational Films, and waited for George to call.

First on Lucas's agenda that first day was a tour of the studio. "Traditionally," he remembered later, "what a student did is go there, and he could choose what department he wanted to be in. You know, the editorial department, script department, whatever." George asked to be assigned to the animation department, where he was least likely to have to deal with other human beings.

A staffer led him around the lot. It was "completely empty." They wandered quiet, potholed paths between idle soundstages. The paint on the buildings was peeling. The animation building stood deserted save for a caretaker, employed to keep an eye on the equipment no one was using. Seven Arts, the production company that had bought the studio, hadn't quite got going yet.

As a result, said George, "my choices of what I was going to do were extremely limited." Only one solitary picture was filming on the lot: a Broadway musical adaptation by the name of *Finian's Rainbow*, starring a sixty-eight-year-old Fred Astaire, dragged out of semiretirement to dance on the big screen for the first time in a decade. The crew were, just then, shooting a big number down in the jungle, the adaptable outdoor set at the bottom of the backlot. The *Finian's* crew had turned it into the script's main fictional location: Rainbow Valley, Missitucky, to which Astaire's cheeky Irish rogue absconds with a pot of gold stolen from a leprechaun.

George winced deeper with every new word of the film's description. The thing sounded like his worst nightmare.

"They're the only people on the lot," the Warner Bros. employee repeated.

They assigned George to watch the shoot. Maybe he'd learn a thing or two.

George had only ever come near a feature film set once before, earlier that summer, way out on location in Page, Arizona: *Mackenna's Gold*, a Columbia Pictures Western starring Gregory Peck and Edward G. Robinson, and directed by J. Lee Thompson, an English director in his fifties. An old-Hollywood picture made by old-Hollywood people—the cinematographer, Joseph MacDonald, had started out in nineteen *thirty*-one—for a sizeable $7 million budget. Via more "scholarships," producer Carl Foreman had picked four film school graduates—two from USC, two from UCLA—to come on location for six weeks and each make a ten-minute documentary about the production.

George's peers went along with Foreman's brief: One made a little film about the cowboy horse wranglers, one made a little film on director Thompson, one made a little film about Foreman himself. George, on the other hand, spent his time shooting a four-and-a-half-minute tone poem in the desert. Shots of the orange sun dissolving into close-ups of dry grass and humming transmission towers. Clouds moving in marshmallow time lapse over the barren landscape. George was desperate to direct motion pictures, but this was the only kind of movie he wanted to make. Not Hollywood. Hollywood was calcified, boring. Its idea of creativity was *The Sound of Music*. George hadn't particularly cared for movies as a child, anyway. His loves had been loud music and fast cars, stuff that made you *feel*. He'd have been a race car driver, if he hadn't crashed his souped-up Autobianchi Bianchina as a high school senior, wrapped himself around a tree and nearly died. That had cured him of his need for speed, and only after that had he fallen in love with film—but underground film, direct cinema, avant-garde, 16mm.

He rode back to California with the other three students at the end of June, with his experimental movie in his bag and $800 in his back pocket—almost the entire salary that came with the Columbia scholarship, and which he'd dutifully saved rather than spent. George was like that, too. Cautious. Convinced, also, that he was destined for something bigger. He'd held that conviction ever since he'd survived that car crash. He should have died. Three days before his high school graduation, a mediocre student, living an uneasy peace with a strong-willed, conservative father. Spending his nights cruising up and down the Modesto streets, listening to the radio, drag racing, looking for girls. Nothing on the horizon except more road, one night at a time.

Then came that afternoon. Driving back home from the library, a little fast, in the yellow Autobianchi convertible with the engine he'd punched up himself. An illegal left turn into the road to the family ranch, a Chevy Impala—also driven by a careless seventeen-year-old—roaring in at ninety miles an hour from the opposite direction, wide and *fast*, filling his field of vision. Smashing into George's cartoon minicar, which suddenly felt as flimsy as it was. The Autobianchi flipped, rolled, bounced, like a ten-cent die-cast Midgetoy. The resonant, rib-cage-rattling crunch of metal grinding and ripping.

He should have died. The car only came to a stop when it smashed into a walnut tree by the side of the road. In the picture they showed him of the wreck when he woke up in the hospital, nearly two weeks later, his beloved roadster had looked beyond mangled, flipped upside down and twisted like a crushed Coke can against the tree, which had been half uprooted by the impact. His steering wheel was in the grass. His seat hung out, upside down, like a lolling tongue.

He should've died—only he'd been flung from the car on the third of its barreling rolls when his racing seat belt snapped, even though racing seat belts, bolted to the floor of the car, were specifically designed to keep the driver strapped against his seat in the event of a high-speed collision. Instead of remaining trapped inside the car, to be pulped by crumpling metal, George had been thrown free.

And *that* should have been when he died, pinned under the rolling vehicle or busted limp against a tree like a puppet with its strings cut. But the rail bar he'd had installed across the convertible, miraculously, shielded him just long enough for him to hit the ground with his chest—his shoulder blade breaking, his lungs bruising on impact, his consciousness knocked out of him. Bright blood poured down his face from a slice across his forehead.

By the time an ambulance arrived, George's heart had nearly stopped. His breathing was barely perceptible. Once loaded in the back of the ambulance, George started vomiting; his skin turned blue. It was nearly four miles to Modesto City Hospital. Six, seven minutes, even with the sirens blaring and the late-afternoon traffic clearing out of the way. A long time for a scrawny kid without a heartbeat.

And yet George Lucas had lived. An emergency blood transfusion, two weeks in intensive care, four months in a hospital bed—but he'd lived. As summer turned to fall turned to winter, as the rest of his class attended graduation and, weeks later, helped their families put up the Christmas decorations, George lay up in his bed at Modesto City and thought, "Maybe there's something else for me. Maybe there's a reason I survived this accident that nobody should have survived . . . I should be dead."

Every day was an "extra day" now, he decided—a "bonus." He had nothing to lose, he could do anything he wanted—because he must be meant for something different. Something *special.*

Why else would the universe conspire for him to live?

Finian's Rainbow wasn't special. The Warner Bros. employee sat George down in an empty office on the lot while they made the arrangements for him to observe the shoot. The minutes dragged. Outside was a mild, warm summer day, and here he was, five years after the accident, trapped again between four walls.

He considered how he might get something worthwhile out of this scholarship he had won. Writing was out of the question—George *hated* writing. He loved operating a camera, finding something beautiful and interesting to compose for the eye, and he loved editing, leaning over the cutting bed in the dark, handling the supple rolls of film, shaping an experience out of the reels. But camera and editorial were union departments, and the film guilds were a notorious catch-22 to get into. You needed a union credit to get in the union, but you need to be in the union to work on a union picture, which was the only way to get a union credit. All of which meant, in practice, that you didn't get in at all—unless you knew someone who already worked at the studio to grandfather you in. And once you were in the guild, that was the only job you could do anyway. An editor was an editor and a cameraman was a cameraman. That was one reason George had wanted to hang in the animation building: Animators, at least, made their own movies.

Maybe everyone had been right, George thought, *when they said there was no point in film school, and that you couldn't get a job in the industry.* Studios might give film students scholarships, but they had never given a film school graduate a picture to direct—never.

It was only the first morning of six months at Warner, and George was bored out of his mind already. The studio employee had left him with a call sheet for *Finian's Rainbow*—a list, issued every shooting day, of the scenes to be filmed; the cast, crew, and materials needed to shoot them; and the tentative start and end times for the work. George picked the form up, intending to read down the roll call of names, but he didn't make it past the first line.

It read: "Dir. Francis Coppola."

He knew the name. Every film student did. Francis Coppola was only five years older than George, but he was something of a legend already. As a theater student at Hofstra, he'd won awards for his directing and all but remodeled the college's entire drama department after himself. At UCLA film school, he'd made all the best films and earned a reputation as a screenwriter. One story went that he'd stayed up all night before his physical for the draft, chugging back coffee, hoping being wired and twitchy and then fainting of exhaustion mid-medical would get the army doctors to fail him. As he avoided sleep, he typed out an entire eighty-page feature film screenplay, in one uninterrupted flow, just to kill the time—and then won the prestigious Samuel Goldwyn Writing Award with it. Eventually, he'd ditched UCLA without graduating to go work for exploitation producer and king of the B-movies Roger Corman, and then he had somehow managed convinced Corman to let him direct a black-and-white horror picture to be released on the bottom of one of Corman's exploitation double bills. Somehow he parlayed *that* into writing screenplays for the legitimate studios, becoming one of the highest-paid writers in town almost overnight, driving a Jaguar and living in a mansion—and *then* he used his screenwriting paychecks to buy the rights to finance a million-dollar passion project, *You're a Big Boy Now,* to direct himself. Just three months before George walked onto the Warner Bros. lot, Coppola had presented that film at the Cannes Film Festival, the only American picture the French selection committee had deemed worthy that year. Only twenty-eight, and his second film had premiered at the world's most prestigious festival, in the same competition as Antonioni and Volker Schlöndorff and Robert Bresson.

And then Coppola had only come home and submitted *You're a Big Boy Now* as his "thesis film" at UCLA so the university would finally have to give him his degree. A Cannes-approved feature film playing alongside everyone else's fifteen-minute, 16mm, half-baked shorts. Now, this call sheet said, Coppola was on the Warner lot, making the only picture still going under the new ownership.

Another name caught George's eye. Howard Kazanjian, listed as a second assistant director, was a recent USC graduate. He and George were friends, were both Delta Kappa Alpha.

George decided to give Howard a call. This scholarship sounded like a dud, but maybe Francis Coppola, at least, would be worth meeting.

· 2 ·

BEYOND THE RAINBOW

The whole family agreed: Little Francis had no talent. He was creative enough; he liked to write and have a good time. But he wasn't his father, Carmine, first flute for the NBC Symphony Orchestra, nor was he his brother, Augie, five years older, handsome and popular and good at everything: school, sports, the arts. "In my family, that's what the issue was," Francis said later. "My father had talent and my brother had talent. I didn't and my sister didn't and my mother didn't—no one else did."

Those were the rules in the Coppola household on 212th Street and 86th Avenue in Queens. A nice house in a quiet neighborhood and, within, a family system that revolved around the dual suns of Carmine and Augie. To be a great man was life's ambition. Great men, or the idea of them, were everywhere. Right at the end of the block, behind the trees, traffic hummed on the Grand Central Parkway Robert Moses had built and was fighting to expand still. Carmine commuted to Rockefeller Center and took his seat in the orchestra inside Studio 8H to be conducted by the genius Toscanini, earning wages he invested into the Tucker sedan, brainchild of innovative auto entrepreneur Preston Tucker. Francis's middle name, Ford, commemorated the Detroit hospital where he'd been born in 1939, itself named after Henry Ford. "Ever since I was a little kid," Francis said as an adult, "I was raised to be successful and rich. If you were raised as I was, everything you do is to make your family proud of you."

Only, he wasn't sure how. His mother, Italia—or "Mammarella," as everyone called her—was affectionate and encouraging, but even she respected the family hierarchy: If Francis ever did something good, she thought, it was probably because Augie had set the right example or otherwise led the way. Mammarella knew greatness, too. Her own father, Francesco Pennino, was an acclaimed and widely published composer who, back in Naples in the old country, had played the piano in cafés in accompaniment to one of his buddies, a young tenor by the name of Enrico Caruso.

By the time he was nine, Francis boasted a face drawn with a cartoonist's pen—big oval ears and a big nose and a full, smirking mouth, and sweeping eyebrows over Mediterranean, almond-shaped eyes, bright and inquisitive—and hid a growing sense of dread behind it. He was getting older and falling short. Francis's uncle Anton, by the time *he* was nine, was singing at the Met, in the choir for Puccini's *Turandot*! "Dear Mommy," Francis wrote in a little letter to Mammarella around that age, "I want to be rich and famous. I'm so discouraged, I don't think it will come true."

Then came the polio. A stiff neck, first, and a long wait in the hallways of Jamaica Hospital, kids along the walls, piled in gurneys three or four high. Kids wailing, locked in iron lungs. They sent him home to 212th Street, where he burned with the fever, first, and then the pain, "and then," Francis said, "you can't move your legs." He woke up that morning and swung his body over the side of his bed, and nothing below his waist did what he wanted it to do. He crashed onto the floor and had to call for help. It was sometime in the second half of 1948, or maybe it was 1949. Francis, later, would only tell people he'd been "about nine." He never liked to talk about the illness itself. His back and entire left side, from shoulder to foot, remained paralyzed for nearly a year. These were the early years of the epidemics, when everyone was scared, when people avoided someone with polio like it was—quite literally—the plague. A miasmic infection that spread invisibly and struck suddenly and seemed to prey particularly on children.

Francis, for all his perceived lack of talent, was a loving child who thrived on the warmth of others. Suddenly, he was alone, in his upstairs bedroom over a street that flared with the sounds of children playing games and riding their bikes. No parents would let their kids come up and see him. As he regained his strength, Francis played with puppets and practiced his skill at handling a ventriloquist's dummy. He watched television—"a lot"—especially on Sundays, when *The Horn and Hardart Children's Hour*, a variety show with a cast of little children, aired on NBC in the morning and *Super Circus* aired on ABC in the late afternoon, featuring ten-year-old Scampy the Clown. Those were his friends and soon became inspirations. Carmine had a tape recorder he used to put down music, as well as an 8mm camera on which to shoot home movies. Francis experimented with both. He recut family memories into narratives, performed voice-overs and lines of dialogue and sound effects, and synchronized the sound to the picture. The technology captivated him. It didn't matter what *had* happened in those home movies; what mattered were the fancies Francis's imagination turned them into. In time, he got his hands on the family's 8mm projector, and that was how, finally, he got neighborhood kids to visit: by charging admission. "I had a little movie company there on 212th Street in Queens," he said, the whole process in the literal palms of his hands, from the uncut film to distribution. "I made money out of them, too."

Maybe he had some talent after all.

His luck turned, but like a twist out of the tragic operas his father loved so much, Carmine's own star fell, as if their fortunes were on the opposite ends of a seesaw. By 1951, little Francis was recovered, left only with a slight limp he would retain for the rest of his life, but Carmine was out of a steady job. He had gone to see Toscanini and handed in his resignation.

"I want to conduct," he told the maestro. He'd watched Toscanini do it for years. How hard could it be?

"You're a fool," came Toscanini's reply.

Carmine found his gamble hard going. The Coppolas moved out of the house in Queens, bounced around the country as Carmine picked up a gig on a touring show here, a temp spot conducting an orchestra there. The paterfamilias curdled like milk gone bad. When he was frustrated or angry, which was often now, every part of his face turned downward: the dark eyebrows, the strong hawkish nose, the scowling lips. Brown bags appeared under his eyes and never went away. He took other people's successes as a personal insult.

Francis went to the movies. Discovered Eisenstein. He grew tall. His shoulders and chest broadened. Augie was gone by now, studying philosophy at UCLA. It was left to Francis and sister Talia, seven years his junior, to weather Carmine's unhappiness. Mammarella requested they finish every bedtime prayer with the same incantation: please, God—"let Daddy get his big break."

The Coppolas swung back East and settled, in what was either a cruel irony or another attempt to manifest a better future, in Lake Success, Long Island. Francis, after years of ricocheting from school to school, still felt like a weird outsider. He liked to play with hidden microphones and blow up homemade remote-controlled explosives in his backyard. But he also started to write. Stories, plays, verse. He ghostwrote love letters to pretty girls on behalf of inarticulate friends and charged for the service. He graduated high school and won a drama scholarship to Hofstra. He went up to Nassau County and was one of the university's star students, writing and directing plays that became campus sensations. He graduated in 1960, went across the country to UCLA, enrolled in the cinema department, and quickly became a collegiate celebrity there, too. At twenty-six, he became a well-paid screenwriter.

By the time Warner Bros.–Seven Arts offered him *Finian's Rainbow* two years later, Francis could have picked any other project at the studio. He didn't like the script, didn't like the show's clumsy civil rights politics, didn't like working for studio executives who questioned his every decision. He certainly didn't like the proposition of making a musical for $3.5 million in three months when that kind of picture usually took twice the time and twice the money. But he'd said yes anyway. Because if you were raised as he was, everything you do is to make your family proud of you, "and I thought frankly that my father would be impressed."

He called Carmine, who was still on the road, schlepping from state to state with Mammarella in tow. A road show production of *Half a Sixpence*, a new house every few weeks, staying in places like Chicago's Croydon Hotel, forty years past its best and scheduled for demolition, where aging vaudeville performers haunted the lounge, the smell of decline sweating off the hallway wallpaper. Francis told his father he was adapting a Broadway hit to the screen for Warner Bros., full of lovely musical numbers Carmine knew and loved already. He asked Carmine to come to California and work on the picture, arranging orchestrations and additional connecting music.

Carmine couldn't say yes fast enough. He quit the road and moved himself and Italia to Los Angeles. He was fifty-seven and here, finally, was a break.

Francis felt proud to be able to offer it to him.

George went down to the jungle and recognized the film's director immediately. He was—other than George himself, Kazanjian, and a few members of the cast—the only person around who looked under forty years old. He and George were also the only men on set to wear beards.

Coppola was filming a musical number entitled "Look to the Rainbow," staged around a large fake tree, under which sat Fred

Astaire. His young co-star, the singer Petula Clark, kicked the song off, before Astaire stood and took over. Three choreographed sections followed: In the first, Astaire walked around the set, singing; in the second, he and Clark shared an Irish step dance under the tree; finally, the old entertainer danced away down a country road, the children of Rainbow Valley following him like a pied piper.

The work didn't look complicated to George, and yet it dragged, take after take. Astaire and his choreographer, the magically named Hermes Pan, never stopped rehearsing. Kazanjian and an assistant choreographer did their best to prepare the rest of the dancers accordingly. Petula Clark disappeared when she wasn't needed, going off with some of the other young actors, to light and share a discreet joint off set somewhere.

Coppola looked every bit the hotshot screenwriter, in his short-sleeve button-down, a chunky watch and ring on his right wrist and hand. He wore hip, square-framed black eyeglasses not too dissimilar to George's own.

He did not, to George's outside eye, look entirely in control.

Francis called for another take. They'd only given him eight days on location, and his Rainbow Valley was repurposed from Joshua Logan's *Camelot*, a bigger-budget Warner musical that had wrapped in the spring. He craved the freedom to experiment—as he had at Hofstra, as he'd been encouraged to by Roger Corman.

"I was faking it," he said later. He'd come in with the best of intentions, but the picture had ground his ideas out of him by the second week of shooting. It wasn't just the lack of time and money. Francis was also contending with Astaire, who was a gentleman but uncomfortable with such a young director, who he thought of as a "hippie," even though Francis was a married man who brought his elder son to set and vastly preferred espresso and red wine to smoking grass. He was dealing with Hermes Pan, who disapproved of Francis's roving camera and tendency to improvise the dancing. He was dealing with

Petula Clark, whose publicist husband kept asking to rearrange her shooting schedule to maximize her tax position back in Britain. There was the English entertainer Tommy Steele, playing Og the leprechaun, who kept slipping into his extroverted shtick, mugging and hamming it up and derailing scenes Francis wanted subtle and quiet.

The schedule slid past him. He had to keep the whole picture in his mind even as they shot the scenes out of order, in "little pieces. And that's the whole game of directing," he remembered. "Directing takes a lot of concentration and being able to be blind to certain problems and just focus where you should be focusing." He had never had so many different things to focus on, and he knew he was failing, at least some of the time, and failing some of the time was enough. A great picture, after all, is an accumulation of the correct choices.

The pressure made him indecisive, and doubting himself made him impulsive. Kazanjian, as second AD, was in charge of keeping the day-to-day filming running smoothly. He would draw up a call sheet, only for Francis to turn up to the lot in the morning, veins laced with strong double espresso, in the mood to shoot something else entirely. Or Francis would conceive of a genuinely great shot, something that called for special resources, "a Titan crane or . . . more or fewer dancers," but then neglect to tell anyone about it until it was time to shoot, when he'd turn to Kazanjian and ask where his crane and dancers were. Kazanjian felt like he was spending half his time on the phone, or running from department to department, covering for his director's screwups. Occasionally, he told Francis they couldn't shoot what he wanted to shoot—*you can't film a dance number the dancers haven't rehearsed yet*, he'd say. Then Francis turned gloomy and self-reflective, and filming slowed further.

The shoot had started on June 26 and was scheduled to end in late September, but Kazanjian could tell they wouldn't finish on time. The weekly cost reports would show "set striking and construction" as the culprits, though the reality was more complicated. The film would turn out fine, if unexceptional. Everyone could just see its driving forces—Coppola; Astaire; Pan; the now departed Jack Warner, who had green-lit the damn thing and chosen both the director and his stars—were on different pages. Francis, oftentimes, didn't seem to be on the same page with himself.

Astaire danced. Astaire sang. *Look, look, look to the rainbow, follow it over the hill and stream . . .* Coppola called cut, conferred with his star or the heads of department, and the crew reset.

As he waited between setups, Francis spotted the skinny kid in a sweater talking to Kazanjian. He wasn't hard to pick out. For starters, he was young and bearded, and for seconds, he didn't appear to have a job to do. *Another hippie*, Astaire might have said.

The crew went for another take. During the next break, Francis noticed the skinny kid was watching him, "always looking at me." He walked over to Kazanjian, who was setting up the next shot.

"Who's that?" Francis asked, gesturing in the newcomer's direction.

"Well, he's observing you," Kazanjian answered.

Francis turned and walked to the kid, who was now, with great focus, watching the crew. "What are you looking at?" Francis asked.

"Nothing much," came the reply. There was a gentle tremor to his voice, the hint of a nasal whine, at odds with the self-possession in his manner.

Kazanjian shuffled over. "George, this is the director, Francis Coppola. Francis, this is George Lucas." He explained George was from USC, had won the Sam Warner Scholarship, and had been assigned to observe the shoot.

"Can I hang around?" George asked Francis. It was Coppola's set, after all, not Warner's, or Seven Arts', or Kazanjian's. George believed a movie belonged to its director.

"Sure," Francis answered, "as long as you let me know if you have any suggestions or ideas about how to shoot the picture."

It sounded like grace. Truth was, Francis could use all the suggestions and ideas anybody had.

George hung around for about a week, growing friendly with Francis. Then he went to Kazanjian and asked to be taken off the picture.

"I have no interest in Hollywood movies," he said. "I have no interest in watching these people do this stuff, it doesn't interest me." It wasn't Kazanjian's call, so George went back to the production department. He asked, again, to be assigned to the animation department.

They reminded him there was nothing active being made in the animation department. George answered that he didn't care. He'd seen cameras lying around in the animation building, as well as short ends—sections of unexposed film shorter than a full roll, which studio pictures didn't use but film students were accustomed to making the most of. If he could just get in there, with only the caretaker to worry about, he'd find a way to borrow a camera and some film and use his six-month scholarship to, stealthily, make a movie. He'd done that kind of thing at USC all the time, working the system to get more than the Department of Cinema allocated. He'd have a picture in the can before the Warner–Seven Arts brass even knew what he was doing.

He was waiting for approval when Francis, visibly upset, found him.

"Why do you want to get off my movie?" he asked.

"Well," George answered, in his adolescent quiver, "'cause it's boring, and, uh, there's nothing to do."

"Look, stick around, and I'll give you something to do. Come up with one good idea every day."

Neither of them could remember, years later, whether something in Francis's tone had convinced George, or whether there had been more of a back-and-forth. Maybe the Warner production department had simply turned down George's request. Either way, the next day, George was back on the grass set in the jungle, this time with a Polaroid camera around his neck. He'd start by scoping out the set; then he'd take a picture, let it develop, and bring it to Francis. *How about this angle for a shot*, he'd ask. Francis liked that. It was proactive, actually helpful.

"You're doing it all wrong," George told Francis about a setup one day. Francis liked that, too—the "chutzpah."

Francis started taking George to dailies, so he'd have someone beside him whose judgment he could trust. "That really was my strength, editing picture," George recalled. "Francis's strength was working with actors and writing, and so, in the end, we became a good match."

Good—but not perfect. Francis was nearly six foot tall, overwhelmingly Italian. He looked perpetually rumpled, with a booming voice and free with a curse word. He was a married man who adored his sons, four-year-old Gio and two-year-old Roman. George was five-six, soft-spoken, always neatly, if casually, dressed, fond of burgers and milkshakes. He lived, "more or less full-time," with his twenty-one-year-old girlfriend, Marcia Griffin, an assistant film editor with a wispy voice and a sweet personality. Francis was pragmatic; he'd made his first movie paychecks rewriting and recutting soft-core nudie flicks on the sly. George resented working for hire so much that even this brief time on the Warner Bros. payroll seemed to pain him. Francis's larger-than-life gregariousness, his showmanship, were run through with a streak of shyness. George's introversion, his tendency to pepper conversations with an old-fashioned *gee* or *gosh*, barely hid the pulsing purpose that powered his decision-making.

Late in the evenings, after wrap, Francis and George and Kazanjian sat in the director's office, nominally planning the next day but, more often than not, shooting the breeze and planning the future. Francis wanted to make personal films, like the Europeans. He was under contract at Warner Bros.–Seven Arts to write several more films: an original called *The Rain People*, as a vehicle for actress Shirley Knight; a passion project entitled *The Conversation*, about a surveillance man on his fiftieth birthday, tormented by the dark consequences of one of his wiretaps; and an adaptation of Hawthorne's *The Scarlet Letter*. He was thinking of directing *The Rain People* next;

after that, everything depended on the success of *Finian's Rainbow*. *The Conversation* struck him as a daunting challenge, and he kept picking at its script. The idea had come to him in a conversation with filmmaker Irvin Kershner, who was sixteen years older than Francis and liked to engage with younger filmmakers, many of whom affectionately called him "Kersh," including George, whom he'd taught at USC. As a child, Francis had enjoyed eavesdropping on family and friends using little radio microphones, and Kershner had told him about Hal Lipset, a San Francisco private detective notorious for the ingenious ways he taped incriminating conversations—once hiding a microphone in a bar of soap to record a private conversation between two men naked in a steam room, and later demonstrating how an even smaller transmitter could be hidden in the olive in a martini glass, with a fake toothpick as an antenna.

Francis conceived *The Conversation* as a noir about a man a bit like Lipset, only haunted by the way his recordings are used—and torn when he begins to suspect a couple he has been paid to record are in mortal danger. The film would be bleak—about guilt and consequences and ambiguous moral dilemmas. Francis wanted Marlon Brando for the lead. He wasn't sure what kind of picture it would be beyond that, but that was both the fear and the attraction. Some filmmakers—like George—started with an image. Others, of which Francis was one, started with an idea, and behind the idea a question. Oppugnant impulses weren't a sign of confusion to him, but of promise.

George brought friends from USC to hang out: Walter Murch, but also a burly, bombastic young writer named John Milius. Francis's old UCLA classmate Carroll Ballard dropped in. They, too, had movies they dreamed of making, but they all knew Hollywood was a closed shop, accessible only by personal favor or nepotism.

Summer turned to September. War raged endlessly in Vietnam. Jim Morrison, who had been Francis's roommate at UCLA, took his band, the Doors, on *The Ed Sullivan Show*, to sing their number one hit "Light My Fire," and he sang the word *higher* live on air, even though Sullivan's producers had ordered him not to, because *higher* suggested drugs and lawbreaking. Network television was just that stuck-up. It was puritanical censorship, repressed and repressive. Sometimes, for all his ambition, Francis thought George was right. How could you make anything truthful for a system like that?

George told Francis about the underground cinema of the Bay Area, where he'd grown up. Francis floated the idea of their moving to San Francisco together, to make personal films there. It'd get them away from Hollywood. One day, Francis opened his closet and showed George what he'd been stashing inside: film stock, reels, bits of equipment.

"Someday when they finally throw me out of here," he said, "we'll have enough and we can make another film."

"Film is power," Francis told Milius. "If you have enough film, all you need is a camera, and I have one of those, too. I can do anything I want."

I'm willing to die by his side, Milius thought. Francis had that aura.

The *Finian* shoot spluttered to a wrap on November 4, weeks late, $1.5 million over budget. Francis, worn out, left the technical postproduction to Warner–Seven Arts staff. The studio gave him permission to move ahead with *The Rain People*. In late January '68, the abstract science-fiction film George had made as his graduation project at USC, *Electronic Labyrinth: THX 1138 4EB*, won the top prize at the third National Student Film Festival. Best animated student film went to *Marcello, I'm So Bored*, directed by Milius. George had edited that one, too. Everyone at USC had known Lucas was a standout talent—"he was special," says one of his classmates—but the awards were covered by the trade and mainstream press, and now George's name appeared, however briefly, in the copies of *Daily Variety* and the *Los Angeles Times* delivered to every Hollywood producer's front step. *Time* magazine ran a feature profiling George and Milius, alongside an intense twenty-five-year-old NYU film school graduate named Martin Scorsese, whose first feature, *Who's That Knocking at My Door*, had recently premiered at the Chicago International Film Festival.

George's ball began rolling. Mike Medavoy, a hungry agent at the boutique agency General Artists Corporation (GAC), read the *Time* magazine article, "and I went and asked my secretary," he recalls, "to see if any of them [were] in the Western phone directory." Milius was, "and he had just done a short film with George Lucas. And then, you know—there was a list of names, and I just wrote the names down." GAC had about twenty clients on the books, and only two, the actors Tony Bill and Carol Burnett, were under fifty. "As a young agent," Medavoy said, "I seized on the notion that the only way I would ever have any leverage was to sign up the young filmmakers I believed would revolutionize the business." He snapped George and Milius up.

Sometime in February, as Francis was casting *The Rain People*, George paid him a visit. He told Francis that Carl Foreman, the producer of *Mackenna's Gold*, was interested in producing a feature-length version of *THX 1138 4EB* for Columbia Pictures. It meant working for a Hollywood studio, but George needed the opportunity, and he needed the cash. His father had lent him the money for his tuition. Graduation had come and gone. George Lucas Sr. expected to be paid back.

"Don't go over there and work for them," Francis admonished George. "I'll get you a job to do it over here." He liked "the stinky kid," as he had started calling him. He could tell George's nascent star was rising.

"You'll come along on *The Rain People*," Francis told George, weaving a strategy out of thin air, as he would do time and time again throughout their friendship. "I'm gonna make this tiny movie with about fifteen people. You can be the assistant art director, the assistant director, the assistant camera, and the assistant everything, and you can write your script, and you'll get paid to write your script if you can work from four to six in the morning. We're just gonna travel around the country and torch some cars." They'd be far away from Hollywood and its meddling executives. George could write in peace.

George liked that idea, and he liked the idea of working with Francis. There was only one problem.

"I can't write," he said. "I'm not a writer." He told Francis he had planned to co-write the feature with Matthew Robbins, a friend from USC who had come up with the original idea for *THX 1138*.

Francis shook his head. "If you're ever gonna be a director, you've got to become a writer," he said.

"I'm an awful writer," George protested. "I hate plots. I hate screenplays."

"You have to learn," Francis insisted.

George thought for a moment. Driving around America with a small crew, working on a guerrilla-style shoot, getting paid for it . . . that did sound like "a great idea," he remembered later. He had started to wonder if he could shoot his own feature film as far away as Japan, eventually, to give it an otherworldly feel. Maybe, doing it Francis's way, he could learn to work for a studio like Warner Bros. without having to live in LA.

"Well, okay," he said finally. "Okay, we'll do it here."

·3·

REALITY ENDS HERE

When Bill Couturié first transferred to the University of Southern California's Department of Cinema, he was sent to the edge of campus, to take his classes in a barn. "The editing rooms were literally stalls for horses," he remembers. "I think the hay was out of it, but it was still very primitive. Funky, funky, funky." Alumni and faculty alike recommended not telling anyone in the industry you were attending a film school. Kids enrolled in the cinema department to watch movies and smoke dope or to dodge the draft, or both. Some—the driven ones—enrolled to get access to cameras, lights, and film. A film degree from USC wasn't worth the paper it was written on, but an outstanding, award-winning short film might open doors. This unproven theory was based on the young career of one—just one—alumnus of the department.

"I was there two years after George," Couturié says. "That's how it was. Life at USC was broken into BG and AG: before George and after George."

Lucas had arrived at the film school in the fall of 1964, crashing at a friend's place in Malibu. An old racing-circuit acquaintance, the Oscar-nominated cinematographer Haskell Wexler—twenty-two years George's elder—was his only contact in the film industry, met on the track when George was a car-mad teenager, and Wexler had promised him a part-time job to pay his way. Once in town, George learned Wexler couldn't honor his offer, not even at his own company, because George wasn't in the union. George felt the sting. He was, at heart, a small-town child of the '50s. He believed in quintessential American virtues of meritocracy, individualism, and freedom—in this case, Wexler's freedom to hire whoever he wanted, as well as George's own freedom to take that job and prove himself good enough to hold it. Hollywood, he felt, had already "shut [him] out," and he found it "extremely unfair." Then and forever, he had a way of taking things personally.

He presented himself at the USC campus, his wallet considerably lighter than he'd expected and his outlook gloomier. The incoming class numbered about eighty students, double the enrollment in '63, which itself had been double the size of the year before that. On the first morning, the head of the camera department, Gene Peterson, stood up in front of the young men—and they were nearly all men—and shook his head.

"I don't know what you guys are doing here," he said. "I don't know what you think you're going to achieve, but here's my advice: get out now. You can still get your money back. Because there are no jobs for you."

"All of those teachers then were in their late thirties to late forties, maybe early fifties," remembers Walter Murch, who, along with George, was part of that incoming class. "And they had been riding the sled of Hollywood downhill since 1946. Here we were twenty years later, which was basically their entire working life, and it had been one of Hollywood descent, and they had taken refuge under the umbrella of a university . . . They were very cynical about Hollywood and didn't hold out much hope for us."

On the second day of classes, about a third of the students failed to show up. Murch did come back, but only because he was on a scholarship. "From my point of view," he says, "they were paying me to go, so . . . I'll stick it out. But we were all afraid, somewhere, of—what *will* happen when we graduate?"

The son of still life painter Walter Tandy Murch, the younger Walter had grown up on Riverside Drive in New York City, recording sounds he found in the wild on a tape recorder, cutting and juxtaposing music off the radio with noises he picked up holding his microphone out the window. Like Francis, Murch was of the first generation for whom portable film cameras and sound equipment were "available as consumer item[s]," he recalled, and he experienced what he called "a kind of delirious drunkenness" at his ability to take "ordinary sounds and arrang[e] them rhythmically, creating a kind of music on tape." You figured it out as you went along.

Murch, keenly intelligent and ravenously curious, sailed through prep school on the Upper West Side and moved to Baltimore to study liberal arts at Johns Hopkins. There he became friends with a kid from Pennsylvania named Caleb Deschanel, as well as Matthew Robbins, also from New York, who hailed from a family much like Murch's: middle-class, artistic, supportive. In their next-to-last year, as nineteen-year-olds, Murch and Robbins set off for Europe, enrolling at the Sorbonne in Paris. They took classes in art history and French literature, "sending our work, our essays, back to Johns Hopkins to get credit," Robbins says. "And it was while in Paris that we got involved in movies, because of the Cinémathèque," the famous film center and screen archive spearheaded by preservationist Henri Langlois. "You could go for, like, six francs or something, and see three movies for six francs, it was insane—and then take a break at like six o'clock and come back at seven and see three more movies and come out at half past midnight." They rode their motorcycles through France and Italy, through Spain, North Africa, and Greece. They met girls, absorbed the Nouvelle Vague, Carlos Saura and Jean Rouch, Fellini and Antonioni.

"I came back to the United States buzzing with the idea of film,"

Murch remembered. They still had no idea what they were going to do with their lives, until one day Robbins's older brother Daniel, a Fulbright scholar who worked as a curator at the Guggenheim, got involved. "If you really want to go to a film school," he told Matthew, "there's only three: there's NYU here [in New York], there's UCLA, and there's USC."

Murch found the concept of a moviemaking school "incredible, delicious, almost absurd." He applied to all of them and, "miraculously," won a scholarship to USC.

Los Angeles it was, then: Robbins applied and was accepted, too. Murch, newly married, set off cross-country with his wife, Aggie, on the back of his motorcycle. Robbins loaded his Ducati in the back of a Volkswagen bus and followed. They found apartments right next door to each other, between USC and Chinatown to the north, and headed off together, black spiral-bound notebooks in hand, to see where they would be studying. USC was a private school with, Murch remembers, a reputation as "a finishing school" for Hollywood's elite.

"We arrived at this campus with palm trees and a big tower which had a globe on it, to symbolize 'world learning,' and it was just so incredibly vulgar to us," Robbins says. They followed directions across the property, through a Spanish gate, and finally found a board-and-batten shack, built, using leftover barrack lumber, as a temporary classroom building during World War II, and never since improved upon. A sign over the door read: "Reality Ends Here."

Unlike crosstown UCLA, where the cinema department was folded into the theater department and the curriculum favored artistic expression, USC's program emphasized the practical and technical aspects of filmmaking, or learning by doing. But the equipment was old and insufficient. The cameras were old navy-surplus Kodak Cine Specials, black-and-silver rectangular boxes that jammed all the time. Many of the light meters didn't work because their glass was broken. The dozen or so Moviola editing machines had the look of antiques, film stock rationed as if a world war were still going on.

"It was," Robbins says, "kind of a dump."

Murch was in the darkroom one afternoon, developing some pictures, when the door to the hallway opened and closed and a short, skinny kid in glasses entered the room. Murch couldn't quite make him out in the dim red light, though he'd seen him around: George Lucas didn't speak much, but he had an intense presence. Murch kept working on his photographs as George stood against the wall and watched him.

"You're doing it wrong," George said finally.

"Get out of here," Murch growled back. "What do you know?"

He soon found out. Early in 1965, the students directed their first shorts, in Herb Kosower's animation class. The assignment: to create a one-minute film, using only still photographs cut together to convey a sense of either movement or emotion. Everyone went out to take a few photographs and assembled them into a sequence, awkwardly reaching for some semblance of dynamism or feeling. George, in contrast, pulled over fifty photographs from back issues of *Life* magazine—including shots of Martin Luther King Jr., dead soldiers, the KKK, Bela Lugosi, a basketball jump shooter, monkeys, puppies, a public health announcement entreating readers to "Help Stamp Out Runny Noses," policemen unleashing dogs and horses at fleeing African-Americans, a swimsuit model standing in tall grass, couples embracing, and the word *LOVE*, atomized into abstract, extreme close-ups—and shuffled them together, smash-cutting and dissolving. He double-and triple-exposed a dancing woman so her hair seemed to bounce. He panned from faces to hands to create the impression of someone waving, and across crowd shots to give the feeling of people running. He inserted a skip, a fraction of a second long, over a close-up of an eye, to make it look like it was blinking.

He broke down one photograph—showing a policeman, his dog, and a Black civilian—into three close-ups: the civilian's startled face, a white hand clutching his collar; the policeman's clenched features, eyes hidden behind sunglasses and cap visor glinting; and finally the German shepherd's open, lunging jaws, from which George almost immediately match-cut to another policeman's baton as it swung for a man's head. The four images and their juxtaposition created an immediate, visceral impression of violence. George set his images to percussive calypso music taken from the main titles of Marcel Camus's *Orfeu Negro*. Few of his fellow classmates had even thought of using a soundtrack, let alone considered the technical challenge of creating one. George, meanwhile, perfectly timed every one of his cuts to the syncopated beat. He interrupted the score near the end of his allocated minute to play the film's only line of spoken soundtrack: a preacher shouting over a crowd to "please not the oppressor, for Hate stirreth up strife, while love covereth all sins!" The film ends with three title cards slowly receding from view: "ANYONE FOR SURVIVAL" and "END," dissolving into a question mark.

Where did this kid come from? Murch asked himself. *He's a Modesto farm kid. How does he know how to do this stuff?*

"Nobody there, including the teachers, had ever seen anything like it," George said later. It was his first proper assignment, and already, "I realized I was able to run circles around everybody else."

Suddenly, he had a lot more friends in the class. "If you went up and saw a student film and said, 'Gee, this is kind of a boring film,' you just didn't ever associate with that guy," Murch said. "But if you went and saw an exciting film, you became friends with this guy. That was the way we all got together." George's films weren't just exciting; they were—as Robbins put it—"the most electrifying things you had ever seen." A small group coalesced fast and firm around him. George bonded with Murch over their shared love of editing and related to Howard Kazanjian's stolid friendliness and no-frills dependability. Willard Huyck, who had come to USC to study journalism, then switched his major to cinema without telling his parents, became a friend because they both loved fine art and the French New Wave. In his second year, needing a roommate to split the $150 rent on a place in Benedict Canyon, George took in Randal Kleiser, who also loved fine art. Kleiser would come home in the evenings and find George painting, canvases "like Margaret Keane, the girls with big eyes." He figured Lucas would become a production designer.

"George made a few friends at USC and decided that's about all he needed for the rest of his life," Huyck said. He was driven. He didn't do drugs. He didn't party. He made films, "ate it and slept it 24 hours a day," he admitted. He'd found his calling, the reason he had dodged death in the wreckage of his Autobianchi. "There was no going back after that."

"George was a quiet person at USC," remembered Kazanjian. "A quiet and patient person, until he [got] fired up."

Or, as Murch puts it: "Yeah, talented. But, you know . . . kind of a blowhard."

George also befriended John Milius, a blustering, larger-than-life Jewish twenty-year-old, born in St. Louis but raised in affluent Bel Air. Milius, who claimed surfing as his religion and dying in Vietnam in a blaze of glory as his life's ambition, was five foot eleven but gave the impression of being several inches taller, a bear of a young man with a round face and a strong nose and hairy forearms the size of many people's thighs. He longed to join the pantheon of great, larger-than-life writers he lionized—Hemingway, Faulkner, Steinbeck, Kerouac—and, before failing his army medical due to chronic asthma, had dreamed of enlisting with the marines to "go prove [himself] in battle." In truth, he was a privileged young man, raised by a father who had become so rich selling shoes in Missouri he'd retired and moved the family to California when he was only fifty-six. The closest the young Milius had ever come to danger was the months he'd spent, as a boy, at Lowell Whiteman boarding school in Steamboat Springs, Colorado, skinning rabbits and sleeping under the stars with other well-off boys sent away for being troublesome at home. He'd chosen USC for film school, he said, because it trained the elite. As if making black-and-white short films were a director's equivalent of being accepted into West Point.

Along with George, Milius was the star of that class, the one his peers thought most likely to succeed. His tastes ran much more mainstream than George's. The two of them liked to sit on the grass outside the film buildings and chat girls up as they walked by, though Milius did most of the catcalling. He teased George for doing so much chasing women and so little catching them, though no girls ever stopped for him, either. George protested that he did fine for himself, even dismissed his alleged conquests as "dumb things." This was before George finally got a part-time job, working as an assistant to the editor Verna Fields, a USC teacher who also cut newsreel and propaganda footage for the United States Information Agency. At Verna's, George met Marcia, another assistant; she was small and lovely, with dark hair and elfin ears. She had a joyful sense of humor and happily identified as a "motormouth." Milius, along with everyone else, was jealous of George for claiming her attention. He told George his girlfriend was prettier than him, smarter than him, and, worse still, a better editor than him.

When Milius wasn't trying to get laid, he and George held court on that same grass, surrounded by other film students, and talked movies. One day, everyone was out there praising Stanley Kubrick's Cold War comedy *Dr. Strangelove*, and they got to talking about ideas for a similar satire of the Vietnam War. Milius brought up Joseph Conrad's novel *Heart of Darkness*, a book their screenwriting teacher had told him was so unadaptable for the screen, even Ben Hecht and Orson Welles hadn't been able to crack it. "It was like waving a red flag in front of a bull," Milius remembered. He told his classmates that he had first read *Heart of Darkness* in Colorado, in the middle of winter, laying a trap line, carrying a knife and a rifle. He felt that, to survive in the woods, you had to become the woods, the same way that to survive the jungle, you had to become part of the jungle.

"You give yourself to that anger, that's exactly what *Heart of Darkness* is, and Kurtz had become part of that," he lectured. "He's given himself to these forces, he's befriended them." Milius had friends coming back from Vietnam, and he was so inappropriately, obscenely jealous. He plied them with questions about the experience. They spoke of being swallowed up by something primordial and visceral; of doing drugs to cope and experiencing the savagery of war like a psychedelic trip. All the fresh, groundbreaking stuff that people like Verna Fields had to censor and edit out.

That would be how he would adapt *Heart of Darkness*, Milius said: in Vietnam, as an allegory. Kurtz as America, consumed and corrupted.

"You should write this down," George said.

Milius started doing just that, in scraps of scenes and ideas that came to him over the coming weeks. He kept the central throughline of *Heart of Darkness* as a guide: As Charles Marlow, in the novel, travels downriver into the "blank spaces" of Africa to find Kurtz, an ivory trader who has "gone native," so Milius's own Marlow, renamed Willard, would go into Vietnam to recover or terminate Colonel Kurtz, a Special Forces officer who has gone insane. But Milius refused to read Conrad's book again so he would be inspired only by the emotion he had felt in the woods in Colorado, and he wasn't sure how to shape the journey itself, what anecdotes to use, what tone to strike.

"Put all the neat stuff in it," George said.

By early summer, Milius was getting somewhere. One hot day, he sat on a bench under the sun with classmate Mike Rachmil and said, "Mike, I want to run this by you." He told Rachmil he was writing something set in Vietnam and calling it *Apocalypse Now*, a riff on one of the more popular slogans on hippie peacenik badges of the day, "Nirvana Now." George was maybe going to direct it, in a cinéma vérité, low-budget style, like Gillo Pontecorvo's *The Battle of Algiers*, which had come out the year before.

Rachmil said sure, he'd listen.

Milius told Rachmil to imagine coconut trees, seen in a haze. Rock music on the soundtrack. Skids of helicopters, as Milius wrote in his draft screenplay, hard shapes that glide by at random. And then, without warning: bombs, the jungle ripped apart in a bright red-orange glob of napalm flame.

He pitched Rachmil the whole story while they sat on that bench, from first frame to last. It took him two hours. Rachmil, sitting sweating under the sun, hung on every word, "spellbound." All he could think was:

This is insane.

· 4 ·

THE FEAR THAT THRILLS

The first minute of George Lucas's *Electronic Labyrinth: THX 1138 4EB* is all black screen. The next minute and a half is made up of grainy close-ups, in the style of a surveillance camera, showing a man and a woman communicating, almost unintelligibly, over a radio. The strings and Gregorian chanting of the Yardbirds' "Still I'm Sad" kick in over an endless card of the endless title. A runaway in an all-white jumpsuit, the numbers 1138 tattooed across his forehead, runs down a maze of all-white passageways, tracked every step of the way by an electronic surveillance system. Torturous mind-control techniques are applied through speakers and screens.

It was an alienating, anti-commercial short film. On the student circuit, it played like a blockbuster. At UCLA's red-brick-and-tile Royce Hall, where the National Student Film Festival awards were held the evening of Sunday, January 21, 1968, crowds of curious kids from colleges up and down the coast turned up to see it—and to catch a glimpse of George Lucas, the graduating student rumor said was apprenticing under Francis Coppola, himself the biggest celebrity in the film school community.

Invisible in the throng that night sat a wide-eyed twenty-one-year-old with a mop of brown hair and the eager, expressive enthusiasm of a teenager. He was in his third year at California State College in Long Beach, pursuing a bachelor of arts. Cal State didn't have a film department. That bummed him out. Young as he was, he had made dozens of shorts and thought of himself as a filmmaker already. To tell the truth, movies were Steven Spielberg's whole life.

But he looked around himself as the theater filled, and his heart sank. As a seventeen-year-old in Phoenix, he had written and directed a whole feature film, *Firelight*, for five hundred bucks, shooting weekends and in the evenings after school, devising all the special effects himself for a story about scientists chasing UFOs. They had even shown it at the local cinema. The paper had celebrated him as a precocious prodigy. The summer of '67—around the same time George and Francis met—Steven had gone on the bus tour at Universal Studios, snuck off during a bathroom break, and somehow convinced Chuck Silvers, the studio's head librarian and head of editorial, to issue him a three-day pass around the lot so he could come back and see how everything worked.

"The only thing I want to do," Steven told Silvers, "is direct before I'm twenty-one."

Silvers had encouraged him, told him his dream was "really original and terrific." Surrounded by real film students inside Royce Hall, however, Steven no longer felt very original. "I realized that there was an entire generation coming out of NYU, USC, and UCLA," he said later: hundreds of kids as young as he was, as talented as he was, as hungry as he was, who shared the same dream and studied in environments where they could exercise their creativity. From being ahead of schedule, he suddenly felt like he had fallen behind.

Of all the films shown that night, *THX 1138 4EB* blew his mind and filled him with dread. It made him "jealous to the marrow of my bones," he said. "This little movie was better than all of my movies combined." At the end of the night, feeling like a fraud and an outsider, Steven filed out of the hall and followed a small pack as it made its way to the after-party. There, he sought out the director of *THX 1138*. George was only a year and a half older than him, but the gulf was daunting. He'd won the National Student Film Festival award, been on real film sets, worked with Coppola. He could even grow a full beard, for God's sake.

Steven inched forward to George, introduced himself, and told him how much he admired his film. As he told it later, he and George vibed right away. "We just became friends," he recalled. George's experience was different. When he and Steven crossed paths again, almost exactly a year later, and Steven brought it up, George confessed he couldn't remember meeting him at all.

Steven Allan Spielberg, born a week before Christmas in 1946 in Cincinnati, Ohio, had lived all over the place and never really fit in. His dad, Arnold, worked as an electrical engineer, and the family, which consisted of Steven, three younger sisters, and their mother, Leah, followed him wherever the work called.

In the early days of 1952, just weeks after turning five years old, Steven saw his first movie on a big screen, in Haddon Township, New Jersey. His parents told him they were taking him to "*The Greatest Show On Earth*," and little Steven was so excited—he had never been to the circus before. He imagined a big-top tent, elephants, giraffes, a lion tamer. Instead, he found himself standing with them outside a building in town, waiting in line for hours in the freezing cold with dozens of other people. They filed into the structure, and Steven saw rows and rows of red seats, all facing a big red curtain. He took his own seat by his parents, and within minutes, the curtain parted to reveal a huge screen. Steven's chest stung with betrayal.

"You said you were taking me to a circus," he whined.

Soon, however, he was spellbound. He didn't understand much of the story on the screen, the grown-up dialogue and interpersonal tension, but he was dazzled by the Technicolor hues, the huge, emotive faces, the staged circus acts. Near the end of the picture, the circus train crashes into another locomotive, a loud, violent collision, a horrible wreck that pushed Steven back into his seat as if he'd felt the whiplash himself. He sank down, averted his eyes, reached blindly up for his parents. He muttered that he wanted to leave. "It was a really terrifying, traumatic thing," he said later, "and it never left me. My first movie was a movie that scared my pants off, and I'll never forget that."

And he didn't. As soon as he stepped back outside into the dark gray cold of January, his small hand in the warmth of his mother's palm, the train wreck took on the quality of a dream, just as real and just as false. His parents told him it hadn't really happened. No one had been hurt. Steven went home to his own electric train set. He laid it out so it would crash, over and over again. His father told him to stop or he'd have to take the train away. Steven didn't stop. He made the little wrecks bigger and bigger. He found new, creative things to crash the locomotive into. He tinkered with speed and the layout of the tracks, and studied the way the boxcars and cabooses tipped. For the first time, he took a fear and asserted control over it. It wasn't happening to him; *he* was happening to *it*. "I was the one causing something," he remembered, and immediately, his mind made a connection: "something that was going to maybe have a chance to scare other people, but no longer myself."

Movies, little Steven found, walked the line between wonder and terror like a tightrope. And the people who made them—people Steven learned were called "directors"—controlled the emotion. Directors weren't scared of the unknown. They led you into it and decided what you would find.

In New Jersey, Steven attended Hebrew school and went to synagogue. He was eleven when his family moved to Phoenix, Arizona. A neighboring family welcomed them by standing out in front of their house, chanting, "The Spielbergs are dirty Jews."

There didn't seem to be any other Jewish kids in Steven's new school. Around his birthday, every house in the neighborhood was strung up with lights and decorations, front windows bright with a lit-up pine tree—every house except his. A week after his own birthday, every kid in town ran out into the snowy street with their own presents. New bikes, new sleds, new comics. Except him.

He already lived prey to many deep-seated, private fears. His nails were perpetually chewed to the quick. He was petrified of the dark. He was anxious in confined spaces. He had such a keen imagination he came up with things to dread faster than a hack writer had ideas. He was scared of the uncanny tremor of the strings inside his mother's piano. He was terrified of the tree outside his window, swaying and creaking at night, and the shadows it threw, like monsters, onto the wall of his bedroom. He was terrified of the clouds in the sky, morphing into "gigantic fists, gigantic faces." There was a slowly expanding crack in the plaster above his closet door, and Steven, who didn't understand the house was just settling, was sure it was some kind of portal, a gate unspeakable horrors crawled through at night, to hide in the closet, behind the furniture, under the bed.

The simple facts of reality were terrifying, too. That family, out on the sidewalk. The rest of the neighborhood, who went along with it. Steven's whole life, he'd been around older Jews who spoke of "the Great Murder." In Cincinnati, there'd been a group of them who didn't speak English in Steven's grandmother's living room one day, there to learn the language from her. One of the men extended his arm and showed Steven the numbers tattooed against the skin. The man bent his forearm and turned the 6 into a 9, and then back. So much of life felt that way. Light as a magic trick, heavy as unspeakable pain. Something awesome and otherworldly moving unseen, just out of frame, and it was unclear whether it was wondrous or apocalyptic. The line between the two, little Steven felt in his gut, was thrillingly and terrifyingly fine.

Phoenix was where teenage Steven's sense that he was different metastasized into shame. Compared to life in New Jersey, being a Jew in Arizona was like being an alien on planet Earth. He rode his bike down the suburban streets in 1957 and 1958—white picket fences, sprinklers spitting over emerald green lawns, kids playing catch with their dads in dry hot weather all year-round, the orange hue of the air so different from the gray back East—and desperately wanted to fit in. "I was not like everybody else," Steven said later of the lesson Phoenix taught him. "I just wanted to be accepted. Not for who I was. I wanted to be accepted for who everybody else was."

He rejected the conservative button-downs his parents wanted him to wear. He told his classmates to call him "Stevie," or Steve. For a time, when he was alone, he duct-taped the tip of his nose back toward his forehead, hoping to get rid of his "schnozz."

He found a purpose entertaining the neighborhood kids. He told scary stories about the bogeyman and invited boys to his basement, where he'd built a guillotine out of a shoebox and decapitated his toy soldiers. He laid out a huge table for war games between little green GIs and plastic cowboys and Indians, choreographing the action like a play. When a toy was hit by an arrow, he hammered a nail through it, splattered the dying hero with ketchup.

Most of all, he made movies. When Steven was about twelve, his father, overworked at the local RCA plant, let him operate the family Kodak Brownie, an 8mm home movie camera. He filmed family getaways, jumping out of the car before they arrived at the campground so he could shoot establishing shots of his father parking the vehicle. He set up his Lionel train set and re-created the climactic wreck from *The Greatest Show on Earth*. He earned his Boy Scout badges by making a short stop-motion film about a gunfight. By the age of thirteen, he had begun directing an entire forty-minute war film, with friends as his cast and crew, which would take him three years to finish—but he saw it through, filming weekends. Other kids turned fifteen or sixteen and got cars and played sports and chased girls. Steven stuck with his movie. Directing was how he made friends. Behind the camera, he could boss around the kids who usually bullied him on the playground, made fun of him for his flattop and his big eyeglasses, which looked even bigger because he was so scrawny. He screened the movies at home, collecting coins for charity. His little sisters sold popcorn and Popsicles. He took to thinking of himself as a film director. It wasn't a hobby, or an aspiration. He simply was.

His new identity was a barrier against the heavy silences and resentful nighttime arguments at home, where Arnold and Leah were on the long, painful road to separation and divorce. Steven's father went away on business more often than before. His mother's exuberance—she played music, she danced, she ripped up and down the neighborhood in her army-surplus jeep—gave Steven joy, but also made him stand out even further from the crowd. She was in love with Arnold's friend and former assistant Bernie Adler. Steven found out when he was cutting together footage from one of the family camping trips and he saw the way Leah and the ever-present Bernie acted when they thought no one was watching. He pulled his mother into the dark closet he used as an editing room and showed her, hoping for an explanation. Leah fell to the ground, crying.

"Please don't tell your father," she begged. "Please don't tell your father!"

Steven didn't tell. Years later, Leah and Bernie would marry. Some of the more conservative, repressed neighbors whispered, unkindly, that it wasn't clear who the Spielberg children's true father was.

Steven escaped into his movies, comics, and science-fiction magazines. And the sky.

He loved the telescope in the backyard. He cherished the night his father, years earlier, had dragged him out of bed, a thermos of coffee in one hand and blankets slung over his arm.

"Come with me," Arnold whispered.

He hurried Steven to the car in his pajamas. Steven trembled, more in fright than at the cold. They drove a half hour in the darkness, out into the desert, and then, as Steven remembered it, suddenly there were dozens of people on their backs in the sand, eyes turned skyward. Arnold pulled the car over onto the side of the road and killed the engine. He led Steven to where the people were and spread the blankets onto the ground, laid out his old army knapsack as a pillow. They both lay down. Arnold pointed at the sky, and told Steven a comet would soon appear, predicted by science and men trained to study space. He told him everyone else had stayed up into the middle of the night to see it, too.

For a moment, nothing happened. The stars shone intensely. A canopy of bright desert dust floated eerily in the air.

Something flared, burned brightly against the sky, and disappeared.

And then again.

Like falling stars, Steven thought.

He was still only eleven. The Spielbergs had just moved to Phoenix. His parents had yet to drift apart from each other. The world made him feel alone, but home didn't. Yet.

A meteor shower lit up the sky.

Steven's memory of the night would grow and glitch over the years. Sometimes he remembered it happening in New Jersey. He claimed Arnold's naming of the shower was set in stone in his mind, though in some interviews he recalled a Leonid shower and in others a Perseid. Sometimes he remembered he had wondered about the source of the lights, and others he said he had decided, there and then, that he would one day make a film about a benevolent force coming from the stars. Sometimes the crowd was two hundred, sometimes more; Arnold would chuckle and shake his head and say that, as far as he recalled, no one else had been out there with them.

The sky filled Steven with the same rush that had overwhelmed him that other time his dad had taken him somewhere dark and unexpected, surrounded by other people who knew better than him what to expect. The circus that wasn't a circus, back in Haddon Township. The black screens of the cinema and of the sky both came to life, and Steven Spielberg felt confusion, awe, excitement, and fear.

The kind of fear that thrills.

Steven turned sixteen. He finished his war film, called it *Escape to Nowhere*, and entered it into a statewide amateur film competition. It took first prize, a reward that consisted not of money, but of a near-professional kit of filmmaking equipment: a 16mm Kodak film camera, a set of lenses, and a collection of film books. Arnold couldn't afford to buy all the 16mm film he knew his son would tear through, so he had Steven exchange the Kodak for an 8mm Bolex H8 Deluxe. It was a chunky matte-black beauty. When Steven donated the books to the school library rather than hoard them, Arnold—also fueled by guilt over his absences and the fraying of his marriage to Leah—bought him a projector and a sound recorder. Suddenly, Steven wasn't just a filmmaker in his own mind. He had a filmmaker's gear. And filmmakers made feature films.

Still just a high school sophomore, Steven painstakingly wrote out a sixty-seven-page script entitled *Firelight*, inspired by that night watching meteors flash against the sky. The screenplay told of a scientist in a troubled marriage who crosses paths with a UFO expert investigating alien abductions. Steven borrowed kids from the school drama department and filmed for six months, all over Phoenix and out at Camelback Mountain, on a budget of $500 generously and entirely provided by Arnold and Leah Spielberg.

Steven came up with a myriad of effects, using makeup and quick dissolves for a scene in which the UFO expert is disintegrated by the aliens, or placing floodlights high up on the sidewalk to mimic moonlight in the countryside. He recorded sound effects from home and laid them over the raw film. In the end, the film ran longer than two hours. They screened it at the Phoenix Little Theatre on March 24, 1964. Even though the Little was a struggling playhouse anyone could make use of—just a decade earlier, L. Ron Hubbard had booked the very same main stage for repeated lectures on a new science he had "discovered," which he called Scientology—the achievement felt momentous. Steven was only seventeen. The screening was packed. Statewide news outlets covered the event, called him a prodigy and hyperbolically compared him to Cecil B. DeMille.

The very next day at the Spielberg home, a "For Sale" sign went into the front lawn again, luggage filled the trunk of the car, and Steven waved goodbye to his friends. The family moved to affluent Saratoga, California, where Arnold was starting a new job at IBM. They were the only Jews there, too. Saratoga High was gentile, preppy, and cruel, and Steven remembered his final high school year as "hell on Earth." He got beat up every day. Got used to the hot sting of being hit in the face, the taste of gravel and blood in the back of his throat. On at least one instance, a classmate passing him in the hallway threw a handful of coins on the ground and ordered Steven to get down on his knees to pick them up. "You want it, don't you?" the boy sneered.

There was no relief at home, either. Arnold and Leah's anger at each other was evident now, like a creature that had been lurking in the depths finally breaking to the surface. Arnold knew about Bernie. Divorce proceedings began and turned ugly. Vietnam hung over everything. In December 1964, Steven turned eighteen and registered for the draft; in March of the following year, American troops landed in Da Nang, and by the end of December, nearly two thousand Americans had died there. Steven longed to show someone *Firelight*, blow their minds, get a job directing at a film company, but only college could keep him out of the war. He dreamed of film school, but his grades weren't good enough for USC, UCLA, or NYU. He found a place at California State College at Long Beach, which didn't have a film department—but it was, at least, only an hour's drive from every Hollywood studio.

His parents split up almost the same month as Steven graduated from high school, another time a milestone of success was shaded with sadness. Arnold took a lease on an apartment in Brentwood in Los Angeles, and Steven moved in with him. In the fall of '65, he started classes at college. Within two years, he had snuck off the bus on the Universal lot, met the studio librarian Chuck Silvers, and began ditching classes.

Being enrolled at college kept him out of the draft—but nowhere did it say he had to attend.

· 5 ·

I LIE TO YOU ALL THE TIME

On New Year's Eve 1967, three weeks before Steven met George at Royce Hall, Francis and his wife, Eleanor, went to dinner at their friend Bart Patton's house. Francis had met Patton, real name Phillip Bardwell, at UCLA, and then hired him as an actor on the horror film *Dementia 13*, the first picture Roger Corman had trusted him to direct. That was the shoot on which he'd met Eleanor, too. She was a slim, dark-haired visual artist, born and raised in Los Angeles, working as the film's underpaid art director. Francis loved being around her. She found his chaotic energy intoxicating. They'd married impulsively in February of '63, boarding the Union Pacific train to Las Vegas with a dozen friends and family members in tow. On September 17, their first child, Gian-Carlo, was born. On the 25th, *Dementia 13* was released in B-movie houses and drive-ins, on the bottom of a cheap Corman double bill. Francis had become a feature film director and a father—his two most dearly held dreams—within a week. He freely confessed that he hadn't thought the marriage "would be forever," but Ellie had got pregnant, and he had always wanted kids. Italian-American culture was all about family, and Francis adored his own siblings; he still feared the sharp, biting loneliness experienced as a bedridden, quarantined child with polio. Ellie was attractive, intelligent, loving, stimulating—"bird-like and kind," remembers Walter Murch's wife, Aggie, with "a wicked sense of humor"—and she was more mature than her new husband, too. Francis was only twenty-three when they tied the knot—Ellie was twenty-six—and he had a wandering eye. He couldn't help daydreaming of all the options that might be on offer should he become famous. Women were one of the reasons he worked in show business in the first place—he had vivid memories of the pretty girls who had shared the stage with his father, and of the chorus girls and the Rockettes, with their long smooth legs, on the nights when Uncle Anton conducted the orchestra at Radio City Music Hall and Francis and August were allowed backstage. Years after his wedding, Francis joked about settling down too soon: if he had waited until he'd become an "important director," he said, "I could have married Rita Hayworth!"

He'd kept in touch with Patton as he became a sought-after screenwriter and Patton began producing films, first for Corman and then, briefly, at Universal. Patton had married even younger—at twenty-one, to classmate and actress Mary Mitchel—and as his career stalled, he found Francis was equally disillusioned. Writing screenplays on assignment was a grind. One day, Francis visited Patton at Universal, shortly before Patton was dismissed, and they walked around the lot venting to one another. Somehow they found their way to the balcony of one of the theaters on which MCA-Universal shot one of their many variety television shows. A crew of go-go dancers, including, Patton remembers, a young Teri Garr, stood in skimpy outfits on the stage below. The two men watched them for a while. Patton talked about other girls he knew, the ones who danced in bikinis in the beach pictures. Francis shook his head wistfully.

"God, Bart, I envy you," he whispered. "I can't wait to get out of this writing."

Patton looked over. His friend, he says, was "drooling."

Soon afterward, Francis quit the contract screenwriting gig and put all his money into his first film, *You're a Big Boy Now*. Now, just a year later, *Finian's Rainbow* was complete, Francis had well and truly "got out of this writing," and Patton felt like celebrating. He asked Francis and Ellie to ring in 1968 at his home in Nichols Canyon, up on the hills between Hollywood Boulevard and Mulholland Drive.

Patton remembered how much Francis liked girls. So, as a cheeky joke, he hired his kids' babysitters, Melissa Mathison and Maureen Hughes, to serve dinner. Melissa and Maureen were pretty and halfway through their senior year in high school, still just eighteen years old, best friends since grade one. Patton asked them to dress up as French maids. He figured he'd get a laugh, some elbowing in the ribs at the naughtiness of it. He certainly didn't expect the joke to set in motion a relationship that, within a decade, threatened to tear Francis's family and career apart.

Everyone called her Missy. Her family lived down the road in Nichols Canyon, and her father, Richard Randolph Mathison, was the managing editor of the magazine *Fortnight*, and the LA bureau chief for *Newsweek*. He knew everyone. In a crowded house—she was in the middle of two sisters and two brothers—Missy was quiet and reserved. She didn't speak a single fully formed English word until she was three years old, a situation so concerning her mother finally sat her down and said, "Missy, you really need to start talking."

"Okay," little Missy said. "I will."

She was able to speak—she just had never felt the need or desire.

She hated having her picture taken, too. If someone stepped up to her with a camera, she turned away or rushed at them to block out the lens. In one set of cherished family photos, Missy is shown in every print weeping and burying her head against her father's shoulder; they were the best pictures the photographer had managed to get out of her. Every single picture as she grew up seemed to show two smiling sisters, two smiling brothers—and Missy, second eldest, her head turned down.

She looked in the lens for school photographs, though, because the nuns said she had to, and you didn't disobey the nuns. Missy grew quietly through elementary and junior high, and entered Providence High School, an all-girls Catholic prep school in Burbank. Providence was a unique kind of place, off Buena Vista Park between the Warner Bros. and Disney lots. The school was religious enough to have nuns teach classes, showbiz enough that Jack Lemmon emceed the '68 senior talent show. More than one of Missy's classmates remembers waiting for the bus and waving to an old, frail Walt Disney as he was helped into his car to be taken to nearby St. Joseph Hospital, where, for much of November 1966, he underwent radiotherapy in a futile attempt to rid his lungs of the cancer created by a lifetime of chain-smoking filterless cigarettes. Missy's senior yearbook photo shows her with big eyes, smooth skin, and straight, glossy blond hair. She had a long face and a slender neck. Big, pearly white teeth filled every inch of space between her upper and lower lips. She was so reserved that her future brother-in-law, who met her when she was fifteen, assumed for a while that she was mute.

"She was a sweet person," remembers classmate Kaja Fehr. "She was very artistic." The two of them passed notes during class and bonded over their type-A sisters, who were running against one another for student body president. Fehr, who was later diagnosed with dyslexia, struggled with coursework, and Missy made sure to hang out with her the night before every test so she could help her cram. "She did it so lovingly and without any judgment."

The Mathison family home up in the Hills was always full of writers. Mostly journalists, but their dad knew Rod Serling, too, and the genre writer Richard Matheson (no relation). Family legend has it that Aldous Huxley had once babysat the older Mathison children. Missy's sister Melinda remembered being "treated . . . like an intelligent, almost-adult person from the time I was 6 or 7 years old"; she would go on to graduate from Stanford and become Ventura County's first female judge. If Missy knew what she wanted to do when she grew up, she didn't let on. She came alive mostly around younger children. "I was the babysitter for the entire Hollywood Hills area, Nichols Canyon area, for a long time," Melinda says. "And then, when I went off to school, Missy stepped in." She was a natural. She listened, she cared, she understood the peculiar loneliness of young childhood. She had a capacity to make room within herself for another person's needs. Her silence created space she welcomed the children into.

Only with Maureen, the friend she had made when she was five, did Missy allow herself to be silly. They liked to dress up in matching outfits, often with a flourish copied from a film they liked. New Year's at the Pattons' was that kind of occasion: a bit of fancy dress in a home they both knew and in which they felt comfortable. Missy hadn't expected Francis Coppola, a decade older than her, large and funny and charismatic.

Francis hadn't expected Missy, either.

In the New Year, Missy started babysitting for the Coppolas, looking after four-year-old Gian-Carlo and two-year-old Roman while Francis and Ellie worked. Little boys adored her, and Gio was no different. She returned to Providence for spring term a new person.

"Her senior year, she started to come out and shine like crazy," says Kaja Fehr. She seemed, suddenly, empowered. Francis had that effect when he turned his attention and praise onto you. No one but he knew when, exactly, "Francis fell in love with her," as Fehr puts it. "She was babysitting his kids when he fell in love with her. I think she was eighteen or so." It was almost as if Francis, as much as his sons, was the Coppola to be looked after. "Francis was very childlike," Fehr says. "He loves to talk about his childhood, and you can see him as a child sometimes, aside from the fact that he's a brilliant genius. I think the children inside them completely related."

When not with Missy, Francis spent more and more of his time meeting with George, to plot *The Rain People* and their break toward independence. If they could make *The Rain People* as Francis conceived it, on the road away from Hollywood, with portable equipment, it would become a model for *THX 1138* and every film of theirs after that. They would no longer need backlots, soundstages, or pencil-pushing studio executives. Ideally, one or more of the films would make enough money that they could, one day, fully finance a film themselves, with unbridled freedom.

"Francis had intended *The Rain People* as a small film," remembers Bart Patton, who served as his producer. "It became about a yearlong project."

Coppola had written a simple story, about a housewife who runs away from home one morning in the family station wagon, unsure of her own motivations. She travels across the country, picking up a brain-damaged college football player along the way, untangling her desires as the two of them stop in small towns and motels. The plot was inspired by a story Francis had come up with at Hofstra, by bits of Tennessee Williams, and by an incident from his childhood, when his mother, after an argument with Carmine, left home for two days and announced she would be staying in a motel. Unlike in real life, where Italia returned after forty-eight hours and normal life in the Coppola household resumed, Francis decided his script would end badly, though he wasn't yet sure how. He would figure it out as he went along, using resources as he found them. A surviving copy of the first draft of the screenplay is dated July 2, 1968, three months into filming.

The lead role, Natalie, had been written with the actress Shirley Knight in mind. For the part of the football player she picks up, Jimmy "Killer" Kilgannon, Francis cast James Caan, an old Hofstra classmate. Caan had grown up in Sunnyside, Queens, where he played three-on-three hoops on concrete courts tucked between buildings, hit baseballs across littered dirt fields, and learned "about things like respect and loyalty." Sunnyside was like "a jungle," he remembered, "and you can smell it." His father, Arthur, paid the rent dealing meat, lugging cuts of kosher beef from truck to restaurant kitchen, and Jimmy had to hose the stick and stench of cow blood out of the family car anytime he wanted to borrow it so he could take a broad on a date. "I wasn't going to be a butcher," Caan decided, "and that's what was waiting for me at the end of the road. So I jumped ship."

He enrolled and dropped out of school after school, looking for a major that caught his attention, but no colleges offered degrees in his preferred topics of "girls, ball, beer." He grew tall, strong, and charming, with baby blue eyes, that rasping Queens voice, and a strong, jutting lower jaw he could roll left or right to express anger, attraction, impatience. From the neck down, he was covered in hair—front and back. He got into football, boxing, martial arts; got so banged up he was covered in so many stitches and scars that the famed *Los Angeles Times* sportswriter Jim Murray later joked Caan wasn't born, "he was embroidered." He eventually dropped out of Hofstra without graduating, too, but he'd caught the acting bug and stayed in New York, enrolling at the Neighborhood Playhouse on East 54th Street and honing his craft under Sandy Meisner, who felt acting was, above all, about paying attention to the other person in the scene with you, and to the emotions that live under the words.

In class, Caan met another actor, nearly a decade older than him, named Robert Duvall. Duvall had already been working in theater and television; previously, he'd saved money and roomed with another Playhouse classmate, Dustin Hoffman. Now he and Caan became friendly. Duvall was resilient, hardworking, and dedicated to acting. His father, a retired admiral, had hoped Robert might follow him into the navy, but the only thing the kid was good at was acting, so he encouraged him to pursue that instead. Robert started in summer stock, made his way up to off-Broadway, earned himself some television gigs. In 1962, the writer Horton Foote recommended him to play Boo Radley in the film adaptation of *To Kill a Mockingbird*, which Foote was writing, and Duvall made his film debut.

By that time, Caan had moved out to Los Angeles, got a small part in Billy Wilder's *Irma la Douce*, then more substantial roles in two out of the great Howard Hawks's final three films. Duvall liked Los Angeles less than Caan did. He was less traditionally handsome than his friend. His hair was thinning already. His nose was a little pointed, his upper teeth a little crooked. He didn't drink, didn't smoke, didn't own a car. He liked country music, and he liked being involved with one woman at a time. Neither he nor Caan was really sure where he fit in the old Hollywood system, with its domineering directors and off-the-assembly-line process. They worshipped Brando, valued authenticity. Neither of them wanted to be movie stars. Caan turned down starring TV roles that would pay him handsomely but fail to challenge him; Duvall figured being Steve McQueen or Robert Redford "must get boring."

So, as Francis was casting *The Rain People*, Caan took him aside. He knew a guy, he said, who could play one of the characters. Francis met Duvall and liked him, and cast him as Gordon, the third-most-important part in the picture—and the darkest: a highway patrolman who pulls Natalie over befriends her and attempts to rape her.

The crew numbered just ten. Patton produced with Ron Colby, another friend of Francis's from Hofstra. The two men were assisted by Mona Skager, a publicist Francis had met at Warner Bros. when he was just starting out as a student screenwriter, hired by the studio to come in at night and doctor screenplays on the cheap. He'd been self-important then, too. Skager came out of the copy room late one night and bumped into him, big and odd-looking in a white mackinaw coat with red and yellow stripes, "his little wife," Ellie, as Skager remembers her, by his side.

"May I help you?" Skager asked.

"Well, I'm Francis Ford Coppola," he answered grandly.

"Well, that's nice," Skager said. "May I help you?"

He liked that she took no bull, so in 1968, he reappeared, and asked Skager if she wanted to make a movie.

"What would I do?" Skager asked.

"You can be the night caterer, the production secretary, and the script supervisor," Francis said.

"Well, I can do two out of the three, but what does a script supervisor do?"

"Ah, don't worry about it," Francis said. "You'll figure out how to do it."

Forty-seven-year-old Bill Butler served as the cameraman, on what was just his second feature film. He'd been recommended to Francis by William Friedkin, a cocky young director Butler had worked with at a television station in Chicago. The boom operator, James Sabat, had never worked on a feature before. A handful of other young people—including Ellie and her brother Bill—tagged along as do-it-all assistants. George would film a documentary about the making of the picture, write *THX 1138* between shoot days, and try his best to serve as Francis's assistant.

The convoy—consisting of a camera van, Francis's larger editing-suite-cum-production-office modified Dodge Frank mobile home, several cars for the cast and crew, and the station wagon Shirley Knight drove on screen—left Long Island and snaked through Pennsylvania and Virginia. George and Francis had designed the Dodge together—cameras on one side, sound equipment on the other, Steenbeck in the middle, dolly track on the roof. Wardrobe hung everywhere inside the cabin, swinging as they drove. George painted the words *HAL 9000* on the side of the vehicle, after the computer in Stanley Kubrick's *2001.*

"We borrowed everything," Mona Skager says. "Cars, everything. We had nothing. It was made on a shoestring. We didn't know where we were going. We would just follow disasters, like a train wreck—we would go, and then Francis would rewrite the scene to the train wreck. And then we'd shoot the train wreck." She realized she had been hired to be the grown-up on the crew. "I present a picture. I wear jewelry and I wear clothes and I wear shoes. I look very straight. But this crew were all hippies." At every stop along the way, Francis would choose a hotel and Skager was the first to go in, to make a good first impression.

They traveled through eighteen states over the course of sixteen weeks. When she was at the wheel of the station wagon during scenes, Shirley Knight drove wherever she wanted, taking turns as she pleased. "I had really no idea where we were going from day to day," Caan remembered. It drove him crazy—nearly, he said later, to a nervous breakdown. The whole time, Francis paid for everything out of his own pocket, reinvesting his earnings from *Finian's Rainbow*, as well as his meager $50,000 fee for *The Rain People*, into making his film the way he wanted. "If you're not willing to risk some money when you're young," he proselytized in front of George's camera, "you're certainly not ever going to risk anything in the years that follow."

As they drove into West Virginia, Francis and George shaved their beards, and everyone cut their hair short, out of fear a pack of hippies caravanning through the South would draw attention, judgment, maybe even violence. The cast and crew meandered and shot in pieces, then stopped in a succession of cheap, joyless motels Skager found last-minute. George would put down his camera and start writing, and Francis would give him pep talks about the power of authorship: how a man who wields a camera is dependent on who hires him, but the screenwriter is the original starting point, the only person on a picture who isn't interpreting someone else's creation. Writing, as Francis saw it, was freedom—a gateway to control. ("Francis will tell you what he really always wanted to be was a novelist," says Matthew Robbins.) You had the money or you had the story, and the dream was to have both; until he put words on the page, George, for all his talent and drive, had neither. But George was easily distracted. One morning, sitting in the lobby of one of the motels, he nudged Skager and pointed at an old episode of *Flash Gordon* playing on the reception television. He told her that was the kind of thing he wanted to make some day.

Early in the summer, after six or seven weeks of filming, the crew entered Nebraska. Colby, driving ahead, lit on the small town of Ogallala, in the grasslands off the I-80. Its main feature was an Old West strip dubbed Front Street, built just five years earlier to commemorate the days the town was a wild and lawless stop along the Pony Express, complete with undertaker and cowboy saloon. Colby parked his car and waited for the rest of the *Rain People* crew. Francis pulled up, took a look, and liked what he saw. "There were many good places that suited our story," he remembered. "The people were nice." It was a sleepy, out-of-time spot, far away from the political upheaval that rocked America's bigger cities. Francis decided to shoot the rest of the film there. He took over a local shoe shop to turn into a production office, and the cast and crew settled in. They would spend the next two months in Ogallala.

George's script came along, slowly and painfully, every sentence like pulling a tooth. He showed Francis a few pages.

"Boy, you were right," Francis said. "You *can't* write a screenplay!"

George kept at it. He became friendly with Duvall and started picturing him as his lead, the eponymous THX 1138.

"I'm writing this script and I really want you to star in it," George told Duvall. The actor liked the idea of a lead part. He didn't often get those.

"George was very slight," says Skager. "He didn't weigh a lot, and he wasn't very big. So he shot everything from below the coffee table. He couldn't lift the camera. He got a lot of crotch shots." He filmed Francis screaming at a Warner Bros. executive down the phone, filmed Francis and Shirley Knight getting into arguments. Francis, as captured by George's camera, delighted in the chaos and tension. His strength—and his vulnerability—lay in his own emotional commitment to the picture. He never seemed to make the film from the outside. He climbed in, poked at the material until he found in it parts of himself that were uncomfortable and unresolved. As he tinkered, Knight's character, Natalie, began embodying his own anxieties. Francis was twenty-nine years old. He had been married for six years and fathered two sons, and he felt cleaved between that life—family, bloodline, dignity—and a roiling lust for new adventures and new women, for young, admiring, adolescent sex and love. Filming *The Rain People* was a fantasy of its own, one of freedom, with everything he needed to live and work packed into a circus-like caravan, no fixed address.

The Rain People opens with Natalie climbing out of bed in the early hours of the morning and slipping silently out of her marital home, without waking her husband. When she tells her parents what she has done, her mother cannot understand it.

"He's just gonna wake up and find you gone?" she asks.

Natalie can never articulate why she has left her husband. Her anxieties over family and responsibility clash with confused emotional cravings. Guilt weighs heavy on her shoulders, never more than when keeping secrets makes her feel dishonest—or when she abandons someone she does not fully love but feels she must care for, be it her spouse or Jimmy Caan's aimless Killer Kilgannon. The camera holds her face in close-up, over and over again, searching.

"I'm sloppy," Natalie tells her husband. "I lie, I lie to you all the time." When she does come clean, still unable to articulate what moves and motivates her, it is scorn, not understanding, with which he meets her.

"I'm not impressed with your goddamn honesty," her husband barks down the phone. "You're stuck out there with yourself, and you don't like it."

In the film's final scene, when Natalie is in the trailer owned by Robert Duvall's highway patrolman, Gordon, facing the melodramatic consequences of her own irresponsibility, the film reveals Gordon as disturbed and predatory, broken by the loss of his own wife—not through abandonment but death. When the film flashes back to the house fire that took her life, it is Ellie Coppola, uncredited, who plays the dead wife. Idealized and inert. Loved beyond words, and the source of destabilizing pain.

This was the personal filmmaking Francis had escaped Warner Bros. to embrace. There, on the page and on the screen, he used the bubble of making a picture to interrogate himself. He wasn't sure he liked the answers, or even knew what they were.

After a few weeks, it became apparent that the people of Ogallala liked having the film crew in town, too. One day, the "city fathers," as Francis thought of them, came to see him with a proposal. "If you kids stay here," they told him, "we voted that we'll help you and we'll make some sort of a movie studio."

Francis thought, *In Ogallala, Nebraska?*

He and George got to discussing it. The only reason any filmmaker needed to be in Los Angeles was the facilities—the studios' backlots, their editing suites, their mixing stages, the warehouses full of lights and C-stands. But the equipment existed now to work outside of that system: They had both used it at film school and were using it now. They preferred to shoot on location, like the Europeans did, rather than soundstages. There was money to be spent outside of the studio system, anyway: Roger Corman had financed his first B-movies with self-funding and private equity; New York filmmakers were finding cash from all sorts of places. Why couldn't they do the same thing, on a more refined scale? *The Rain People* was all but in the can, George had *THX*, Francis had been writing *The Conversation*, Milius had *Apocalypse Now*. That was nearly a slate already.

George argued for San Francisco Bay as a possible home. Out on the road with their caravan, they already felt "like Robin Hood and his band," as Francis put it. "Imagine if we went to a beautiful city like San Francisco and implanted ourselves as a filmmaking community. We would have independence, and we'd still be close enough to LA to be able to draw on talent from there."

It happened that, before starting work on *The Rain People*, Francis had agreed to appear in a panel discussion in San Francisco as part of a conference held by the Associated Council of the Arts. But filming had dragged on, and it was impossible for him to leave Nebraska. He sent George in his place.

Lucas arrived at the Hilton Hotel in Union Square for the talk on June 7 under a cloud of gloom. Millions of Americans on the West Coast had stayed awake past midnight on the 5th to watch live coverage of the shooting of Robert Kennedy at LA's Ambassador Hotel. Twenty-four hours later, the nation had woken up to confirmation of Kennedy's passing.

George, once he was on the event stage, found himself in a combative mood. On the panel with him sat his former USC instructor Arthur Knight; *New Yorker* critic Brendan Gill; the editor of *Film Quarterly*, Ernest Callenbach; and a local filmmaker named John Korty, who at thirty-two had already made four films, including three features and an Oscar-nominated animated documentary short, *Breaking the Habit*. He'd produced and directed them all from a barn in Stinson Beach, a community of three hundred or so inhabitants nestled against the ocean on the north side of the Golden Gate Bridge in Marin County, never once having to set foot in a Hollywood studio or put up with an executive's notes and commands.

George listened as Knight complained that film schools were "oversubscribed," and that young people today could have their parents buy them a handheld camera and immediately pretend they were filmmakers. Knight thought the closed shop of the old days lead to higher-quality pictures. "All you have to do today to be a moviemaker is put your eye behind a camera," he asserted; experience and skill were no longer valued. Callenbach agreed that only "a few interesting American films" had been made in the preceding few years. The tone was academic, staid, a little glib. When his turn came, George threw the civility over like a table.

"The cigar-chewers are beginning to realize that their prime audience is young people," he announced, "and that they don't know this audience, or understand it. They keep making films the old way and then wonder why nobody goes to them." He talked up *The Rain People* as a model of creative freedom. "The studio hasn't even seen a script," he said, "and won't be allowed to cut it afterwards. This is a major change—the independency to make personal films. Before, all the studios did was countermand us."

Korty watched and listened. He had been looking forward to meeting the notorious Francis Ford Coppola, but he was taken with the skinny kid in blue jeans and tennis shoes who had showed up in his place. Korty, too, had contempt for the "cigar-chewers," a term he also used when his turn came to speak. Making a movie wasn't the real challenge, he opined—booking it in theaters was. "The cigar-chewing distributor wants you to bring the film to him at nine in the morning so he can watch it in a screening room while he makes telephone calls," he said. Hollywood had no respect for movies, no understanding of quality.

Afterward, George told Korty they were both clearly fighting the same fight: Korty from outside the studios, George from within. They ran to find a pay phone and called Ogallala. George had to tell Francis. Making personal pictures independently, away from the studios, wasn't just possible.

John Korty was already doing it.

·6·

DO YOU WANNA BE A FILM DIRECTOR?

After watching *THX 1138 4EB*, Steven returned to his routine: two packed days of classes in Long Beach, trying his best but fundamentally uninterested, and the rest of his week on the Universal lot, bouncing from department to department with the energy of A. A. Milne's Tigger.

"I was on the outside of a wonderful hallucination that everyone was sharing," he said, from film school students like George to the employees on the backlot. "And I wanted to do more than be a part of the hallucination," he added. "I wanted to control it. I wanted to be a director." Though he didn't realize it, the word set him subtly apart from the likes of Francis and George, who wanted to be *filmmakers*, a more encompassing term, one that, to them, was a philosophy rather than a job description, and meant being an artist rather than an employee. Steven might not have thought about it so deeply, but George had. He told people, vehemently and often, how much he resented the word *director*.

Whenever he could, Steven convinced the Universal employees humoring him to take their paintings down off the office wall so he could project one of his short films up against the bare paint. Their feedback was usually kind, but they all told him that 8mm home movies didn't play well. If he wanted to be taken seriously, he had to shoot something on 16mm or, better still, 35mm. The size and quality of the image was one of the differences between his childish shorts and George's *THX*, which *felt* like a real movie. Immediately, Steven took a job in the university lunchroom, stocking his schedule in Long Beach even fuller, and saved up for professional film stock.

On July 6, a month after George met John Korty, Steven rolled cameras on the first project he had ever shot on 35mm film. The short was called *Amblin'*, the budget $15,000, most of it provided by a small-time band manager and aspiring film producer Steven had met named Denis Hoffman. It was artier than anything Steven had ever shot before, something closer to the abstraction and expressionism of George's film school work. Over a twenty-six-minute runtime, a young man carrying a guitar case meets a free-spirited young woman, and they hitchhike across the Mojave Desert. When they reach the ocean, he opens his case and reveals it contains not an instrument, but wing tip shoes, a suit, shirt and tie, deodorant, mouthwash, and toilet paper. Sad and bemused, the girl leaves him there and walks away alone.

Steven cut the film himself and had it finished by the fall. He showed it to Mike Medavoy, who he had heard about through other young filmmakers. Medavoy was impressed and took him on as a client. Steven also showed the film to Chuck Silvers at Universal, who was equally impressed, and told the young man to leave the print with him. One rainy evening soon after, Silvers called the office of Sidney Sheinberg, Universal's vice president of television. He told the secretary it was urgent.

Sheinberg was just thirty-three but intimidating, the shrewd and hard-nosed protégé of MCA head Lew Wasserman, the single most powerful man in the entertainment business.

"Jesus Christ," he snarled at Silvers down the phone. "I'm in the middle of a goddamn meeting, arguing with these people."

"Sid, I've got something I want you to see," Silvers said.

"I've got a whole goddamn pile of film here. I'm going to be here half the night. I'll be lucky to get out of here by midnight."

"I'm going to put this in the pile for the projection booth," Silvers insisted. "You really should look at it tonight."

Sheinberg paused for just a second.

"You think it's that goddamn important?" he asked.

"Yes, I think it's that goddamn important," Silvers answered. "If you don't look at this, somebody else will."

Silvers put the phone down, walked the print to the screening room, left it with the projectionist, and went home.

When he came in the next day, a message was waiting for him in his office. It asked, simply:

Who is Steven Spielberg?

"They want to talk to you," Silvers said urgently when he managed to reach Steven at home. "When can you be here?"

Steven raced to Universal City Plaza, without taking the time to call Medavoy. He had wanted this for too long, imagined it for too long. He entered the Black Tower, Universal's headquarters, a thirty-six-story skyscraper of black aluminum and glass. Someone showed him up the elevator. Sheinberg sat behind his desk, austere in his suit and tie, looking out the window. He turned as Steven entered.

He'd expected a man in his late twenties or thirties. Instead, here was a scrawny-looking kid with a long face, smooth cheeks, and a high school nerd's haircut, wearing nothing more formal than a button-up shirt and a pair of slacks. Sheinberg blinked and recovered.

"Sir," he started—Sheinberg called everyone *sir*, at least when he wasn't screaming at them—"sir, I liked your work. How would you like to go to work professionally?"

Steven stammered and mumbled. His heart pounded in his chest.

"You sign a contract and start in television," Sheinberg explained.

He made direct, piercing eye contact from behind the square lenses of his heavy eyeglasses. "If you do a few shows and other producers like your work, you can—maybe—branch out into feature films. You should be a director."

"I think so, too," Steven said. Sheinberg was struck; the kid even *sounded* young.

"Hopefully you're going to have a lot of success in your career," Sheinberg said, softening. "And a lot of people will stick with you in success; I'll stick with you in failure."

Sheinberg had liked *Amblin'* precisely because it was the opposite of *THX 1138* and all the facsimile student films that came in its wake—"a lot of stuff that was very technical," Sheinberg said later, "all white" and sterile. "But this was a human story."

He offered Steven the standard entry-level deal: a seven-year, exclusive contract with Universal to direct whatever episodes of television he was assigned to, starting at $275 a week, maybe $300. A golden opportunity, shaped like a cage; an infernal old-time Hollywood pact of the Jack Warner kind. Steven was keen, but something in Sheinberg's fatherly tone brought to mind the image of his own father—the real one, the one who was paying his rent and his tuition.

"Well," Steven said uneasily, "I haven't graduated yet."

"Do you wanna graduate college or do you wanna be a film director?" Sheinberg snapped.

Steven wanted to be a film director.

"I quit college so fast," he said later, "I didn't even clean out my locker."

On July 4, 1968, as the *Rain People* shoot was winding to a close, George and Francis traveled to John Korty's home studio in Stinson Beach, between redwood trees and white sandy beaches, in search of their own dreams. They arrived in two of the beat-up station wagons, producer Ron Colby riding with them, as well as Ellie and little Gio and Roman. As the cars slowed in front of the run-down old barn Korty used as his headquarters, Francis hesitated. *This*, he thought, *is what George has been making a big fuss about?*

But then, as Korty remembered it, "Francis and George walked in and their mouths dropped open." Inside the barn were an editing facility, a screening room, and storage for film and sound equipment. A perfectly independent personal film studio in an idyllic community shielded from the avarice and commercialism of Hollywood.

"This is what I want," Francis announced.

They had dinner and shot fireworks into the darkening sky.

Francis had recently visited Vancouver, and it had been, until that time, his preferred place to relocate. He pushed George to do like a draft dodger and consider moving to Canada. ("If he'd gone to Vancouver," George said later, "I'm not sure I would have gone with him.") The visit to Korty's barn, in the end, settled the matter. The Coppolas stayed a few days at the Mark Hopkins hotel in San Francisco, and Francis fell further in love with the idea. They could sell their house in LA, he told Ellie excitedly as they strolled through the lobby. "You should move up here with the children," he insisted.

George stayed in San Francisco to hunt for possible headquarters, and in early August, Francis took another trip, this one to Europe, in search of equipment and inspiration. In Germany, he attended a trade show in Cologne and put down a fortune on state-of-the-art postproduction equipment—Keller-Elektro-Mechanik (KEM) flatbed editing tables, a sound mixing bed—and arranged to have them shipped to California. Then Francis headed to Denmark. On a previous trip to Europe, he had heard of a Danish filmmaker, Mogens Skot-Hansen, who ran a film company, Laterna Film, that operated independently, owned its own editing equipment, and gave young people their starts. Francis wanted to see how Skot-Hansen was pulling it off. "Part of the bohemian idea of people doing shows goes back to my Hofstra experience; socially it had been so much fun," Francis explained, "and I always missed in film the sense of sitting around with your friends at the café and the pretty girls and that kind of theatre life."

Skot-Hansen, erudite and well-connected, loved everything about movies. Laterna Film—named after the *laterna magica*, or magic lantern—was headquartered outside Copenhagen, in a grand white villa surrounded by a park and gardens. Inside was everything one might need to make a picture: plentiful offices, spacious writing rooms, and, in the cellar, editing suites. Young filmmakers worked for Skot during the day and made use of the facilities to cut and mix their own films by night. Throughout the building, Skot displayed items from his extensive collection of early cinematic devices: magic lanterns, and also praxinoscopes, zoetropes, zoopraxiscopes.

"It looked like a very consolidated film company, which it wasn't," remembers Dorte, Skot-Hansen's daughter, who was twenty when Francis visited. The grand white villa was leased from the municipality of Copenhagen, and it was never certain Skot would make the next month's rent. The museum-worthy collection had been amassed at flea markets, not auctions. The work Laterna produced to support itself consisted of workmanlike documentaries and short films, with the odd commercial and television series thrown in. (Among those being shot in 1968, when Francis was in Copenhagen, was an eight-episode series, *Hemmelig Sommer*, starring, in his debut, a twelve-year-old child actor by the name of Lars von Trier.)

Francis and Skot hit it off right away. "They clicked," Dorte Skot-Hansen says. "They were both entrepreneurial, interested in doing many different things. They both thought: anything can happen, so you have to try it." Francis ended up staying for three weeks, "kind of as an apprentice," Dorte Skot-Hansen says, which mostly meant "hanging around." The restless Francis briefly considered making an improvised, low-budget picture in Denmark, Corman-style, and had Laterna employees drive him around Copenhagen, scouting locations. In the evenings, Francis picked up Dorte in a borrowed car, and the two of them traveled the city's "death route," as the local students called it, a wild tour of central Copenhagen's most notorious bars and taverns. Dorte was twenty, a decade Francis's junior, and her parents weren't too sure about the appropriateness of their going drinking together, but he was never ungentlemanly. "He was easy to be with," she says, "charming, fun, interested in everything." One weekend, everyone drove out to the Skot-Hansen summer house. Skot played the piano; Francis danced with Dorte and her girlfriends.

"I saw this mansion, and the pretty blond girls I'd always associated with Denmark, and the editing rooms and so on," Francis said later, "and when I came back I told George Lucas that we too had to get a mansion somewhere."

When Francis finally set off for America again, Skot gifted him one of the zoetropes from his own collection. The zoetrope was an optical toy from the late nineteenth century, a cylinder with slits cut vertically on the outside and images painted on the inside; when spun, the images, viewed through the moving slits, appeared to move. The word *zoetrope*, Skot told Francis, was a portmanteau of Greek root words, its meaning variously translated as "wheel of life," "movement of life," or—in France's preferred translation—"life revolution."

Francis loved the zoetrope. It harked back to the magic of early cinema, to the daring and vision of the men who made those optical toys and machines—each of them part artist, part engineer, part speculator and businessman. More personally, it would remind him always of Skot's little paradise: independent, youthful, free-spirited.

Francis headed back to America. Just as he did, Skot embarked on his most ambitious undertaking yet, producing and co-financing Peter Brook's adaptation of *King Lear*, with Paul Scofield in the title role. It was a gamble that stretched Laterna Film to its limits, but might, finally, make the company's international reputation. The shoot was grueling, on snow-covered and wind-beaten beaches; the budget kept growing, from $400,000 to $2 million. When the film finally came out in 1971, the reviews were poor, the business worse. Laterna Film shut down soon after.

"Skot lost a lot of money on that movie," his daughter says. He suffered a stroke less than a year after *King Lear*'s American release and spent the next twelve years in a home, until his death in March 1984. "It was part of the reason my father had a stroke," says Dorte, "that he was trying to cope with this disaster." She pauses for a moment. "I wish he had stayed with the documentaries, and that he had not made *King Lear*, but he had to try it. That is the film business, sometimes."

Francis made it back to New York in time for the gala premiere of *Finian's Rainbow* at the Penthouse Theatre, on the corner of 47th and Broadway. Warner Bros. put him up in a suite at the Plaza, and Francis brooded. George had agreed a mansion sounded idyllic, but they couldn't afford any of the places he found available. The expensive equipment Francis had bought was on a boat from Europe, but they still had nowhere to put it when it arrived. With *Finian's Rainbow* about to be released and *The Rain People* still in postproduction, they hadn't been able to find financing for *THX 1138* yet, either.

Francis had changed as a man in the year since wrapping *Finian's Rainbow*, and perhaps he dreaded coming face-to-face with the work of a filmmaker he felt he had now outgrown, and having that filmmaker be misunderstood as the person he was now. In any case, when the film critic Joseph Gelmis dropped by the Plaza in the afternoon to interview him, hours before he was due to step out onto the red carpet, he found Francis "nervous and under great emotional stress."

In a conversation in which he would have been expected to talk up his picture, Francis instead blamed the studio for turning the film's release into "a big fancy roadshow," blamed Hermes Pan for doing an "abysmal" job of choreographing the dance numbers, blamed actors Don Francks and Tommy Steele for turning in poor performances. He reminded Gelmis his shooting budget and schedule had been just a fraction of what bigger musicals usually got.

"It's come to the point where I just want to get out altogether. I just want to go do my own thing," he said. "And I may do that. I'm fed up. It takes too much out of you."

He wasn't in want of studio offers—he told Gelmis he had recently turned down "lots of big pictures," including "half a million dollars for . . . another musical"—but he only wanted to make personal films now, films that were *his*, for better or worse. He confessed to feeling responsible for George. He'd convinced him to turn down the sure-thing offer from Carl Foreman to produce *THX 1138* at Columbia, and now, "let's say *Finian's Rainbow* is a big flop," Francis speculated. "It's going to hurt George more than anybody . . . I'm saying, 'If you want me, you've got to give George Lucas his break.' Well, if suddenly they don't want me, then George has got a problem." Fail once, and it was back to the assembly-line grindstone—or slip out of the business altogether. And if he—the first film school graduate to make a studio movie—failed, then would any film school graduates get hired again?

"What I'm thinking of doing, quite honestly, is splitting," Francis told Gelmis again, as their time together wound down to a close. "I'm thinking of pulling out and making other kinds of films. Cheaper films. Films I can make in 16mm . . . All I know is that I'm tired. It's not just opening-night jitters. I've been thinking about this now for six months. I'm tired. I never knew that so many people wished you failure. I didn't realize. Let somebody else have the headaches . . . I really feel I could make an important film. It may take ten years. But I feel it's possible . . . If it means I've got to work on $6,000 films in San Francisco, then I guess that's what I have to do."

He paused. The afternoon light was dimming over Central Park on the other side of the window glass, streetlamps twitching to life on 59th Street.

"I don't know," Francis said finally. "I'll probably do another big picture now. I really need the money."

· 7 ·

TEST-TUBE BABY

Finian's Rainbow rolled out across America to mixed reviews. There were those, like the *New York Times*'s Renata Adler, who found it "joyless," and Joe Morgenstern, for *Newsweek*, who dismissed it as "fake, its sentiments always bogus." Even the critics who liked the film liked it almost in spite of itself, like Pauline Kael, who praised Coppola in the *New Yorker* for doing "pretty well, or probably as well as could be done short of rethinking the whole thing." Only Roger Ebert seemed genuinely impressed. He thought it was "the best-directed musical since *West Side Story*."

The film grossed a solid, if unimpressive, $11.6 million for Warner Bros.–Seven Arts—only a fifth of the cash raked in by *Funny Girl*, the musical that became the year's biggest hit, but a healthy profit all the same, on a film Francis had made, all told, for about $4 million.

Francis and George sat together in Francis's office on the Warner Bros. lot and debated what to do next. They could probably convince the studio to finance *THX 1138* now, but Francis, whose mood was as volatile as the weather, wanted more. He wanted a deal big enough to bankroll their dream of an independent studio in San Francisco—a deal that could pay for the mansion, pay for the equipment, pay for all of it. That deal was bigger than one movie; he needed a slate of films to dangle in front of executives, a package worth gambling on. The only projects he had to offer were *THX 1138* and *The Conversation*. To make a slate, they needed more.

The first person Francis called was John Milius. After graduating from USC, Milius had joined classmate Willard Huyck as a script reader at American International Pictures, the low-budget distributor that often released Roger Corman's pictures. AIP fired him after two weeks, on the grounds of his generally being a prick, but rehired him quickly, and he and Huyck got their first on-screen credit soon after, for rewriting the exploitation thriller *The Devil's 8*. With that credit in the bag, Mike Medavoy started booking Milius more rewriting gigs, and even sold a couple of his own, not-very-good spec scripts. Milius was pretty happy. He was making a living from his pen, like his literary heroes. He was improving his craft. He had recently finished a treatment for a movie to be called *The Crow Killer*—eventually retitled *Jeremiah Johnson*. It was the first script of his he really liked, drawing on those days in the mountains in Colorado, and the first one he'd be truly proud to have his name on. He made almost thirty grand a year and could live on fifteen, and he was left alone, without a boss hanging over his shoulder, to smoke cigars and scratch drafts out in longhand on his yellow legal pads. He didn't have to work in an office, and he didn't have to go back to lifeguarding. What else did he need?

The Crow Killer was a Warner Bros. movie, so Francis met him on the lot. Though five years younger than Francis and with much less experience under his belt, Milius thought of them as equals: Coppola had been the first to break into the industry, he was the second, everyone else trailed behind them. Spielberg—who Milius had met briefly after the screening at Royce Hall, where Steven was shy and Milius, wearing a giant cowboy hat, was flirting with the girls and knocking back drinks—was in television, and nothing he'd directed had aired yet. George had not made a film since graduating.

Francis told him about the plan to move to San Francisco, start an independent studio. He was on the lookout for writers.

"How much do you need to live on?" Francis asked.

"$15,000," Milius answered.

"Well, I'll get you $15,000 to do your Vietnam thing," Francis said, referring to *Apocalypse Now*. "You and George."

It wasn't a great offer. Milius's multiple drafts on *Crow Killer* had netted him, in all, almost $80,000, and he had an offer on the table for another rewriting gig, which would pay him $17,000. Universal had recently extended him a seven-year contract of the same kind Steven had signed, allowing Milius to write and maybe even direct television.

And yet Milius saw Francis's proposal as a fork in the road. He could stick to the path of the studio hack and "rewrite some piece of crap that would probably be rewritten by somebody else," or he could "go do my own thing." The great men he admired—Steinbeck, Hemingway, John Ford—would only choose one way.

Milius told Francis he was in. He went back to AIP and filled Huyck in, and Huyck declared himself ready to move north to San Francisco, too. If Milius knew any other young and hungry screenwriters, Francis said, they were welcome to follow.

Soon after, Matthew Robbins's phone rang, and the voice at the other end introduced itself as Jeff Berg. He said he was an agent at Creative Management Associates, and a colleague of Mike Medavoy's.

"I hear you might like to write screenplays," Berg said. "Would you like to write?"

". . . Yeah," Robbins answered. He wasn't sure what an agent did or was.

"I can make that happen," Berg said. "Lemme take you to lunch."

Berg was right—Robbins *had* started thinking about becoming a screenwriter, an ambition he discussed mostly with Hal Barwood, another former USC classmate, though neither of them had actually sat down at a typewriter yet.

Berg took Robbins to a local diner, bought him a hamburger. "Milius tells me you want to write a movie," he said. "What you got?"

Robbins wasn't too sure how to respond. The whole thing was dreamlike, like a scene in an old movie. He experienced the same uncanny sensation he'd felt the first time he'd held a copy of *Daily Variety* in his hands. He'd run his finger along the green logo at the top and thought it looked unreal, like a movie prop, something out of *Sunset Boulevard* or *The Bad and the Beautiful.*

"What have you got?" Berg repeated. "Because Francis has made a deal with Warner Bros. to develop seven feature films, and you can get guild minimum, which is $5,000, and you and Barwood can split it, and I'll get 10 percent."

Robbins and Barwood got to work.

Then Francis and George enlisted Korty, and then a documentary filmmaker named Steve Wax, also out of San Francisco, who wanted to make a film about student counterculture. Francis went on a sailboat outing with his former UCLA classmate Carroll Ballard, whose second film, *Harvest*, a nonfiction work about farming commissioned by the US Information Agency, had just been nominated for the Academy Award for Best Documentary.

"There is no way one can work within the system," Ballard agreed. "The best chance is to get out of L.A." Francis could use his name, too.

Francis took his lineup to forty-six-year-old Warner Bros. chairman Ted Ashley and his thirty-eight-year-old vice chairman and head of production John Calley. The two men had just come into their positions, installed after Seven Arts sold the studio to the Kinney National Company, a parking lot and cleaning services conglomerate. Ashley had been a successful agent, and Calley had years of experience in television and film production. All the same, Francis knew that a young suit in a new corner office was often anxious to make his mark; Ashley and Calley were smart and aggressive and eager to make the studio into a home for a new generation of filmmakers. As Francis saw it, they were susceptible to a sale.

His pitch to them was simple: He, Francis, would bring the studio several other young filmmakers just like him—including George Lucas; John Milius, the hottest young script doctor on the lot; Academy Award nominee Carroll Ballard; and Academy Award winner John Korty—each of them with an idea for a movie aimed at a youthful audience, ready to be fleshed out into full screenplays at the drop of a first draft fee. For a small price—and entrusting Francis to oversee the projects as a producer, through a new company he called American Zoetrope—Warner Bros. could tie down a whole slate of projects from the finest film school graduates in America, starting with the feature film adaptation of the most sensational, celebrated student film ever made: *THX 1138*.

This was, Francis suggested to Calley, more than an opportunity: It was a privilege.

Calley bit. The studio would fully finance *THX 1138* and put up another $300,000 for Francis and George to start their studio. In exchange, Warner Bros. would have right of first refusal to the scripts Francis pitched, including *The Conversation* and *Apocalypse Now*, drafts of which were expected to be ready to read around the time *THX 1138* wrapped filming.

Francis and George hit the phones again—the clock was ticking now. They gave up on their dream of a genteel hilltop mansion. A music producer on Folsom Street, in the heart of San Francisco, had listed his second-floor space for rent; they would lease it and start there.

Francis met with Mona Skager and asked her to be American Zoetrope's "secretary-treasurer"—the adult in the room, once again.

"How would you like to move to San Francisco?" he asked. He pitched it to her like the *Rain People* shoot, but more organized: a little studio of their own, with no unions to worry about, no one telling them what to do or how to make their films.

"Sounds good to me," Skager replied.

George called Murch.

"Francis needs someone to cut the sound and mix *The Rain People*," he said.

"Great," Murch answered.

"But it's in San Francisco," George added.

"Great," Murch repeated. He'd found a job cutting commercials for Haskell Wexler's company, but he didn't love living in Los Angeles, a city he thought of as an unfinished jigsaw puzzle, its pieces—your house, a good restaurant, a family doctor—distantly scattered from one another. He loaded a truck full of sound equipment, and his wife, Aggie, drove them up to Northern California, Murch asleep in the passenger seat, their six-month-old son in his lap. They couldn't afford a place in San Francisco, so they bought a houseboat in Bolinas, a few miles from Korty's barn in Stinson Beach. George and Marcia, who were married in February in Pacific Grove at First United Methodist, a little church among the pines, bright with the sunlight pouring through its mosaic stained glass windows, rented a small house at the top of a hill in nearby Mill Valley for $120 a month. Francis and Ellie bought a big Victorian mansion with four floors, nine bathrooms, and an elevator, right on Broadway in the heart of San Francisco.

Like the "pied piper," Matthew Robbins says, Francis led the way to the Bay Area, and to the Bay Area, the others followed—each according to his means.

And then the phone in Francis's office at Warner rang. The operator told him the caller was one Steven Spielberg, from MCA-Universal. Francis, with a shrug, accepted the call.

A nasal, nervous voice came down the line. "I'm a young director working at Universal," Steven told Francis on the phone. "I've just done my first TV show, and I'd love to come over."

Steven had dropped out of university on January 31 and started shooting his first television job the very next day. "Eyes," written by the creator of *The Twilight Zone*, Rod Serling, was a chapter in the horror anthology *Night Gallery*, starring Joan Crawford as a wealthy blind woman who pays a doctor to transplant a desperate gambler's eyes in place of her own. Filming lasted nine days, and Steven thought he'd done okay. He'd been overwhelmed, but Crawford had graciously empowered him every step of the way, and the studio producers admitted he had talent, even if they groaned at his occasionally wacky, arty choices—like an establishing shot filmed through a chandelier dangling from the ceiling, or a surgical operation scene he'd shot so suggestively it was hard to tell what, exactly, was happening. As he looked ahead, the first person Steven wanted to connect with again was George, who always seemed one step ahead of him. Steven made little short films; George made the short film that won the National Student Film Festival. Steven signed a TV contract; George joined Francis Coppola at Warner Bros. Steven finished shooting a TV episode with Joan Crawford, only to read in the trades that George was about to direct a *feature film*.

George didn't remember meeting Steven, but he and Francis were intrigued by the phone call. On the recommendation of Caleb Deschanel, they had watched *Amblin'*, curious about "this kid who was trying to do a 35-millimeter film," George said, "which was a big deal at the time." George magnanimously decided *Amblin'* was "good," even "professional. He knew what he was doing." He told Francis they should let the "kid" drop in.

Steven drove over to Warner Bros. for lunch. He was nervous. Francis had an aura and, at least as far as Steven was concerned, so did George. Most people met the kid from Modesto and saw a shy, reluctant young man in a button-down shirt—but Steven looked at him and felt what he had felt that night at Royce Hall. "I was a little bit in awe of him," he recalled.

They took each other's measure as they ate. In their respective recollections, Francis, usually the center of gravity at any meal, fades into the background. "That was the first time I actually talked with Steven," said George. "He was the youngest director at Universal; I was the youngest director at Warner Bros . . . But I was already impressed. He was 22, directing TV shows. I hadn't directed anything yet, so I thought, *Oh my God, he's ahead of me.*"

Steven was planning a film he wanted to shoot in San Francisco himself, if Universal gave him a green light. It was a sex comedy retelling of "Snow White" featuring, in lieu of dwarves, "seven guys . . . who run [a] Chinese food factory." Jeff Berg's father, Dick, was producing. The three men talked about Zoetrope. Francis was still ambivalent about the whole move. Now that he had sold both the studio and his friends on a dream of independence, he was considering doing another studio picture first. He wondered if he could have his cake and eat it, too.

It struck Steven that George, rather than Francis, drove the pair's dream of independence in the Bay Area. "George was this kind of maverick from Northern California, an independent filmmaker who was always extremely proud that he had very few attachments to Hollywood," Steven said, "and I was essentially a test-tube baby, incubated on the lot at Universal Studios, raised inside the establishment, and very proud of that."

Zoetrope didn't appeal to him, and besides, he was one show into a seven-year contract. The vice president of television had promised to stand by him, in success and in failure. He was developing a feature. Things were going well.

He drove back home and reported for work the next day. Within weeks, Universal rejected his dreadful "Snow White" idea, and offered no alternative assignments. Steven was dejected. Medavoy came by Steven's little rented bungalow, with its framed movie posters on the walls and its waterbed in the bedroom. He made Steven's comfort lunch—peanut butter and jelly sandwiches—and told him not to overthink it. The company had a long list of directors under contract and he was the most junior; he had to wait his turn. He didn't tell Steven the whole truth: that Universal was a mess; that the seven-year contract had been a bad idea; that, with the exception of

Sheinberg, the studio brass thought Steven was good but not great, not worth upsetting the apple cart over. Medavoy didn't say that, in his heart, he agreed with them. Steven would make a very good journeyman one day, and his encyclopedic knowledge of film made him very good at copying other people's stuff. But it wasn't clear his work had a distinct personality.

Francis and George packed their lives up and moved to the Bay, to start their alternative Hollywood. Steven, tethered to the dimming light of a failing studio, stayed behind.

He wouldn't work again for a year.

Part Two

YOUNG MOGULS

American Zoetrope is a new film company located in San Francisco engaged primarily in the production of feature motion pictures for theatrical release but anxious to develop into the overall media field that includes television, documentaries and educational films.

. . . The essential objective of the company is to engage in the varied fields of film making, collaborating with the most gifted and youthful talent using the most contemporary techniques and equipment possible.

—From the press release booklet announcing the foundation of American Zoetrope and calling for business, 1969

· 8 ·

AMERICAN ZOETROPE

"We were aware," says Walter Murch of the opening of American Zoetrope, "from a cinematic point of view, that we were putting our flag on the moon."

In the fall of 1969, Francis finally began setting up the company's offices on the second floor of 827 Folsom Street, on a noisy strip of parking garages and automobile service shops, cheap loft spaces leased by artists and recording studios, and—on a nearly three-block stretch starting at the corner of 7th Street—bathhouses, clubs, bars, and sex-toy shops, the "sexual centre" of gay San Francisco. Mona Skager, a no-nonsense girl from Duluth, Minnesota, raised in strict Catholic schools, stoically told friends she'd moved to "wine country," which she felt was only half a lie: Everyone on Folsom Street, she joked, was a drunk.

"What we're striving for," George told the *San Francisco Chronicle*, "is total freedom, where we can finance our pictures, make them our way, release them where we want them released and be completely free to express ourselves. That's very hard to do in the world of business. In this country, the only thing that speaks is money and you have to have the money in order to have the power to be free."

At 827 Folsom, Francis stripped the plaster from the walls, revealing the bare brick, and from the ceilings, exposing wood beams. His equipment arrived from Germany, and the air was thick with dust as it was carted in through entrance doors Francis was still having installed, rescued from the old Fox Theatre after its demolition. The editing flatbeds were set up upstairs, the portable Eclair cameras stored away. Murch rode his motorcycle thirty minutes each way from Sausalito and parked the bike on the curb, indistinguishable, at first glance, from the Harleys waiting outside the neighboring leather bars, and oversaw the installation of his brand-new KEM mixing table into the warehouse's unfinished basement.

San Francisco was the antithesis of film-obsessed Los Angeles. It was hippies and counterculture and anti-Vietnam sentiment; it was Scott McKenzie's melodious entreaty to visitors to wear flowers in their hair. It was Jefferson Airplane and the Grateful Dead and Hunter S. Thompson and *The Dharma Bums*. Long before all that, it was the California gold rush and the Pacific railroad. Even the wind and drizzle felt highbrow compared to LA's relentless, monotonous sunshine. "Literally my only experience in L.A. was going to college," Lucas, a Northern California native, later remembered. He had no interest in sticking around for more.

San Francisco had no film industry to speak of, with the exception of Korty out in Stinson Beach and a handful of underground experimental filmmakers in lofts and vacant storefronts, but it had culture. The *Chronicle*'s star columnist, Herb Caen, called the city Baghdad-by-the-Bay; he wrote poetic odes to its "crowded garages and the empty old buildings above them, the half-filled nightclubs and the overfilled apartment houses," to "the great bridges and the rattle-trap street cars."

George went out onto the city's streets on Monday, September 22, and started filming *THX 1138*. His budget was $777,777. Francis had more or less pulled the number out of thin air. He knew Warner would only green-light the film if it cost them less than a million—

and seven was his lucky number, so: seven hundred seventy-seven thousand seven hundred seventy-seven dollars.

THX 1138 was an early instance—maybe even the first—of a young filmmaker using a short film as a calling card for a feature-length adaptation. The plot was an expansion of the original *Electronic Labyrinth: THX 1138 4EB.* THX 1138 is a worker in a sterile dystopian future in which the government controls the populace through the regular, mandatory use of emotion-suppressing drugs. People, like drones, are assigned mates and required to wear white uniforms and shave their heads. Sexual intercourse is prohibited. They confess in booths and receive the "blessings of the State." Through a mix-up, THX is briefly off his drugs, and experiences feelings and sexual desires; he has sex with LUH 3417, a surveillance worker, leading the State's android police force to detain and attempt to reprogram him.

Joining Robert Duvall as the lead were Donald Pleasence, as a coworker who is imprisoned alongside THX, and Maggie McOmie, as LUH. Pleasence had just starred as the villain Ernst Stavro Blofeld in the fifth James Bond film, *You Only Live Twice*, but McOmie was an unknown, spotted by Murch and Ron Colby in a local production of *Marat/Sade*. Everyone shaved their heads for their roles.

Over forty days, George and his small cast and crew crisscrossed San Francisco, taking advantage of the corners of the city that felt, themselves, like locations from a dystopian future. They shot at the airport and in unfinished, unopened tunnels of the Bay Area Rapid Transit system. They shot in the bowels of the Oakland Coliseum. George wanted it to feel like a film *from* the future, not *about* the future. Extras were recruited cheaply from the nearby Synanon addiction recovery center. The crew moved quickly, sometimes running from cops walking over to check their filming permit—they usually didn't have one.

George gave his actors little direction. "We didn't have a lot of takes," McOmie recalls. "Two, three. I just did what they told me to do." She didn't mind her nude scene with Duvall. She was attracted to him, he was attracted to her, it was the '60s, and prudishness was square. That suited George, too. Having written the sex scene, he wasn't too sure he'd be at ease staging it. (George felt uncomfortable with sex scenes because he was inhibited. Francis didn't shoot many sex scenes, either, but he suggested later his reason was the opposite—he was such a horny person that, when he tried to film romance on-screen, "I do it with such an emotional charge, I become timid and turn away.") George hired Caleb Deschanel as his nominal second unit director for a handful of shots he didn't have time to film himself, and Deschanel enlisted Matthew Robbins to help him. Murch, who had co-written the script, designed the sound. In many ways, the project felt like a USC short film, just bigger.

They wrapped in late November. Francis agreed George could install one of the editing machines in the attic of his little house in Mill Valley, because George couldn't stand the noise of construction at Folsom Street, and he thought the place looked like a nightclub.

"How is it possible I'm the only one with any vision around here?" Francis boomed.

Though he'd found the money for the expensive German equipment and the bespoke front doors, Francis told George the company couldn't afford more than one work print of its first movie, so instead of working in parallel, George cut the picture during the day—and then Murch had to take over and work on the sound by night. At breakfast, Murch would update George on his progress, George got back to work, and Murch went to sleep for the day.

They took a short break in early December and made their way out to the Altamont Speedway, an hour east of San Francisco, where the Rolling Stones were headlining a free concert festival, optimistically billed by some as "Woodstock West." The Grateful Dead, Jefferson Airplane, Santana, and Crosby, Stills & Nash were booked as support acts. The documentary filmmakers Albert and David Maysles and Charlotte Zwerin had been filming the Stones throughout their US tour. Expecting thousands to attend at Altamont, the Maysles brothers, through Haskell Wexler, put a call out for local crew.

George was given a camera with a long 1000mm telephoto lens, and he and Murch—the latter carrying his field sound recording equipment—were assigned to a hill at the outer edge of the speedway. The music started, George rolled, and his camera jammed after a hundred feet, barely into the first reel of 16mm film. That was his day done. It wasn't until much later, when they let the Maysles brothers screen their raw footage in one of the unfinished Zoetrope editing suites, that George and Murch learned that the Hells Angels hired by the organizers to work security had beaten up multiple people in the crowd throughout the day, and that an eighteen-year-old man, Meredith Hunter, had been stabbed and beaten to death after pulling a gun on the bikers after they yanked him away from the stage. Already, in August, as George and Francis were moving north, members of Charles Manson's "Family"—a commune of young people with a seemingly hippie lifestyle, from sing-alongs to free love orgies—had brutally murdered actress Sharon Tate, celebrity hair stylist Jay Sebring, and five other people, over two nights, in their homes in the Hollywood Hills. That, and now Altamont: peace and love, drug-taking and psychedelic music—the youth movement on which Francis had sold the staid executives at Warner Bros. had, all of a sudden, turned repulsive and toxic.

Five days after Altamont, the finishing touches were put to the American Zoetrope "studio." Francis entertained a reporter and photographer from the *San Francisco Chronicle* the day before the opening party, mocking the studios—in LA, he said, they made deals, but here people made films. The *Chronicle* writer thought Francis looked youthful and unserious, "rumpled as if there were 30 dwarfs playing handball inside his clothes." He was bearded again, and wore a V-neck sweater and a long striped scarf, his hair in a black mane down his neck to his shoulders. George was upstairs, working. Korty, in a black suit and tie, leaned over the pool table in the main room. Ellie dropped by to help with the final arrangements. She hung Marimekko fabrics on the walls; carefully arranged transparent, inflatable plastic chairs for the guests. She painted diagonal orange and white stripes in one room, blue and white stars up and down the hallway.

"Who's the most beautiful woman in San Francisco?" Francis suddenly asked the photographer from the *Chronicle*.

"Joanna Kobrin," the photographer replied. She was the wife of a psychiatrist in the city, and had appeared in *Bullitt*.

"Invite her," Francis ordered. "Invite them all. My wife is giving me four hours off during the party."

Ellie raised an eyebrow. "If you can get anything accomplished surrounded by a thousand people, be my guest," she said.

Francis hammered in a few nails for show and paused to make a joke about "George's four-grand lens," a 1000mm 4.5 telephoto he said George had insisted he *had* to have to shoot *THX 1138*, even though it was more expensive than any other object in the building. He seemed euphoric.

"I'm 30 years old," he proclaimed. "It's the '70s, we've survived, and we've completed our first film." He paused. "And all the beautiful women in San Francisco will be here soon!"

Twenty-four hours later, Friday night, the guests got their first look. Every young artist in San Francisco came and danced. Visitors walked up the stairs from the street and emerged right into the main room of American Zoetrope, without even a landing; the first thing you saw was the pool table taking up the center of the room, massive and felted in pastel, "and then against the wall was this huge, antique espresso machine," remembers Richard Chew, an editor working with Korty at the time, "and on the opposite side across the pool table was a glass-top table, where there was always a young lady as the receptionist, wearing a very short skirt, to greet all the visitors." Displayed pride of place was Skot-Hansen's gift: the zoetrope that lent the company its name.

The "lounge," as Francis called it, gave a relaxed, even amateurish first impression, but it hid arguably the most sophisticated independent film studio in America. Over three floors, Warner Bros.' money had paid for seven picture editing rooms; three screening and mixing rooms; studios for props, costume, and wardrobe; even a refrigerated unit for storing film. Some of the equipment was so advanced no one else in America owned its like. Upstairs were three offices, within shouting distance of each other around the central hallway: one for Francis, one for George, and one for Murch. (Francis insisted they were not offices, but *workrooms*.) "Right now, I guess you have to have one person running things, and I'm it," Francis said, but in the long term, American Zoetrope would belong, in spirit, if not in the incorporation papers, to all three of them. "I don't want to be Louis B. Mayer around here."

Poets and gorgeous women populated the opening party's guest list. Francis served sushi—"the first sushi that any of us had ever eaten," Murch remembered. He put his new Eclair cameras on display, and people started picking them up and walking out with them, like they were party favors. Drunk guests stumbled into the brand-new screening and editing rooms and spilled their drinks until the floors and the expensive German equipment were crusted and sticky.

"There was a lot of dope being smoked and a lot of sex," Milius said. "It was a great time."

"We have the means of production!" Francis announced.

As early as the next week, when work proper began, tensions flared. Mike Medavoy, who represented half the filmmakers involved with Zoetrope, felt pretty sure Francis, in fact, "wanted to replicate the studio system"—though Medavoy didn't see that as a bad thing. The old studios were family businesses, after all, nothing like the factory line of modern Hollywood. The moguls—Mayer, Thalberg, Laemmle, Goldwyn—had been gamblers, not bean counters. Their companies were benign autocracies—Francis would have emphasized the *benign* bit. After a while, however, everyone else at Folsom Street rankled against the second part: autocracy.

"It was never a cooperative venture," remembered Carroll Ballard. Francis seemed to live lavishly enough, but everyone else was paid so little it was, Ballard said, "practically non-earning." With George and Murch across the Golden Gate Bridge, feverishly editing *THX 1138*, the studio quickly descended into chaos. Even with "Mona Skager running things with an iron fist," as Drew Takahashi, an animator who worked for John Korty, puts it, "there was always a loose assortment of people coming in and going out, making things at Zoetrope but semi-independently." Francis tried to engage with the anti-establishment spirit sweeping the city, but it didn't come naturally to him. Some of the Zoetrope collective started making a film about Eldridge Cleaver, of the Black Panthers, leading Francis to run around the building, frantic, demanding to know whose idea it was, because Jack Warner had heard about it and called him and threatened him with the FBI. One young filmmaker, a professed communist, confronted Francis, and demanded to know why Francis drove a Porsche.

"Well, it's . . . my car," Francis stuttered.

"That means you're just one of the bosses," the youngster shrieked. "You're no different than J. P. Morgan or any other capitalist who's exploiting us!"

He ranted until Francis cut him off. "It's my car," Francis boomed, "and I'm gonna drive my car, because I'm the big guy here! You're not the big shot, I'm the big shot!"

A little while later, as a show of solidarity, he loaded Ellie and the kids into the Porsche to attend an anti-war rally. They wandered around the crowd for a while, like tourists, and when they came back to their parking spot, the Porsche had been stolen.

"Francis had no concept of failure whatsoever," George recalled. "He was convinced we were going to take over the world." As George would learn, Francis could get knocked down hard—and then he'd come back up swinging.

Equipment vanished, most likely stolen. Aspiring local filmmakers turned up at all hours of the day, expecting to hang out and drink cappuccinos and talk Francis into financing their films. Local high school students mixed with the staff at the Thursday night film screenings, everyone piling plates high with Chinese takeout Francis paid for. He ran his business like he ran a film set—on vibes. He moved too fast for business plans, profit-and-loss statements, and careful consideration, but also too fast to dwell on losses or learn his lesson. For a few weeks, his charisma papered over the cracks. One filmmaker compared him to Manson. "Francis had this Mansonesque effect on all of us," he said. "If he'd told me to stab [Ted] Ashley, I probably would've stabbed Ashley."

"Francis always lived on the edge," Bart Patton says, more mildly. "He'd mortgage his grandmother if it could get him some extra money." Discontent grew in the wake of his haphazard leadership. Ellie's brother Bill complained that he had yet to be paid for the work he'd done refurbishing the warehouse. Down in Los Angeles, George's old classmate Chuck Braverman began hearing rumors about "the Zoetrope thing." The word, as he remembers, "was that Francis was broke half the time."

The state-of-the-art German flatbeds were Francis's studio in a nutshell: They weren't very reliable, they didn't work very well, but they were, Takahashi says, "pretty damn cool." The sound mixing console was gigantic, with gates for four different reels and machinery so complicated it demanded exquisite precision. No one wanted to even try using it, but no one wanted to tell Francis, either, because he was so proud of it. It was the future, and Francis loved nothing more than the future. The past, he romanticized; the present, he moved too quickly for.

The espresso machine was the same. "Three and a half feet high, round as a manhole, all chrome with a gold eagle on the top," describes projectionist Colin Michael Kitchens. "No one ever tried to get that thing to work—no one except Francis. It was so intimidating."

In all the chaos, it was hard to get any work done. Bart Patton tried to produce an adaptation of Henry Miller's *The Smile at the Foot of the Ladder*, for which he met with the French mime Marcel Marceau, but it went nowhere. Carroll Ballard's *Vesuvia*, an original screenplay about "a young man [who] returns home from a foreign war and begins a regression into fantasy and madness," was stalled, as was Korty's *Have We Seen the Elephant?*, the logline for which read only, "The Gold Rush of 1849 haunts contemporary America." Only George, Murch, and Milius seemed grown-up enough to approach the opportunity offered by American Zoetrope like what it was: a job.

"Francis wanted us to be artists, like him," Milius said. "He wanted you to go out and write your scripts and if you couldn't do it, if you went to him and whined and said, 'Gee, I need some help,' he didn't have much regard for that . . . He expected you to be independent and he was giving you a wonderful opportunity to be independent of anybody else. But people did go to him and complain and whine all the time. All the time."

Steve Wax, also a UCLA graduate, was set to write and direct *Santa Rita*, named after the jail in which students participating in the Berkeley Free Speech Movement were held and abused in 1964 after the "People's Takeover" of the university. His writing partner, Stan Adler, loathed Francis. "Sure, there was the giant cappuccino machine, the pool table, refrigerators stocked with Coors, DIY work schedules, flexible deadlines, and the scintillating company of budding geniuses," Adler wrote of Zoetrope years later. "But there was also Francis—an uber filmmaker with boundless arrogance and imperious bearing. I remember him at an afternoon party lying in a hammock reciting *Henry V* in a John Wayne accent and patting the butt of any woman who passed by." One day early in 1970, Francis asked Wax and Adler to come in and update him on the progress on their script: Months after the announcement of the Zoetrope slate, the two men were still mired in conducting research and interviewing witnesses. They were no longer sure about the film's title and,

Adler admitted, had yet to "pin down some basic considerations like character, plot, scope, title, etc."

All the same, and even though Francis was paying for development on the film—neither Wax nor Adler had ever made a feature—Adler bristled at being summoned. He decided it was "an opportunity to teach Francis a thing or two" and, he claimed, "teaching Francis a thing or two was something that everyone in the building wanted to do."

They went into his office and sat down on the couch. Francis asked how the writing was going.

"When could I expect to have something halfway complete?"

Wax hemmed and hawed—it was a complicated story, controversial real-life events, people weren't collaborating . . .

"How far along are you?" Francis asked.

Close, Wax said.

How close was close, Francis wanted to know. The script was meant to be done already.

"I need a little more time," Wax said.

"You don't have any more time," Francis said.

At this point, Adler stood up from the couch and took a deep breath. "Francis, do you mind if I say something?" he asked. Francis looked at him, seemingly unsure of who he was. Without waiting for an answer, Adler launched into a speech about the *balance of the film*, asking Francis to imagine a baseball bat poised on the tip of his finger, spinning an analogy in which he and Wax were slowly crafting the bat's handle, which was the script, so it could extend into a perfectly weighted barrel, which was the film, which would "hit the ball out of the park. That's what we're getting close to," Adler concluded. "*Santa Rita* will be a shot heard around the world!"

Francis blinked. *Santa Rita,* he knew then and there, would never get made. *Vesuvia* was never made, nor was Patton's adaptation of Henry Miller. The screenplay Robbins and Barwood were writing fell by the wayside, victim not of their work ethic but of their inexperience.

In all the excitement surrounding the studio, Francis was neglecting his own script of *The Conversation*.

Luckily, Milius was getting somewhere. Back near the end of 1968, he had screeched up to the Calabasas Park Gun Club, north of Malibu, in his beat-up cream-colored station wagon, shotguns and ammunition clinking around in the trunk, fast-food containers and yellow legal pages sliding across the back seat, his dog panting at the window. The trap and skeet range had just opened, and Milius, gun enthusiast that he was, had come to check it out. The manager, Steve Kanaly, was newly returned from duty in Vietnam, where he'd served as a radio operator in the First Air Cavalry. His stories fascinated Milius. As he booked him in, or set up the trap house, Kanaly told Milius about riding in helicopters with the doors open and your feet on the skids, loudspeakers hanging off the fuselage, blasting rock 'n' roll music. He told him about rigging mini-guns onto the Chinooks, loading a tracer every fifth round. Tracers were bullets with a pyro built in, so they'd light up when fired, Kanaly explained; they'd go up when it was dark and spray a jungle area the size of two soccer fields with lead, the rate of fire so quick, Kanaly said, that you pulled the trigger and you unleashed what looked like a flow of lava, a solid string of fire, onto anyone unfortunate enough to find themselves below.

"Anything in there," Kanaly told Milius, "gets *obliterated*."

At first, Kanaly says, Milius's interest appeared to be pure curiosity. But John was still obsessed with the war, and he had been growing frustrated with his early drafts of *Apocalypse Now*. His characters were derivative. His battle scenes read like every other battle scene in every other war picture. His words didn't capture the absurdity and brutality he imagined the conflict to have, and that, Milius came to fear, was the problem: No matter how often he had fantasized about war, no matter how much he had read about it, he had no firsthand idea of what he was writing about.

As they hung out and shot, Kanaly told Milius about the day-to-day of Vietnam, about the heat, the isolation. He told a story about an officer he knew who'd showed up in the jungle wearing a cowboy hat, acting out "all this macho stuff," giving all the companies sobriquets because he didn't like their official names. Milius eventually explained he was writing a screenplay for a friend of his to direct. They wanted to shoot it low-budget, almost like a mock documentary. Kanaly fed him more and more stuff. Slowly Kanaly felt Milius's questions change. "He was working," Kanaly says. "Our conversations became more directed towards a clear understanding of how combat worked."

Seeing Milius making steady progress, Francis invited a producer he'd known from the Corman days, Gary Kurtz, up to San Francisco. Kurtz had attended USC in the early '60s, a few years before George, and cut his teeth as an assistant director on films including Bart Patton's *Beach Ball.* He was a quiet, gentle man, raised a Quaker, a firm believer in the testimony of peace. When he was drafted into the marines in '66, interrupting his film career just as he was getting it started, he spent his three years in Vietnam wearing an empty pistol holster as a symbol of his pacifism. He carried a 16mm Bell and Howell instead, serving as a combat cameraman. He had only just got back home and was looking for work. Times were hard. Studios were making fewer movies than ever; one-third of union crew members were unemployed.

Francis put Kurtz up at his house and told him about the film Milius was writing for George.

"He and John Milius and the others were all talking about the lunatics taking over the asylum, and the studios were dead, and we're going to have the power now," Kurtz said. Francis told Kurtz he was the only producer he knew who had actually been to Vietnam, and maybe he and George should meet. He drove Kurtz out to George's house in Mill Valley while *THX 1138* was being edited and introduced the two men.

George told Kurtz that the project had started as a mix of *Heart of Darkness* and *Dr. Strangelove*, but Kanaly's stories were inspiring

Milius to turn it into something more like Robert Altman's recently released satire *M*A*S*H*, only more absurd, more sadistic, more heartless. "Just an evil dark screenplay"—Milius grinned—"the most violent movie ever made." Francis didn't think Ashley and Calley would go for it. Maybe Kurtz could look around on George's behalf, see if another studio wanted to set the picture up. Kurtz agreed.

Early in the spring of 1970, Warner Bros. reached out to Francis and insisted on being shown something for their money. Ashley and Calley had seen the photographs of the pool table and the espresso machine; what they had yet to see, however, were any scripts pages, or any footage from *THX 1138*, even though it had wrapped filming back in November. The executives requested a screening of the full cut on the Warner lot in May, and delivery of the developed screenplays by the same date.

George and Murch raced to get the movie ready. Late one night, around ten PM, Murch was sitting in the basement on Folsom, laying the temporary sound mix, when Francis stepped in the room. He had trusted George the whole way, given him the freedom he'd promised. He had yet to see a single foot of film.

"Do you mind if I watch?" he asked.

"No, sure," Murch said.

Francis sat down and watched Murch work for a half hour or so, and then got heavily back to his feet.

"Well," he sighed, "it's either a masterpiece, or masturbation."

It would be up to the studio to decide which of the two.

· 9 ·

BLACK THURSDAY

In George's words, the industry had opened a crack, and Zoetrope had formed, off to the side but still behind city walls, coffers briefly full of studio money. There were no women directors or writers on the American Zoetrope slate, nor were there any people of color. Francis, George, and Murch thought of themselves as progressive, and it would have been unfair to suggest the responsibility was theirs alone, yet it remained a fact that they had come out of overwhelmingly white male film school programs, hired white male above-the-line collaborators, and almost certainly did not think twice about it. The crack had opened for younger white men—but scarcely anybody else.

Stephanie Rothman, a filmmaker who had directed pictures for Roger Corman as successful and well received as any of his male protégés, never managed to break out of exploitation films, not even to direct episodic television. The screenwriter Nancy Dowd, a UCLA graduate and, later, Academy Award winner, chose to resort to male pseudonyms or uncredited jobs to keep working.

"The fact that the door had opened a crack for women didn't mean dick," said Joan Tewkesbury, screenwriter of *Nashville* and frequent collaborator of Robert Altman's. "Any women I knew who had any aspirations of directing or getting into it was not working."

The dynamic repeated at home. Francis hired pretty girls to sit in miniskirts at the front desk and cracked jokes about having affairs while Ellie neglected her art and raised their kids. Repeatedly, Marcia suggested to George that *THX 1138* was a cold, unfeeling film, and that he perhaps needed to breathe some emotion into it. But when she spoke up, she made him angry. She didn't understand abstract filmmaking or visual storytelling, he said. He insisted they do it his way, not hers.

He respected her—she knew that. But that respect reached only to a point.

In May, Murch and Francis flew down to Los Angeles with the cans that contained the director's cut of *THX 1138*. George had not been invited.

"This is your first film," Francis reassured him before he left. "We're all learning, we're all trying something new here. It would be crazy to think we're going to hit the bull's-eye the first time."

George knew his friend well enough to know Francis was preparing him for a gut punch. He wondered if he would even get his work print of the film back. There was, after all, just one. Just in case, he and Murch made a plan. While Francis prepared for the screening, the two of them prepared for a heist.

Shortly after Francis drove onto the Warner lot for the screening, Murch rolled up to the gate himself, in Hal Barwood's Volkswagen minibus, Matthew Robbins and Caleb Deschanel crouching unseen in the back. He told the security guard he was the editor on *THX 1138*, and the guard waved him through. He drove the bus to the Warner Bros. water tower, just outside the executive screening room, and parked.

Inside the building, Francis found himself surrounded by suits: not just Ashley and Calley, but the vice president of production, the head of business affairs, and the head of the studio story department, standing by the blood-red seats like a jury. Staff carried the *THX 1138* work print into the projection booth and prepared the reels for the screening. Francis and the executives took their seats.

Outside, Murch checked his watch and began counting the minutes until the end of the show.

As the film played, Francis could feel the executives growing unhappy. The house lights came back up, and they rounded on him as one.

"Wait a minute, Francis," one of them said. "What's going on? This is not the screenplay we said we were going to do. This isn't a commercial movie."

"I don't know what the fuck this is," Francis muttered.

At the same moment, Murch, Robbins, and Deschanel hopped out of the VW bus and hurried to the back of the screening room. They knocked on the door, and Murch popped his head round it.

"I'm here from the *THX* cutting room," he said casually. "You guys got a work print here for me?"

The projectionist and his assistant nodded. Murch, Robbins, and Deschanel crowded into the room, grabbed all the reels as quickly as they could, and loaded them into the van. They were off the lot before the suits were done excoriating Francis.

Inside the screening room, an agreement was reached. Francis conceded changes could be made to make the film more accessible, and the studio assigned an executive, Fred Weintraub, to oversee the modifications. Francis flew back up to San Francisco to deliver the notes to George, which consisted mostly of moving some of the more exciting material to the front of the picture, which at that point was a slow burn. One particular request was for the "freaks," as Weintraub called them—the hairy dwarves who appear near the end of the film—to be moved to the beginning, to titillate and weird out the audience. "You gotta put them up front," Murch remembers Weintraub insisting. "Freaks up front!"

George shook his head.

"Forget it," he said. "I'm not doing any of that stuff."

He resented Francis for not standing up for him. When Coppola complained that American Zoetrope was bleeding money, and that he needed *THX 1138* finished, George retorted that he wasn't the one responsible for throwing $300,000 out the window. He hadn't bought the pool table, or the espresso machine, or the state-of-the-art equipment for ten postproduction suites they didn't need. As George saw it, while Francis played the impresario on Folsom Street, he'd been the only one actually making a movie.

Marcia tried to suggest the studio had a point, which made George even angrier. "When the studio didn't like it," she said, "I wasn't surprised. But George just said to me, I was stupid and knew nothing. Because I was just a Valley Girl. He was the intellectual."

Francis and George threw blame and recriminations at one another. George learned that Francis had charged some of Zoetrope's overhead to the *THX 1138* budget, and accused him of cheating him. When Mona Skager sent him a bill for $1,800, costs for long-distance calls George had made on the Folsom Street telephone to recommend Marcia for editing jobs with other filmmakers, George felt insulted and deeply hurt. He had to ask his father for a loan to pay Zoetrope back.

"I would never have done that to a friend," Francis conceded. "Mona was way out of line." But George didn't buy his apology.

"I always believe that that incident was one of the things that pissed George off and caused a breach," Francis said.

He took to driving out to George's house in Mill Valley nearly every day, partly to try and restore their friendship, partly to nudge his friend into making the tiniest of changes to the *THX* cut—anything that might placate Ashley and Calley. He had convinced Weintraub that cutting down the runtime in the second half would make a difference, and George, reluctantly, agreed to try.

Spring turned to summer. Francis finished a new draft of *The*

Conversation and reached an agreement with Gene Hackman to play the main character, Harry Caul. Hackman had already been nominated for an Academy Award for Best Supporting Actor for his work in *Bonnie and Clyde*, and was about to film his breakout starring role in *The French Connection*, directed by Francis's pal William Friedkin, but he was not yet a household name, and no one seemed interested in financing *The Conversation*—already a difficult picture—with a nobody in the lead. Francis put the project aside again. His prospects seemed nonexistent.

And then Francis was sitting on George's couch one day when the house phone rang for him. He answered, spoke for a few minutes, and returned to the editing room. He said the call was from Peter Bart, an executive at Paramount.

"They've just offered me this Italian gangster movie," Francis told George. "It's like a $3 million potboiler based on a bestseller. Should I do it?"

The book was called *The Godfather*, by Mario Puzo.

"I don't think you have any choice," George said. "We're in debt. You've gotta get a job." He sounded like his own father.

Francis dithered. He was aware of the novel, about a Mafia don, Vito Corleone, and his three sons, navigating gang warfare in New York in the decade following World War II. It had become an immediate smash hit on publication, spending more than a year on the *New York Times* bestseller list. But Francis's experience of reading the book was a disappointment: *The Godfather*, he thought, was tacky pulp fiction, "filled with sex and silliness."

He didn't want to do it. And why did George get to be so precious about his freedom, refusing to make any changes to his picture, yet at the same time tell him to farm himself out as a gun for hire?

"Francis," George said, "we're going broke. They're gonna chain the door. You have to do this, we have no other alternative. We need the money."

They had the same conversation over and over again, for weeks.

Francis urged George to make changes to *THX 1138*; George pushed Francis to accept Paramount's offers. Francis reported that the studio had assigned a low-budget specialist, Al Ruddy, to produce the picture. He complained that, while the book was set in New York in the 1940s, Paramount wanted to film in St. Louis and set the action in the contemporary 1970s, all to save money. The fee on offer was a meager $75,000—at a time when Mike Nichols, just a few years older than Coppola, was being paid $1 million to direct *Catch-22*. And anyway, Francis repeated, the whole idea of Zoetrope was to make personal films, films only they could make. Why else were they fighting Warner Bros. over a handful of cuts?

One day Murch was in the house with them, and George was at it again. "Just suck it up and do it," he told Francis. Murch kept getting caught in the middle, Francis pulling his hair out, George prodding and pushing. "Francis, just roll over and do whatever they want you to do," George said. "Just grab the money and run. They want you to shoot it in St. Louis, shoot it in St. Louis. Then we can use that money and make our own films."

Francis was still fretting, late in the summer, when he flew down to Los Angeles to meet with Paramount about the project. Hal Barwood met him at the airport in Burbank in his VW van, Matthew Robbins sitting in the back. As Barwood drove them down the I-5 toward the city, the purple sky dimming all around them, Francis thumbed his copy of Puzo's novel.

"What do you think I should do?" he asked them.

Robbins reached over and took the book out of Francis's lap. He flicked it open to a random page. A scene of the Mafia dons, debating whether they should get into the drug business. One line of dialogue caught Robbins's eye: "In my city," says the head of a Detroit mob family, "I would try to keep the traffic in the dark people, the colored . . . they are animals anyway. They have no respect for their wives or their families or for themselves. Let them lose their souls."

Robbins raised his eyebrow. He, too, had thought *The God-*

father was a cheap period potboiler, but what he was reading had the wherewithal—and *balls*—to address white crime families deliberately flooding Black neighborhoods with drugs? That felt pretty hip.

He handed the book back to Francis. "Do it," he said.

Francis did have some interest in making a film with a Mafia setting, but Paramount was an industry joke. Adolph Zukor, who had founded the business back in the 1910s, remained in charge well into the 1960s; the joke went that he still called his company president, seventy-seven-year-old Barney Balaban, "the boy." The films Paramount made were as stodgy and old-fashioned as its leadership, the accounts bleeding money so bad that Zukor had sold both the studio's film library and its physical headquarters in Times Square in desperate attempts to stem the losses. Finally, in 1966, the studio had been swallowed up by Gulf+Western, a growing international conglomerate built by Charles Bluhdorn, a forty-year-old Austrian-born businessman with an elusive background. Bluhdorn didn't know movies, or have much passion for them, but he liked public acclaim, and he liked the idea of being seen with movie stars. In the words of one film executive's wife, he "bought Paramount to get laid. It's that simple."

The hard-nosed, combative Bluhdorn moved Zukor and Balaban out, and hired as his new head of production a thirty-six-year-old former actor who had yet to successfully produce a picture. Robert Evans had the looks of a matinee idol and the strutting swagger of a playboy, and was primarily driven, by his own admission, by a "big-time" obsession with "pussy." Bluhdorn had hired him after reading a profile of him in the *New York Times*—written by Peter Bart, who Evans immediately brought on board as his head of development. Evans was a shrewd businessman, a clever hustler who had made a small fortune selling women's clothes with his brother in New York. He had friends in the mob—he thought of Sidney Korshak, lawyer for the Chicago Outfit, as his own consigliere—and he had both good taste and the courage to bet on it.

All the same, the industry laughed. Charlie Bluhdorn, an awkward foreigner with no Hollywood connections, had taken over a studio, and instead of hiring Irving Thalberg, he'd read a fluff piece in the Arts & Leisure section of the *Times* and hired a guy whose only notable acting role was that he'd once *played* Irving Thalberg. It was like an old landed gentry sneering at the nouveau riche. Broadsheet papers called Evans "Bluhdorn's Folly." The tabloid rag *Hollywood Close-Up* was more direct, and nicknamed him "Bluhdorn's Blow Job."

Bluhdorn, for his part, saw some of himself in Evans. He'd built Gulf+Western up from a little auto-parts company in Grand Rapids, Michigan. People had made fun of his ambitions then, too, but he was cold and clear-eyed. The question he asked the most—about any topic—was: "What's the bottom line?" And the bottom line on Robert Evans, thought Bluhdorn, was that, like himself, he was an outsider who would, as Bart put it, "beat them at their own game."

"What did I have to lose?" Evans recalled, years later. He wasn't interested in the game of executive musical chairs played by lifelong studio suits. He thought of himself as a handicapper—not a blind gambler, but someone who analyzes the game and plays the odds—and he saw no downside. "I had plenty of green and was holding the dice as well. For me, the worst thing that could happen is that I'd crap out." He could always go back to New York to sell dresses and flirt with socialites.

Evans put his chips on youth. "The strongest period in Hollywood history was in the thirties, when most of the creative people were young," he said. "The trouble is that most of them are still around making movies." He made quick strides in turning the studio around, green-lighting hits including *Barefoot in the Park*, *Rosemary's Baby*, and *Love Story*, the last of which made his new wife, actress Ali MacGraw, into a star. Bart found future bestsellers to adapt while the manuscripts were still in galleys, and Evans had a knack for pairing those properties with the right directors. He was good, too, at making friends—actors like Jack Nicholson and Warren Beatty, directors like Roman Polanski, politicians like Henry Kissinger. When Bluhdorn questioned his decisions, Evans brushed him off.

"If you're giving me the store, let me run it."

Bluhdorn would laugh and turn to Martin Davis, his second-in-command, who disliked Evans. "Marty," Bluhdorn said, "I told you the kid's got balls."

Evans had been in on *The Godfather* from the start, when he'd lent author Mario Puzo some money in exchange for the film rights to the book. Gangster films hadn't made money since the days of Jimmy Cagney, but Evans had an ace in the form of a fresh approach: He was going to hire an Italian to direct the thing for once.

"That's what brought the magic to the novel—it was written by an Italian," he said. "The film's going to be the same."

Bart said he knew a young director who fit the bill: Francis Coppola, up in San Francisco.

"Are you nuts, Peter? He's crazy."

"Brilliant though," Bart insisted.

"That's your esoteric bullshit coming out," Evans countered.

Word came from New York: Burt Lancaster, Oscar winner and three-time nominee, wanted to produce the film and play the don, and Bluhdorn would hand it over to him if Evans didn't get his own plans in motion. It didn't matter that Lancaster, talented as he was, was a square-jawed, chestnut-haired Irish Protestant—nothing like the Sicilian gangster.

Coppola it was, then.

At first, Francis liked the flamboyant, irreverent Evans. He liked Bart, too. He picked up Puzo's thick gangster novel again, this time with a pen in hand, scribbling carefully as he turned the pages, sniffing for a way into the material. What he found "lurking within" was the potential for a family saga of Shakespearean dimensions: "that of a king with three sons, each of whom had inherited an aspect of his personality. I thought that if I could just extract that part of the book and make the film about that, then I could work up some enthusiasm for it."

"Coppola will make the picture on one condition," Bart reported to Evans. "That it's not a film about organized gangsters, but a family chronicle. A metaphor for capitalism in America."

"Fuck him and the horse he rode in on," Evans groaned. "Is he nuts?"

"Doesn't matter." Bart smiled. "He's Italian."

On September 28, 1970, with debt collectors threatening to carry Zoetrope's assets down the stairs and out onto Folsom Street, Francis signed his contract with Paramount, agreeing to direct *The Godfather*. He would be paid $75,000 and 6 percent of the net profit. If he was lucky, it would be just about enough money to keep American Zoetrope from shutting down. At the last minute, John Calley, the head of Warner Bros., attempted to scupper the deal.

"Don't use him, Bob," he warned Evans on the phone. "His company owes us . . . Whatever money you pay him goes directly to us." Calley couched the call as a courtesy, letting Evans know that hiring Francis financially benefitted a rival studio. But he might also have hoped American Zoetrope *would* go bankrupt so Warner Bros., first creditor in line, could lay claim to all the company tenuously owned—from its state-of-the-art editing beds to John Milius's *Apocalypse Now*—without having to pay a penny for it.

Evans ignored Calley's advice. The announcement of Coppola's hiring had run in the trades already, and if Coppola was in that much debt, he'd be inclined to play nice, anyway. It was a win-win, as far as Paramount was concerned.

What Francis hadn't told Evans was that he had reached another kind of agreement, this one with himself. If he was going to compromise his career and make a gangster picture, then he was sure as hell going to do it his way.

He took Ellie, the boys, and several friends on a sailing trip to

Europe to celebrate. They stopped in beautiful Sorrento, on the Bay of Naples, for the film festival there. In that beautiful town of pastel buildings and lemon groves, overlooking the sparkling water, Francis came across a short, stocky, long-haired young film programmer who introduced himself as Martin Scorsese.

"I'm used to being the youngest one at gatherings like this," Francis remembered. "But here's Marty, only twenty-seven . . ."

Marty, it turned out, was from New York, had grown up without much money on the streets of Little Italy, trying to steer clear of the gangsters who constantly threatened to kill his uncle, a small-time troublemaker. Marty had already made a sort-of-autobiographical low-budget feature, *Who's That Knocking at My Door*, starring a friend, Harvey Keitel. It had taken him two years, rewriting scenes all the time, shooting nights, weekends, whenever Keitel could get away from his job as a court stenographer. Most of the $70,000 budget had come from Marty's NYU film teacher, Haig Manoogian, and friends around town. The final result was rough around the edges but profoundly sincere; it had won Marty a few influential admirers, among them Roger Corman and the film critic Roger Ebert. Marty was married with a daughter, but right after *Who's That Knocking* premiered at the Chicago Film Festival, he'd turned to his wife, Laraine, sitting by his side on the plane back to New York, and told her he was leaving her. He was going to be a Hollywood filmmaker.

Marty remembered Francis from a loft party in New York a year or two earlier, when Francis had come to give a talk to NYU students like him, and had exhorted them to be ready to lose everything for their movies, to be willing to die for their movies. That speech had changed Marty's life. Finally, he'd thought, here was someone who felt about pictures the way he did—as if they were life or death.

Sorrento, however, was their first time meeting directly. They sat with other directors for long lunches under the shade of the trees and argued about movies. Late at night, they went out for grappa or coffee, talked about their Italian roots, their Catholic faiths. When he got home from Sorrento, Marty said, he would be moving to Los Angeles.

Francis expected they would see each other there.

Six weeks later, Francis was back in the Zoetrope offices and preparing for his own trip down to LA. George and Murch had completed a new cut of *THX 1138*, one not meaningfully different from the one they'd screened for Warner Bros. in May, but, Francis hoped, sufficiently changed to show goodwill. He had also managed to get eight of his writers to finish drafts of their screenplays, and he had twelve copies of each bound in leather, one for each president and vice president at Warner Bros. He packed them tightly into a long silver box embossed with the American Zoetrope logo. George thought it would backfire. The small-business owner in him—his father's voice, essentially—knew the executives would find the presentation frivolous, a symbol of Francis's self-importance and profligacy. Korty, for his part, took one look at the box and suppressed a smile.

"Gee," he said dryly. "That looks like a coffin."

It was Thursday, November 19, 1970. George's friend Willard Huyck picked Francis up at Los Angeles airport and helped him load the box into the back of his car. It was so heavy Francis had thrown his back out carrying it.

They drove to Warner Bros. Huyck helped Francis get the box into the screening room and waited outside. After two hours, Francis emerged, "looking different," Huyck recalled, "and sort of crestfallen."

The screening had been a disaster. "They went ballistic," George remembered. Calley, especially, was incensed.

"I can't believe you made this film," he spat at Francis. "I hate it so much." In his speech before showing *THX*, Francis had made a big deal of how he had let George "go off on his own and make this movie," how it was a prototype of the Zoetrope way: promising filmmakers given complete freedom. He had misread the room. Calley turned the concept around on him.

"How could you let him make this thing?" he asked. "Didn't you do anything about it?" The picture was a loser, he railed; no one in their right mind would know what to do with it. It had no appeal, he predicted, to anyone.

Ashley rendered his judgment on the spot. The studio had a contractual agreement to distribute *THX 1138*, and they would honor it. But they were keeping the print this time, and they would have their in-house editor, sixty-year-old Rudi Fehr, recut it as they saw fit. What's more, Francis could take his ninety-six bound screenplays back on the plane with him. Ashley didn't want them, nor did he want to pay for them. The studio demanded its $300,000 back.

Huyck rose to his feet when he noticed the crushed look on Francis's face.

"Well," he asked, "what happened?"

"Well," Francis said, "they thought that the scripts looked really neat in the box."

Francis returned to Folsom Street, where the staff were waiting, knowing how much rode on the meeting. He was exhausted and dispirited, but he gave it to them straight. Many of those listening were blindsided. Until that very moment, Bart Patton says, Zoetrope felt like "a going concern—and then, one by one, everyone was pink-slipped." Francis asked him and editor Robert Dalva to stick around and keep the commercials division going, bring some money in, but that didn't last long. Another one of Francis and George's miscalculations. "San Francisco wasn't much of a film center," Patton says. "It was just a location. A place where people came to film."

Murch, for his part, figured there was still hope. "We were sort of like Wile E. Coyote run off the cliff," he says. "Something might happen. We'll come up with something."

He tried his best to make Francis feel better about *THX*. "It hasn't been released yet," he told his friend. "So who knows? Maybe the studio didn't like it, but maybe the people will like it."

George, for his part, fumed. "It was insane," he said later. "I wish I had filmed it. It was like bringing an audience to the Mona Lisa and asking, 'Do you know why she's smiling?' 'Sorry, Leonardo, you'll have to go back and make some changes.' "

He was proud of the film. He thought it was good. Who cared what the suits thought?

He took another couple of trips to Los Angeles, bargained with Rudi Fehr over every cut. In the end, Fehr, with Ashley's approval, trimmed four minutes off the movie. "There was no point for them to do it, other than exercise some power," George fumed. "*We can screw around with your movie, so we're going to.*"

"It's an injustice," Matthew Robbins agreed. "It was as if they took your little 4-year-old daughter and they said, 'We know how to make her better,' and they cut off only one finger—and then they gave her back to you and said, 'Now she's fine. She has nine out of 10 fingers—I mean, come on, nine fingers out of 10 is not that bad. What's your problem?' "

Irvin Kershner, who had just directed the Sean Connery picture *A Fine Madness* for Warner Bros., remembered the studio was "reluctant to release" *THX 1138* at all. He lobbied Ashley to change his mind.

Francis seemed not to take sides, and George seethed. "You're gonna let them cut it?" he asked Coppola. "You're not gonna go down there and stop 'em?"

"Just cut these five minutes out and we'll call it a day," Francis argued. "Otherwise they're not gonna release it."

George hadn't expected them to win their fight against Warner Bros.—they had no leverage—but he also had not expected Francis to club, so easily, *with* the studio.

To his friends, George insisted he would never trust a studio again. Privately, he knew his career might be over, and he knew, too, that he was done with Francis. If he was going to grow, he would have to grow without him.

"Francis was a good commander," Milius argued. "He knew to fall back to the hills and fight a different kind of war. [But] the guys saw him as a traitor who had gone to the screening and now joined the great gray-suited masses of those in the bureaucracies . . . That just wasn't true."

Even Francis's deal to make *The Godfather* was, suddenly, held up against him. "Everybody who knew Francis felt he was selling out," said Caleb Deschanel.

Korty moved out of his Folsom Street cubicle and back to Stinson Beach. George, too, stopped coming to the warehouse. Instead, he incorporated a company of his own. He called it Lucasfilm Ltd. and headquartered at his home in Mill Valley.

"I had always regarded George as my heir apparent," Francis said later. "He'd take over Zoetrope for me while I went out and did my personal films." As Francis saw it, George had made *his* personal film, talked Francis into going back to work as a hired gun for a studio, and jumped ship. "Everybody utilized Zoetrope to get going, but nobody wanted to stick with it," Francis complained. "Zoetrope was picked clean. Everyone had used it, no one had contributed."

He held on to the lease at Folsom Street. Mona Skager stayed on and endeavored to rent out the editing suites. Every penny they made went straight to Warner Bros. Francis turned his attention to *The Godfather*, but he was discouraged. The film had been hard enough to get excited about before. It was even more so now that he knew his fee would go to repaying Ted Ashley and John Calley.

He left George with one last piece of advice.

"You gotta make a movie that's about people," Francis told him. "*Real* people."

His tone was a little snide, but he believed every word of it.

"Something funny," Francis added. "Don't do anything with robots in it."

· 10 ·

I BELIEVE IN AMERICA

In early 1971, George went down to USC to show *THX 1138* to the students in the cinema department. Bill Couturié, an outspoken young man who had originally enrolled as an architecture student but transferred into film, attended the screening almost out of spite. Around the university's hallways, George was talked about like a mythical figure. Instructors compared every student film to his. "They showed us *THX* [the short film] like once a week," Couturié remembers. "We were so sick of hearing about George, and how he hooked up with Francis, and how he was making big pictures now." As Couturié saw it, every film student thinks of himself as a hotshot filmmaker already, waiting to be discovered—and instead of discovering them, teachers were banging on about this other guy? It was like going out with a girl who couldn't stop talking about her ex-boyfriend.

Couturié and his classmates filed to the department's screening room that night to watch the feature adaptation of the short film they kept having to study. George appeared to introduce the picture, and resentment rippled through the rows of seats. "He was just a bearded little guy," Couturié says. The lights dimmed. The film played.

"There is no audience tougher in the world than film students," says Couturié. "We hated it. We loathed it. And we dumped on it."

Most of the young people left straight after the screening. George did the honorable thing and took the five or six who remained down to the student union and bought them all cherry Cokes, told them he was happy to answer any of their questions. It was awkward, and he was downbeat. If Warner Bros. didn't like the film, *and* his wife didn't like the film, *and* film students just a couple years younger than himself didn't like it, then maybe he had actually made a bad movie. Or at least a movie without an audience.

Someone asked him what he planned to do next. "I have two projects in mind," George answered. "Though I can't figure out which one to do." One was called *Apocalypse Now*, and it was about Vietnam. It sounded "very heavy," Couturié says, even bleaker than *THX 1138*.

"Ugh," one of the kids said. "That sounds horrible. What's the other one?"

"It's less developed," George answered, "but it's an idea about the last night of high school, when you all go out with your friends and get drunk."

"Obviously," Couturié remembers, "we thought: *That sounds great. Do that one!*"

George had been thinking about Francis's advice. If he were to make a film about "real people," and make it personal, then it would have to be about people he knew. His mind turned to his high school years, cruising the Modesto strip, listening to the radio. He could make a film about that, he thought. As he'd mentioned to the USC students, *Apocalypse Now* was a possibility as well, though Milius's dance card was full—he was in demand now, sometimes credited on-screen, as he was for his biopic of Evel Knievel, and sometimes not, as he was for substantially rewriting Warner's hit thriller *Dirty Harry*. George also kept returning to the idea he had mentioned to

Mona Skager while filming *The Rain People*: a feature adaptation of *Flash Gordon*. Francis took him to lunch to build up his courage before his meeting with the King Features Syndicate, which owned *Flash Gordon*, but George came back disappointed: The company had already sold the rights to the comic strip and television show to Italian producer Dino De Laurentiis.

"Well, I'll just make up my own thing," George said, despondent.

"Yeah," Francis commiserated. "What do you need *Flash Gordon* for?"

"I'll call it *Star Battles*," George said, "or *Star Wars*, or something."

In March, Warner finally released *THX 1138*, without much fanfare. Critics liked it, mostly—Roger Ebert thought it was "special," and the *New York Times*'s Vincent Canby professed himself wowed by it—but George fumed at the few negative notices. If studio executives were idiots who demanded changes to the *Mona Lisa*, then critics were vandals who covered her in their own garish spray paint.

The film made no money. "I did warn you it doesn't involve the audience emotionally," Marcia tentatively suggested.

"Emotionally involving the audience is easy," George grumbled. "Anybody can do it blindfolded. Get a little kitten and have some guy wring its neck."

Francis echoed Marcia's advice. "Don't be so weird," he told George when they spoke.

Fine, George decided. "I'm going to show you how easy it is," he told Marcia. "I'll make a film that emotionally involves the audience."

Mario Puzo was a large, warm man in his early fifties, with slicked-back black hair and heavy-rimmed black eyeglasses framing a cinder block of a head. He often held a cigar tucked between fore- and middle finger; his fleshy lips broke easily into a smile. Life hadn't been easy on him. He'd grown up on the streets of Hell's Kitchen, steering clear of the local tough guys and helping his mother, who raised her seven children alone after Mario's father, diagnosed with schizophrenia, was committed to Pilgrim State Hospital, never to return home. Donna Puzo had come to America from Naples and she was "ruthless," Puzo remembered; when he sat down, as an adult, to write up Don Vito Corleone, it was his mother's voice he heard in every line of dialogue that flowed out of the typewriter. "Mario told me that all of the great dialogue, those quotable lines he put into the mouth of Don Corleone, were actually spoken by [his] mother," said Francis later. "*An offer he can't refuse, keep your friends close but your enemies closer, revenge is a dish that tastes best when it is cold*, and *a man who doesn't spend time with his family can never be a real man* . . . [all] sayings he heard from his mother's lips."

Mario graduated high school and went to work for the New York Central Railroad, and was shipped to Germany to see out World War II. When he returned, he enrolled at the City College of New York on the GI bill and started writing. His first short story was published in 1950, his first novel in 1955. He married, had five children, paid the bills by writing trashy stories under a pen name for magazines with titles like *Male* and *True Action*. He wrote another novel the world paid no attention to. He indulged in food and gambling and dug himself into a hole of debt. He'd been a professional writer for nearly twenty years, and he was beyond broke. "It was time," Mario's son Anthony later recalled, "to put up or shut up."

Mario's publisher, G. P. Putnam's Sons, had long been asking him for a novel about the Mafia. He was Italian-American, born and raised in Hell's Kitchen, parents from Naples—surely he had enough material to fill three hundred dramatic, salacious, saleable pages?

Puzo started writing *The Godfather* in much the same mindset as Coppola when he agreed to direct its adaptation: His artistic integrity had led him to insolvency, with no choice other than to accept a project he felt in his heart to be beneath him. He had never been involved with the mob, had always toed the line. He accepted Putnam's modest $5,000 advance and set to work, crafting the rules and honor system of the Corleone family "entirely from research," inventing unforgettable scenes of murder and mayhem even though he personally abhorred violence of any kind. "I wrote it to make money," he stated plainly.

It was a novel written on a monkey's paw. It gave Puzo the fame and fortune he'd gambled for, but it also became the one thing he would forever be remembered for.

Francis loved Mario as soon as he met him. Puzo reminded him of some of his uncles: "so much fun to be with, so warm and wise, funny and affectionate," dedicated to his wife and children. Puzo had already written a first draft of the screenplay. Francis put it in a bag and took it to Mill Valley. When George and Marcia had first moved to the sleepy little town, Francis had followed them and bought a house at nearby 8 Laurel Street—and then tried to buy every adjoining property bounded by the nearest four streets. One of the homes he did manage to buy, right next door, was a small one-bedroom summer cottage built in the 1920s for a nephew of Leland Stanford's and known affectionately as "the Nest." Francis turned the Nest into his writing studio, and now he walked from the main house to the little cottage, laid out Puzo's draft, cracked open his annotated copy of the novel, and got to work.

"I had maybe 15 pages," most of the film's opening scene in which Don Corleone welcomes requests and favors on his daughter's wedding day, Francis remembered, when a screenwriter friend, William Cannon, dropped in for a visit.

"You want to see the first 15 pages?" Francis asked him. Cannon said yes, took a seat, and began to read.

"Francis, you did such a good opening on *Patton*," Cannon said, referring to a biopic Francis had written back in his days as a contract writer. That script opened with a uniformed General Patton, standing in front of a huge American flag, delivering a speech to the troops, but addressed as if to the audience. "That was such a striking opening, couldn't you do something more like that, something more unusual, that kind of gets you into it?"

Francis mulled and came up with another monologue, this one very different in tone and scope, delivered to camera but in tight close-up instead, with an off-screen audience of one: an undertaker in the darkness, pleading to Don Corleone for vengeance. Patton's speech had been about his country, spoken with vulgarity and fire, with patriotic passion and bellicose braggadocio: "Americans," Francis had written for Patton to say, "love a winner and will not tolerate a loser. Americans play to win all the time."

This time, Francis's character was not a general, but a common man broken by violence done to his family. Francis put his fingers to the typewriter's keys and wrote the speech's opening line:

"I believe in America."

As the book's popularity grew and grew, putting pressure on Paramount suddenly to deliver not a low-budget gangster flick but an event picture, Francis's interest also expanded. "People don't remember it," he said later, "but maybe a third, if not more, of the book concerned this young woman, Lucy Mancini, and her private anatomy problems and [her] love affair with the doctor who fixed them." He cut all that stuff out. He imagined a film about power, about family, about the corruption of the soul.

I believe in America.

He clipped the scenes he liked out of the novel, arranged them into five Shakespearean acts, and placed them into a binder. On *Finian's Rainbow*, he had become overwhelmed by the sheer number of small decisions a director had to make every day, and on *The Rain People*, he had perhaps let himself be too much of a hostage to fortune, following opportunities and obstacles as they arose. This time, he would be open but prepared. He read and reread his chosen chapters. He covered them in notes and scribbles, turning the binder into a prompt book much like the kind directors and stage managers use in the theater—a guide to staging the play. For each scene in the book, he typed up a synopsis with its key beats, the important "tone and imagery," the "core" of the moment he needed above all to preserve—and, for every scene, a listing of "pitfalls" to avoid, including, sometimes, a "note to me." ("This is tough," reads one. "Think about it, AND BE PREPARED, FRANCIS.") He jotted down details about his own Italian-American family, texture he could use to make the Corleones real. Bottles of anisette on the sideboard. Undershirts showing through dress shirts. Browning sausage before you start a meat sauce. ("Francis," Puzo wrote back on the script when he read it, "gangsters don't brown, gangsters fry.")

Francis finished his draft and split it in two parts. He sent Puzo away to rewrite the second half, and relocated to his home in San Francisco to revise the first, walking down every morning to nurse an espresso at Caffe Trieste in North Beach and go over the pages. When they were done, they swapped and rewrote each other. Then, knowing Puzo loved to gamble, Francis suggested they decamp to a suite at the Peppermill Resort Hotel in Reno, to finish the shared work. For weeks, the two men sat and talked and wrote. Coppola typed up dialogue; Puzo scratched out his notes and corrections onto the fresh pages. They ordered bacon and eggs from room service at all hours of the night—or pasta, pizza, lasagna. Mario liked to wear exercise clothes, "though I don't recall any exercise going with it," Francis said. When they got stuck, Francis fretted, and Mario rode the elevator down to the tables, taking chances until he was fed up with losing. Then he'd strut back into the suite with "a smile and a twinkling eye."

It became one of the lessons Francis took away from his time with Mario, in that casino in the Nevada desert: "If you hit big losses," Francis remembered, "you could escape upstairs to continue working." You hit them like snags under the surf: If you're still going, then they haven't sunk you.

As they wrote, Francis found his own beating heart in the pulpy pages of Puzo's novel. He understood the Corleones as a family much like his own. He understood Michael, the brother who can't fight his own nature. He understood Fredo, the brother who lives in the shadow of more charismatic siblings, mirroring his own childhood feelings toward Augie. The Corleones were a family like many Italian-American families.

"What people don't understand is that a gangster's job is not to go around killing people," Martin Scorsese said years later, when he was about to embark on his own mob picture, *Goodfellas*. "A gangster's job is to make money. Someone gets out of line, and it ruins making the money for everybody, and he's got to go. It's simple. It just happens to be their line of work."

Francis and Puzo wrote a similar idea into *The Godfather*. A sort of motto, a capitalist self-justification that worked as a counterpoint to "I believe in America." A line we hear from several characters, but which Michael Corleone only utters when he finally joins in the killing:

"It's not personal. It's strictly business."

That was what America told you, as far as Francis saw it. That it was only business as, literally or metaphorically—firing you after decades in a job, say, or taking your films and your company away from you because it had done the math and you weren't worth the money—America blew your brains all over its nice Ivy League suit.

Very early on, Francis had made his mind up on two of his leads. He wanted Marlon Brando—once Hollywood's hottest actor, but now box-office poison, with a reputation for difficulty and unprofessionalism to boot—to play Don Vito Corleone, the eponymous godfather. And for years, he had admired Al Pacino, an intense Italian-American stage actor, who he had first seen at the Belasco Theatre on West 44th in New York in 1969, starring in a new play, Don Petersen's *Does a Tiger Wear a Necktie?* Francis was blown away by the actor, who starred in the play as a teenage addict, and afterward sent word to him that he wanted to meet. Not at the stage door, not even in New York, but at the Zoetrope warehouse in San Francisco.

Pacino, whose phobias ranged from paying rent to licking stamps onto envelopes, didn't like leaving home, but Francis had also sent him an original script he had written, "a wonderful love story about a young college professor with a wife and children who has a love affair with one of his students"—"it really was special," Pacino remembered—and the actor was sufficiently intrigued to get on a plane. He spent five days in San Francisco, eating Italian food and drinking red wine. Francis seemed the inspiration for the main character in his script, a bit "like a college professor himself," Pacino thought. He visited the American Zoetrope building on Folsom Street, still being prepared for its official opening later in the year, and thought it had the odd, tense energy of a bunker full of hippie radicals. He liked Francis, though, and agreed to star in the love story, but soon after he returned to the East Coast, the project, for lack of financing, died. Pacino didn't mind much; his heart was on the stage. As a child, he had discovered "an energy within myself that . . . I could channel," a liberating, exhilarating focus he could only tap into when performing in front of a crowd, an act he approached as a quasi-religious search for truth and self-knowledge. He felt it had saved his life by liberating him from himself. ("My favorite quote of Michelangelo's," Pacino once said: "Free me of myself, Lord, that I may please you.")

Then, in early 1971, Pacino's phone rang, and it was Francis on the other end again.

"I'm going to be directing *The Godfather*," Francis told him, "and I want you to do it."

Pacino paused. He knew of the book—everybody did—and he wondered, *How did they give him* The Godfather*?*

While reading Puzo's novel, Francis had pictured Pacino as the don's youngest son, Michael Corleone, described by the author as "handsome in a delicate way," with skin "a clear olive-brown that would have been called beautiful in a girl." To Francis, Pacino *was* Michael Corleone. No one else would do.

By the time *The Godfather* was in preproduction, Pacino had made his film debut in Jerry Schatzberg's *The Panic in Needle Park*, playing a hustler and heroin addict, but the film would only be released when *Godfather* had started filming. The actor's star power, even to those who saw the film early, was not evident. Robert Evans liked his male stars traditional—strong-jawed, light-haired, preferably blue-eyed. Pacino was dark, moody, five foot five, with a soft and sometimes mumbling delivery. Evans suggested Robert Redford, maybe Jack Nicholson.

Pacino himself was reluctant even to consider *The Godfather*. He hadn't enjoyed his time on *Needle Park*. Film, in contrast to the stage, felt so fake, so contrived. You played to the lens and the lights, with a wired microphone snaking up under your clothes and a boom hanging over your head, acting out scenes in chunks and pieces, take after take. He didn't feel able to find a continuity of performance, to condition himself into a place of truth and authenticity, values he had been taught were paramount by acting gurus Uta Hagen and Lee Strasberg.

But, Pacino said, "I didn't have a choice. Francis wanted me." He'd go along with Francis and audition, and that would be that.

His attitude shifted during the screen tests. He could tell Francis was rooting for him, wanted him and him alone, and it was a rush, the best feeling an actor could have. And the script . . . Francis's version of Michael was quiet, understated, "there," Pacino thought, "but not quite showing up," until out of nowhere he blows bullet holes through gangster Sollozzo and corrupt cop McCluskey. The character had growth, continuity. Pacino began to see a part he could play—a part he *wanted* to play—and he saw in Francis a director he wanted to follow. From his acting teacher Charlie Laughton, Pacino had learned about the Flying Wallendas—a daredevil circus family known for performing their perilous high-wire tricks without a safety net. One day in Detroit in 1962, Laughton told the young Pacino, the Wallendas were doing their famous chair pyramid—four of them walking in a line across the wire with a bar connecting them over the left shoulder, two more standing across that bar with another bar over their shoulders and, sitting on a chair balanced on that bar, founder Karl Wallenda's pretty seventeen-year-old niece, Jana Schepp. That night, according to Laughton, the front man at the base, Jana's brother Dieter, had faltered, mumbled, "I can't do this," and the pyramid collapsed. Dieter and one of Wallenda's sons-in-law were killed; Wallenda's son Mario's injuries left him paralyzed. Karl and his brother Herman managed to hang on to the juddering high wire. They caught Jana long enough for an emergency net to be stretched below them, but when Jana dropped, she bounced off the netting and injured her head. Karl damaged his own pelvis in the fall.

The very next night, Karl and the other members of the family well enough to move were back under the big top and walking the wire once again. Someone asked Karl why, and how, he did it. "Life," he answered, "is on the wire. Everything else is just waiting."

"I understood immediately why Charlie was telling me this," Pacino later wrote in his memoir, *Sonny Boy*. "It stuck with me for a long time. Life's on the wire, man. That's my acting, my life. When I work, I'm on the wire. When I'm going for it. When I'm taking chances. I want to take chances. I want to fly and fail . . . It's what's kept me alive."

In this, Pacino found a kindred spirit in Francis. He, too, needed the wire.

Evans resisted. Francis played along, shooting screen tests with every young actor he could find—his friend Jimmy Caan; Pacino's friend Martin Sheen; even a New York actor named Robert De Niro, who had featured in a couple of low-budget satires by an independent filmmaker named Brian De Palma. "Everybody tested for

Michael," De Niro recalled. "The whole fuckin' city tested for Michael." Francis kept going back to Pacino.

As he worked to convince Paramount to hire the young unknown, Francis also pushed for Brando. This time, Evans was keen—it was showy casting, and Evans liked showy—but Paramount bean counters in New York did the math, and wired word that the studio would not, under any circumstances, approve the actor for the role. He was the wrong age and the wrong look, he was difficult, he was washed up. Instead of giving in, Francis called Bart Patton and a couple of San Francisco friends and drove down secretly to Brando's house to film an unauthorized screen test. Brando emerged for Francis's camera with his hair slicked back and tissues stuffed into his cheeks to give his face the hangdog look of an old bulldog. He discarded the pages Francis had brought and improvised some lines around the house, in a quiet but powerful rasp, moving with the measured slowness of a man who knows all eyes are on him. They screened the footage in New York, and suddenly, as long as he agreed to work for scale and profit points, Brando had the part. He immediately lobbied on Pacino's behalf.

"He's got something. Use him," Brando told Evans. "Pacino, he's a brooder."

"I'm looking for an actor, not a brooder," Evans answered. "He's tested three times, hasn't cut it."

Still, Brando's opinion gave the producer pause. If the greatest actor of all time recommended "the dwarf," as some in Hollywood called Pacino, then maybe there *was* something there.

Evans made a last-gasp offer to Jack Nicholson, who dreamed of working with Brando, but turned the film down because he felt, as Francis did, that Michael should be played by an Italian-American actor, and then agreed to hire Pacino on the condition Francis cast Jimmy Caan to play Michael's hotheaded older brother, Santino "Sonny" Corleone. Then the producer flirted with the idea of hiring Henry Kissinger to play Don Corleone's consigliere, Tom Hagen—

"he['s] Cary Grant with a German accent," Evans insisted—but Francis laughed him off and offered the part to Caan's *Rain People* co-star, Robert Duvall. With four weeks to go until production and knowing Evans was running out of time to argue, Francis, with the help of casting director Fred Roos, a close friend and fellow UCLA alumnus, rounded out the cast as he saw fit. Diane Keaton, an actress he had seen and liked in musical theater, signed on to play Michael's love interest, Kay Adams. Roos brought in another hardworking theater actor, John Cazale, to play the last Corleone brother, the weak-willed Fredo, and Francis cast his own sister, Talia, to play the sister, Connie.

Then a new problem arose. Pacino had failed to disclose that, while the long round of auditions and callbacks dragged on, he had taken another part, this one in MGM's *The Gang That Couldn't Shoot Straight*, which was scheduled to shoot at the same time as *The Godfather*. He was already in rehearsals. Pacino asked MGM to release and replace him. The studio refused. Neither Francis nor, now, Brando wanted to proceed without him. Suddenly, *The Godfather* was stuck.

Enter Evans. He had fought against Pacino, but now that the deal was done, it was done—once you played your card onto the felt, you stuck with it. He called his lawyer, the Chicago Outfit attorney Korshak. Korshak, the story goes, called Kirk Kerkorian, the multi-millionaire owner of MGM. Fewer than twenty minutes later, Irwin Winkler, the producer of *The Gang That Couldn't Shoot Straight*, got his own phone call, from Pacino's agent David Begelman.

"The iffy deal we had for Pacino" wasn't binding, Begelman told the producer, and the actor was leaving Winkler's picture immediately.

Almost at the same time, Evans got his own furious call, from MGM's president, James Aubrey, screaming down the line: "You no-good motherfucker, cocksucker, I'll get you for this . . . The midget's yours."

Pacino signed on to star in *The Godfather*, Winkler replaced him with Robert De Niro, and both films kept going. The next time Evans saw Korshak, he asked him how he'd managed to get MGM to let go of Pacino in less than half an hour. Korshak shrugged and reminded Evans that Kerkorian was then building the largest hotel in Las Vegas, the MGM Grand—and the mob ran Vegas.

"I asked him," the lawyer said simply, "if he wanted to finish building his hotel."

Evans had pushed all his chips to the middle of the table. Bluhdorn's accountants in New York were less confident. While still in preproduction, before he had rolled a single foot of film, Francis landed at Los Angeles International Airport after a location-scouting trip—only for a Western Union employee to push an urgent message into his hand. It was from Freddie Fields, Francis's agent at CMA.

"Don't quit," read the wire. "Make them fire you!"

· 11 ·

THE FAMILY BUSINESS

The Godfather shot in New York from late March to early July. From the first week, Francis feared he would lose his job. The studio expected a cheap, quick, reliable crime picture, just the kind of product Francis couldn't bring himself to deliver. "Fast, good, cheap: pick two" was one of his favorite expressions, and he wasn't going to let Paramount pick fast and cheap at the expense of good. The studio hovered over him. They hadn't liked his cast, and they didn't like what they saw in the dailies. Allegations that the film was anti-Italian, encouraged by the New York mob, made them nervous.

"I was 29 [actually 32]," Francis remembered later. "I had no power. They could easily push me around, which they did and tried to." Within just a few days, with only the opening wedding sequence in the can, rumors rippled across the set that Paramount wanted Pacino fired and his director with him. Francis cut some of the rushes together, hoping to impress his bosses, and his heart sank. He sent word to Pacino to meet him that evening at the Ginger Man, a French restaurant on 64th Street. When the actor arrived, Francis was at a table with his two children and Ellie, at the time heavily pregnant with a third. Francis didn't stand up.

"You know how much you mean to me, how much faith I had in you," Francis said. He cut his steak awkwardly. "I don't think it's working. You're not working."

He showed Pacino the rushes the next day. The actor just shrugged. It was the opening sequence; Michael was meant to be withdrawn, almost invisible. He would unfold over the course of the picture. That's what acting was.

Francis couldn't afford to wait for Evans to catch on. He told Ruddy to move one of the film's showstoppers—the scene in which Michael shoots rival gangster Sollozzo and corrupt policeman McCluskey dead in an Italian restaurant—up several days in the schedule. He took his time with it, fifteen hours with the three actors around the table in a little eatery in the Bronx, the air thick with cigarette smoke and heavy with the fizzing heat emanating from the film lights. A tense meeting, Pacino's eyes anxious and furious, and then the eruption of violence, the blood spurting over the white tablecloth, the shocked shriek of a fellow diner. Evans watched the dailies when they came in to the Paramount screening room in Los Angeles, and suddenly, there was no more talk of firing Al Pacino.

Francis's job remained on the line. His openness on set read as indecision; the texture with which he wanted to layer the picture seemed indulgent. Costs kept rising, and the accountants blamed the situation on the director. Hadn't they told him they should shoot the thing in St. Louis?

On Thursday, April 15, Francis sat at home with Ellie, who was nine months pregnant, and Marty Scorsese, back in New York to visit family, and turned the television to NBC to watch the Academy Awards. Two hours into the show, the actors Sarah Miles and George Segal walked to the dais and announced the winner for Best Original Screenplay: for *Patton*, Francis Coppola and Edmund North. It was Francis's first Oscar; he hadn't gone to the ceremony because he thought, if he left New York, someone else would be directing *The Godfather* by the time he came back.

"How are they going to fire you now?" Marty asked, beaming.

Francis figured they'd find a way. Not much later, the *Godfather* shoot moved to Filmways, a studio in East Harlem, for some of the interiors, and one day, Francis was sitting in one of the toilet stalls when he heard two crew members walk into the bathroom.

". . . film's a load of shit," he heard one of them say.

"That asshole director doesn't know what he's doing," the other agreed.

Francis held his breath and, as quietly as he could, raised his feet up onto the toilet seat—so the men wouldn't see and recognize his shoes.

In May 1971, George flew to Europe with Marcia, the first foreign trip they had ever taken as a couple. It wasn't a romantic getaway. *THX 1138* had been selected to feature in the Cannes Film Festival's Directors' Fortnight, an out-of-competition showcase of new worldwide films. The festival would not be paying George's costs to attend the screening, but George was determined to go anyway—not for the experience, not for the holiday, but because he needed to sell his next picture.

Over the previous month, George had enlisted Willard Huyck and Huyck's wife and writing partner Gloria Katz to help rewrite his fifteen-page treatment for the film Marcia and Francis had been urging him to make—originally called *A Quiet Night in Modesto*, now retitled *American Graffiti*. It turned out, to George's great frustration, that writing emotions wasn't as easy as he'd claimed. The story in the treatment was personal to George, inspired by specific experiences and feelings, but it was too transparently calculated, Huyck said, to make "a nice, simple piece of good Hollywood entertainment." George's agent, Jeff Berg, and his producer, Gary Kurtz, shopped the treatment to the studios, but no one bit.

George and Marcia were running out of money. Columbia asked George to direct *Tommy*, the film adaptation of the Who's rock opera—but George turned them down. Producers adapting the hit Broadway musical *Hair* had George on a list of possible directors that also included Gene Kelly and Hal Ashby—but George turned them down. He turned down the crime thriller *Lady Ice*, even though it came with a screenplay co-written by Alan Trustman, who had written *Bullitt* and *The Thomas Crown Affair*. It didn't matter how broke he and Marcia were, and they were *broke*; George described his situation at the time as "destitute." He wasn't interested in making other people's films, not even once. The universe hadn't saved him from the wreck of that car so he could settle and take a paycheck.

He flew down to LA first. He hated playing the Hollywood game, but Berg and Kurtz had made it clear it helped to sell a picture if the director deigned to show investors his face, maybe answer some questions. George didn't have the money for a hotel, so he slept on the couch at Francis's house. He drove around the flat concrete expanse of the city, agonized through the meetings. No one wanted to make his movie. He was still a kid, scrawny and soft-spoken. His first feature had made no money and won no awards. He didn't even have a script.

He and Marcia flew to New York next. George wrangled a meeting with the new man in charge at United Artists, David Picker, who was director-friendly and actively looking for films to build his first full slate as CEO. He was young—thirty-nine—and had helped bring the Beatles and James Bond to the studio, all while shepherding serious adult pictures like *Midnight Cowboy*. He was friendly with Truffaut, Bergman, and Fellini. He was happy to hear Lucas out.

George made his pitch: a nostalgic, crowd-pleasing comedy-drama for young audiences, about friends cruising the streets of a small California town on the last night of summer vacation before heading off to college, with a soundtrack of wall-to-wall rock 'n' roll hits, so watching the film would feel like listening to the car radio. It wouldn't cost much. The main characters were young, and the studio could get promising unknowns to play them. The material was accessible and relatable to people across the country, from coast to coast, and it targeted precisely the youth audience studios claimed to be desperate to connect with.

Picker didn't say no, but he didn't say yes, either.

"Well," he started, "in a week or so I'm going to the Cannes Film Festival . . ." He gave George an apologetic look: The market that ran parallel to the festival was one of the busiest two weeks of the film industry year, and Picker would be hearing pitches from dozens of filmmakers there, some of them with scripts and casts attached. He couldn't commit to anything until he had heard them all out. "I'm sure you understand," he added.

"*I'm* going, too!" George blurted out. "I have a movie there."

"Okay," Picker conceded, "come and see me *there*."

It wasn't much, but it was something.

The Lucases stayed the night with Francis in the little apartment he was renting for himself, Ellie, and the boys—Gian-Carlo, now seven, and Roman, five. George found his friend "in severe trauma." Francis was six weeks into shooting *The Godfather*, and he was certain Paramount had lined up Elia Kazan to take over the movie. He went to the set every day expecting to get fired; then he came "home" to Ellie, who was also feeling alienated and uncomfortable. Zoetrope had failed, he had two kids to feed and a third on the way, and he wasn't "at all confident . . . that I'd ever get another job." The whole thing was hell.

George knew he had pushed Francis to take on the job, back when Francis was in similar financial straits to the ones George was in now. George was the one who'd insisted Francis face the music and do it, the one who reminded him you need money coming in to cover the money you owed—who had chided Francis the way his own father had, in the past, chided him. And yet here George was, refusing to take his own advice. Acting, as he often did, as if settling, as necessary as it was for everyone else, was beneath *him*.

Or maybe George knew himself. Francis had the energy for those battles, even an appetite for them. At times, on *The Rain People* and now on *The Godfather*, he seemed to relish the siege mentality, the feeling of us against the world that could be stoked in a crew like a fire when time, money, the studio, were all enemies. Francis was fed by it. George . . . maybe George knew already that the same fire would feed *on* him.

At four in the morning that night, George and Marcia were woken off the couch by Francis and Ellie running frantically across the dark room, stumbling and crying out apologies. Ellie was in labor. They rushed out the door and to the hospital. Three hours later, George and Marcia left the apartment for the airport. It was May 14, George's twenty-seventh birthday. They landed in London, and George called back to New York. Francis told him Ellie had given birth to a girl, Sofia. She and George shared a birthday.

The only people on the *Godfather* set to have any faith in their director, it seemed, were the actors. Francis, as he had done on *The Rain People* and would try to do again and again, had cast actors whose real-life dynamics he felt mirrored those of their characters on the page. Never did that alchemy work better than on *The Godfather*. Caan and Duvall, who were more experienced, treated Pacino with all the affection and ribbing older siblings reserve for their kid brother; all three of them—as well as fourth brother John Cazale—looked up to Brando, the actor they all idolized, the way sons do to a father of whom they are in awe. Visitors to the set on any given day might have seen Caan and Duvall mooning each other, Brando reading his lines off hidden cue cards (in one instance, a huge chalkboard sign propped up in a tree; in another, sheets of paper taped around Duvall's body), and Francis looking serious and alone. His sister, Talia, felt, at times, like she shouldn't have been on the movie, put in a position to see her older brother so vulnerable.

Paramount wanted the film violent, explicit. Classy wasn't what they had in mind when they bought Puzo's book. Working for Corman had taught Francis that all he needed were a few set-piece moments: Michael shooting Sollozzo and McCluskey dead, Luca Brasi garroted to death with his hand pinned to a bar top, Sonny machine-gunned to shreds at a tollbooth. Caan asked how many squibs were wired to his body for that last one and was told 147, and not to put his hands too close to any of them during the take or his fingers would get blown off. He thought of chickening out, but there were pretty girls on set watching.

One day, Evans invited his friend Robert Towne to visit the set. Towne was a sought-after "script doctor," known around town for fixing the script to *Bonnie and Clyde*. He'd done favors for Evans before, and he knew Francis a little from the old days, when they'd both cut their teeth working for Corman. The tall, bearded, long-haired writer spent a few hours watching Francis work, then sat in a screening room at the Paramount Building in Times Square to watch four hours of dailies, with Francis by his side.

"That is without question the best footage I've ever seen," he told Coppola when it was over.

Francis's heart skipped with relief. Towne, he said later, was "the first and only person who told me *The Godfather* wasn't a failure." The two men agreed, however, that the film was missing a resolution to Vito and Michael's relationship. Towne suggested writing a final scene for Brando and Pacino together, one that would show the love and respect between the father and the son—but also Don Vito's melancholy resignation that his youngest and most promising boy was following in bloody footsteps he had hoped to steer him away from.

That sounded great, Francis said, but whatever new pages Towne wrote, he had to shoot them tomorrow.

Towne carried a copy of Francis's script back to his hotel room, read it, took notes, felt his way into the picture's voice. He sat typing until four in the morning. In the pages he handed Francis at the crack of dawn, Michael sits in the garden listening to his father as Vito breaks down the chess moves to come—"Barzini will move against you first," he says, "he'll set up a meeting with someone that you absolutely trust, guaranteeing your safety, and at that meeting, you'll be assassinated"—before pausing and, unexpectedly, confronting his age, his enforced semiretirement, his legacy. He asks after his son's family, apologizes for fretting, turns his eye to the past. He grows forgetful, distracted. He apologizes for not handing Michael a better, more legitimate inheritance—Senator or Governor Corleone, he says, rather than Don.

It was a short, quiet scene—three or four pages, under four minutes of screen time in the end—two men sitting at a table under the trees. But it was everything Francis wanted *The Godfather* to be.

Francis started believing in his film. He wanted so badly for it to be great, it was like his life depended on it. Late in the schedule, the cast and crew were out at Calvary Cemetery in Queens, filming the funeral of Don Corleone. Under a hazy gray sky, a somber Michael Corleone sits by the coffin as it is about to be interred, watching family, friends, and fellow mobsters pay final tribute to his father, each tossing a single rose onto the casket. Then one of Michael's lieutenants, Tessio, asks to speak to him, and takes him aside to pass on a message from rival gangster Barzini, requesting a peace meeting—one Michael knows, from advice his father has given him in Towne's new scene, is a trap.

Up until that exchange, the scene is wordless, a complex choreography of eyelines and body language. The crew shot all day, wrapping only when the sun began to set. Pacino said his goodbyes and made his way through the burial plots to his trailer, feeling good about his day's work and excited about the short ride home and a cold beer or two. Ahead of him, a man sat on a tombstone in the dying light, "weeping like a baby[,] profusely crying." Pacino was startled when he recognized his director.

"Francis, what's wrong? What happened?" Pacino asked.

"They won't give me another shot," Francis answered.

He wanted to keep filming, but he'd lost the light. The sunset wouldn't match the rest of the day's takes. He wanted more, and he was devastated.

As he continued on to his trailer, it occurred to Pacino that maybe this picture was going to be worth something after all.

Another plane, and George and Marcia were in Cannes. *THX 1138* screened, and George couldn't reach Picker. The fortnight of the festival ticked to a close, and still he couldn't pin him down. Finally, he cornered the executive on the terrace of the palatial Carlton Hotel, where most executives stayed, and pitched him *American Graffiti* again. Told him he could have the rights to the picture for just ten grand. It wasn't much money, especially if George had to share it with Huyck and Katz, and it's unclear where George came up with the $10,000 figure in the first place, though there are stories. A week in Cannes wasn't cheap. "From what I hear," Mike Medavoy recalls, George "needed money to get out of his hotel room. And he went to David Picker, and said, *Look, I need five thousand dollars, and I'll option you these two projects.*"

Whether it was five each for two projects, as Medavoy recalls, or ten for *American Graffiti*, the sum on the table, George remembered later, amounted to essentially "nothing." It was exactly the kind of arrangement George's father had warned him against, back when George had first told him he wanted to be a filmmaker. *Don't ever go into business with your hobby*, George Sr. had advised his son, *because you'll be taken advantage of and you'll be doing stupid things. Doing things for love instead of money.*

Picker thought about it for a moment.

"Okay, we'll do it," he said finally. "Or at least, we'll give you the ten to write the script. Do you have any other films?" A standard Hollywood question: What else you got? Can we get dibs on the next one, just in case this one hits?

"Well—" George hesitated. "I have this sort of space opera thing. It's sort of an action-adventure film in space."

"Okay, we'll make a deal for that, too." They shook on it: $10,000 for United Artists to option the rights to *American Graffiti* and the "sort of space opera thing" George had been dreaming of, titled, at that point, *The Star Wars*.

The meeting had taken only minutes. It was such a good deal for the studio, and for such an inconsequential amount of money, that, years later, Picker admitted he couldn't even remember making it.

George had never been a good traveler. He went back to Marcia, settled their hotel room bill, and braced himself for the long journey back home.

· 12 ·

UNICORNS

The Godfather wrapped in August 1971, after three and a half months in New York and a brief stint in Sicily. Francis dove straight into cutting, with Peter Zinner and William Reynolds as his editors, and Murch, with whom he'd grown close, as his sound mixer. Even then, Murch says, "there was a big trough period where it looked like the film was not going to work. The studio kept hammering, and Francis was resisting . . . The feeling on *The Godfather* was: this is long, and dark, and self-indulgent." Robert Evans wanted Francis to get rid of the score he had commissioned from Italian composer and conductor Nino Rota. He thought it was pretentious.

"If you boys don't fight for this music," said Murch's wife, Aggie, "there's not a decent pair of balls between you."

Francis took a copy of the movie to Rome to show Rota in October. On the night of Saturday, November 13, shortly after coming back, he threw a party at his house to unwind. George and Marcia were there. There was something quaint about George and Marcia. Francis liked to call them "country mice"—happy and simple and, he'd add only a little dismissively, "sort of romantic, like kids picking oranges in an old Jane Powell movie." Marcia loved Francis's gatherings. The editor Richard Chew, who spent weeks on Folsom Street, remembers her as "very social," which George decidedly was not.

On this evening, George was particularly disengaged from the merriment. He had kept in touch with Steven Spielberg as Steven returned to work, directing a couple more TV episodes and then a feature-length television movie, *L.A. 2017*, which aired in January of 1971—the story of a time-traveler caught in a dystopian future Los Angeles, where the populace lives underground to escape deadly pollution, while a fascist government polices them through the use of law enforcement psychiatrists. George had watched it on NBC, amused. It wasn't quite a rip-off of *THX 1138 4EB*, but it was close—a "friendly homage," he thought, with the benign haughtiness of an older sibling watching their kid brother imitate them. Since then, Steven had been handed the reins of another TV movie, *Duel*, based on a short story the genre author Richard Matheson had published in *Playboy*. On its face, *Duel* was simplistic—a traveling salesman on a business trip gets into a confrontation with a tank trunk, driven by an unseen driver, who pursues him along the road, trying to kill him—but word in LA was that young Spielberg had turned it into something electrifying. Something far more impressive than the kid had any right to make, given the thirteen-day shooting schedule, four-hundred-grand shooting budget, and strict seventy-five-minute runtime.

The buzz about *Duel* was so strong it thrummed up the coast to San Francisco, and the film was premiering on the Saturday of Francis's party, so as the other guests mingled and drank Francis's red wine, George kept an eye on his watch. ABC's Movie of the Week started broadcasting at 8:30 PM and he was keen not to miss it. He figured he would let Marcia dance, give Spielberg's little movie ten or fifteen minutes, see what it was like, and then return to hovering on the fringes of the good time. Shortly before 8:30, he drifted away from the laughter and conversation and climbed up the stairs. He found a room with a television and turned over to ABC.

"I remember very distinctly," he said years later, "I started watching—and I couldn't stop."

At the first commercial break, he leapt out of his seat and ran down the stairs. "Francis, you've got to come see this movie," he said. "This guy's *really* good."

Francis refused to be taken away from the fun. George ran back upstairs alone and sat there for the next hour, the lit television screen reflected in his eyeglasses, absorbed in Dennis Weaver's desperate, sweaty escape from the monster truck. The party roared on through the ceiling beneath him, but George could no longer hear it. George responded to *Duel* as a piece of art not all that different from the mood poems he longed to make himself. A red car chased down dusty roads by an ugly truck as vividly designed as any human character; expressive sound design of the kind George and Murch were obsessed with. From the simplest of ideas, Steven had created an experience, not with plot, not with dialogue, but almost purely out of sound and images. George was "very, very, very impressed."

Steven was proud of *Duel*, though his dream contract at Universal had become instead a nightmare obligation.

"TV for me wasn't an art form," he said later. "It was a job . . . I felt that it was like working in a sweatshop, and I wasn't getting any of that stimulation, that gratification that I even got making 8mm war movies when I was 12 years old. I didn't have that passion, because television sort of smothered the passion."

Duel, a prestigious Movie of the Week, was finally his breakthrough. Critics loved it; executives took note. It was even scheduled for a theatrical release in Europe. Tentative offers came in. Jeff Berg set Steven up with Matthew Robbins and Hal Barwood, to see if Steven might be a fit to direct a script they were shopping, a science-fiction adventure called *Star Dancing*. Steven liked the writers, and the evocative concept art they had commissioned from a Boeing design illustrator named Ralph McQuarrie, more than he liked the project. He passed, but he and Robbins and Barwood remained friendly. He worked with a pal, the actor Joseph Walsh, on a screenplay about Walsh's gambling addiction, following two friends who can't resist the lure of an elusive big score. Steven felt he could relate to the characters. It was a bit like show business—the "excitement," Walsh said later, but "underneath all that, there is a trap. There is a sadness." James Aubrey, the MGM executive who had screamed down the phone at Evans over Pacino breaking his contract, was keen on green-lighting it, on the condition it starred Dean Martin, with whom MGM had a working relationship, and was set and shot at the Circus Circus Hotel & Casino in Las Vegas, which MGM owned. Steven brought Walsh's screenplay to Universal, to which he was still under contract, but Sheinberg wasn't interested. He declined to release Steven from his contract to work for Aubrey. Steven felt like he was treading water.

"You're better off *not* being under contract," his agent Mike Medavoy told Steven, "because everything Universal does is not very good. You gotta get out of your contract, and out of Universal."

"I can't do that," Steven answered. "I've become really close to Sid Sheinberg, I can't get out of it."

"No studio is going to give you a movie, and then you go back to Universal, and they can't work with you again because you're under exclusive contract to Universal."

"I can't get out of it," Steven repeated.

Medavoy shook his head. "You need another agent," he said. He flogged Steven off to his colleague Guy McElwaine, a smooth and charming agent who had come to CMA from a career as a publicist.

Steven had reason to feel discouraged, but his new agent turned out to be a gift. McElwaine, who had once been Frank Sinatra's public relations man, was old-school showbiz slick. He wore large eyeglasses with smoky lenses, and checked tweed jackets and paisley ties. His skin was a perpetual leathery tan. He liked a martini. You'd meet him and he'd talk and talk, giving you the impression he liked nothing more than the sound of his own voice—until you realized he had, somehow, negotiated you into a deal, as smoothly as his curveballs baited hitters into swinging, back when he played minor league ball after graduating from USC. He'd been in the business a long time; knew the unspoken rituals, the difference between lines you could cross and lines you couldn't. McElwaine recognized the clients—like Warren Beatty and now Steven—who needed not just representation but hand-holding. Their confidence was outsize yet brittle. He also understood, as Medavoy hadn't, that Steven was hungry to know more about the business, and how to play it. So, as he waited for Steven's television contract to run its course, McElwaine took the initiative. He drove his young charge around, meeting executives, teaching him about the bottom line. He drove Steven to the house of Terry Semel, who ran distribution for Disney, so Semel could explain how films were sold and exhibited and how box-office revenue was divvied up. "Terry must have talked for about four hours straight," Spielberg remembered. "I was taking notes, and at the end of the day I knew more about distribution and exhibition than I ever wanted to." Semel took note, too: It wasn't often he met a director who cared about the ins and outs of what he did.

In a touch of serendipity, around this time, Universal shook up its executive hierarchy. Lew Wasserman, while retaining Sheinberg as the head of Universal Television, was also handing him the reins of the motion picture studio. Richard Zanuck—president of 20th Century Fox and youngest son of Darryl Zanuck, the co-founder and chairman of the studio—had just been fired by his father, in no small part for having the temerity to question why sixty-eight-year-old Darryl was spending so much of the company's money developing vanity projects for his mistress, twenty-four-year-old French actress Geneviève Gilles. The younger Zanuck was shrewd, hardworking, and charismatic. He'd already rescued Fox once, in 1963, when the fiscal disaster of *Cleopatra*, an out-of-control epic starring Elizabeth Taylor and Richard Burton, had come close to sinking the company. (The situation was so dire, Zanuck had to shut the studio down for a while, just to stem the financial bleeding.) Zanuck had now found a new job as an executive vice president at Warner Bros., but Wasserman was working to poach him and his partner, David Brown, to a first-look deal as independent producers at Universal. They would buy their own material and develop it. They would have the pick of directors on contract to work with.

McElwaine said he'd set up a meeting. Maybe Steven had something he could bring them.

Francis finished editing *The Godfather* in the New Year. George helped, cutting a brief montage of crime scene photos and newspaper headlines about the war between the Corleones and rival families. He bailed Francis out when the director realized he hadn't shot enough footage of empty hallways to intercut into the tense scene in which Michael finds his hospitalized father abandoned and vulnerable to assassination: Why not, George suggested, just use the trim ends on the existing shots—the seconds of footage before the assistant director called *action* and after he called *cut*? Studio editors usually discarded those as scraps, but George had learned to use every second of available film at USC.

All throughout the editing process, Paramount let it be known they expected the film to be a bomb. Evans fought Francis over every decision. "Francis and I had a perfect record," Evans wrote later, "—we didn't agree on anything." He canceled the film's scheduled Christmas 1971 release, and pushed Francis until he was happy.

"You don't know what you've got, Francis," Evans told him enthusiastically in the final days. "We've got a shot at being remembered."

By now, Francis was exhausted.

"I'm tired of listening to your hype, Evans," he moaned.

Evans stood his ground. He thought *The Godfather* could be one of the biggest films ever, make over $50 million.

"Only *Gone with the Wind* and *Sound of Music* hit those numbers," Francis argued.

"Yeah, and we will too," Evans said, "if you don't fuck it up."

"And you'll buy me a Mercedes, too, if it does, huh?"

Raise or fold. Evans looked into Francis's eyes.

"You're damn right I will," he said.

Francis forgot all about it. He just wanted to be done—and in February 1972, he finally was.

Those were "the happiest days that I can remember," he insisted two decades later, "when *The Godfather* was over and I didn't have to go there anymore." The film wouldn't be released for another month, and he had no prospects on the horizon. When Evans asked him if he would be open to quickly rewriting a screen adaptation of *The Great Gatsby*, Francis leapt at the chance. The film was months into preproduction already, but no one liked Truman Capote's screenplay. More inconveniently still, Evans had only ever wanted to make the movie because *Gatsby* was his wife Ali MacGraw's favorite book and Daisy Buchanan her dream role, but now MacGraw had gone off and started fucking Steve McQueen, and then had the gall to suggest she and McQueen might star in the movie together. Evans resentfully cast Robert Redford as Gatsby and replaced MacGraw with Mia Farrow. "I bought *The Great Gatsby* as a wedding gift," he told *People* magazine, "and I took it away as a divorce gift."

Francis didn't know F. Scott Fitzgerald's novel very well, but he was anxious about supporting his young family and he needed the money. There was no harm in doing Evans and Paramount a favor, either. He'd store up some goodwill in case *The Godfather* was a failure.

He left Ellie and the kids behind and checked himself into L'Hôtel, on the Rue des Beaux-Arts in Paris, the small hotel in which Oscar Wilde had spent the last eighteen months of his life, exiled and disgraced. The surroundings matched Francis's romantic, melancholy mood. For three weeks, he stayed in Wilde's room, number sixteen, and banged away at his typewriter. When he found that

Gatsby and Daisy barely speak to one another directly in the novel, he bought a book of Fitzgerald's short stories and liberally stole lines of dialogue to put into their mouths. He had thought of the job as a job and himself as a hired hand, but as usual, once he got started, the material spoke to him. The reinvention and performance of the self. The unattainability of one's dreams. The false promises of love and wealth. He wrote it all down at a wooden desk by the doors to his small, private stone courtyard, bright in the warm early-spring light.

He flew back for *The Godfather*'s gala premiere at the Loews State theater in New York on March 14. Everyone was there: Evans and MacGraw, putting on brave faces; Puzo, looking like a delighted father of the bride, in his dark tux and ruffled white shirt; a grinning Jimmy Caan with knockout blond Sheila Ryan on his arm; a long-haired Pacino, his gaze hazy from the booze he'd drunk to deal with the anxiety, standing with his beaming, beautiful girlfriend, Jill Clayburgh. Francis avoided the cameras. In the surviving pictures of the night, he stands awkwardly on the patterned carpet next to the peacocking Caan and his beauty queen date. He wore a velvet suit with a chunky bow tie and a long scarf and seemed underdressed among the black, uniform tuxedos. The expression on his face is closed and uneasy.

They played the picture, all three hours of it. The audience gasped when Pacino blew holes through McCluskey and Sollozzo; they cried when Brando's don keeled over, dead among the tomato vines of his garden. When the credits rolled, they cheered.

At the after-party at the St. Regis hotel, Henry Kissinger and his partner Nancy Maginnes hung out to drink and eat. Jack Nicholson turned up, wearing a newsboy cap, looking a little stoned. Evans and MacGraw pretended to be in love. Francis dropped the whole thing into his memory hole; on at least one occasion, telling the story of the premiere years later, he said he was still in Paris when it happened.

The next day, he left it to Ellie to update him on the first box-office returns.

"It's a big hit," she told him. "There are lines around the block at five theaters in the city."

It was the news Francis hadn't dared hope for, and yet, in the moment, he couldn't bring himself to acknowledge it. "Yeah, yeah," he answered, "but I've got to finish the *Gatsby* script."

The Godfather, it turned out, was far more than a "big hit." Unexpectedly stellar reviews celebrated its arrival. Pauline Kael, in the *New Yorker*, complimented Francis for taking Puzo's "trash," "unreadable" novel and turning it into an epic "with the spaciousness and strength that popular novels such as Dickens' used to have . . . Coppola has not only done his best but pushed himself farther than he may realize." She compared Francis to the painter Renoir and his film to classics *On the Waterfront* and *From Here to Eternity*. The critic for *Newsweek*, Paul Zimmerman, echoed Evans's prediction: *The Godfather*, he predicted, would be "the *Gone with the Wind* of gangster movies—both in its artful, intelligent control of gaudy material and in its certain sensational box-office success."

The five cinemas showing the film in New York were so overwhelmed by demand they ran the film around the clock. Local businesses complained to the press about the long lines blocking access to their storefronts. By the time it opened in Los Angeles on March 22, the movie had already grossed $13 million—twice its shooting budget—in a single week, in a single city. On March 24, *The Godfather* "went wide," opening in cinemas across the rest of the United States, and the pattern repeated itself again. It packed every house. It had legs. Pacino, Caan, and Duvall became household names overnight. Brando was again hailed as a great, singular American artist. And over and over, critics, writers, columnists, and scholars praised Francis: for his seeming control of every frame, for turning popular entertainment into great tragedy, for blurring the boundary between genre picture and work of art. Hollywood filmmaking, as Francis had found it in the late '60s, had been a cultural irrelevance. It churned out manipulative tearjerkers and creaky roller-coaster rides. Francis had done what no other American director of his generation had yet managed: He had made a film that excited and titillated as entertainment, but also pushed the bounds of the medium. His picture had "touched greatness"—as Kissinger put it—and also outgrossed every entertainment picture in memory.

In the summer, on the exact day *The Godfather* passed $50 million in revenue, Francis and George went down to the nearest Mercedes dealership and bought a dark blue 1972 Mercedes-Benz 600 Pullman—the same model, Francis boasted, as the pope's. The car cost roughly $38,000—about $200,000 in 2025 dollars. Francis told the salesman to send the bill to Robert Evans at Paramount Pictures.

By early September, *The Godfather* fulfilled Zimmerman's prediction and overtook *Gone with the Wind* as the highest-grossing film in American history. Weeks later, the film became the first picture ever to clear $100 million at the domestic box office. It opened in Europe and South America and found success there, too; in Italy, nearly twenty-two million admissions were sold, the second-most of any film ever. Shares in Gulf+Western, which owned Paramount, quadrupled in value by December. At the end of its theatrical run, *The Godfather* had grossed $133 million in the United States, and an estimated $250 million globally. It had not just broken every record but smashed them to pieces, bringing in more than the highest-grossing pictures of the previous three years (*Love Story*, *Fiddler on the Roof*, and *Butch Cassidy and the Sundance Kid*) put together. Cultural historians would say later that Hollywood's renaissance had begun with *Bonnie and Clyde* in 1967, but *The Godfather* earned nearly three times more. It earned almost ten times as much as *Easy Rider*, another contender to the title of era-defining, turn-of-the-tide movie. The film studios had taken notice of those two films, but *The Godfather* was a whale. It was popular entertainment as exciting, as artful, as culturally significant as great fiction or the art that hung in museums. And *everyone* went to see it.

The film's success made Francis giddy. The world had decided he was no longer "a shy kid from Queens, a perpetually bad student who had been temporarily paralyzed by polio": Now he was "the young man who'd caught lightning in a bottle." No longer "an obscure, impoverished young director/writer"—but "a house-hold name."

He was not the only Coppola to see his life changed by the Corleones. Francis's father, Carmine, had contributed music to Nino Rota's score, and the film was his first taste of acclaim in a long time. Francis's sister, Talia, was praised for her portrayal of Connie, a breakthrough in her own career. August, the older brother Francis had looked up to his whole childhood, was uninvolved in the picture, and its release drove him into a crisis of identity. He'd been the promising one, the talented one, the eldest destined for greatness. He'd earned his doctorate when Francis was still making ten bucks a week editing nudie flicks; he'd become an esteemed professor of literature while his little brother struggled to establish himself as a filmmaker. Now entering middle age, Augie, intelligent and a touch flamboyant, used to the minor celebrity of being immediately noticeable on any campus he called home—with his bald crown, flowing dark hair down his neck, and collection of handmade scarves—became, overnight, the less celebrated of the two Coppola brothers. August loved the opera, too; had married an artist, too; had brass espresso machines installed in his offices, too. He did all these things before Francis, but now, the world saw him only as a facsimile of his little brother.

"I just wanted to be his kid brother," Francis remembered, but "when *The Godfather* came out and suddenly Francis Ford Coppola was somebody, he couldn't be August Floyd Coppola anymore because it seemed as though he was copying me—but I was copying him, and that caused the heartbreaking issue that went on and on throughout my life." August, who had always looked after him, suddenly turned cold.

Francis's marriage also changed. He was suddenly surrounded by fawning fans and giddy yes-men who told him every idea that came out of his mouth was a slice of genius. Every studio wanted to work with him now. Only Ellie dared to question him, sometimes, and it opened a distance between them. Francis took it personally. Why did his own wife doubt him when no one else did?

Missy didn't doubt him. She had moved away from Los Angeles and enrolled at UC Berkeley, just across the bay from San Francisco, to study political science. When with Francis, she was like "the girl who has a crush on her professor," he said later—impressionable, impressed, unconditionally supportive. In the same way he told Ellie to spend more time making art, Francis suggested to Missy she should be a writer. She had the potential to be more than a student and part-time babysitter. She loved films; maybe she could work on one of his.

Evans's own life was turned upside down by *The Godfather*. He was no longer a joke, and there was no longer talk of Paramount firing him, but stress over the picture had given him a case of debilitating sciatica, which he self-medicated with alcohol and cocaine, and his amphetamine-fueled workaholism was part of what had driven MacGraw away. He had almost missed the birth of their son, Joshua, because he was busy in casting sessions, arguing with Francis. Looking back on *The Godfather* twenty years after its release, Evans wrote in his memoir of Francis's "bearish looks, great smile, and operatic manner," his bravado and his stubbornness, and the emotional immaturity that he felt lurked within. "At the core," Evans wrote, "he was a scared, prepubescent kid."

He was also, Evans thought, one of the great seducers—and one of the great liars. "Till this day," he wrote in 1994, "I doubt whether his own wife really knows who he is."

Both resounding failure and overwhelming success lay character bare, and *The Godfather* was as overwhelming a success as any filmmaker had ever had. The scared, prepubescent seducer was now globally famous, wealthy beyond his wildest dreams, vindicated in his creative instincts. He resented his beautiful, talented wife, who had met and fallen in love with him when he was an awkward, struggling young writer-director, for not idolizing him with the same fervor as his beautiful, talented mistress, with whom he spent more and more time.

"My life before and after that film," Francis remembered, "—it was night and day."

Steven, too, was crushed by *The Godfather*. After *Duel* aired on ABC, the feature film offers he'd dreamed of had finally started to come, and he was thrilled—at first. Every script that came across his desk was for an action film. The industry still perceived him the way Medavoy had: as a competent, creative genre director. No more or less. The versatility he had shown across television projects was perceived as a lack of personal style. His ability to bring *Duel* in so quickly was taken not as a demonstration of ambition, but as proof he had matured into a reliable journeyman.

Steven developed two new film projects he thought Zanuck and Brown might go for. He had an idea for a science-fiction picture about regular people coming in contact with aliens, inspired by his own feelings of awe and wonder that night from his childhood when his father had dragged him out of bed to watch a meteor shower. *Firelight*, the $500 home movie feature he'd made as a teenager in Phoenix, had explored the same idea, and shortly before *Duel*, Steven had written a variation of it up as a short story entitled "Experiences." He was a boy of images, and no visual compelled him more, then, than colored lights dancing and flitting—magically, inexplicably—across the dark night sky. It was everything he loved about cinema. It was Walt Disney's *Fantasia*; it was the enormity of David Lean and the danger of Alfred Hitchcock; it was the hazy borderline between illusion and reality, the spiritual and the scientific.

It was also a nonstarter. The executives at Universal were not interested in anything redolent of green saucer people from Mars. That was for Roger Corman, cheap B-movies, drive-in theaters. Truth be told, the special effects Steven needed to make his vision come true, to properly conjure the "kind of scary that tickles," didn't exist. Even if they did, they would be expensive, and he was wise enough to the business, by now, to know no studio in town was giving him $20 million or more to direct his first theatrical feature.

The other film Steven wanted to make was more grounded, and based on a true story. Back in 1969, he had read an article in the *Hollywood Citizen-News* about a real-life "Bonnie 'n' Clyde" in Texas. Twenty-two-year-old petty criminal Robert Dent, newly released from prison, and his wife, Ila Faye Holiday, had kidnapped a highway patrolman and driven three hundred miles across Texas, pursued by a caravan of over a hundred police cars, because Dent "want[ed] ten or fifteen minutes to talk to my kids," who were staying with his father-in-law. Dent and Holiday had only been married a year, and the young man hadn't intended to get into trouble. They'd set out early morning to reunite with their kids—actually Holiday's from a previous marriage—and when a police car pulled up behind them, cherry lights flashing, Dent panicked and sped off. He and Holiday eventually stole a highway patrolman's car and took him hostage. Dozens of police cars chased them all the way to their destination. News vans and an ambulance soon joined the convoy. Helicopter news crews hovered overhead. Curious locals lined up by the road to wave the parade on. By the time Dent and Holiday reached the house where the kids were staying, a county sheriff and an FBI agent were already there waiting for them. They killed Dent as soon as he opened the door, with a shotgun blast that sent his body flying back down the front steps and into the dirt.

It was a story of tragic stupidity, but one Steven was drawn to. He and Dent were the same age. He imagined being a father that young—and did not need to imagine the longing felt by the members of a broken family. But he also calculated that a riff on *Bonnie and Clyde*, recently a huge success, had the potential to kick-start his own career. He was desperate to escape television, for every reason imaginable. "First, there's a lot of money in features," he explained. "And then there's that old-fashioned thrill of getting in your car, driving around the corner, and watching people standing in line to see your movie." The itch was maddening. He had to scratch it.

But Universal immediately turned that idea down, too. Two dumb kids kidnap a cop and drive slowly for hours before one of them gets blown to pieces? They couldn't imagine *anyone* wanting to buy a ticket to that picture. Dent and Holiday had no scope, no motivation; frankly, the whole thing sounded dark and depressing.

Steven had nothing. He was, again, at the mercy of the screenplays being offered to him. In February of '72, around the same time Francis sat in Oscar Wilde's final room in Paris, Steven picked one script out of the pile. Producers Arthur Gardner and Jules Levy had a revenge picture entitled *McKlusky* ready to go at United Artists with thirty-seven-year-old rising star Burt Reynolds, and they wanted Spielberg to direct it. Steven said yes, and Sheinberg agreed to loan him out to UA. Spielberg met with Burt Reynolds and went location scouting across Arkansas. He later remembered, alternatively, spending either "two and a half months" or "five months" in preproduction for the picture. Doubt crept in. The more Steven thought about it, the less *McKlusky* felt like a meaningful step up from *Duel*, and the less it felt like *him*, too. It would be a picture, as Reynolds put it, "made in the South, about the South and for the South," a world foreign to Steven.

In the middle of preparing *McKlusky*, Steven took his seat at the cinema and watched *The Godfather*. The Paramount mountain filled the screen. The screen went black. The slow, mournful, ominous trumpet solo filled the room, and then, still over black, the undertaker Bonasera's first line descended on Steven like thunder from the cinema's speakers: "I believe in America."

Steven was glued to his seat for the next three hours. "I was pulverized," he remembered. "I also felt that I should quit, that there was no reason to continue directing, because I would never achieve that level of confidence and the ability to tell a story such as the one I had just experienced. In a way, it shattered my confidence." Twenty-five years later, he would continue to insist that "I've never made a movie anywhere near as good as *The Godfather*."

He stepped back into the fresh outside air, dazed, admiring, inspired, demoralized. It was not unlike the intimidation he had felt, several years earlier, when he'd first seen George's *Electronic Labyrinth: THX 1138 4EB*.

He had grown past that. He could grow past this.

Soon after, Steven resigned from *McKlusky* and went in search of something more relevant—and more personal. Francis had taken a best-selling book, a popular, thrilling yarn, and found a way to inject his own heart into it. Steven thought he could do something similar with the tragic story of Robert Dent and Ila Faye Holiday. He remembered Matthew Robbins and Hal Barwood, George's USC friends, who he'd liked when he'd met them. He decided to give them a call.

In the end, *The Godfather* made more than enough money to keep the Folsom Street offices open a little longer. It won three Academy Awards, including Best Picture and Francis's personal second, shared with Mario Puzo, for Best Adapted Screenplay. Francis—as much as the movie—had become bankable. The San Francisco Opera hired him to direct *The Visit of the Old Lady*, though he had never directed opera before; the Geary Theater put him in charge of a revival of *Private Lives*, though he hadn't directed a stage play since Hofstra. His name, not his expertise, would put butts in seats.

The trendy auteur theory, popularized in the 1950s by French critic François Truffaut and his colleagues at the magazine *Cahiers du Cinéma* and translated into English in 1962 by *Film Comment*'s Andrew Sarris, held that directors, not producers or studio heads, were the authors of their films—but in the old days, even the greats, like

Hawks, Cukor, or Capra, had been employees under contract, their careers shaped by the material assigned to them by the studio heads. If they had authorship, it was not always with work they originated. Filmmakers of Francis's generation, on the other hand, were freelancers. They chose their projects, and in doing so were perceived as the authors—not just by critics writing for *Film Comment* or the *Cahiers*, but by the public.

"What happened in the '70s was that films that didn't fit into anyone's models started making money," says Paul Schrader, then a film critic himself. Looking for a pattern, executives and their marketing men saw only one: the directors.

Francis had understood this earlier, maybe, than anyone else. He had branded and marketed himself, the way a movie star might, since the Corman days. That was why he'd drummed up such a racket about American Zoetrope, pushing himself into photographers' cameras, inviting journalists to write profiles about him. He had an ego, sure; he liked the sound of his own voice. All the same, for a man who did not control the capital, notoriety was one path to autonomy. Studios promoted themselves and so he should promote himself.

"Ten years ago," wrote critic Stephen Farber in the *New York Times*, "the idea of building a promotion campaign for a movie around the personality of the director would have been virtually unthinkable. Since then the auteur theory, and the media's restless search for new celebrities, have turned the director into a superstar." Money morphed the auteur theory into a sort of unicorn theory: the idea that there were some filmmakers who were rare and imbued with genius, able to create magic. Studio heads weren't sure what this new, youthful moviegoing audience wanted, but they thought they could recognize a unicorn, like Francis, when they saw one. And, Paul Schrader says, "once you have one unicorn . . . you ask, why aren't there any more unicorns in the woods?"

Days after the release of *The Godfather*, George came to Francis. United Artists had dropped *American Graffiti* after reading his hodgepodge screenplay—Huyck and Katz had written a draft, another old USC classmate called Richard Walter had written a draft, George himself had gritted his teeth and written a draft—and declined to pursue *The Star Wars* any further. Huyck and Katz gave the screenplay another pass, lightening its tone, and Universal was interested in making that version, but only if George restrained himself to a very low budget—and if Francis, the biggest unicorn in the woods, lent his name to it as a producer. They couldn't pay him, but he would get 10 percent of the film's profits in exchange for the favor.

Francis hesitated. George wasn't asking for his involvement because he trusted or wanted him; he was asking because Universal wanted to be in business with the man who had made *The Godfather*, and to be able to advertise *American Graffiti* as such. Besides, *THX* had made no money, and *Graffiti* was another low-cost picture, with a premise that sounded pulled from one of Corman's now long-outdated teen pictures. Ten percent of nothing, Francis told himself, was nothing.

On the other hand, he always liked to help a friend in need, or support work he found worthwhile—after all, that had been one of the original ideas behind Zoetrope. If they were going to be independent again one day, Francis needed allies as in demand as he was now—a new slate of films, an ecosystem. He needed other unicorns. One of them might be George.

He thought of financing *American Graffiti* himself. George had told him he could make it for under a million dollars; it would be a stretch, but Francis could afford it now. If he did, he and George would own the picture outright. Even if it barely broke even on first release, they'd control the eventual profits, forever.

He asked his wife what she thought. Ellie read George's script and told him, unenthusiastically, that she didn't think it was worth it. Francis agreed to the Universal offer and let them put his name on the movie.

"The thing that killed us was her reaction to *Graffiti*," said Francis later. "I was ready to finance *Graffiti*. Then I kind of pulled back and that was, of course, a $700,000 movie that grossed $200 million. Movie history would have been different if I had."

Much later, after *American Graffiti* had come out and the profits had started pouring in, Francis did the math. Had he owned the film, it wouldn't just have made enough money to keep American Zoetrope going.

It would have made him enough, he said, to buy struggling 20th Century Fox—outright.

· 13 ·

AMERICA'S FELLINI

Universal budgeted *American Graffiti* at $777,000. Francis's favorite number again. The studio couldn't wait to advertise the picture as brought "from the man who gave you *The Godfather.*"

Over the next several weeks, as Huyck and Katz labored on a shooting draft, George flew down to Los Angeles nearly every week to cast the movie, meeting every young actor he could. When in town, he stayed on Matthew Robbins's couch at the house in Benedict Canyon, and for a while, Steven Spielberg and Hal Barwood would appear at the door in the afternoon, eager to work on their own project, the script for the Holiday-and-Dent story, now called *The Sugarland Express*. By the time George came home in the evenings after a day of meetings and auditions, Steven and Barwood would usually still be sitting around the kitchen table with Robbins. George took a seat alongside them. Someone made or, more likely, ordered dinner. They ate, talked, hung out, got to know each other. George and Steven shared a love of adventure movies, serial television, comic books—and bitching.

"I mean, we're constant complainers," Steven said later. "We love complaining to each other."

They were at the start of a four-year period that Scorsese, who had finally moved to Los Angeles, would later describe as the happiest time of all their lives. Marty needed it; his life was in upheaval. He was intense, skittish, allergic to seemingly everything, from horsehair to paint pigments. He sometimes wore white gloves to stop himself from biting his nails. He spoke very fast, and had thick bushy eyebrows that rose and fell as he expressed himself. He was endlessly curious and engaged. He was so sensitive that, in the words of David Field, an executive who worked with him later, he was like "a man born without enough skin. Everything came in at him at incredibly full strength, at a level of reality most of us screen out."

He had caught the disease of film early on. Born in Flushing, Queens, in the cold of November 1942, raised in Little Italy in downtown Manhattan, he had the kind of upbringing typical of New York Italian-Americans of the postwar generation: His Sicilian grandparents remembered the old country, his parents worked in the Garment District, his friends played and fought on the street and grew up to become gangsters and priests. When he was only a few years old, his asthma was so bad he spent days alone with a vaporizer in a tent in his bedroom; the only time he saw a human face was when someone pulled open the tent, peered in to see how he was doing, and vanished again. When he was allowed out into the loud, violent world, Marty, naturally susceptible to awe, fell under the spell of ritual: that of the movie house, where his father took him on Saturdays, with its red curtains and sticky floors and its projected images of larger-than-life human faces, magnified in close-up, and that of the Catholic Church, where his family went on Sundays, with its robes, songs, and candles, its echoing floors and its painted images of larger-than-life martyrs and saints, mythologized in the Gospels. Both were places of transformation and revelation. The stories told inside them developed a sense inside *him* that everyone—from hardworking laborers to junked-up sex workers and gangsters—was a unique human being, with a soul as worthwhile as any other. From

Elizabeth Street, where his family lived, it was only a block to the Bowery, which "at that time was the end of people's lives," he later told the author Mary Pat Kelly. "They were dying in the streets there. I watched them become dehumanized and watched everybody else dehumanize them. And you begin to feel it in yourself."

He enrolled in an all-boys Catholic high school in the Bronx and longed to be a priest. *If Jesus were here now*, he would think throughout his life, *he'd be on Eighth Avenue and Fifty-Fourth Street with the prostitutes and drug addicts.* In the end, however, he didn't have the restraint required to become a man of the cloth—he liked sleeping in too much, he liked women too much, he liked food too much, he feared loneliness too much. He graduated and enrolled at New York University, where he majored in English, with an eye to becoming a filmmaker, so he could make movies about people like him, neighborhoods like his, problems like his.

"My whole life," Marty said, "has been movies and religion. That's it. Nothing else." He pursued filmmaking the way believers commit to the priesthood. He watched pictures obsessively, repeatedly, indiscriminately, with a technical mind that took easily to the uses and power of lenses, depths of field, and aspect ratios. The frame in which he saw the world was one tensed between idealism and guilt.

He married young, still a student, to his NYU classmate Laraine Brennan. She was a dark-haired, dark-eyed beauty from suburban New Jersey. She knew he was a genius, she says, right away. On their first date, he took her to see Marcel Carné's black-and-white *Les Enfants du Paradis*. They married at St. Patrick's Cathedral in May 1965 and moved into a little apartment in Jersey City; a daughter, Catherine, named after Marty's mother, was born in December. You do the math.

Marty and Laraine had bonded over their common dream: to be at the heart of a thriving independent New York–centric film world, alongside the Maysles brothers, who had an office up in Harlem, and Jonas Mekas, founder of the Film-Makers' Co-Operative and

Filmmakers' Cinematheque. Now they were young parents, broke, and terrified of a world that, Laraine says, they felt was "being disassembled" around them: the war in Vietnam, the assassinations of Robert Kennedy and Martin Luther King, the killing of unarmed students by the National Guard at Kent State University. Marty held down a job at CBS News, editing footage flown back from Vietnam, with orders to cut out "all the bloody parts" that might shock American viewers. "It really affected him," Brennan says. "He came home upset, like he'd spent the day in a slaughterhouse." He had insomnia. When the baby woke up crying in the night, he rocked her to sleep in the darkness, and watched *Psycho* or an old B-movie on the flickering television.

Marty made his first film, *Who's That Knocking at My Door*, in fits and starts over the course of two years, with a young actor, Harvey Keitel, found through an ad posted in the paper. When it played festivals, some in the industry took notice. Marty got an agent in Harry Ufland, who worked at William Morris; to Laraine, Ufland represented an industry and a culture that "did not practice monogamy or sobriety." Temptations swirled around Marty. Drugs. Hustlers. Women.

"Marty grew up in the most loving family you could imagine," Brennan says. "I think he thought it came in a bottle like that—that marriage was easy, that it took care of itself. And it just wasn't like that." He couldn't see how to reconcile his life at home with the life he wanted. As his life had split into a fork when he was young—left, become a priest; right, become a filmmaker—now he saw two paths: One stayed with Laraine and stretched ahead into years of making underground, black-and-white films for no money, living in an apartment, one of millions of souls stacked onto each other across New York. The other led to Hollywood and—Ufland whispered in Marty's ear—fame, wealth, and respect. Or, in Biblical terms, 1 John 2:16: "the lust of the flesh, the lust of the eyes, and the pride of life."

Marty chose Hollywood. A voice inside told him he had to be

famous before he turned thirty, and he was twenty-eight already. Laraine's mother had just been diagnosed with cancer, and Marty told Laraine he had to leave now, when her family was distracted. He couldn't let the Brennans confront him, change his mind, hold him back. He felt the guilt and the shame. He decided it was a cost worth paying.

"I wanted more space in Martin's life than he could learn to give," Laraine says now. "It hurt that I took us seriously but—I thought—Marty is willing to let that go. That thought was very hard. But I realized: The sun was going to come out every day, and every day my daughter would want breakfast, and I was going to have to feed her." She did not have the luxury of selfishness.

Marty left for Los Angeles in January 1971. He rented a lonely apartment in the Hills, pinned a poster for Vincente Minnelli's *Two Weeks in Another Town* above the bed, found work as an editor and an assistant director, and did his best to fit in. He grew out the long hippie hair, even tried wearing beads. He started dating Sandy Weintraub, daughter of Fred Weintraub, the Warner Bros. producer George had accused of mutilating *THX 1138*. Marty didn't really know anyone else. "You know, I was a kid from the Lower East Side who never went anywhere and then I'm in a strange town with no friends and I'm alone," he remembered. "And the only guy who would come around would be Brian De Palma and he'd take me to all these people's houses and everything."

Fellow New Yorker De Palma knew Marty from a class they'd taken together in '63. He'd made the move to Los Angeles a year before Marty, lured out to make his first studio film, *Get to Know Your Rabbit*, for Warner Bros., but then the producers had fired him before he could complete his cut of the picture. He only found out the film was finished and being released when he came across a tiny ad Warner Bros. had taken out in the *New York Times*. He and Marty would sit at the fountain in the center of the Warner lot and moan about how badly the studio treated them. De Palma was scathingly funny. He was a tick under six feet, with a close black beard and hair that was receding on the top, long down the sides, to cover ears that stuck out a little. He carried himself with an easy alpha male quality. He drove Marty out to a pretty A-frame house on Trancas Beach and told him his friend Jennifer Salt, an actress he had met in the early '60s, lived there with her roommate, the Canadian-American actress Margot Kidder. Jennifer and Margot paid only $400 a month for the lease, but the place was far nicer than either Brian's or Marty's digs. They started hanging around there all the time.

"Everyone used to come to Trancas Beach because the girls cooked, and we had lots of parties," De Palma says. "Margot knew Steven Spielberg—that's how I met Steven—and Marty was learning to drive, and I knew Marty because we both lived in town and used to hang out. And George came in and out of town as he was working on *American Graffiti.*"

Kidder had soft eyes, cheekbones and a chin so fine they looked carved, and an easy, generous laugh. She was sharp and curious and politically engaged, with a sardonic, self-deprecating wit that hid mood swings and periods of intense emotional distress. She hailed from the mining city of Yellowknife in Canada's Northwest Territories, literally closer to the North Pole than Los Angeles. At ten years old, she wondered if she was crazy. She had first tried to die by suicide at age fourteen, swallowing a handful of codeine pills in the days following a painful breakup. When she was eighteen, another boyfriend got her pregnant and arranged an illegal abortion, performed in a hotel room where Kidder was made to lie naked in the bathtub by a woman who then filled her uterus with Lysol. She had become an actress because she figured that, wearing a character's skin and speaking a screenwriter's lines, she could let her real self out, in all its anxieties and contradictions, and not be judged.

All the boys were in love with her. She was going out with De Palma then, but over the years, she'd hook up with more than a few of them; later in life, she liked to joke that if she wrote a memoir, she'd call it *I Fucked Everybody*.

She was great fun to be around. "When I party," she said, "I *party*."

De Palma noted that, with the exception of Steven, they'd all been through the same baptism by fire: They had all been fucked over by Warner Bros. "I got fired with *Get to Know Your Rabbit*. Marty was working [as an editor] on *Medicine Ball Caravan*, which was a mess, not because of his work but how it was ultimately finished. And Francis and his whole company, they, you know, ultimately threw him off the lot with all the stuff he had developed. And of course George also. I mean, I was at the opening of *THX*. We were all experiencing the same rejection from Warner Bros.—we had a lot in common." Even Milius, who was liked at the studio, had had to deal with his name being taken off *Dirty Harry*, even as he felt he deserved credit for every line.

The crowd grew. No one had any money, so when word got out that there was a house out in Malibu, where two beautiful girls who didn't mind sunbathing topless also cooked delicious meals and hosted every exciting young filmmaker around, it rang along the coast like a siren call. Paul Schrader was smart, intense, and self-interested, so abrasive that a group of writers who shared an agent with him once threatened to leave the agency en masse just to get away from him. His wife had kicked him out and he briefly lived in his car, eating junk food and drinking himself to blackouts, cruising from porno theater to porno theater. There was no one he didn't fall out with, back then, and was in the throes of a cocaine addiction that could make him behave, in the words of his girlfriend Beverly Walker, like "a truly amoral person." He angled for every opportunity he could get while shit-talking everyone behind their backs and, as he grew more confident, to their faces. Over the years, he'd call De Palma "artistically weak . . . Skate fast on thin ice. That's his story. That's his con."

The one person he seemed to admire was Milius, who Schrader

nicknamed "the Master of Flash" in his *Los Angeles Weekly News* column. George had first brought his old USC classmate along to Trancas Beach, and Milius was so over-the-top everyone took him with a hefty grain of salt. The only exceptions were Steven, who was in awe of him, and Schrader, who wanted to be him. Milius took them skeet shooting. After that, Steven and Schrader both started buying their own guns. To someone like Schrader, who had grown up under the strict discipline and repression of a Calvinist household, Milius's bombastic political posturing and gleeful provocation were downright inspiring, as were his glorification of weaponry, his coarse masculinity, his disdain for any kind of consequence to his own statements and actions. Great men made things happen and didn't stick around to sort out the rubble, but so did small, fucked-up men. Milius and Schrader both had the propensity to think of themselves as the former, even when they acted like the latter.

Producer Tony Bill came by and brought producers Julia and Michael Phillips, who lived just down the beach. George brought actor Richard Dreyfuss, who he had cast as the lead in *American Graffiti*. Dreyfuss was high-energy and a little pretentious. He had known since the age of eleven that he was—to use the term he prefers—manic depressive. His first memories were of his father Norman's crutches and canes in the hall closet of the family home in Bayside, Queens; Norman had gone to war and been so badly injured in the Battle of the Bulge that he spent two years in hospital, emerging a different man, cold and distant and avaricious. He moved the family to Beverly Hills and worked all hours. Later he left Richard's mother as she was diagnosed with thyroid cancer. She died alone; he remarried three times. Richard seemed intent on rejecting everything about the man. He went to state college; he devoted himself to acting; he declared himself a conscientious objector when drafted for the war in Vietnam, and put in two years of alternative service as a clerk in a hospital. By the time George cast him in *Graffiti*, he'd only worked in television, and in small roles in a handful of pictures—one line in Mike Nichols's *The Graduate*, a couple in *Valley of the Dolls*, a few scenes as Baby Face Nelson in Milius's *Dillinger*—but he made demands and turned down offers as if he were already a star. He was funny, difficult, lustful, infuriating.

"It was such a romantic time," Kidder remembered years later. "Everyone was young and passionate and convinced they were going to change film forever." They'd go out on the beach, smoke pot, take magic mushrooms. Milius surfed; Kidder skinny-dipped. Marty, George, and Steven sat fully clothed in the sand—Marty even kept his socks and shoes on—squinting against the wind, forearms white with the pallor of too much time spent in movie theaters and editing rooms. They were all embarrassed and awkward around the women—all except for De Palma, who had earned his master's degree at Sarah Lawrence, the only man on an all-female campus, and felt comfortable with women, be it one-on-one or in a group. It conferred on him a funny, juvenile kind of status around the other filmmakers: *He* knew how to talk to girls!

They didn't see, yet, that some of them—Kidder, Schrader, the producer Julia Phillips, and, quietly, Marty—were more vulnerable to the drugs than everyone else, more susceptible to getting hooked. Only Steven and George refused to partake. George was too straight. Steven watched his friends get high with a touch of curiosity, maybe even interest, but he was simply too risk-averse. Back in college at Long Beach, all his roommates had been high, all the time. They called the apartment cat Daytripper, fed it LSD, watched it jump out the fourth-floor window. More than once, Steven had to be the one to drive one of his roommates to the emergency room as they flirted with an overdose in the passenger seat. He watched the shenanigans on Trancas Beach with the quiet longing of a young man who knows he's too square to ever be the life of the party. He knew, in his heart, that he belonged with people like Matthew Robbins, who loved books and history, or Hal Barwood, who had married his teenage sweetheart and whose favorite hobby was to play board games while his wife knitted or bent over jigsaw puzzles.

But Trancas Beach was a charmed place. Kidder was the youngest of the group, younger even than Steven—she was twenty-three in 1971, De Palma eight years older. They were into making love, not war. They wanted to get rid of the old, greedy institutions, from the Hollywood studios to the military-industrial complex. "We were just a bunch of kids," Kidder said, "who had no money and wanted to change the world. We really loved each other."

De Palma wrote Margot a movie, *Sisters*, in which he also cast Jennifer Salt. That film would be a departure for De Palma, who was known for his comedies: This one was a dark Hitchcockian thriller about separated conjoined twins, one of whom is a murderer. He planned to go back to New York to shoot it, on a half-a-million-dollar budget provided by Roger Corman's old business partners, American International Pictures. It was a lurid genre picture, but smart and ambiguous—a combination soon to become De Palma's trademark.

"At that time, movies were the center of the social conversation," remembers Paul Schrader. "If you wanted to know what was going on in society, you went to the movies. There were all these-*isms*, feminism, socialism, and you believed—and you were right to believe—that movies were important. And film critics became important because they were writing for people who thought movies were important. That was a unique window. It coincided with the old financial infrastructure of Hollywood falling apart. No one could figure out how to make money, real money, and that opened the window."

This was a point Francis hammered home in seemingly every conversation. He wasn't around much, but when he was, he talked, a lot. Studio executives, he felt, were there for the taking. They were either old and past it, or green and starstruck, rocking up with pockets full of money to take over a business they didn't yet understand. "If you believe it enough and if you say it enough," Francis told everyone, "they'll let you do it."

"We don't *have* to be Hollywood," Schrader agreed.

The group cruised Los Angeles in their cars, went out to eat together, found obscure screenings of obscure films. "You had to go somewhere new every night," Schrader says, "to a different rep house, or there'd be a 16mm print of something shown on a sheet in someone's living room." They watched trashy films on scratched-up prints in dingy Hollywood Boulevard picture houses. Marty and Steven went to foreclosure sales and tried to collect pieces of old memorabilia, "to keep the old Hollywood alive" in their own little apartments.

Francis remained on the fringes of the group. He was slightly older and had a family already, and his desire to do more than just direct set him apart. "Francis was more ambitious," De Palma says. "George wanted to create a studio outside of the system, as did Francis."

De Palma gladly took money from any producer who put it up. He knew about scrambling for just enough cash to make just the next movie; it's what he'd done his whole life. The warehouse on Folsom Street intrigued him. "Marty and I went up together," he remembers. "I remember very distinctly going to the Zoetrope offices. It was the first time we had seen a flatbed editing machine—we sort of looked at it with amazement. It was sort of a wonderland to us."

He and Marty didn't need an empire outside of the system. They dreamed only of making films. Wasn't that enough?

When he wasn't hanging out at Trancas Beach, Marty kept working. He met the independent filmmaker John Cassavetes, who gave him a job in the sound department on his current project, *Minnie and Moskowitz*. He met Roger Corman, who liked *Who's That Knocking at My Door* and offered him a job directing *Boxcar Bertha*, an exploitation flick about railroad bandits in the Great Depression. Marty had twenty-four days and less than half a million dollars to get the picture in the can, and he took the job as seriously as he took everything. He locked himself in his motel room on location in Arkansas and sketched out every frame of the movie, pinning the drawings up onto the walls. He tried to make the story his own by having the protagonist killed, graphically, by crucifixion. *Boxcar Bertha*—with its trademark Corman combo of blood, nudity, and sneaky progressive politics—made its budget back twice over and earned a handful of decent reviews, but when Marty screened it for Cassavetes, his mentor put his arm around the young man's shoulder and kindly said, "Marty, you've just spent a whole year of your life making a piece of shit. You're better than that stuff, don't do it again."

Marty told Cassavetes about a script of his own he wanted to make called *Season of the Witch*, written with his friend and former classmate Mardik Martin, an Armenian who had grown up in Baghdad and lived in New York when the Iraqi Revolution erupted and the regime took his father's life. The film was about a young Italian-American man from Little Italy, Charlie, torn between his Catholic faith, his loyalty to his destructive friend Johnny Boy, and his work as a small-time mafia crook. Marty had written most of it before moving to LA, sitting at night in Mardik's Plymouth Valiant. It was cold and uncomfortable, but the car was a safe space from their wives. Mardik smoked; Marty wheezed. They made fun of the best-selling book of the season, Mario Puzo's pulp thriller *The Godfather*, which was being advertised everywhere. "To us, it was bullshit," Martin remembered. They scribbled scenes onto blank pages. *Season of the Witch* was inspired by Marty's father, his uncle, his friends. The script still needed work, though.

"So do it." Cassavetes shrugged.

Corman was up for financing and producing *Season of the Witch*, but only if Marty moved its setting to LA, rewrote the characters to be African-American, and made it blaxploitation. Cassavetes disagreed.

"Make films about what you know," he told Marty.

The same push and pull Francis felt: Did you make films about yourself and hope the world saw themselves there, too, or make films you thought the world wanted to see and endeavor to find a way into material otherwise foreign to you?

Marty followed Cassavetes's advice. Jon Voight agreed to star as Charlie, but then dropped out; Marty cast his old friend Harvey Keitel instead. Then, at a Christmas dinner hosted by critic Jay Cocks in the dying days of 1971, De Palma introduced Marty to a twenty-nine-year-old actor from New York who had appeared in several of De Palma's low-budget movies back East.

"You used to hang out with so-and-so and so-and-so," the actor said with a squint, naming a couple of kids Marty knew from the old neighborhood.

"Yeah," Marty answered. "How do you know?"

"I'm Bobby."

"Bobby?" Marty repeated, and then it hit him. They'd grown up two blocks from one another off the Bowery, moved with different crews, only friendly enough to wave and nod at each other. He remembered the guy's last name—De Niro.

"Bobby," he said again. "Oh my God."

De Niro told him he was friends with Keitel, too, and had seen *Who's That Knocking at My Door*. "That was a really terrific movie."

"I have this script . . . ," Marty said. De Niro read *Season of the Witch* and was keen to play Charlie. But he liked Marty, and back then, he took roles for the experience, not the cachet. He was open to one of the smaller parts. Back in New York, he bumped into Keitel in the Village.

"Careerwise, *I* should be playing Charlie," De Niro ribbed him.

"You know who you should play?" Keitel answered. "Johnny Boy."

"And that clicked," De Niro recalled. "I played Johnny."

Marty started bringing De Niro around to Trancas Beach. They became friendly with Schrader, who, like them, was preoccupied with the compulsions and constraints of faith, and, like them, thought in images and ideas more than words. Schrader, when he'd first come across Scorsese, had smirked at the small, intense young man's ambition.

"When I first met Marty in 1972," he recalled, "he told me that there were two books he wanted to make, *Gangs of New York* and *The Last Temptation of Christ.*" The former was a nonfiction book by Herbert Asbury about gang warfare in 1860s Manhattan; the latter a controversial revisionist novel by Nikos Kazantzakis, in which Jesus Christ, after his crucifixion, wakes up to a life in which he has rejected his calling and lived a long, normal, human life with Mary Magdalene as his wife. Said Schrader, "It struck me that these were rather grandiose ambitions for someone whose most important credit was a Roger Corman film."

Season of the Witch was interesting, though. Marty found six hundred thousand bucks through some independent producers—a little bit more than his *Boxcar Bertha* budget. He made the film his way, going so far as to fly back to New York (most of the film was shot in California) to pick up specific scenes in the same buildings where he'd grown up, so the texture of the walls felt right. Francis lent him three thousand dollars, so he could pay for permission to film during Little Italy's actual Feast of San Gennaro, after the film's producers had refused, knowing the money would go to the mob, who all but ran the festival. In the edit, Marty built the soundtrack from songs he loved—the Rolling Stones' "Jumpin' Jack Flash," the Ronettes' "Be My Baby," but also "Addio, Sogni Di Gloria"—"music I heard on the streets where I lived, in the neighborhood, in the tenements. You often have one song coming from one window, another coming from another—opera, rock 'n' roll, Frank Sinatra."

Season of the Witch—renamed *Mean Streets* during production—changed his life. National critics hailed him overnight as one of the great young American directors; studios and movie stars left messages and sent screenplays. Laraine watched from afar. She had little access; friends had called her as the divorce was finalized, apologizing that they could no longer be her friends—"they had made a choice, and they chose Marty." He was thirty years old and famous, as they'd all predicted he would be. The only part of it Laraine couldn't believe was that she wasn't there with him when it happened.

For Marty, it wasn't enough. Something insatiable remained in him, like a hungry spirit in his gut, condemned to always be craving. Roger Ebert, already one of the arbiters of hip, watched *Mean Streets* and wrote that, given ten years, Marty would become America's Fellini. The next time Ebert saw Marty, he found the filmmaker anxious, his thick eyebrows tightly knotted. Marty looked up at him and asked:

"Do you really think it's going to take ten years?"

· 14 ·

HARRISON FORD IS NOT A GOOD NAME FOR YOU

In late June 1972, George returned to Northern California and started filming *American Graffiti*. Kurtz had broken the schedule down to twenty-six nights. That was all George had to revive his career and make his film about real people: less than a month. Francis's casting director, Fred Roos, had helped George put together a dream cast of young talent: Dreyfuss, Ron Howard, Candy Clark, Cindy Williams. A struggling young actor and model named Suzanne Somers was cast as the beautiful blond in a white Ford Thunderbird who mouths "I love you" as she drives by Dreyfuss's character early in the night, sending him on an obsessive search to find her again. For the tiny part of street racer Bob Falfa, Roos dug up a twenty-nine-year-old carpenter from Illinois, Harrison Ford, who had once been a contract player at Columbia but had long since been let go. Ford was classically handsome and devastatingly charming, but the studio, after putting him under contract because of his obvious charisma, had had no clue what to do with him. The standard procedure was to build new faces up through bit parts, but Ford's powers couldn't come through as an uncredited bellhop (*Dead Heat on a*

Merry-Go-Round, 1966) or an uncredited motorist (*Luv*, 1967). The studio tried him out in a small, credited part in *A Time for Killing*, a Western directed by Roger Corman, his first for a legitimate studio, but they fired Corman halfway through, and no one associated with the film did well out of it.

Ford tried to make his own opportunities happen. He became friendly with Jacques Demy, one of the leading lights of the French Nouvelle Vague, and Demy's wife, Agnès Varda. They hung out at the French couple's little rented house in Beverly Hills, smoking Marlboro cigarettes and "listening to the Doors, the Mamas & the Papas, Jefferson Airplane, Buffalo Springfield," recalled Varda. She shot little test sequences of Ford on the back deck. Demy wanted to cast Ford as the lead in his first English-language picture, *Model Shop*, which Columbia was financing. The studio's president, sixty-year-old Leo Jaffe, didn't see it.

"Forget him," Ford remembered Jaffe saying. "He has no future in this business." He gave the part to Gary Lockwood, who had mostly appeared on television. Demy went off and made *Model Shop* in the summer of '68, and it came out in early 1969, buried on the bottom of double bills, and tanked. Demy never worked in Hollywood again; Gary Lockwood went back to supporting roles.

Columbia's vice president, Jerry Tokofsky, thought spending any more time on Harrison Ford was a waste. Ford protested that he hadn't been given the opportunity to exercise his craft.

"The first time Tony Curtis ever appeared in a movie he delivered a bag of groceries," Tokofsky told Ford. "You took one look at that person and you knew that was a star. You ain't got it, kid."

Ford countered that maybe Curtis should have delivered the bag of groceries like a guy delivering groceries, not like a movie star—wasn't that the definition of acting?

He'd always had a big mouth. Even in his twenties, he acted like the phrase *he doesn't suffer fools gladly* had been invented just for him.

Tokofsky didn't like his name, either.

"Harrison Ford is not a good name for you," he asserted. "It sounds, I don't know, *pretentious*."

He told Ford to come up with a stage name. Ford fished in the back of his mind for "the stupidest name I could think of," and suggested *Kurt Affair*.

Tokofsky decided not to renew his contract.

Ford's career was dead before it had ever really started. He was "out of my depth," he later said, in almost every arena of his life. "I had a young family . . . I didn't know where I was going, how I got there."

In his free time, he fixed up his and his wife Mary's own home and found he had a knack for carpentry. He did little jobs in the neighborhood. Sometime in 1970, when the Brazilian musician Sergio Mendes, who lived in nearby Encino, mentioned to a friend that he was thinking of building a recording studio in his backyard, the friend answered that he knew a cheap, easygoing carpenter with shaggy hair and lots of free time. Mendes hired Ford on gut feeling; the actor had to borrow books from the local library to figure out how to pull off the biggest job he'd had yet.

Ford found life was better standing on a roof, shirtless in the beating sun, tools on your belt and a joint between your teeth, than it was shuttling from rejection to rejection. Famous people who had found success in the world he couldn't enter hired him regularly. He built a deck and renovated part of the Malibu home of Joan Didion and John Gregory Dunne, who had just written the screenplay for *The Panic at Needle Park* together and were adapting Didion's novel *Play It As It Lays* for the screen. Became friends with them. Some clients insisted Ford couldn't build for shit; the carpentry was a cover for pot dealing. They said he hid the weed in a bull fiddle case. Dunne wrote later that he'd had to fire him after six months—the job was supposed to be done in two—describing him as "an out-of-work actor" with a crew who "sniffed a lot of cocaine." Instead of grumbling at the firing, Ford said that he understood, man, and pulled Dunne, ten years his elder and more than a little curmudgeonly, into a "soul-brother handshake."

"He was the most charismatic guy I ever met," insisted Griffin Dunne, John Gregory's teenage nephew, already interested in being an actor himself. The actor Mark Hamill, when he finally met Ford, confessed that "from day one . . . I thought, *This guy's like . . . Steve McQueen? Gary Cooper? John Wayne?*" It was a generational gap. Ford's peers could tell he had star quality. Older people—among whose ranks stood most of Hollywood's film executives—saw a sloppy, irreverent hippie.

By the time Fred Roos put Ford forward for *American Graffiti*, he hadn't worked as an actor in three years. He enjoyed the time away from the routine of home. He and some of the other actors—Dreyfuss, Paul Le Mat—terrorized the local Holiday Inn, smoking dope, getting drunk at all hours, climbing the hotel sign and launching themselves into the pool. On set, Ford was pigheaded. He refused to trim his hair down to the '50s buzz George wanted and instead bought himself a cowboy hat to cover up his '70s shag. He and George had little in common, except maybe this one thing: If they did anything, they would do it their way.

Early in the shoot, George called his cast together, apologetic about the film's low budget and honest about the need to film quickly.

"The movie's going to be a major hit," he reassured them, "and you'll all be a part of it."

Somers looked around her castmates, all unknowns like her, and thought, *What a bunch of losers.*

Dreyfuss, who didn't think the film would do well, either, was often grumpy. George's own optimism soured whenever Universal executive Ned Tanen flew up from Los Angeles to visit the set. The film's publicist, Beverly Walker, understood Tanen was everything George hated—an executive without taste or conviction, known in the industry for "trying to cash in on whatever is the current vogue"—and besides, George had "a ridiculous, dramatic intransigence" about authority. To him, Tanen's mere presence was interference. He felt vindicated when Tanen started bothering him about changing the film's title. *American Graffiti* was no good, Tanen said; it didn't mean anything. He sent George and Francis a memo with sixty alternatives he and the studio marketing department had come up with, including *Wild Is the Blood*, *The Cherry Coke Summer*, *Pals 'N Gals*, and *Make Out at Burger City*. He told Walker they couldn't sell the movie as a car picture—car pictures always bombed—not understanding that cars were George's passion.

George ignored Tanen's ideas, and he ignored Tanen when he came to the set, sending Walker to babysit him in his place. Most nights, after an hour or so, the wounded Tanen left.

"George alienates everybody," Walker says, "so he always needs somebody else to front for him." That was her role and, she felt, Gary Kurtz's, too.

George even grated at Francis's presence. As a producer, Francis came to set occasionally, gliding into San Rafael in the middle of the night in the blue Mercedes-Benz. The production couldn't afford trailers—the actors and extras shared one Winnebago—so when George and Francis wanted to hold a meeting, they climbed in the back of the parked Mercedes. Many of the crew found Francis more approachable than their quiet, collegiate director, in his varsity jacket and his blue jeans, crouching behind the camera as if he resented all the attention.

The shoot was the talk of the small town of San Rafael. Added excitement was provided by the presence of Haskell Wexler, who flew in every evening from Los Angeles to help George, his protégé, capture the look he was after—gleaming chrome cars, bright neon diner signs, sapphire night skies. None of the actors knew "much about George Lucas," remembered Ron Howard, "but everybody was very impressed that Haskell Wexler was *killing himself* to come work on this movie. I mean, it was insane."

Wexler was a legend, an Academy Award winner for *Who's*

Afraid of Virginia Woolf?, and popular with young Hollywood for his vocal anti-establishmentarianism. He'd first organized a workers' strike in his twenties—at his father's own electronics factory. He was *cool*—rocked a little mustache and double denim, had served in the merchant marine with Woody Guthrie, had survived ten days in a lifeboat after a German U-boat torpedoed his ship in the Indian Ocean. He carried the guilt of his privileged upbringing everywhere he went, felt a duty to pay forward the good fortune of his birth. Several young filmmakers, George among them, thought of Wexler almost as a surrogate father.

To help George on *American Graffiti*, Wexler flew down to Los Angeles at dawn and shot commercials all day before returning at sunset. He slept on the plane both ways. He landed soon after the sun went down and was driven onto set just as the locals turned out in droves to watch the old cars being lined up and down the streets. Among them was the nine-year-old son of writer Jack Fincher and nurse Claire Mae Fincher. Young David Fincher had dreamed of making movies for the past eighteen months, ever since he had watched Robert Crawford's Emmy-winning documentary about the making of *Butch Cassidy and the Sundance Kid*. He had always known movies were fake, but he had never thought about the details the television special revealed: the stunt doubles, the repeated takes, the huge and unsung company of people it took to put two hours of entertainment together. "It was the ultimate magic trick," he remembered. Even the science behind film astonished him—if you played twenty-four still photographs one after the other fast enough, they looked like they *moved*?

His parents told David that films were made in a place called "Hollywood," so he was shocked and thrilled when he heard that one of them was being shot just down the road from their house in San Anselmo. He stood on 4th Street and watched the young, bearded man in a USC varsity jacket who seemed to be the director. The man looked twenty years younger than David's father, and here he was: making his own movie.

Soon after, David came home from school and went to work. He hopped on his bicycle, a bag full of the evening edition of the *Marin Independent Journal* slung over his shoulder, and cruised through San Anselmo, tossing papers onto subscribers' driveways and front lawns. He came home when the satchel was empty and watched as the neighbor two doors down from his house opened his front door, walked down to the end of the driveway in his bathrobe, and bent down to pick up his newspaper. The neighbor was George Lucas.

"Hi," David called out.

"Hi," George answered.

"It was demystifying for me," Fincher recalled. "It wasn't just behind the Bel Air gates that [movies were] happening . . . Coppola was shooting *The Godfather* at the Marin Art & Garden Center and on Shady Lane in Ross. Kids in my second grade class were showing up with shaved heads because they had been in Lucas's *THX 1138*."

Every kid on his block wanted to be a moviemaker, all of a sudden. Because they could see it.

· 15 ·

PARANOIA IN NORTH BEACH

Francis, now flush, could afford to spend much of 1972 writing. He took *The Conversation* out of a drawer and finished a new draft on August 18, shortly after George finished filming *American Graffiti*, then revised it again until September 29. He completed a third pass on November 22.

He went straight into filming. Paramount, thrilled with the success of *The Godfather*, happily picked up the bill. Gene Hackman played the lead, surveillance man Harry Caul. Francis's confidence was higher than it had ever been. He changed the shooting schedule day by day, following his instincts. He coaxed a performance out of Hackman unlike anything the actor had committed to film before, and Harry Caul became another expression of how Francis felt about himself: physically imposing, the center of gravity in any room, lauded by his peers as a leader—but also wounded, awkward with women, and haunted by the possible consequences of his actions. Francis loaded the character with bits of himself. Caul's mastery of audio recording equipment mirrors Francis's lifelong obsession with the same gadgets, and Caul talks of suffering from polio as a child. Hackman was a novel presence, and Francis surrounded him with regulars: Teri Garr as Caul's girlfriend, John Cazale as his assistant, Robert Duvall as the Director. He threw a small role to the young man Fred Roos rated so highly, the carpenter with the dazzling smile and the little chin scar that George had just put in *American Graffiti*. Harrison Ford told Francis proudly that he had decided to play his character, the devious antagonist Martin Stett, as a homosexual, though what he meant by that, beyond colorful shirts and a smoldering pout, wasn't immediately clear.

For his crew, Francis reused many of the heads of department George had employed on *American Graffiti*: Aggie Rodgers as his costume designer, Murch as his supervising editor. Francis had been impressed enough by Haskell Wexler to hire him as his cinematographer, but fired him only days into filming—they had a disagreement about backlighting, and neither Francis nor Wexler was known for compromising—and replaced him with Bill Butler, his cinematographer on *The Rain People*. And he hired Missy as an assistant, too, though uncredited. It was the first time she spent an extended amount of time on one of his sets. An excuse, perhaps, to see each other more often, and in plain sight.

Francis retained the lease on the warehouse on Folsom Street, renting out the space and equipment to cover the rent. When local actor Colin Michael Kitchens, known to everyone as Mike, was hired as a projectionist, there was such little money on hand, he did double duty as a janitor, looking after the facility from the sound mixing suites to the front step, which was not infrequently covered in human excrement when he arrived in the morning to unlock the doors, presumably courtesy of Folsom's unhoused, or one of its late-night revelers. By that point, Kitchens says, "that facility was about Walter [Murch]. Walter was the person who made it a comfortable pair of shoes. He is the biggest mensch. I always say: I didn't get to direct, I didn't get to act in films, but the prize is I got to work with Walter. He's calm, he's funny. There's a reverence for him all around the Bay Area."

Soon after Kitchens arrived, Francis, having moved up in the world, decided to leave the Folsom Street warehouse behind. He bought and renovated the historic Sentinel Building—previously owned by pop band the Kingston Trio—and installed offices and sound mixing facilities throughout the distinctive copper-green flat-iron building at the intersection of Kearny, Columbus, and Jackson. This was a much more glamorous location than Folsom Street: Across the street from City Lights Booksellers, and another block from the newly opened Transamerica Pyramid, the tallest skyscraper in the city, the Sentinel sat on the border between North Beach, San Francisco's Little Italy, and the city's financial district. The top floor of the Sentinel became Francis's penthouse, where he lived and worked when in town. He renovated the whole thing and invited friends over to show it off. It was "the ugliest decorated place I'd ever seen," remembered Jimmy Caan.

Francis moved the rest of the Folsom Street facility, including the editing and mixing suites, to Pacific Avenue, across the street from the Sentinel. He said he'd run a little theater company there, a magazine, too, maybe a radio station and a restaurant. He would cook the food in the restaurant himself, or at least design the menu; he would direct the stage plays. He wanted Kitchens to oversee the move.

"Francis liked to think of himself as at the edge of the future," Kitchens says. "Avant-garde. He thought of himself as seeing movements." He talked about Preston Tucker all the time, invoking the automobile designer as a model. "The man who foresaw seat belts, safety—and no one appreciated his innovations," Kitchens recalls. "Francis related to that. He wanted to be this old-world figure who cooks for his family—and then he wanted to be this visionary."

Walter Murch instead compares Francis to the indefatigable nineteenth-century French novelist and entrepreneur Honoré de Balzac, who wrote and published eighty-five novels in the final twenty years of his life, some of them masterpieces. He, too, had been a larger man of prodigious energy, enormous appetites, and manic productivity, often motivated by a suffocating burden of debt. Even Francis's penchant for a double espresso struck Murch as an echo of the Frenchman, who supposedly drank more than fifty cups a day to keep himself going. "There's that lovely quote where he was having dinner in a social environment," Murch says. "A woman was sitting next to him at the table and didn't know who he was, and asked, *What do you do, M. Balzac?* And he said, *Madame, I am a machine that turns coffee into ink.*"

Francis "has always wanted to be in this wonderful community of artists at the moment that people would talk about later as some golden era," Ellie wrote later. "He tried to make it happen in San Francisco. He dreamed of this group of poets, filmmakers and writers who would drink espresso in North Beach and talk of their work, and it would be good . . . He spent a lot of money and energy trying to make it happen."

He recommended his friends for jobs. At some point in 1973, his phone rang; on the other end was Ellen Burstyn, calling from the set of *The Exorcist.* She had a script called *Alice Doesn't Live Here Anymore*, about a widow looking for a fresh start on the road with her preteen son, a film much like *The Rain People* but warmer, funnier. Warner Bros. would finance it on her name alone.

"I'm looking for a director who's new, exciting, and unknown—do you know one?" Burstyn asked. Francis told her to track down an unreleased film called *Mean Streets*. Marty got the job.

Everyone at Zoetrope called the Sentinel, simply, "the Tower." The nearby Northpoint Theatre, on the corner of Bay and Powell, was chosen to hold a preview screening of *American Graffiti* in January 1973, attended by George and Francis, as well as Ned Tanen.

Tanen was pissed off before he even set foot in San Francisco. Maybe it was George's treatment of him during the shoot, or maybe it was having to work on the weekend—the preview was scheduled at ten AM on the morning of Sunday, the 28th—but Robbins and Barwood were on the same plane out of Los Angeles, chatting amiably with Jeff Berg, when Tanen shoved past them to get to his seat. After the plane landed, he hurried to the taxi lane so he wouldn't have to share a cab with the three others, though they were all going to the same place.

He glowered at the crowd of eight hundred people filing into the cinema. Robbins and Barwood found Francis and George standing with Marcia, Walter Murch, and Gary Kurtz. They watched as Tanen stomped to a seat in one of the front rows and sat down like a child in detention.

The audience whooped and cheered and clapped all the way through the picture. They danced in the aisles. They were on their feet as the credits rolled, and so was Tanen, who powered back up the aisle, grabbed Kurtz and Francis by the arms, and pushed them to the back of the theater.

"That film is not ready to be released," he growled.

George and his friends rushed up the aisle and gathered around.

"This film is a disaster," Tanen said. "I'm so disappointed in you, George."

Marcia froze. *Oh my God, here we go*, George thought. *It's THX all over again.*

But then Francis exploded.

"What do you mean?" he exclaimed. "You should kiss this kid's feet!"

"You stacked the audience," Tanen asserted. "It doesn't matter to me how it played now in front of this group, my point is that I don't see the work. You were given our notes and you were responsible for making these changes and I don't see the work. You've had six weeks to make changes . . . I'm not happy."

"What are you talking about?" Francis screamed. "You were just in the theater for the last two hours! Didn't you just see and hear what we all saw and heard?"

"I'm not talking about that," Tanen said. "We'll see if we can release it."

"You'll see if you can *release it*?" Francis roared. "This kid has killed himself to make this movie for you. He brought it in on time and on schedule. The least you can do is thank him for that!" Something pent-up and uncontrollable was flooding out of him. He reached into his pocket for a wallet, or a checkbook. "You know what," he continued, "if you hate it that much, let it go. We'll set it up someplace else, and you get all your money back. Let's go, right now."

Tanen stared in confusion and disdain for a moment.

"That's not what I'm here to do," he said. "Don't be ridiculous."

"You should get on your knees and thank this kid for saving your career!"

Tanen shook his head and threw up his hands and turned on his heel, storming out of the theater without responding.

Francis's theatrical flourish became the stuff of legends. "I wish I'd been there to see it myself," Steven said, "because it's the best story to come out of Hollywood since the late 1940s."

"Francis really stood up to Ned," George remembered later. "I was pretty proud of him."

In the following days, Universal formally requested changes, a demand George ignored. Tanen felt humiliated. Gary Kurtz and Beverly Walker, separately and behind George's back, worked on the executive to find a solution, and eventually, the studio hired Verna Fields, who had mentored George and Marcia a few years earlier, to implement their changes without George's approval. It wasn't much, a trim of a scene here and there, adding to a loss of about four minutes, as much to save Tanen face as anything else. "Nothing was changed, nothing was lost," says Walker, who had seen the film before and after Fields's edits. "She was making those changes she thought would, psychologically, satisfy Tanen."

George was livid all the same. Principles were binary; betrayal was betrayal.

"The critics will probably like it," Tanen said in the end, in an attempt to be conciliatory. "It's a good, solid critics' film."

He was wrong. When *American Graffiti* came out in the summer, it was a slow-building but gigantic hit, earning the studio—and George personally—millions upon millions of dollars. Critics unanimously loved it. It won George an Oscar nomination for Best Original Screenplay, and Marcia a nomination for Best Editing, though George shared his with Huyck and Katz and Marcia had to share hers with Fields.

George spread his profit points around, sending money to the main cast, his co-writers, and even his lawyer Tom Pollock. He rankled at Francis getting his contractual share—in the end, about $3 million. George's own cut was four times as much, but "the amount of money that George had to send to Francis upset him," said Willard Huyck. Francis, in turn, bristled at the suggestion that $3 million was a disproportionate payoff for him to receive. Without him, there would have been no *American Graffiti* at all. Executives had only ever wanted to be in the George Lucas business because of Francis Coppola.

"I had the job in Hollywood, I had the credits, I had the money, I had the houses," Francis protested. George, Murch, the young film school graduates who had roamed the Zoetrope halls—they had all been "broke," Francis said, "and I took them all with me and used everything I had to fund their, and my, projects." Now that everyone was reaping the benefits of his faith, they had the nerve to criticize him?

George expected that Francis would share some of his money with Gary Kurtz, since they were both credited as producers. Francis disagreed; he said George had hired Kurtz, not him, and surely George could spare some cash out of his much larger pot. George also felt they had an agreement to split some of the profits with Haskell Wexler, and again Francis denied it. Finally, Francis gave in, but weeks passed and he didn't pay Wexler. For George, this, too, was black and white.

"Francis was questioning my honesty," George said. "He was accusing me of being like him, and that upset me . . . It was one of the reasons we drifted apart more than anything else."

Another reason was *Apocalypse Now*. Columbia Pictures was now interested in the film, and Milius had completed a screenplay. George dispatched Kurtz to look for locations, and Kurtz heard of some spots they could use in the Philippines. He and George made plans to film some footage there, some at home in the US, and maybe even sneak a small Japanese crew into Vietnam to shoot documentary footage on location to splice into several sequences. They could blend fiction and nonfiction in the same way Haskell Wexler had done in 1969 on *Medium Cool*, about a news photographer caught up in the riots at the 1968 Democratic National Convention.

George went to meet Francis, and told him Columbia Pictures was willing to pay for development on *Apocalypse Now*. They would send Kurtz to the Philippines for a second scout and pay Milius for a fresh draft of the screenplay. Columbia was even enthusiastic about George's unorthodox directorial vision. They were willing to make the film for $2 million.

There was only one holdup to Lucasfilm and Columbia signing an agreement: Francis, through American Zoetrope, still owned *Apocalypse Now*. That fact in itself annoyed George. As he saw it, Francis had never explicitly asked for his permission to package *Apocalypse Now* into the original Zoetrope deal with Warner Bros. in the first place. More inconveniently still, that agreement granted Zoetrope 25 percent of the film's eventual profits—twice what George, as the director, would be receiving. (He split his own quarter share with Milius.) George argued that he was no longer the novice film student he was when that original deal had been made. Now he was Francis's equal, with two films of his own under his belt, and besides, it had never been Francis's film to claim in the first place. He—not Francis—had set up this deal at Columbia. He—not Francis—would be directing the movie. Gary Kurtz—not Francis—would produce it. Francis wouldn't actually do *anything* on the picture—why should he make a quarter of the profits?

"I've got a chance to make this, Francis," George pleaded.

Coppola wasn't interested in ceding the rights to the film to a studio. He already regretted letting someone else finance *American Graffiti*—"he never got over it," George said—and he refused to let go of *Apocalypse Now*. He and George had to own it—that was the whole definition of independence.

The deal with Columbia died. And so, for a long time, did George and Francis's friendship.

· 16 ·

FROM *SUGARLAND* TO THE VINEYARD

Steven Spielberg ended 1972 and started 1973 finally doing what he had dreamed of from the age of twelve: directing a feature film. He loved the screenplay Robbins and Barwood had written for *The Sugarland Express*. Producers Darryl Zanuck and David Brown were impressed, too. When Goldie Hawn, already a television star and an Oscar winner, joined on to play Lou Jean Poplin, the script's version of Ila Faye Holiday, the picture was suddenly a go. Her status made Hawn, not Steven, the most powerful person on the project, but Hawn was self-deprecating and easy—she liked to make jokes about her Oscar to put people at ease—as well as keen. "She was only two years older than me," says William Atherton, who played Clovis, the fictional version of Robert Dent, "but she was an Adult with a capital *A*, and a great businessperson."

The *Sugarland Express* cast rehearsed for two weeks and then set off for Texas, where Steven got to shoot happily unencumbered by the looming presence of the business. Milius's friend Steve Kanaly, who played one of the cops chasing down Clovis and Lou Jean, a role he'd obtained on Milius's recommendation, could tell immediately that Steven was special. Milius had cast Kanaly as Pretty Boy Floyd in his own directorial debut, *Dillinger*, and as a director, Milius was direct, minimal, no-nonsense. He was well prepared, treated every sequence to be shot like a battle to be won. Steven was different. "He was six scenes ahead in his mind all the time," Kanaly says. "You had to slow him down."

"I never met anybody who loved movies as much as he did," Atherton says of Spielberg. "Being on set with him was a joy. He created a great, warm atmosphere." He left the actors mostly to themselves. "Steven isn't as interested in acting as he is in other things about film," Atherton says. "When he's casting, he casts actors who know how to act. He goes by instinct on people and their abilities, and what they represent." Then he left them to it.

With the camera, however, Steven was exacting. He and cinematographer Vilmos Zsigmond took great pains with every shot. He was quick and decisive in the edit, working particularly well with Verna Fields. *The Sugarland Express* hit cinemas in March 1974, but by then, Steven was already preparing for his next picture. Starting your next picture before the previous one came out was another trick Steven had learned from studying studio executives. Build your next bridge, he liked to say, before you burn the last one.

"Steven wanted to be a studio director," says Atherton. "He stormed the studios. He wasn't going out with a handheld—though he could do it, and do it brilliantly—but it wasn't what he wanted. He wanted to be a studio director, with the power and all the technical tools that come with it."

He wanted his second film to be big. Guy McElwaine set him up for a meeting with his old agent, Medavoy, who had just taken over from David Picker as vice president at United Artists, with a brief to bring his ethos as an agent—young filmmakers, hip material—to the company's slate. He still thought Steven was nice, a little insecure, a little unremarkable, but *The Sugarland Express* suggested he might be more than that.

"You have a choice of films," Medavoy told him, laying out some of the screenplays the studio had in development. "What would you like to do?"

"I'd like to do a James Bond film," Steven answered. The series was two movies into its Roger Moore era.

"Aside from *that*," Medavoy replied, "what would you like to do?"

The answer came in the form of another project, one Medavoy had once controlled, but now, conveniently, belonged to Zanuck and Brown at Universal. There was a book Steven had come across in Zanuck's office—like *The Godfather*, it was a pulpy genre novel with a catchy hook, though the subject was very different. It hadn't been published yet, and it was the author Peter Benchley's debut, but Steven had read it and found it captivating.

Its title was *Jaws*.

George mourned *Apocalypse Now* and turned his mind toward outer space. United Artists had passed on *The Star Wars* when they passed on *American Graffiti*, so George was free to shop the space opera elsewhere. He took the treatment to Universal, in spite of his dislike for Tanen, and the studio offered him $25,000 to write and direct—barely more than the twenty they had paid him for *Graffiti*. George pushed for more, and Universal called talks off altogether. Francis showed the treatment to his friend William Friedkin, on the off chance Paramount would be interested—Francis, Friedkin, and Peter Bogdanovich had a collective deal at that studio through their shared production outfit, the Directors Company, under which Charles Bluhdorn had agreed to let them make virtually any films they wanted, with unlimited creative control, as long as each picture's budget came in under $3 million. This was how Francis was making *The Conversation*, and how Bogdanovich was making *Paper Moon*. Bluhdorn, desperate to sign up even more young directors, had told the three men they could each bring in a protégé, too, and the terms would apply to that apprentice's own project of choice. (Bogdanovich took the piss by walking into Paramount with Orson

Welles and announcing that the sixty-two-year-old genius was the "promising" filmmaker he would mentor. The Directors Company didn't last long.)

Loyal to a fault, Francis brought George's treatment for *The Star Wars* to Friedkin and Bogdanovich for their approval. Friedkin took one look at it.

"What's this shit?" he croaked.

Finally, Jeff Berg found a warm ear on the head of Alan Ladd Jr., a vice president at 20th Century Fox. Known by family and friends as "Laddie"—to set him apart from his namesake father, star of the classic Western *Shane*—Ladd was laconic, likeable, and loyal. He had more hands-on experience than the average suit, having worked both as an agent and as an independent producer before becoming a studio executive.

Laddie loved *American Graffiti*. He asked Berg to bring George in. George duly pitched his science-fiction labor of love, doing his damnedest to sell Laddie on his story of a mystic knight and his robot companions from a galaxy far, far away, engaged in battles by "lazer sword" and spaceship dogfights created via state-of-the-art special effects. Laddie listened and hoped George couldn't tell he had absolutely no idea what the hell he was talking about. The title alone—*The Adventures of Luke Starkiller, as Taken from the Journal of the Whills, Saga 1 of the Star Wars*—was migraine-inducing.

George finished his pitch and took a breath. Laddie thought for a moment. The executive was known for his brevity—he'd once turned down a whole pitch just by saying "No" without further explanation. George braced for the worst.

"I don't understand this movie," Laddie said.

George's chest tightened.

"I don't get it at all—" Laddie expounded.

George had heard this too many times to count.

"—but I think you're a talented guy," Laddie went on, "and I want you to make it."

Ladd had always thought of film as a filmmaker's medium. Producing was easy, he felt; "You just have to be moderately intelligent and get along with people," he said, and "in the end, it's the director's ballgame. He calls the shots." In this case, he trusted George to call his. Laddie, too, had grown up on *Flash Gordon* and *Superman*. As a teenager in Beverly Hills, he had taken one of his first jobs, as an usher at the cinema, just so he could watch Errol Flynn swashbucklers five or six times a day, and the boxes he looked to tick in any project remained those that made those adventure pictures so special: "Can you root for the hero and heroine? Can you boo the villain? Is the action fast and furious?" George spoke about these ideas with such vision and passion, and the way Laddie saw it, you invested in people, not pictures.

They agreed for George to deliver a first draft in June, which Fox would then decide to either pass on or develop further. George and Marcia had spent some of their *Graffiti* money on a Victorian house in San Anselmo, twenty minutes north of Mill Valley, and he spent every afternoon from then until the summer sequestered on its top floor, sitting at a custom three-sided desk large enough to spread out his notes. The scenic window gave onto Mount Tam in the distance, hunched and green in the sunlight. For eight weeks, he toiled at his least favorite activity: writing. He came up with character backstories and alien species. He threw ideas from human history together to create his fictional world, like a pick and mix: There would be an evil Empire, like the Roman Empire, though their uniforms and demeanor would be reminiscent of the Nazis. (The Empire's faceless foot soldiers, in George's drafts, quickly became known as stormtroopers.) The guerrilla resistance to Imperial forces was modeled on the Vietcong. George called the warrior-monks who worked with the resistance the Jedi, from the Japanese *jidaigeki*, meaning "period drama," a genre in which his idol Akira Kurosawa had worked frequently. He decided that Eastern Buddhist principles would govern the monks' philosophy, but gave them a motto, *May the Force be with you*, rhythmically adapted from the *May the lord be with you* of Catholic Mass. Outer space, as he described it, had the laser weapons of *Flash Gordon*, the spice mines and moisture farms of Frank Herbert's *Dune*, and starship scuffles modeled after World War II's Battle of Britain. The technology was futuristic, but George's drafts insisted the story took place a long time ago, in the past. The sum total of these ideas was rich, complex, and near incoherent.

Kurosawa's filmmaking bore significant influence on George's plot, too. In the Japanese filmmaker's 1958 *jidaigeki* adventure film *The Hidden Fortress*, two quarrelling peasants agree to help a sword fighter travel across enemy lines to rescue an imprisoned princess, without realizing the bandit is a decorated general. George adapted that narrative almost directly into his first versions of the screenplay, with droid robots in the peasant roles and a Jedi as the sword fighter. As he fleshed out the world and its characters, he revised and rewrote, razed and rebuilt. Characters changed ages, names, occupations, genders, and species. The bickering droids remained. The imprisoned princess, too.

When stuck, he read through comic books and treatises on fairy-tale archetypes and borrowed prints of old serials from the studios, and they distracted him as much as they helped. "When I sit at a desk for eight hours a day, I can't help but think about things other than what I'm supposed to be thinking about," he admitted later. He was enthralled by *Don Winslow of the Navy*, an old Universal film about a naval intelligence officer investigating unusual reports from the Pacific, and the '30s comic *Tim Tyler's Luck*, about a resourceful boy who goes on globe-trotting adventures after being discharged from an orphanage. He toyed with making various characters in *The Star Wars* space anthropologists; one draft followed Luke Starkiller, an adventurer compiling a catalogue of ancient knowledge from archeological evidence he finds on various far-flung planets. Soon enough, though, George realized the idea didn't belong in *The Star Wars*. He wondered what adapting one of those old serials might look like, and this new idea became a distraction and a respite. Every time he grew frustrated with his galaxy far, far away, he played with this different tale of adventure. He wanted his protagonist to have a name both unique and mundane, so he gave him the last name Smith, and then the first name Indiana, after his and Marcia's giant, scruffy Alaskan malamute. Indiana liked to ride in the passenger seat of the car wherever George went—George took that and put it in *The Star Wars*, in the form of space pirate Han Solo's furry co-pilot, Chewbacca, a name derived from the Russian word for dog, pronounced "sobaka." Han Solo himself had started as a green-skinned Jedi, but as George settled on "Luke Starkiller" as his protagonist—a farm boy with a fondness for fast landspeeders, chosen for greatness by a higher power, whose first name, Luke, was George's high school nickname—he transformed Solo into a "burly-bearded" pirate, slightly older than Luke, with a taste for "gaudy" and "flamboyant" clothing. Himself as the hero; Francis as the hero's reckless, rakish confederate.

George handed in his first draft of *Star Wars*—he lost the determiner somewhere along the way—and Laddie liked it enough to encourage him to keep working. 1973 turned to 1974. Money kept rolling in from *Graffiti*. The financial comfort softened George's already flaky commitment to writing. He spent more and more time reading comics, watching serials, cheating on the slog of *Star Wars* with the exciting, no-strings-attached experimentation of *Indiana Smith*. He learned somewhere that Hitler had been obsessed with the occult and decided Indiana would race the Nazis for supernatural objects across the globe. George liked Bond films so, like a spy, Indiana Smith would lead a regular civilian life at home, but government agents would send him on secret adventures abroad. Bond was a Cold War creation, however, and Nazis as antagonists meant setting *Indiana Smith* in the '30s or the '40s. When George thought of a suave, tuxedo-wearing hero from that particular period, he reflexively pictured Humphrey Bogart. He imagined "Indy"—for short—as a mixture of *Casablanca*'s Rick Blaine, the smooth and cynical former gun runner exiled in a foreign land, and Bogart's other iconic character, *The Treasure of the Sierra Madre*'s gold-hoarding Fred C. Dobbs, rumpled and stubbled and sweaty under his dirty fedora. Indiana Smith would blend both personalities.

The James Bond films loomed large over both of George's projects. Back in August, he'd told the *Los Angeles Times* that *Star Wars* was "a combination of *2001*, the Bond films, and *Lawrence of Arabia*," a mishmash so confused it explained his struggle with writing a script that matched the vision. Crucially, Bond films were targeted at younger, primarily male audiences, and for a decade, says Mike Medavoy, who oversaw the franchise while at United Artists, "like clockwork, they made $75 million a movie. So if you just made it for twenty-five, and you grossed seventy-five, plus all the other ancillary rights, you'd wind up making money." 007 was the closest thing the film business had ever had to a surefire bet, and the franchise bankrolled Medavoy's more ambitious, more adult pictures, including *One Flew Over the Cuckoo's Nest*, *Rocky*, and *Annie Hall*, films that won the studio the Academy Award for Best Picture three years in a row between 1975 and 1977.

If George was ever going to be independent from Hollywood, he thought, he wouldn't get there by making abstract mood poems—he needed Bond-like dependable income. His other frame of reference was Disney cartoons, which were also aimed at younger audiences and had a set financial floor—theirs drawn not from a singular intellectual property, like Bond, but from the cachet provided by Walt Disney's name. The original unicorn.

"Those movies always make $16 million," George told a colleague. "Look it up."

Walter Murch prepared *American Graffiti* for international release, then joined Korty's old editor, Richard Chew, to start editing *The Conversation*. Chew's first assemblage of Francis's footage stretched to over four hours. Murch rolled up his sleeves and dug into it, like a mechanic ripping nonessential parts out of an engine. Out went all the scenes Francis had shot about Caul's troubled relationship with his runaway niece. Out went an entire secondary plot about Caul placating disgruntled neighbors. Francis, already the kind of director who mostly stayed out of the editing suite, was busy preparing *The Godfather Part II*, and he left Murch to figure out the structure. Murch distilled *The Conversation* to what he felt had been the heart of Francis's screenplay all along: one man, his job, and the guilt and loneliness that imprison him. He turned the focus of the film more subjective, more visceral. After all, he, as much as anyone alive, understood the intimate sensuality of the act of hearing.

Over the years, Murch had grown even more fascinated by the science of sound, by the fact "a third of the neurons in your brain are dedicated to visual processing," he says, "but a thirtieth of your brain is dedicated to audio . . . The effect that the sound is having on you is somehow co-opted by the big brother of the visual circuits, and interpreted as a visual thing. Which is great for us, because it hides the marionette strings." He rarely had the chance to truly explore how that worked, though he'd applied it to great acclaim in one particular scene of *The Godfather*—the one where Michael meets Sollozzo and McCluskey in an Italian restaurant and shoots both dead. In the moments before Michael pulls the trigger, Murch had laid down the clunking, then the screeching, of an elevated subway train, the metal grinding growing louder and louder as the pressure builds for Michael to commit the crime the audience expects him to commit. "The sound is interpreted as an internal state," Murch says. "That's a metaphorical sound."

On *The Conversation*—a picture all about suggestibility and the tricks the ear plays on the brain—Murch had free rein to play with auditory metaphor. Francis didn't have an ending, and without an ending, he couldn't be sure what the film's shape should be. For Francis, "that was part of making a movie," says Jim Bloom, who worked as an assistant on *American Graffiti* and *The Conversation.* "Looking for an ending all the time, shooting different things."

Murch had access to all the different options in the editing room, and he played around. For a long time, the film didn't work. The editor remained steady. "Films mostly don't work until they're finished," he liked to say. Back in 1970, he'd sat at home with his wife, Aggie, and watched a BBC production of *The Six Wives of Henry VIII* on *Masterpiece Theatre*, and in one episode of the miniseries, Henry's third wife, Jane Seymour, tells him a parable about two thieves, sentenced to death by the French king Louis. One of them requests an audience with the king, which is granted, and when he returns to the gaol, the look of optimism on his face surprises his cellmate.

"The king has pardoned me," he explained, "provided that in a year, I will teach his horse to talk."

"You'll never succeed," the other thief replied. "No one could."

"Well," countered the first thief, "in a year I may die anyway, or King Louis may die, or the horse *may* talk."

It was the kind of irrational optimism you needed in the editing room. Murch would repeat the last line any time his director lost faith: The film might not work yet, the studio might be on our backs, but Francis, *the horse may talk.*

Every other week, Francis would come home from Lake Tahoe, where *The Godfather Part II* was filming, and take a look at what Murch and Chew had put together. He was not like the other directors Chew worked with, whose feedback was so granular: the removal of a single shot, the trimming of a few frames. In postproduction, Francis was scatterbrained and easily distracted. He thought in broad strokes and big pictures, and was more likely to suggest writing and shooting an entirely new scene than to bend over the KEM, finding preexisting moments and beats to modulate.

For a long time, Francis had resisted Paramount's desperation to make a sequel to the biggest film of all time. He was offended to learn the studio had already had Puzo write a draft without his input. Bluhdorn tried to convince him by saying, "You have the formula for Coca-Cola. You're not going to make more Coca-Cola?," but the analogy repulsed Francis. He told Paramount that if they insisted on making a sequel, they should hire Martin Scorsese instead, but the studio wasn't interested. Then Bluhdorn promised to freeze Robert Evans out of the production and let Francis be his own producer. That argument got Coppola listening.

Francis thought of *The Godfather* as a complete, stand-alone film. He could not simply add another story to the back of it, and one of the primary draws of the first film—Brando's Don Vito—was gone and dead. But now that his father was in his sixties, and his own sons, Gio and Roman, were growing up, Francis found himself tempted to tell another version of the father-and-son dynamic in the first *Godfather*. Half of the sequel would reach into the past, to show Vito Corleone's rise to power, and half into the present, to show Michael Corleone's loss of humanity. This time, it wasn't Fredo whom Francis related to, but Michael, powerful and paranoid, anxious about the burdens of success. He intertwined the narrative of young Vito Corleone—ruthless, decisive—with the continuing story of Michael, who feels the heat from all sides. He keeps secrets from his family. He lies to himself. He is most hurt when his wife threatens to take his family and children away from him. He has Fredo killed, a cold excision of the weakness and perfidy in his own blood.

It would be a sadder, bleaker film than the first. Michael, at the end of *The Godfather*, stands in a room lit in warm hues, shaking hands, surrounded by vows of loyalty. At the end of *Part II*, he is alone, hollowed out, in the cold of a vast and isolated compound.

The bulk of the main cast returned: Duvall, Cazale, Keaton, even James Caan in a flashback cameo. For a time, Pacino held out, even as Paramount promised larger and larger paychecks. He only agreed to return after Francis gave him permission to spend a week workshopping changes to the screenplay.

"You're holding me up here," Francis complained.

"I just want a better script," Pacino answered. The thing was almost there, he said: Francis had assembled all the right furniture, but now they had to move it into the house, find where it all fit.

Francis fretted over finding an actor charismatic enough to play a young version of Marlon Brando's don—until Marty showed him a cut of *Mean Streets*. "He looked at it," Marty remembered, "and the next day he called De Niro to play in *Godfather II*."

The shoot was difficult on the Coppolas. Pacino found Francis colder, less friendly. The script was melancholy; shooting on location in Lake Tahoe and the Dominican Republic was lonely. Francis was still sleeping with Missy, whom Ellie knew nothing about. He gave Missy a job on the picture; she dropped out of UC Berkeley, where she'd been studying political science, working part-time in a local bakery, to follow him. He told her she would learn about filmmaking.

By now, Ellie had more or less accepted her own career was on hold. She was a wonderful artist, fascinated and inspired by the natural world, and she needed to create as much as Francis did. As in every marriage, there was a line between being a partner in a pair and letting someone else define who you are, and Ellie sometimes lost track of which side of the line she walked on. She tried to find the time and inspiration to make smaller pieces, in hotel rooms and rented apartments. She was sometimes angry and resentful. She put Francis at the center of her own life, as she felt expected to do—it's what her mother had done, what every good wife had to do—but she couldn't always bring herself to appear fulfilled and excited to do so.

Missy, fourteen years Ellie's junior and new to the experience, could. Francis, when speaking about her later, would say she was "exuberant and full of fun," a relief from the pressures and complications of home. With Missy, Francis was no longer a father with financial pressures and domestic responsibilities, a role he craved but couldn't bear to be confined to. With Missy, he could dance to the Beatles—drive down to the beach in her cherished, battered

Fiat—expound for hours, over hamburgers, about whatever castle he meant to build in the sky. She was intelligent, curious, and sensitive, always empathetic and engaged. In the late sixties, her father, no longer able to support his family from his typewriter alone, had stopped writing full-time and taken a job he hated at the Motion Picture Association, watching three films a day and helping decide on their maturity ratings. In 1971, he and Missy's mother, Margaret, had divorced. Life had grown complicated and uncertain since Providence High, and Missy longed for joy and escape of her own. "When you get into a relationship like that," says Missy's friend Kaja Fehr, "that's so thrilling and so loving and so creative, you just know it's going to last forever."

Francis sometimes put the relationship in cruder terms. "She's the greatest thing in bed I've ever had," he told friends. He was so inconsiderate that Carmine and Italia, visiting the set in Lake Tahoe, were upset to see their son betraying his wife so openly. Ellie felt threatened by all the "adoring young proteges waiting in the wings" for a glance from Francis's wandering eye—but she seemed blind to Missy.

When *The Godfather Part II* eventually came out, Mathison's name appeared in a film's credits for the first time, as a "location assistant." Francis told people she was his personal assistant. "I just got coffee and Cokes for people," Missy said. "I had been working in a bakery. Bringing coffee to Al Pacino was exciting."

"She worked, I think, as a nanny, honestly," remembers Mathison's sister Melinda, a setup that could only have felt dangerous and uncomfortable—hiding directly in Ellie's sight.

Missy didn't seem to have worked out what she wanted out of life yet. "She kind of was in her own head a lot," Melinda says. She took some work as a stringer for *People* magazine, but didn't stick with it. She connected easily with her subjects—including, for one article, a teenage Disney star by the name of Jodie Foster—and she turned in clean copy. But she was desperately reluctant to pick up the phone, chase leads down, impose herself as one needed to report a story. She liked a slower, more reflective pace. She and Francis bonded over words, books. "She loved writers and writing," Francis recalled. She read widely and voraciously, from the nineteenth-century existentialist novel *Hunger* by Knut Hamsun to the books of America's then-new literary sensation Joan Didion. She loved a good story, and now she found herself paying close attention to the craft required to tell one. Around this time, she took a trip to Mexico, with a vague plan to write something out of it—a short story, or an essay.

"I want to see if I can write," she told her father.

Francis thought she might have a talent for it, too.

Mike Medavoy had worked with Dick Zanuck just once, when he had sold the producer, then at Warner Bros., a David S. Ward script titled *Steelyard Blues*, made into a film starring Donald Sutherland and Jane Fonda. "It was a terrible movie," Medavoy says, so bad it played a part in Zanuck and his partner, David Brown, losing their jobs at Warner and moving across town to Universal. So bad, Medavoy remembers, that he felt he owed Zanuck and Brown a favor. The agent controlled two properties at the time: an original script, also written by Ward, entitled *The Sting*, that one of his readers, Rob Cohen, had championed out of the slush pile, and an unpublished novel about a killer shark terrorizing a seaside resort on Long Island, written by struggling author Peter Benchley. Medavoy sent both to Zanuck, with a message saying the two properties were his if he wanted them.

Zanuck wanted *The Sting*, and when he read *Jaws*, he wanted that, too, a desire vindicated when his partner, David Brown, told him he, too, was intrigued about Benchley's book, because he had read a description of it in *Cosmopolitan*, where his wife, Helen Gurley Brown, was an editor.

The Sting came together quickly. Zanuck and Brown bought it for a record fee. Medavoy showed the script to Robert Redford, who was his neighbor in Malibu. Redford liked it, Paul Newman joined on, and Zanuck and Brown teamed the two actors with George Roy

Hill, who had directed them a few years earlier in *Butch Cassidy and the Sundance Kid.* By January 1973, the project was filming in Chicago, and it hit the screens in December, grossing over $150 million. It won seven awards the next April, including Best Picture, Best Director, and Best Original Screenplay. Medavoy's reader, Rob Cohen, parlayed his discovery of the script into a huge promotion, becoming head of programming at 20th Century Fox Television.

Jaws was a harder sell. When Medavoy sent the book to Zanuck, it was still months away from publication and, exciting as it was, the novel was also gaudy, its prose crude and its narrative convoluted, intercutting the gruesome shark killings with subplots about the Mafia and small-town sexual trysts.

"Look," Medavoy told Zanuck one day, "I'm going to give you my client list of directors. Pick one and you can have him." Zanuck chose thirty-seven-year-old Dick Richards, who was an in-demand director of television commercials but had only one feature film under his belt, the low-budget revisionist Western *The Culpepper Cattle Co.* Zanuck and Brown flew to New York with Richards to meet Benchley for lunch at the 21 Club, "and unfortunately," Medavoy says, "Dick Richards kept referring to the shark as a whale."

"This is wonderful, to have this small town terrified by this whale," he told Benchley. The author raised an eyebrow.

"Wait a minute," Zanuck interrupted. "You mean shark."

"Oh yes. Yes."

Benchley poured himself another drink, and Richards described how he would adapt the book for the screen. His vision was compelling until he touched on the film's climax. "Then," he said, "when the whale attacks the boat—"

"Shark!" Zanuck shouted. "Shark!"

After lunch, the producer called Medavoy in Los Angeles, to thank him for the favor. "Everything went great," he seethed, "but the director thinks the shark is a whale!"

A few days later, Medavoy was in London, and Zanuck was back on the phone. "I decided I want to go to Spielberg," the producer said.

"Go ahead," Medavoy answered. He wasn't Spielberg's agent anymore. He directed Zanuck to McElwaine.

Steven signed on quickly and gratefully. *Sugarland Express* wasn't out yet, but the word about the film around the studio lot was good. He liked the book, and he thought of the project as a good career move. *Build the bridge in front of you*, he thought, *before they burn the one behind you.*

He sold Zanuck and Brown on his vision for *Jaws*: He would not shoot it on the backlot tank; he would not shoot it like a Roger Corman B-movie, with cheap special effects shots of puppets and fake boats rocking in front of a matte painting of the sea. "No long shots of a shark intercut with close-ups of faces reacting," as Steven's eventual screenwriter Carl Gottlieb put it, "no cutaways to miniatures, no models. The story and the movie required that you see a boat, and men, and a shark, all in the same shot, on the surface of an ocean with an open horizon." Location scouts flew out to the East Coast to scour for oceanfront locations, and since no believable, filmable-from-all-angles, moving monster shark had ever been built in the history of cinema, Zanuck and Brown hit the phones, putting out calls for a shark wrangler who could train a real great white to perform on camera.

When Steven finally went out to shoot the film in Martha's Vineyard, it became the stuff of legend, stretching out over the entire summer of 1974, so full of difficulties it nearly ended his career.

· 17 ·

YOU'RE GONNA NEED A BIGGER BOAT

By March 1974, Peter Benchley had written one draft of *Jaws*, Steven himself had written a second, and a screenwriter named Howard Sackler had written a third. Though Steven remained unsatisfied with the words on the page, Zanuck and Brown drew up a budget from the latest of the drafts and landed on a number they were happy with: $8.5 million. The absurd idea of using a real-life shark had been abandoned, and production designer Joe Alves prepared plans for a mechanical alternative. Zanuck knew his numbers might be a little off—a film's budget, he said, was like par on a golf course, an ideal number to aim for, and handicapping par for a "course" like *Jaws* was as difficult as playing golf "with new clubs on a strange course with an exploding ball"—but he felt good about the task, and he felt good about Steven. What was *Jaws*, after all, if not *Duel* with a mechanical shark instead of a truck—and hadn't Steven brought *Duel* in like a responsible, frugal old hand?

In a workshop down on the studio lot, special effects specialist Bob Mattey got to work building a shark to Joe Alves's specifications. Mattey, sixty-four, had done everything in his career, from creating the flying spaceships in old *Flash Gordon* serials to constructing the animatronic people used in several of Disneyland's most iconic theme park rides, like the Haunted Mansion and the Jungle Cruise. He was the only person in California with the skill and experience to make the kind of unprecedented automaton required for Spielberg's movie. George, who had grown up on Mattey's work and had started to think of Steven as his "creative compatriot," dropped in one day to observe the progress, bringing Martin Scorsese and John Milius along. The huge shark sat unfinished in a warehouse, with support rods sticking out of its hollow eyes and clamps holding its rubber skin together, the whole thing slightly elevated off the ground, like a car at a body shop. George poked his head into its mouth to check out the inside mechanisms. Steven, for a joke, pulled the lever that shut the shark's mouth, and got George stuck inside. Steven, Marty, and Milius yanked and pulled, forced the jaws apart, and, after several minutes of sweaty, panicked struggle, managed to free George. The four of them hurried off the lot, convinced they'd broken Mattey's expensive work-in-progress.

"It's not going very well," Steven told his friends whenever they asked after the movie. He didn't feel ready to move forward, but the studio kept pushing. An actors' strike loomed, possibly to begin in July. Universal scheduled May 2, 1974, as the first day of principal photography, and expected filming to wrap by the end of June. If *Jaws* didn't go ahead on that schedule, it might never go at all.

Production agreed Steven should film all the land scenes first, while Mattey and his men finished building the shark, and then the crew would finish out at sea. Sheinberg, who remained a mentor to Steven, asked him how he felt about that timeline.

"I'll be four or five days behind by the time we go to sea to shoot the third act," Steven predicted. It wasn't a perfect schedule, but he could work with it.

On April 22, Steven finally hired a screenwriter he trusted in his friend Carl Gottlieb, a thirty-six-year-old who had mostly worked writing television comedy. The two young men flew out East a week later. They stopped in Boston for three days, where, in a high-rise hotel suite, Gottlieb typed out their first set of agreed revisions and Steven held marathon ten-hour-a-day casting sessions.

Steven was anxious. Three main roles headlined *Jaws*—Brody, the city cop turned police chief of seaside resort Amity Island; Hooper, a shark-obsessed oceanographer hired by Brody to shed light on the sudden shark attacks; and Quint, the grizzled, hard-drinking local shark hunter who takes Brody and Hooper out to sea on his fishing vessel, the *Orca*, on a mission to kill the beast—and, with the first day of filming just over a week away, neither Steven nor Universal had had any luck attaching a big star to any of them. Lee Marvin, Steven's first choice to play Quint, had turned him down. Jon Voight, Timothy Bottoms, and Jeff Bridges had passed on Hooper. Charlton Heston, then entering his fifties, wanted to play Brody, and the film's producers were keen on him, but Steven resisted; he thought the star of *Planet of the Apes* and *Ben-Hur* would date the movie and overwhelm the balance of the cast. He suggested a couple of unknowns whom Zanuck and Brown vetoed in turn. Shortly before flying to Boston, Steven was sitting alone at a party in Los Angeles when Roy Scheider, whose turn in William Friedkin's *The French Connection* had earned him a Best Supporting Actor nomination two years earlier, took a seat next to him.

"You look awfully depressed," Scheider said.

"Oh no, I'm not depressed," Steven answered in a small voice. "I'm just having trouble casting my movie."

"What's the film?"

Steven told him, pitching the whole thing from beginning to end.

"Wow." Scheider smiled. "That's a great story. What about me?"

Steven looked at him. "Yeah," he said. "What about you? You'd make a great Chief Brody!"

Scheider was used to playing cops, as he had in Friedkin's picture, but they were usually tough action men, not fallible and guilty, principled but frightened, as Brody was. He happily signed on for a more complex role, and a rare shot at top billing.

This left Quint and Hooper to be resolved. George had a suggestion for the latter.

"Why don't you cast Ricky Dreyfuss?" he asked.

Steven liked the idea, but Dreyfuss passed, too. He didn't find the part interesting. George worked at convincing him. Gottlieb, who was also friends with Dreyfuss, called him and petitioned him to consider it. Dreyfuss flew in from New York to meet Steven in Boston.

"I don't want to make a film, I want to make a *movie*," the director told him.

"I'd rather see this movie than be *in* it," Dreyfuss argued. "I hate the script."

"We all hate it," Steven answered. "That's why we're fixing it, that's why Carl is here, you've got to trust us to make the changes that are necessary."

They kept arguing about it over drinks, over dinner, after dinner. Over the course of the evening, Steven and Dreyfuss shaped and negotiated a version of Matt Hooper with which the actor was happy.

Finally, on April 29, Steven found his third lead, hiring British actor Robert Shaw to play Quint. Shaw was an old hand with twenty-five years of stage and screen work under his belt, from *Macbeth* in Stratford-upon-Avon to villains in *From Russia With Love* and *The Sting*. Immensely intelligent and talented, he also somewhat looked down on his profession, once asking a reporter: "Can you imagine being a movie star and having to take it seriously without having a drink?"

He longed instead to be known for his writing. He drank too much, and could be alternatively a delight to be around or an abusive nightmare. He was electric on the screen, no matter whether the material was good or bad. He was in debt to both the IRS and Her Majesty's Revenue and Customs, and he had eight kids to feed. He was happy to take Universal's money.

With his three actors finally confirmed, Steven sat down with Gottlieb. They stripped Benchley's book down to its main attraction: the shark. The film adaptation of *Jaws* would focus on thrills and scares, clean and hard as bone. A great white shark—evolution's most perfect killing machine—unleashed on Fourth of July vacationers.

Steven and Gottlieb drove their car onto the ferry to Martha's Vineyard, the island south of Cape Cod that Steven had chosen as his shooting location. He had prepared as well as he could. As spring warmed to summer, the *Jaws* crew only confronted one real problem, but it was a big one.

The shark—the one on the poster, the one featured in every set-piece scene, the showpiece on which Steven Spielberg was staking his career—did not work.

The *Jaws* crew set up headquarters in the quaint seaport village of Edgartown, on the west side of the Vineyard. The locals, at first, thought of Steven and his band as little better than "invaders," in the words of resident Edith Blake, but quickly, she wrote, the "turned-up noses" became "turned-up palms," a volte-face the parochial islanders had become very good at over the first few years of the 1970s, as they began to allow new-built developments and affluent new residents into their previously shabby townships and municipalities. Word traveled through the island that *Jaws* had money and Universal was willing to spend it—on labor, materials, bed and board—and the residents' arms, peevishly crossed across their chests, opened in welcome.

On the first day, a few dozen islanders gathered to watch the Californians work. Steven had scheduled a simple scene to get everyone started—a vacationing college student, played by local Jonathan Filley, walks Roy Scheider's Chief Brody along the beach the morning after the shark's first victim disappears, and they find her horribly maimed body in the sand, sticky with salt and seaweed.

The islanders watched and scratched their heads and whispered.

The film people clearly hadn't prepared for the beach—their tripods stuck in the sand; the dolly tracks, designed for flat studio surfaces, wiggled and bumped—or the wind, which kept huffing across the actors' wireless microphones—or the light, which, on Martha's Vineyard, changes by the minute. Steven rehearsed for what seemed like forever, and then shot the scene ten, fifteen, twenty times.

"Don't they see," the bystanders muttered to one another, "the water is different, the light is different?"

Steven and his crew did not see. The first days of shooting ticked slowly by as they learned how to. Then Steven moved his cameras into small boats out onto the sea, still close to shore, and there was more learning to be done. Salt water doused the expensive cameras. Wind and waves threatened to throw the little boats over. Assistant directors drew up shot lists from weather forecasts phoned in from the National Weather Service, not understanding that the weather on the Vineyard changed as often as the hour. Crowd scenes set on the beach had to be pushed back when production realized the waters off the Vineyard remained icy until at least late May. For a scene in which a band of fishermen publicly display the carcass of a shark they have caught, mistakenly believing it to be the murderous great white, the production bought the corpse of an eleven-foot tiger shark in Florida and flew it up from Sarasota, packed in salt, on a chartered plane. The makeup and special effects crew stabbed and poked and "dressed" it with battle wounds. The rigid cadaver stank; the work done to keep it looking real only made it look ghoulishly fake. No one bothered to ask the local fishermen for an alternative, or they would have been told dozens of tiger sharks could be caught just a few miles away anytime.

"They just don't listen," the islanders repeated to each other, shaking their heads.

The repetition involved in the making of any film—set up, rehearse, action, cut, back to one, do it all over again, over and over—boggled the locals' minds, the absurd requirements of filmmaking even more so. For one scene, set in the water and shot day-for-night, Steven's camera and lighting crews zipped up their wet suits and waded into the shallows with their lights, snaking power cables underwater and back to the shore, a tragic accident waiting to happen—because they needed *more* lights, they said, to turn brightest day into pitch-black nighttime.

"No wonder they all go nuts out in Hollywood," one islander said as he watched.

The locals soon grew fed up with Universal's trucks parked along the beach from Monday to Saturday, blocking traffic and closing off their towns' quaint, narrow streets, idling exhaust fumes into the sea breeze. The Californians turned resentful themselves. They muttered about the tedium of the little town. They grumbled about the constant, greedy hikes in their room rates and restaurant bills. "Summer people" began to arrive on the island for the season, gawking at the film crew as if at a zoo. Only Dreyfuss seemed happy. "Waitresses arrived from the mainland," Gottlieb wrote, "and lots of them had seen *American Graffiti*, which was good news for young Rick . . . he made out all right."

In the middle of June, with filming, as Steven had predicted to Sheinberg, four or five days behind schedule, the *Jaws* crew began working out at sea. Zanuck and Brown estimated the final act of the film, in which Quint, Brody, and Hooper go out onto the water to hunt the shark, would take about three weeks to capture. Every morning, Steven's armada of boats set out from Harthaven, four miles north of Edgartown, and stayed out until sunset, a sixteen-strong fleet including a tugboat headquarters, christened *White Foot* ("mother ship," wrote Edith Blake, but also "restaurant, base, 'john,' and towboat"); a big barge repurposed from an old ferry, the *City of Chappaquiddick*, piled with lights and lenses and generators and special effects gear; the SS *Garage Sale*, ungenerously nicknamed because, weighed down with all the equipment needed to maintain and operate the mechanical sharks and their rigs, it was also a monstrosity patched together, like Frankenstein's creature, from the parts of other boats; and finally the *Orca*, Quint's ship, built from an old wooden lobster-boat hull. All around them were several smaller skiffs and runabouts used to ferry actors, crew, and equipment to and fro.

For the first two days, torrential rain battered the boats from morning to wrap. Then the rain subsided, and Steven learned that the electric generators were not built for the rocking and rolling of the sea, which displaced the oil inside the machines and made them malfunction. Then the sun came out, baking the open barrels of chopped fish Quint, Brody, and Hooper throw into the water as bait for the shark. The already queasy cast and crew, still finding their sea legs, delayed the work even further as they leaned over the ships' sides to be sick. Steven spent an hour setting up a shot, only to find the tide was dragging boats away from each other and out of position. The *Orca*, slow and heavy, needed to be pulled by an off-camera motorized boat, but early into the sea filming, the speedboat yanked the old ship too fast, ripping planks out of its hull, sending the actors screaming Mayday as the boat began to sink.

"Fuck the actors!" screamed sound mixer John Carter, standing next to them, his recorder held high above his head. "Save the sound department!"

Nerves frayed. Dreyfuss and Shaw couldn't stand each other. Scheider raged at the cabin fever of being stuck on the stinking, claustrophobic *Orca*. Back on shore one night, Dreyfuss relieved the tension by starting a giant food fight in the hotel restaurant—the kind of scene unlikely to change the locals' minds about their nutty Hollywood visitors.

A week into filming at sea, and Steven was badly over schedule; the spending was over budget and out of control. Crew and locals alike whispered and tattled: He was about to be fired; new producers were flying in from Los Angeles to take over; the whole production would be taken back to the water tank in the Universal backlot, where it should have stayed in the first place. The actors' strike had been averted, but the first week of July, the Vineyard would open for business and tourists would flock to the beaches. Universal had guaranteed its crew would be long gone by then. "We were shooting away, slowly completing those pages in which the actors acted with each other," Carl Gottlieb wrote later, "relentlessly approaching the day when there'd be nothing left to shoot but the shark."

The day came all too soon. On July 1, crew members put Mattey's shark prototype on its platform, supported by flotation tanks, with divers all around to help it into the water. The platform tipped. The shark sank.

In all, Mattey had built three mechanical sharks for Steven's use. The full-size model rode a wooden "sea sled," towed on a line by the SS *Garage Sale*, giving the illusion, if filmed from above the surface, of the great white moving by itself. The other two sharks came in halves—one the left flank of the fish, the other the right—each with an open side rigged to a mechanical arm jutting out from a platform painted ocean-floor green. These two would be used for "hero shots," or close-ups. Crafted after drawings by production designer Joe Alves, all three models had hard rubber skins stretched over neoprene-foam flesh and steel skeletons, their guts filled with cables and pneumatic hoses, so their heads, bodies, and tails could wiggle, and their mouths could hinge open and shut.

Steven called Mattey's creations, collectively, "Bruce," after his lawyer Bruce Ramer. They were marvels of animatronic innovation, so novel that Mattey's harbor workshop, dubbed "Shark City" by the crew and locals alike, was shrouded in secrecy.

They were also virtually useless.

As the crew dragged the dummies out of Shark City and into the Atlantic Ocean, it quickly became evident that here, too, what worked in the shop did not work in the sea. Salt ate at Bruce's rubber skins. Water gushed out of his eyeballs. His plastic parts soaked up water, and his rubber teeth folded back like putty. His circuits were liable to fry when immersed. The sea sled and ocean-floor platforms jammed and froze. The SS *Garage Sale* was so vulnerable to the waves it needed a support boat to keep it upright, but producers Zanuck and Brown—careful watchers of their budget or, in the word chosen by co-writer Carl Gottlieb, "stingy"—hadn't paid for one big enough.

"You're gonna need a bigger boat," someone remarked from shore when the little vessel set out with its monstrous partner. But the producers didn't listen. Nor had they listened when the special effects crew suggested the sharks be tested in seawater in California before being shipped, in parts, to the Vineyard. These were costly mistakes. Each of the sharks was twenty-five feet long, and the full-size model, which took fifteen people to operate, weighed several tons, as big as Alves figured he could believably make a great white. The entire production ground to a halt whenever the message came crackling on the walkie-talkies that one had to be moved or repaired, which turned out to be all the time. The sharks were scheduled for nine in the morning, and at ten, Mattey would estimate they would actually be ready for eleven. Steven and the actors, called to set at 6:30 in the morning and still having shot nothing by lunch, would look up at the unbroken horizon and groan. Scheider read the paper cover to cover; Shaw hopped on a small boat and went golfing; Steven told Dreyfuss about his longing to make a film about aliens. The young director had planned every shot he needed to take and how long he might need to film it, but "it's not the time it takes to take the take that takes the time," Scheider joked. "It's the time it takes between the takes that takes the time it takes to take."

Every time something went wrong—the shark broke down, lunch was late, a storm rocked equipment all over the boat, walkie-talkies fell overboard—someone on the crew would repeat the line that had become the company catchphrase: "You're gonna need a bigger boat." Scheider started improvising the line into scenes, exasperating Steven, who told him to cut it out.

Back in LA, Universal discussed contingency plans. They could send everyone home except the special effects crew, leave Mattey on Martha's Vineyard to do the shark stuff while Steven and Verna Fields edited what they had back in Los Angeles. Spielberg could come back in September, if he needed, for the bare minimum of pickup shots. The movie was already wildly over budget.

Steven refused to go along. He told Fields not to show any rough footage to anyone, not even the studio, until he was ready, and Fields—whom the studio trusted, the same trust that had led Warner Bros. to let her recut George's *THX 1138* without his permission—this time told her bosses that the footage she was cutting was spectacular, and declined to show them any of it. Some of the executives in Los Angeles suggested firing Spielberg—wasn't he just a TV guy, and a kid at that? Hadn't he only made one feature film, and hadn't that film flopped? Sheinberg, who believed in his protégé, refused to listen.

"Keep going," Zanuck told Steven. "Don't despair, you're getting good stuff."

"Good stuff? You saw one shot in dailies."

"But it was a great shot! Get more great shots like that. Tomorrow, try to get *five* great shots."

Every night, Steven sat on the phone at the log cabin, begging Universal executive William Gilmore to let him keep going, and every morning, he went back out onto the ocean, hoping for better. He spent hours rocking on the sea, ABBA's "Waterloo" playing on a loop on his headphones. Eight hours of work, and he'd get one shot, maybe two, sometimes neither of them great. He stared at the sharks as they were lifted out of the water and into their dry docks, like vessels sunk by the enemy. Alves had drawn his sketches from great whites in attack position, when their mouths are wide open. The longer you looked at Bruce, the less menacing he seemed, and the more he appeared to wear a perpetually stupid, slack-jawed expression.

Bruce got a new nickname. Steven called him "the great white turd."

Anxious as he was, Steven tried his best to meet the moment. He'd always wanted to be hip, and in trying to be so, he only became less so. Early in the shoot, he received word that *Sugarland Express* had won the Best Screenplay award at the Cannes Film Festival—Francis took home the Palme d'Or, for *The Conversation*—and for a while, his confidence was high: He was, finally, a proper Hollywood feature film director. Even the *French* took him seriously.

The residents of Martha's Vineyard, however, did not. They smirked at his getup—the $200 jeans with myriad incongruous zippers, the white turtleneck sweater, the aviator sunglasses. They rolled their eyes as he gamely climbed into any boat he needed to—it had been his idea, after all, to shoot the whole thing out on the ocean—even though he couldn't hide how uncomfortable he felt on them. Soon enough, heat, sand, and necessity got the best of his wardrobe, and he started turning up for work in the cut-off denim shorts and humble T-shirts preferred by the rest of the crew.

The unpredictability of both the sea and his sharks meant Steven had to revise himself, as well as the script, simply to keep up—with circumstances, with cuts, and with his own imagination. "Steve is an opportunist," wrote Edith Blake as she observed the filming. "While directing he's quick to see a scene's potential as a springboard for something else . . . One reason many in the crew found it hard to work for Steve Spielberg was his intense concentration when creating. He would become so wrapped up in his moment that the mechanics of the scene never penetrated his head. When he wanted the impossible, he got it, it just took forever." He had an uncanny ability to remember every one of the hundreds of takes shot over the weeks, every angle and every composition. When an idea came, he knew how to shoot it and where it would fit, as if continually assembling scenes in his head. At some point, desperately frustrated with Bruce's endless malfunctions, Steven thought up an unexpected way to entirely redesign the picture: He would craft most of the film's most terrifying sequences without showing the shark at all. He would shoot from the shark's point of view, an invisible menace always lurking, threatening. Cameras were encased in waterproof protection, and the cinematographer, Bill Butler—who had worked for Steven in TV but also shot *The Rain People* and *The Conversation*, and was trained in the Coppola school of improvisation—invented a platform and case so he could shoot from above the water's surface as well as below.

In the evenings, Steven retreated to the pine log cabin Universal had rented for him, where he stayed with his assistant, Richard Fields (editor Verna Fields's son), and Carl Gottlieb. Every night, the hired cook, Adele Francis, made wholesome yet elaborate meals, and Dreyfuss, Scheider, and others drove up to have dinner around the cabin's long table and pick apart the movie, their own parts, the day's difficulties. Shaw dropped in and drank and teased everyone. Steven's "very spoiled" long-haired spaniels, Elmer and Zalman, followed their owner from room to room, humping legs and nipping at strangers. The guests left around nine, and Steven put himself to bed around ten, leaving Gottlieb to work out how to implement the dinner story sessions into new draft pages. Early the next morning, Steven woke up in the dark house, made a hot cup of tea, and read the pages left out for him by the now sleeping Gottlieb. He headed off to set while Gottlieb, over breakfast, typed up last-minute notes and photocopied the pages before cycling them over to the production office. The whole routine had the energy of making a short film back in Arizona, an energy on which Steven thrived. As anxious and hopeless as he often felt, he never lost his sense of humor. He heard crew members and bystanders opine that *the director doesn't know what he's doing* so many times that he began singing the line to himself, loud enough for everyone to hear—"the director doesn't know what he's doing . . ."

• • •

July slipped into August, and Steven was still filming. Crew members moved out of hotel rooms reserved by vacationers and into short-term leases scrounged up wherever they could be found. "I had terrible, despairing days where I could see nobody hiring me again, and I could imagine *Jaws* being my last studio movie," Steven remembered. "I thought I would probably go on to make independent films if I could get doctors and dentists to put up enough money to finance a little movie with four people playing cards in a room." He couldn't take a break; he knew if he left Martha's Vineyard, he could never bring himself to come back.

He led his fleet out early morning, disappearing over the horizon before Edgartown woke up; by the time the tourists in their shorts and sandals wandered to the beach and harbor, the rubber speedboats of the *Jaws* crew were already well into their day of rushing back and forth to the shore, carrying men, women, batteries, coffee, soup. The hot sun traveled across the sky and to the west, and it was only when it set—as late as eight, nine in the evening, as tourists rubbed lotion into their sunburns and went down for dinner and drinks, "as the last light," Edith Blake wrote, "turned the harbor waters turquoise blue and the east purple"—that Steven's "strange little fleet, running lights atwinkle, would trail into the harbor, carrying their exhausted illusion makers home," tired, cold, skin crusted with Atlantic salt.

Mattey got Bruce working well enough, and the pace picked up. Steven filmed the shark's final, desperate attack on Quint's boat. Early in the sequence, Brody leans on the boat's edge, cigarette burning between his teeth, scooping chum into the sea—when the shark bursts out of the foam, inches away from his outstretched hand. The police chief staggers back to his feet in shock, ash lengthening on his cigarette. He slowly retreats into the *Orca*'s cabin, where Quint is setting up a fishing line.

"You're gonna need a bigger boat," Scheider muttered.

That one, Steven decided to keep.

Finally, on September 15, Bill Butler, his camera and lighting men, Joe Alves, and the special effects crew got together one last time to shoot the film's final payoff: Brody blowing up the shark with a well-aimed rifle shot at an oxygen cylinder jammed in its hungry mouth. They dragged the original model of Bruce's head into the water like a sacrificial offering, stuffed it with gallons of red paint and chopped-up squid, and jammed in four sticks of dynamite. They set up every camera they had onto the SS *Garage Sale*, lenses pointed at the rubber beast. They would only be able to do this once.

"Lord, this place will be a sea of blood," Butler said.

They called action. Scheider pulled the trigger, the special effects crew matched his timing, and Bruce went up into the sky in a deafening spray of gore and guts.

Steven wasn't there to see it. A driver had whisked him back to the mainland the day before. He had heard the crew planned to throw him into the sea in celebration—or punishment—for completing the job, but he was sick of the sea. In a Boston hotel, he and Dreyfuss got drunk and grabbed each other by the shoulders. Filming had taken a hundred and fifty days—ninety-five more than originally scheduled. While they were away, sports seasons had begun and ended. President Nixon had been the subject of an impeachment inquiry and resigned and been pardoned.

"Motherfucker, it's over!" they screamed. "It's over! Motherfucker!"

And then Steven went back upstairs to his room and had a panic attack—jaw clenched shut, heart racing, muscles trembling uncontrollably. In the morning, as Alves put an end, once and for all, to the monstrosity he had created, Steven took the first plane back to California.

For months, he dreamed he was still filming. Still out on the sea, still queasy, still chasing the vision he had imagined. He always woke up before he got it.

· 18 ·

INDIANA SMITH AND FRANCIS'S APOCALYPSE

Back in Marin County, George was stalled. *Star Wars* had grown too big, too complicated. He took long walks with his friend Philip Kaufman, a fellow San Francisco–based filmmaker, whose fourth film, *The White Dawn*, had just come out in July, to broadly negative reviews and indifferent business. Kaufman made pictures that were stylish and sophisticated, if a little staid. He held a history degree from the University of Chicago and, as a younger man, had spent time working on a kibbutz in Israel and traveling across Europe, taking teaching posts in various countries. One late-summer or early-fall day, not long after the resignation of Richard Nixon, George told him about this other fantasy idea he had been kicking around. The thing, George told Kaufman, was about this treasure hunter in the '30s, Indiana Smith, who tries to stop the Nazis from getting their hands on some kind of ancient supernatural artifact Hitler might use to take over the world. George saw himself wrapped up in *Star Wars* for years to come, and he thought Kaufman might be a good fit to direct the adventure movie.

"C'mon," he nudged Kaufman. "Let's do this picture, and we'll get Francis or somebody to get us a deal somewhere."

George didn't have a script yet; in fact, he had yet to work out what the artifact at the heart of the picture should even be. It would function as a MacGuffin—Hitchcock's term for the object or narrative device that kicks a plot into gear, like the military secrets in *The 39 Steps* or the uranium ore in *Notorious*. Hitchcock didn't think the nature of the MacGuffin mattered much, and in this, he and George differed—Lucas felt his MacGuffin should be unique and memorable because it defined the tone and the exoticism, even defined the stakes, of the story. He hadn't found any ancient artifact that suited his needs.

Well, Kaufman suggested, had George ever heard of the Ark of the Covenant? A gold-plated chest, built to specifications given to Moses by God on Mount Sinai, carried before them by the Israelites in exile from Egypt. The Ark had since been lost, or hidden; various religious traditions held that its reappearance would herald the day God showed Himself again to gather His faithful. The divine revealed itself in the Ark, and Moses had spoken to God through an opening in its cover. Perhaps, Kaufman suggested, the Nazis in George's film would want to steal this valued Jewish antiquity, imagining it to wield literal divine power.

George felt himself get excited. His experiences on *THX* and *Graffiti* had broken any desire he had to ever work with a studio again. In the best-case scenario, both *Star Wars* and *Indiana Smith* might become properties as reliable as James Bond—and he would own them both.

Francis turned *The Godfather Part II* around so quickly, it was in cinemas for Christmas 1974, just seven months after the release of *The Conversation*. He always asked Ellie and her friends what they thought. "The wives were very close," remembers Aggie Murch. You could count on them to be honest.

"Well, it's a better film," Aggie told Francis after he screened *Godfather II*. "But it won't make as much money."

He was furious, but she was right. *The Godfather Part II* didn't match the record take of the first installment, though it still became Paramount's biggest moneymaker of the year. When Academy Award nominations were announced in late February 1975, Francis was nominated for Best Director, for *The Godfather Part II*; for both Best Original Screenplay, for *The Conversation*, and Best Adapted Screenplay, for *The Godfather Part II*; and for Best Picture twice, for both *The Conversation* and *The Godfather Part II*. Altogether, his two films garnered fourteen nominations. His sister was nominated for Best Supporting Actress. His father, with Nino Rota, was nominated for Best Original Score. Three of the five nominations for Best Supporting Actor went to actors from *The Godfather Part II*. The last film to have achieved that feat had been the first *Godfather*; no film has received three actor nominations in the same category since. No director in thirty-two years had had two movies nominated for Best Picture in the same year. It was the third year in a row that at least one picture Francis had produced was nominated for Best Picture, after *American Graffiti* the year before and *The Godfather* the year before that, and the second time in three years that he had also been nominated for both writing and directing. No filmmaker in history had ever had such a run, let alone one who refused to even live in Los Angeles.

Francis turned thirty-six on April 7. The Oscar ceremony took place the next day at the Dorothy Chandler Pavilion in downtown Los Angeles. Before the event began, Francis, waiting at the back of the auditorium, unexpectedly found himself standing alongside Robert Evans. In his last year as head of Paramount—he was stepping down to become an independent producer—Evans had earned the studio a total of forty-three nods, more than any one studio had ever received in a single year. He was nominated for Best Picture personally, for producing Roman Polanski's *Chinatown*, tied with *Godfather II* for most nominations at eleven apiece, putting him in direct competition with Francis, who had humiliated him when he had asked, and received, the right to ban Evans from his set. Francis said it was a question of creative freedom. Evans, to the end of his days, said Francis just wanted to hog the acclaim to himself.

They stood awkwardly side by side in their tuxedos.

"It's your night," Francis said.

"No, Francis, it's yours," Evans answered.

They hated each other's guts.

Robert De Niro won the first award of the evening—Best Supporting Actor, for his portrayal of the young Vito Corleone. Francis took the stage to accept it on the actor's behalf. In his seat, Evans smiled politely. Halfway through the night, Francis's father, Carmine, accepted his statuette for Best Score, shared with Nino Rota, soon followed by Dean Tavoularis, winner for Best Art Direction. Entering the final stretch, *The Godfather Part II* had collected three awards; *Chinatown*, none. Goldie Hawn and filmmaker Robert Wise took to the stage and announced Francis as the winner for Best Director. Then writer James Michener immediately called Francis's name again, alongside Mario Puzo's, as winner for Best Adapted Screenplay. Robert Towne, who had written *Chinatown*, collected the award for Best Original Screenplay. Nicholson, star of Polanski's film, and Pacino, star of Coppola's, split the vote for Best Actor and lost out to Art Carney, winner for the minor dramedy *Harry and Tonto*. Marty was up on stage next, accepting the Best Actress statue on behalf of Ellen Burstyn for *Alice Doesn't Live Here Anymore*.

All that was left was Best Picture. Evans still held out hope. His good friend Warren Beatty, who had never presented a prize at the event before, had accepted to hand out the final statuette, in the certainty his pal Evans would be the winner. Beatty was as well-connected as anyone. He was never wrong. Smiling, Beatty walked up to the podium and opened his envelope.

"Francis Ford Coppola," he said, "*The Godfather Part II.*"

Evans, stony-faced, did not applaud.

Francis hopped to the stage and motioned to his co-producers,

Fred Roos and Gray Frederickson, to give their speeches first. Frederickson thanked the crew, Roos the cast. Then Francis took his turn. "Thank you again," he said. "We tried to make a film that would be a really good film, and, uh, and thank you very much." He burst into a huge, incredulous smile, and shook the golden statue by the side of his head. "Thank you."

After the show, he made sure to find Evans. "I've lost all the joy of winning," Francis told the man who had, technically, green-lit his movie. He set his face into a disingenuously pained expression and apologized for "forgetting" to mention Evans in his speech. And then he walked away, his three gleaming Oscars clutched tightly in his large hands.

Francis, wealthier than he had ever imagined possible, expanded his romantic, bourgeois business empire. He and Ellie bought the Victorian estate of Finnish sea captain and winemaker Gustave Ferdinand Niebaum in Rutherford, Napa County, an hour north of San Francisco, along with fifteen hundred acres of the surrounding historic Inglenook winery Niebaum had established in the 1870s. Francis's grandparents had bottled their own homemade vino in their basement in New York; now Francis—in addition to the Sentinel Building and the Pacific Avenue complex—owned one of the most celebrated vineyards in American history.

Yet he remained unsatisfied. It rankled that his biggest successes—the *Godfather*s one and two—were works for hire, films in a franchise, jobs he owed to men like Robert Evans. The personal films he originated himself, like *The Rain People* and *The Conversation*, were well received but, inevitably, overshadowed.

Like George, Francis was tired of going to studios, hat in hand, begging for a green light. He needed an expression of his personal vision to be as big as the *Godfather* movies. He needed a personal blockbuster—and he needed to own it.

The cumulative success of the two *Godfather* pictures was

"tremendous," De Palma says. "But you know, success can be very corrosive. You can do some really stupid things when you're very successful."

Soon after buying Inglenook, Francis traveled down the road to Mill Valley to meet George. He had the choice of any film he wanted to make happen next, and he wanted it to be *Apocalypse Now*. It would take months to develop another original screenplay, he argued. Milius's script was ready and, to Francis, it was just the kind of crowd-pleasing action-adventure popcorn flick guaranteed to make them all a fortune.

"Look, I'll finance this myself now," Francis told his friend. "I've got the money. I've finished *The Godfather*; I'll do it." He wanted to know, once and for all: Was George going to direct it? He'd been working at his space fairy tale for nearly two years and didn't seem like he was cracking it. They had the clout now to make a risky picture like *Apocalypse Now* and retain ownership of it. They'd been waiting half a decade.

Francis's arguments brushed *Star Wars* aside as if it were nothing—a pastime—which was an attitude George had grown used to, even from friends. But the timing didn't work for him. And in his conception, *Star Wars* wasn't a mindless entertainment; it was a passion project, no less worthwhile than *Apocalypse*. He thought he'd be ready to start shooting as early as the following January. He was too close to break momentum.

Francis pushed. He was anxious for George to make the film, "on any basis at all." He would pay the same money Columbia had agreed to two years earlier: a $25,000 fee, and 10 percent of the net on top of that.

George stiffened. He reminded Francis tersely that Fox was paying him *a hundred and fifty thousand* dollars for writing and directing *Star Wars*. "I'd like to do *Apocalypse*, because it's a film I really care about, and I'd like to make it," he said carefully. "But I'm already into this. I just can't drop this at this point. I'll do it after *Star Wars*, but I won't do it before."

In that case, Francis said, he was thinking of directing *Apocalypse Now* himself.

"What the hell, I've got it," he said. "Let me do it, just to get it off the boards."

George felt himself grow upset. *It's* my *picture*, he thought. He knew Francis well enough to know the idea of claiming *Apocalypse Now* for himself hadn't just occurred to him, and knew him well enough to know that, riding on the success of *Godfather II*, he wasn't going to do someone else's picture next "just to get it off the boards." Francis had come to him with an agenda, and had made him an offer that—on paper—George couldn't refuse. "I didn't have any control over the situation," George remembered later. "He had every right to make it; he owned it." He felt drained, disrespected.

"If you want to make it," he said, "go make it."

Francis went ahead.

Years later, he admitted he might have brushed his friend aside a bit too casually. "I don't think I ever became conceited," he said, but after the huge success of *Godfather II*, "maybe I became too ambitious and enthusiastic; maybe that's the same thing." He was oblivious to the pain it caused when he took over. *Apocalypse Now* had been on the first Zoetrope slate. "I had financed it and owned the script, but George was busy . . . and John Milius was also busy, and so it fell to me to direct the project." The decision, he insisted, had been "friendly."

His error with American Zoetrope, the first time around, had been to start with small, artsy, personal projects. This time, he would make a blockbuster. *Apocalypse Now* had a simple plot, an exotic setting, and a string of spectacular set pieces. A grandiose, mainstream adventure movie. "I had this idea," he said, "that if I took this war film, and put some terrific stars together with me as director, I could make a picture and own it, too. I'd been around a long time, done a lot of good work, but I still had to go hat in hand to the movie companies. However, if this picture made a lot of money, I could use that money to build my own movie studio."

He had the clout now. He could raise the money and assemble a cast. All that was left, after that, was to go to the Philippines for a few weeks and make a straightforward, entertaining picture, something like *The Guns of Navarone* or *Where Eagles Dare*.

George handed over the research he and Kurtz had gathered over the years, along with a warning. "Francis," he said, "it's one thing to go over there for three weeks with, like, five people, and scrounge a bit of footage using the Filipino Army. But if you go over there as a big Hollywood production, they're gonna kill you. The longer you stay, the more in danger you are of getting sucked into the swamp."

Francis waved him off. In the jungle, in San Francisco, in New York—it was just another movie shoot. How hard could it be?

· 19 ·

WE COULD GET ANOTHER SCREAM HERE

Throughout the dying weeks of 1974, Steven drove to Verna Fields's little house in Valley Glen every day. He sat with the editor as she pieced together the footage brought back from Martha's Vineyard. An insert shot taken in early July, to take advantage of the lighting or a pause of filming, spliced with another shot taken in early September, and both slotted into a scene from mid-August—Steven remembered where everything fit, no matter how disjointed and fragmented the order of filming. In early December, he took a break and went to see Marty's *Alice Doesn't Live Here Anymore.*

Alice—a tender, heartfelt, funny film, so unlike *Boxcar Bertha* or *Mean Streets*—represented another step forward for Marty. It was his first picture for a studio, and the one that introduced him to relationships that continued to be important for him. He hired an eleven-year-old actress named Jodie Foster in a small part; hired George's wife, Marcia, as his editor. When the film came out in December, it grossed ten times its budget and won Ellen Burstyn the Academy Award for Best Actress and Marty a British Academy Film Award for Best Film, his first major trophy. It was so well received

CBS developed a television spin-off, which premiered in the summer of 1976 and ran for nine seasons.

If not yet one of the unicorns, Marty had become at least bankable, and he considered what to do with the opportunity. He still wanted to adapt *The Last Temptation of Christ*, though he knew it would be a difficult project for which to raise financing. He was also reading *Raging Bull: My Story*, the autobiography of boxer Jake La Motta, a former middleweight world champion and rival of Sugar Ray Robinson. De Niro had dropped by the *Alice Doesn't Live Here Anymore* set to give Marty a copy.

"There are some really good scenes, and he's an interesting character," he said.

La Motta was Italian-American like De Niro and Marty, born in the same Lower East Side streets. He had flirted with both organized crime and show business. But "I didn't know anything about boxing," Marty protested, "and I wasn't interested in films about boxing." He read the memoir and felt no connection. In its pages, La Motta recounted raping a neighborhood girl, nearly bludgeoning a man to death with a lead pipe, beating his wives out of blind jealousy—tales told with a thuggish, confessional narcissism that made the truth difficult to separate from invention.

De Niro explained the story wasn't about boxing. It was about guilt and shame and failure, and about the ability, sometimes even the desire, to take a beating. To rouse Marty's interest, he got Mardik Martin to write several drafts, which no one liked, then gave the book to Paul Schrader, who agreed to take his own crack at it.

Marty felt much more attracted to a preexisting script of Schrader's, an original titled *Taxi Driver*. De Palma had been meant to direct it, but he'd passed it on to Marty. *Taxi Driver* followed Travis Bickle, a traumatized veteran marine who works nights as a New York yellow cab driver and slowly sinks into insanity, disgusted at the moral decay he sees all around him. "I almost felt I wrote it myself," Marty recalled. "Not that I could write that way, but I felt everything. I was burning inside my fucking skin."

De Niro was eager to play Bickle, but the dark, sweaty screenplay made studios uncomfortable. Executives questioned Schrader's main character, Travis Bickle, his lack of backstory and neat, tidy characterization. The writer argued the audience didn't need the exposition to understand Bickle. "His problems aren't your problems," he said, "but his symptoms are your symptoms." Show only the symptoms, Schrader figured, and people would be compelled to try and make a diagnosis. *Don't tell me the moon is shining; show me the glint of light on broken glass*, as Chekhov was thought to have said. Travis Bickle was all broken glass.

Now, however, one young Italian-American director had struck gold with two dark, violent films of his own—*The Godfather* and *The Conversation*—and when the same director had vouched for two younger filmmakers, in George and Marty, their films—*American Graffiti* and *Alice Doesn't Live Here Anymore*—had been hits, too. In April 1974, Columbia skittishly signed on to finance *Taxi Driver*, but only after getting Scorsese, De Niro, and co-star Cybill Shepherd to agree to substantial pay cuts. The budget was set at $1.3 million, just under what Marty had been given to spend on *Alice*.

Danger lurked, but in Marty's personal life. The journalist Julia Cameron was twenty-seven, born and raised in Chicago but now living in Washington, DC. She wrote hip New Journalism pieces for *Rolling Stone* and the *Washington Post*. Her family was Catholic, but she had given up on God early, and—without her consciously realizing it—her loss of faith left a void inside her aching to be filled. She swore like an old-time newspaperman and dreamed of a promiscuous, cynical, glamorous life. She drank so much, and so regularly, that erstwhile colleague Hunter S. Thompson, of all people, suggested she cut down. She decided she would only drink while writing if she took amphetamines at the same time, to keep her "lucid."

She was on assignment for *Oui* magazine, *Playboy*'s more hardcore sister publication, when she met Marty. She traveled to New York and took her seat at a table in the King Cole Bar, at the St. Regis hotel, and waited. And then Marty walked in, short and dark. He said hello, and sat down, and she thought—within seconds, she swore—*My God, I've met the man I'm going to marry*. She paused the conversation halfway through and called her mother to tell her as much.

He was so warm, so alive—the wild gesticulations, the rat-a-tat diction. "He was magical-seeming to me," she said. They finished the interview in his hotel suite, in bed.

Laraine had been steady; Julia was the opposite. Marty wasn't a heavy drinker, but he and Julia shared a taste for cocaine. The drug seemed to alleviate Marty's anxieties, his repression and guilt, his obsession with sin. Not everyone liked Cameron—the critic Pauline Kael suggested Marty was only into her because of the sex, and she was only into him for his money—and Cameron's writer friends warned her the relationship would damage her credibility. But she and Marty gave each other something they needed, destructive as it soon turned out to be for both of them.

She left everything to be with him. In Los Angeles, Marty's new girlfriend came off as a country mouse in city-mouse clothing. Many of his friends and peers seemed to look down on her. Magazine and newspaper assignments dried up, on account of Cameron sleeping with one of the people she had been hired to interview. She felt anxious and vulnerable. She drank more. Marty urged her to "use [her] talents," and she tried to turn herself into a screenwriter. She convinced herself she couldn't put pen to paper unless she was loaded first.

Schrader wrote high; Julia Phillips, one of the producers on *Taxi Driver*, had never met a drug she didn't try. Marty, insomniac and often depressed, saw it as self-medication. Wondered if it could help him work, too.

Some white powder to get started.

A Quaalude split and shared with Phillips to even out.

Up all night, watching movies. Working on their picture about a lonely New Yorker who can't sleep. Can't relate to women as full human beings. Can't handle the sin in the world around him and in himself.

Soon after Christmas 1974, Steven showed *Jaws* in work print form—a cut of the film without music, a sound mix, or visual effects—first to Sheinberg, who liked it; then to Zanuck and Brown, who also liked it; and finally had it screened for John Williams, his composer on *Sugarland Express*. Steven had briefly flown to Japan for the release of *Sugarland* there, so Williams sat alone in a screening room on the Universal lot. He was a humble, friendly man, to whom music was as important, and natural, as breathing. "I came out of the screening so excited," he recalled. "*Jaws* just floored me." The shots from the shark's point of view suggested a personification Williams thought he could put into music; sequences of the three men thrown together on their boat to hunt the monster had the feel of an old-timey, swashbuckling high adventure. Williams went home and experimented on the piano. When Steven returned from Japan, Williams sat down at the keys and played the theme he had designed for the shark: a slow, simple E-F-E-F bass line—a primordial sound, "so simple," Williams said, "so insistent and driving, that it seems unstoppable, like the attack of the shark."

Steven laughed out loud. Williams held his gaze. Steven's face dropped.

"You can't be serious," he protested.

"Well, I think when the basses and celli of the orchestra, maybe supported by timpani or contrabassoon . . . ," Williams said. He played it again, a bit longer, E-F-E-F-E-F-D-F, dragging the notes, explaining how the same motif could be played slow, when the shark was lurking, and faster, when it spurred to attack. The theme suggested the great white's movement. The audience's pulse would quicken with it.

"Let's try it," said Steven.

Williams got together a seventy-three-piece orchestra to record the music on a stage at 20th Century Fox in early March, while the postproduction crew worked on the optical effects. George was there; Steven had called him at home in San Francisco to say, "You have to come down and hear [this] yourself." By March 26, the film was ready for its first sneak preview in Dallas. Steven sat in the back with Zanuck, Brown, Sid Sheinberg, and Verna Fields, who turned on a tape recorder and placed it in her lap to take down the audience's reaction.

Sixteen minutes into the film, the shark kills a little boy at the beach, tearing him off his inflatable raft in an eruption of thick, red blood. A man in the audience rose out of his seat, ran past Steven to the lobby, and vomited all over the floor.

Oh my God, what have I done? thought Steven. *A man has just barfed because of my film.* But then the man wiped his mouth clean—and returned as quickly as he could to his seat.

The crowd cheered, screamed, and laughed as the movie unfurled; they filed back into the street afterward humming Williams's theme as, pretending to be sharks, they crept up and startled each other. Two days later, Steven previewed the picture again in Long Beach, to much the same reaction. The audience was so loud as they left the cinema that Sheinberg, his boss Lew Wasserman, and the studio's sales and publicity executives huddled in the men's room. They had never seen anything like this, they agreed. How could they capitalize on it?

Most prestige films, until the summer of 1975, had been platform releases. Like *The Godfather*, they opened in a handful of cinemas, usually in New York and Los Angeles; then they spread across the country, into more and more screens. Eventually, they played the second-run houses. When *American Graffiti* came out, George's parents had had to wait two months for their son's picture to reach Modesto's little local cinema, and part of the film's success was that it ran and ran, playing a year or more in some places.

Universal executives decided it didn't make sense to roll *Jaws* out slowly. They should make Americans everywhere want to go see Steven's film as soon as it came out. Opening weekend.

The men leaned their heads together and began hatching a release strategy. They would book *Jaws* into four hundred, five hundred cinemas nationwide, simultaneously. (Someone suggested six hundred to a thousand, but Wasserman wanted a balance to be struck: enough cinemas the film was available everywhere, yet few enough that the screenings would still be sold out and news stations could show footage of lines around the block, a visual representation of the film's popularity that would drive people to want to see it more surely than any paid advertising.) They would saturate the market in the week or two leading to the film's release—thirty-second ads on every prime-time show on every television network for three days immediately before opening day; actors guesting on every talk show going; Steven touring from city to city; radio ads, newspaper ads, the cover of *Time* magazine. In the end, said Universal publicity director Charles Ramsay, the studio put up "the largest expenditure on advertising of a release in the history of the company."

It was such an unusual release strategy that, when executives at other studios caught wind, they assumed Steven had made such a bad movie Universal had decided to dump it at once all across the country, in hopes of selling as many tickets as possible before bad reviews and underwhelming word of mouth cut the movie's legs out from under it. Marty, who was about to fly back to New York to start filming *Taxi Driver*, heard the rumors and knew Steven would be anxious. The day the movie came out—June 20, 1975—he took Steven for a drive around Los Angeles to see how bad things were. They cruised from cinema to cinema.

At every single one of them, the line to get in stretched to the end of the block and around the corner.

Jaws took in $7 million its opening weekend alone, the biggest first two days of any movie, ever. It made its shooting budget back in less than a week. Universal opened it in two hundred more theaters the next week, and another hundred the week after that. In just seventy-eight days, Steven's film overtook *The Godfather* as the biggest box-office success of all time. *Jaws*, when all was said and done, brought in $123 million in rentals, $37 million more than Francis's historical hit.

A year earlier, on April 5, 1974, Steven's first film, *The Sugarland Express*, had gone wide the same day the hardcover debut by Stephen King, *Carrie*, had hit the shelves of American bookstores. Neither had met great success. But in 1975, as *Jaws* made the most of its six-hundred-screen saturation release, the paperback edition of *Carrie*—cheaper and more widely available—sold a million copies. Both were early triumphs of mass-market capitalism—fruits of corporate America's eagerness to leave the radicalism and division of the 1960s behind, and corral its consumers into a lucrative, hegemonic monoculture, shaped in the boardroom.

But *Jaws* was also a masterpiece in its genre, every drop of its plot exploited for thrills by a filmmaker who kept trying, right up until the end, to find marginal ways to make it better. One of the film's most memorable moments shows Hooper, in a diving suit, exploring underwater at night after Ben Gardner, a local fisherman, has gone missing. Hooper finds the hull of Gardner's sunk boat, a shark tooth planted in the wood. As he approaches to recover it, Gardner's decapitated, bloated head floats out at him from inside the hull of the wrecked vessel, a jump scared that causes Hooper to drop the shark tooth—and film audiences everywhere to throw their popcorn in the air. It was a shot Steven had filmed himself, the kind of thing he'd done as a resourceful kid in Arizona. Listening back to Verna's tape of the Dallas test-screening audience, he'd noticed a gap in the symphony of shrieks and gasps, and matched it to the scene of Hooper underwater.

"You know," Steven told Fields, "we could get another scream here."

The scene, as it was cut, missed a close-up of Gardner's head appearing from inside the boat. After Universal refused to pay for a reshoot, Steven spent $3,000 of his own money to have the prop head driven from storage to Verna Fields's house, and a replica of the boat hull built at the bottom of Fields's humble backyard swimming pool.

It was like being a kid in Arizona again. He put a black tarp up to block out the sun. He pulled a gallon bottle of milk from Fields's fridge and emptied it into the pool to turn the water thick and murky as the Cape Cod seabed. It took a few takes, but Steven got his shot. "On more than one occasion after the film's release," wrote Gottlieb, "Steven and my wife and I would visit the World Theatre in Hollywood, where *Jaws* was playing, timing our visit to coincide with the moment in the film when the head was revealed. The manager would let us in, we'd stand in the back of the theatre, just to watch the sold-out audience visibly rise out of their seats with a collective shriek."

Another filmmaker might have celebrated the successful test screenings and looked forward to his movie being out, but not Steven.

He could always come up with another surprise, another thrill, another scream.

· 20 ·

BLOCKBUSTER

By the summer of 1975, Francis and Steven had become the two most in-demand filmmakers in Hollywood.

McElwaine fielded calls from every executive in town, but Steven, having made his blockbuster, longed to finally make a film that came from his heart. He had sold a pitch to Columbia back in '73 for a sort of larger-scale revisiting of his teenage *Firelight*. Steven mistrusted authority—he struggled to write any story with a man in uniform as the hero—and he conceived the project as a cynical conspiracy thriller about governmental cover-up of UFOs. Columbia had paid Paul Schrader—whose twitchy paranoia and sweaty Calvinist anxiety seemed a perfect match—$35,000 for a first draft of the screenplay.

The success of *Jaws* gave Steven the leverage to ask Sid Sheinberg to loan him out from his contract. It felt like the right time to spread his horizons and work away from the Universal lot.

He sat down to read Schrader's work, and with every new page turned, his heart sank deeper into his chest. He'd asked for a tale of tension and thrilling set pieces, packed with memorable images—like a flying saucer descending on Robertson Boulevard in West

Hollywood—mature and dark, but still an entertainment. Instead, Schrader had written a religious allegory with barely any spaceships to be seen, a bleak Bressonian character piece about a government agent who investigates and debunks UFO sightings, only to be turned, through an almost literal Road to Damascus revelation, into a believer. He'd ditched Steven's title, *Watch the Skies*, and renamed the story *Kingdom Come*.

"I remember when I met with Steven on it, which became an argumentative discussion," Schrader said. The writer felt strongly that a film about alien life should wrestle with the meaning of the divine. The protagonist should be an archetype, a "superman." Steven had no connection to that thematic framework—total depravity, irresistible grace, predestination. He found Schrader's draft joyless, self-indulgent, and "embarrassing." He wanted a film grounded in everyday, ordinary life, with a blue-collar Everyman as the hero.

"I refuse to write a story about the first man to leave our solar system with the sole goal of setting up a McDonald's!" Schrader sneered.

"That's exactly who I want!" Steven insisted.

They parted ways. Steven toyed with the idea of hiring another writer, but he feared being misunderstood again. "I figured," he said later, "the only person to tell the story at that point was the person who's been living with it the longest"—himself. Francis had always said a director should be able to write—that putting your story down yourself was the only way to make a picture that was fully your own.

"So I rented Francis Coppola's suite at the Sherry-Netherland," Steven said. Francis, then in San Francisco getting started on *Apocalypse Now*, kept a permanent New York home at the old neo-Gothic apartment hotel on 5th Avenue and 59th Street. Steven moved in for six weeks in July 1975, with *Jaws* raking in cash at box-office tills around the country. He filled the rooms with books, transcripts, outlandish stories in the *National Enquirer*. He pored over dozens of stories of close encounters with alien life-forms. 1947: Civilian pilot

Kenneth Arnold observes nine silver disc "flying saucers" flying in formation above the Pacific Northwest. 1955: A family in Kentucky claim aliens surrounded their farm and took them hostage, dissecting and experimenting on their livestock. 1961: Barney and Betty Hill, of Newton, New Hampshire, claim to have been abducted, while driving on US Route 3 at night, by humanoid beings flying a rotating, pancake-shaped craft. 1966: Unidentified flying objects hovering over swamps in Michigan are observed by several dozen people, including police officers.

Steven cautiously described himself as "agnostic" about alien life, but privately, he was becoming something of a believer. "I read everything on the market," he remembered. "I interviewed enough people to know that all of them could not possibly be lying." He was intrigued by the classification system invented by J. Allen Hynek, an astrophysicist adviser to the US Air Force on UFO sightings and founder of the private Center for UFO Studies. Hynek's "Close Encounter" scale ranked UFO sightings from 1 ("nocturnal lights") to 6 ("Close Encounters of the Third Kind," or CE3): incidents in which a witness sees not just lights, or craft, but alien life-forms. Hynek, originally a skeptic, had reached the same conclusion as Steven: He could not make sense of how so many people—many of them well educated and rational, some of them trained military men—could be hallucinating or wrong.

Steven reached out to Hynek. He renamed the movie *Close Encounters of the Third Kind*. He invited the acclaimed science-fiction author Isaac Asimov to visit him, and Asimov dropped by the Sherry-Netherland one day, though he had no clue who the baby-faced filmmaker was. He heard Steven out, then told him testily that he "wasn't interested in a film that glorified flying saucers."

At the end of the summer, Steven flew back to Los Angeles with about half a draft ready. The film would be about a man in Indiana who comes across aliens on a deserted road at night, leading to subliminal hallucinations and the breakdown of his family life, much like what had happened to Barney and Betty Hill, and also about a scientist like Hynek, investigating UFOs for the United Nations. Matthew Robbins and Hal Barwood suggested a third plotline about a three-year-old child who is kidnapped by the aliens. Steven spent the next ten weeks hunkered down in his living room, sleeping during the day and writing at night, from eight PM to eight AM, weaving the narrative strands together. He listened repeatedly to "When You Wish Upon a Star," from Walt Disney's *Pinocchio*. The song had the wonder and hopefulness he'd felt as a child, lying with his father in the desert, watching lights streak across the black canopy of the sky.

Marty wrapped his own picture for Columbia, *Taxi Driver*, that same August. Filming had taken place under a heat wave, a sanitation strike, the specter of New York City going bankrupt. The end of the Vietnam War felt like both a relief and a shameful defeat. It was "a cokey movie," producer Julia Phillips wrote in her diary. "Big pressure, short schedule, and short money . . . Night shooting. I have only visited the set once and they are all doing blow."

De Niro had committed to the part of Travis Bickle with the intensity he was fast becoming famous for—obtaining a driver's license and working as a cabbie; losing thirty pounds; obsessively listening to a tape of the diaries of Arthur Bremer, would-be assassin of 1972 presidential candidate George Wallace. Marty committed in his own way, drenching himself in the nihilistic despair that saturated every frame. It was the most violent film he'd made yet, so violent that when Columbia CEO Stanley Jaffe screened a cut in late September, he threatened to take the movie away from Scorsese unless he recut it to avoid an X rating from the Motion Picture Association of America. Marty called Steven, Milius, and De Palma to his house on Mulholland Drive to rant, tears in his eyes. He smashed a glass bottle on the kitchen floor. He could only stop throwing things when they pinned his arms down. He went back to the Columbia lot in the following days and stole the film's work print, sneaking the reels off the property in the trunk of his car. He called Phillips in the middle of the night.

"There's only one way to deal with Stanley Jaffe," Marty said, in a serious murmur Phillips thought sounded like a voice-over. "I'm gonna go out and buy a gun—a little gun, I'm a little person—and I'm gonna shoot him."

He was no longer rational. Coke gave him energy, but it frayed him like an old rope. Marcia sat with him in the editing room well into November, swiveling back and forth on her stool. He popped Quaaludes and washed them down with champagne. In the end, Marty cut a few frames out of the final shoot-out and desaturated all the blood so it looked rusty brown instead of bright red. The MPAA gave him an R rating. Columbia backed off.

Thanksgiving came and went, and Francis, at home in Northern California, rewrote Milius's screenplay of *Apocalypse Now*. He completed a draft on December 3. "The Lucas-Milius script simply took [from Conrad's novel] the metaphor of the boat going up the river and the name Kurtz," and originally Francis had intended to follow the simplicity of this thread. But the more he worked, the more one-dimensional Milius's writing seemed, and the more interested he became in creating a descent into the absurdity and brutality of war, hewing closer to the moral core of *Heart of Darkness*—as much an indictment of the war in Vietnam as Conrad's book had been of white colonial rule over Africa. Francis began, as usual, to see something of his own demons in the material, a question he wanted to ask of himself. The title page of his draft, crediting Milius not as a co-writer but as the author of an "original screenplay" Francis had adapted, was suggestive of his process: a bit of Milius, a bit of Conrad, a heap of himself. The plot was episodic and the ending open. What might Willard meet at the end of his descent into madness? Who would he be? What would any of it mean?

Francis raised $7 million from foreign exhibitors in exchange for the right to eventually distribute the finished film in their own territories, a process known as "pre-selling." Francis promised them a star-studded epic. He announced publicly that Steve McQueen would star as Willard and Marlon Brando as Kurtz, before either of them had signed on the dotted line.

McQueen soon got cold feet at the idea of spending seventeen weeks in the Philippines. Francis offered the part to Al Pacino, who turned him down for the same reason. *Variety* announced Gene Hackman would play the supporting role of Colonel Kilgore, but negotiations fell apart when Francis asked Hackman to work for no up-front salary.

Francis was sure, at least, that Brando would commit to the film. They were great friends, weren't they? *The Godfather* had resurrected Brando's career. He called Brando, and Brando didn't answer. He called Brando's agent, Jay Kanter.

"He's not interested in a part," Kanter said, "and doesn't want to talk about it."

Francis called McQueen's agent at William Morris and offered the actor Kurtz, a part for which he'd only have to spend three weeks abroad. At the same time, he sent the script to Clint Eastwood with a note offering him Willard. McQueen's agent called back, told him McQueen would do it, but only for the same $3 million fee he'd have received to play Willard.

"The film will earn it back in foreign sales anyway," the agent said. He'd done the math; that was what McQueen's name was worth, whether it was for three weeks' work or seventeen.

Word came back that Eastwood didn't understand the script. Francis called James Caan and offered him Willard and a $1.25 million fee.

"Two million," Caan countered.

Francis offered one twenty-five again. They were friends, Jimmy was negotiating, he wasn't going to turn him down.

But Caan turned him down.

One by one, Francis's casting options faded away. Martin Sheen passed on Willard (scheduling conflict). Jack Nicholson passed on

Willard (scheduling conflict), then passed on Kurtz (not interested). Robert Redford passed on both. Francis flew to New York to give Pacino the hard sell, and Pacino didn't say no, but he didn't say yes, either, which, if you knew Al, was a no. As far as Francis was concerned, he'd made all these people's careers—*The Godfather* had made Al Pacino and James Caan; it'd restored Marlon Brando when no one would touch him. Now he was sticking his neck out and needed them, and they turned their backs on him?

A little bit, he might have thought, like when he had staked his name to bring George and the other USC kids to San Francisco to partake in American Zoetrope. Then, too, everyone had fed off him and left him hanging.

Francis grew so frustrated that, when he returned to California, he scooped his five Oscars into his arms and hurled them out the nearest window and into the backyard. Twelve-year-old Gio, ten-year-old Roman, and four-year-old Sofia ran outside to pick up the golden pieces.

On December 13, the board of 20th Century Fox convened for its annual meeting, at which they would decide whether to green-light George Lucas's *Star Wars*. George hadn't given the studio brass much to inspire confidence: a few concept sketches, an ever-changing script full of incomprehensible jargon, a projected budget that had hit $7 million and kept rising. After learning that Fox had closed down its special effects department in a round of cost-cutting measures, George had founded his own special effects company, called Industrial Light & Magic and staffed with a motley crew of college students and engineers in a vacant warehouse in Van Nuys. This upset the suits, too. The development money Fox had been spending on design and visual effects was going, some of them believed, into growing George's own business.

"The board never had enthusiasm for the project," remembered

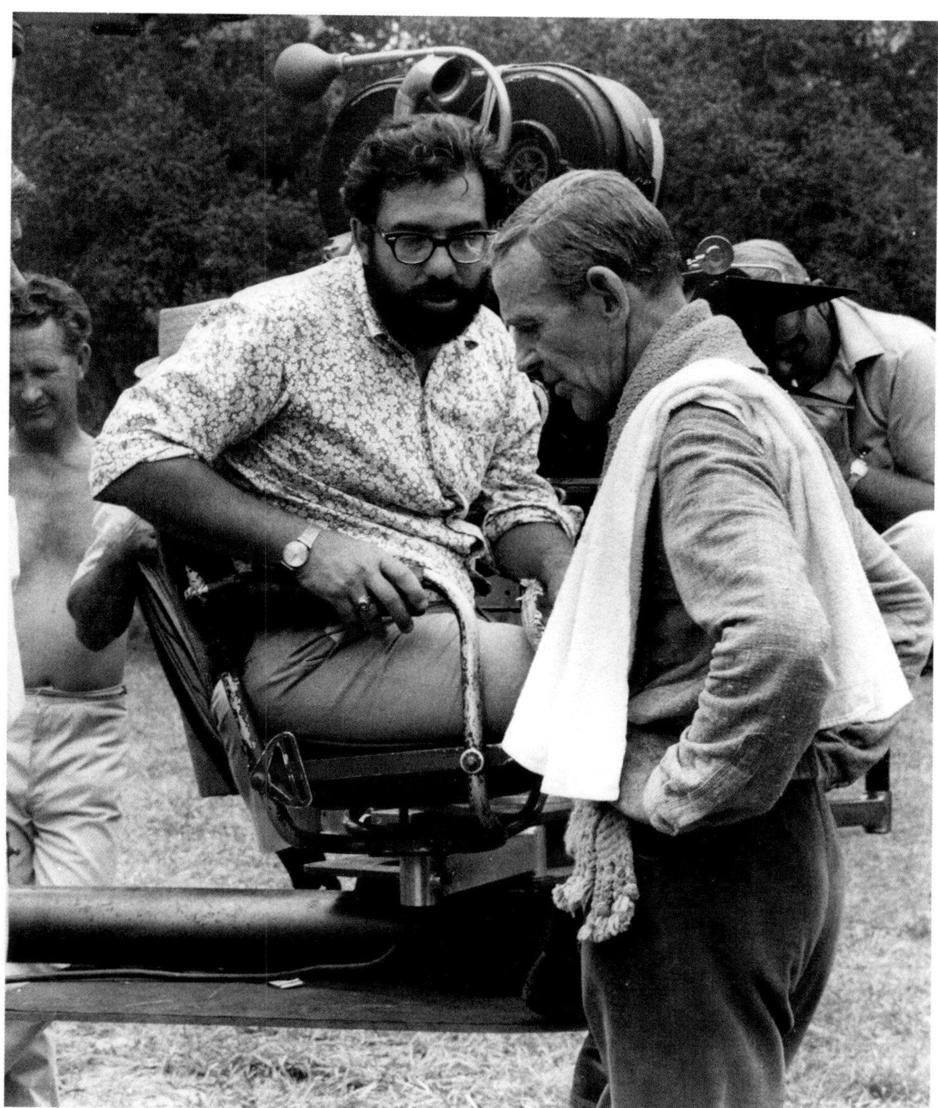

Francis Coppola and his star, Fred Astaire, on the 1968 set of Francis's first studio picture, *Finian's Rainbow*. (WARNER BROS. / PHOTOFEST)

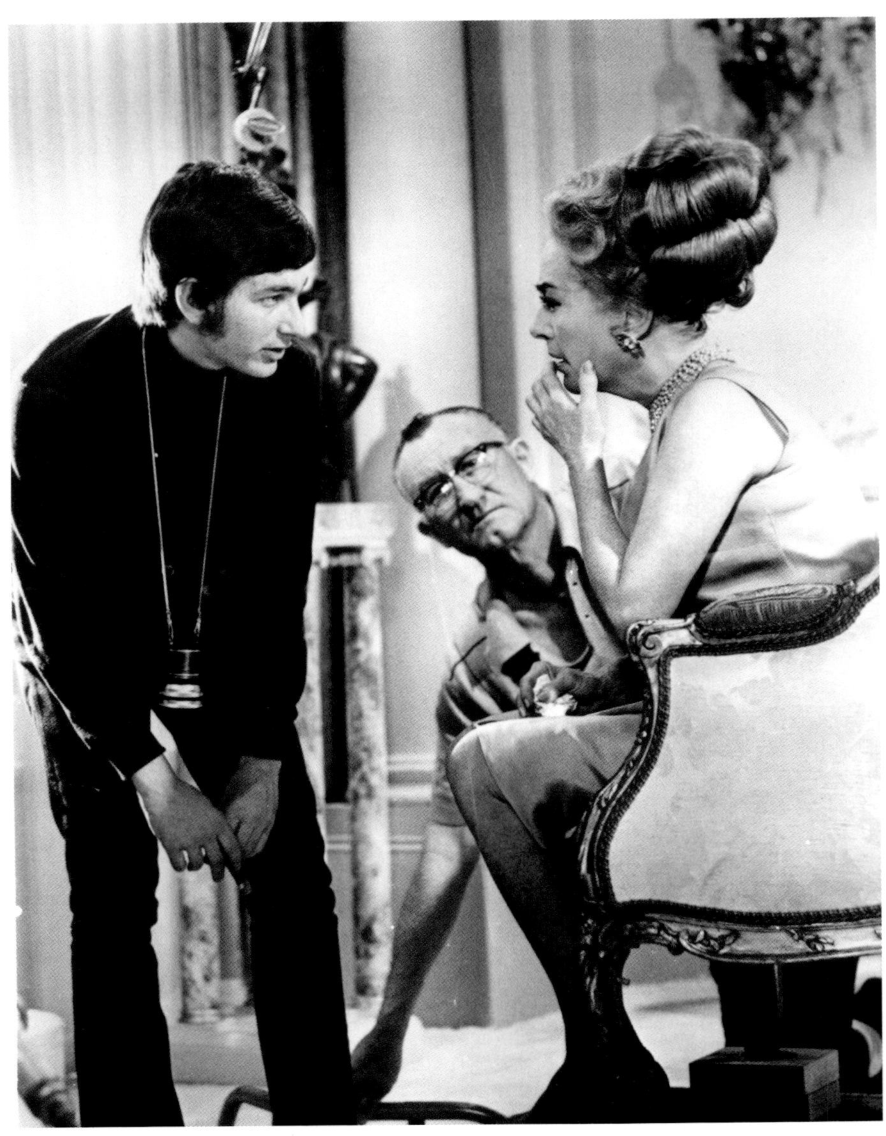

Steven Spielberg directing Joan Crawford in the television series *Night Gallery*, his first professional job, after signing a seven-year contract with Universal.
(UNIVERSAL TV / PHOTOFEST)

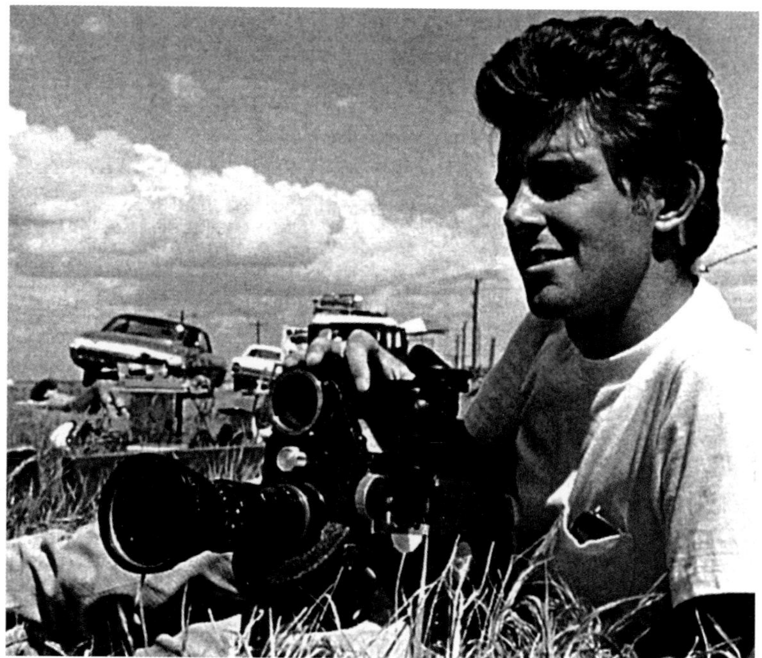

George Lucas with the camera he used to film a behind-the-scenes documentary of the making of *The Rain People*. He had shaved his beard as the crew traveled through the American South. (AMERICAN ZOETROPE / SKYWALKER RANCH)

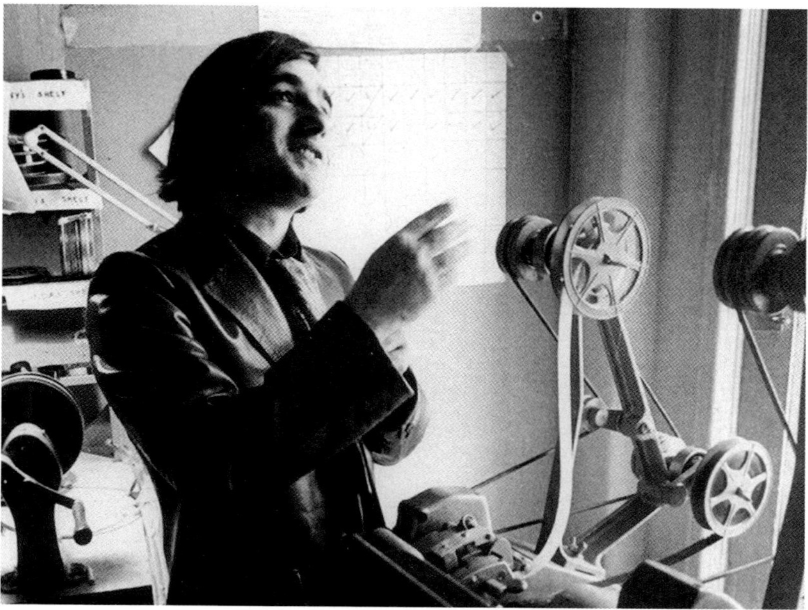

Martin Scorsese in 1969, two years after the release of his first film, *Who's That Knocking at My Door*, and on the brink of leaving for a new life in Los Angeles. (PHOTOFEST)

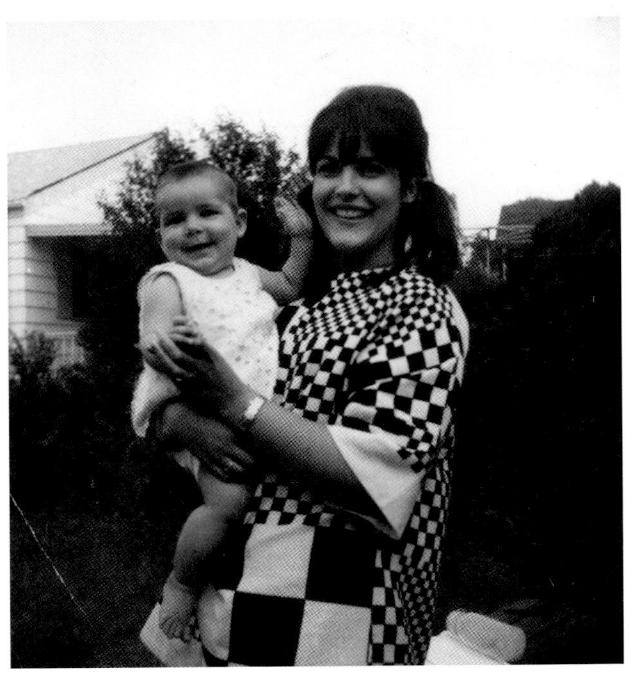

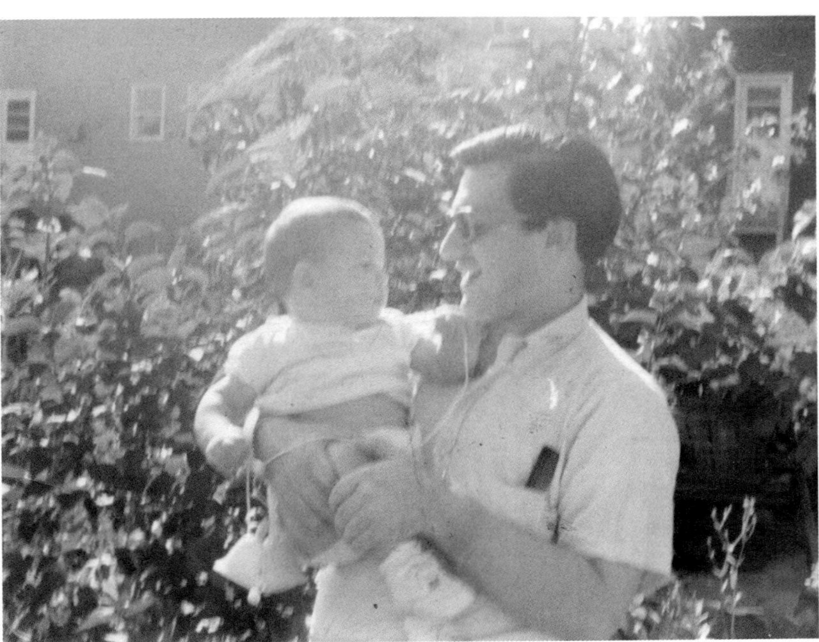

Laraine Brennan and Martin Scorsese with their daughter, Catherine, in the summer of 1965. (LARAINE BRENNAN)

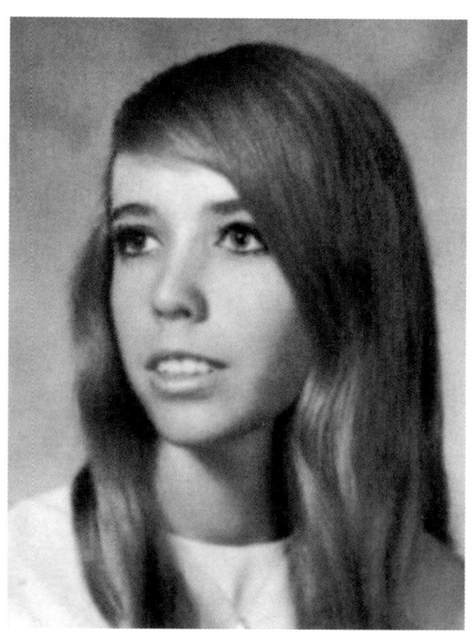

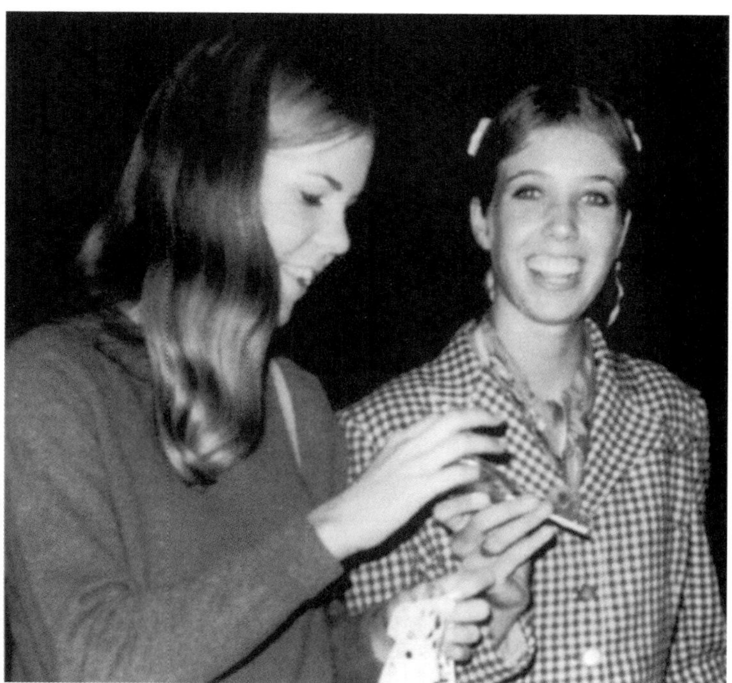

Melissa Mathison (*top, bottom right*) as she appears in the 1968 Providence High School yearbook, her senior year, around the time she met Francis Coppola. (PRIVATE COLLECTION)

Martin Scorsese's NYU classmate and first wife, Laraine Brennan. (LARAINE BRENNAN)

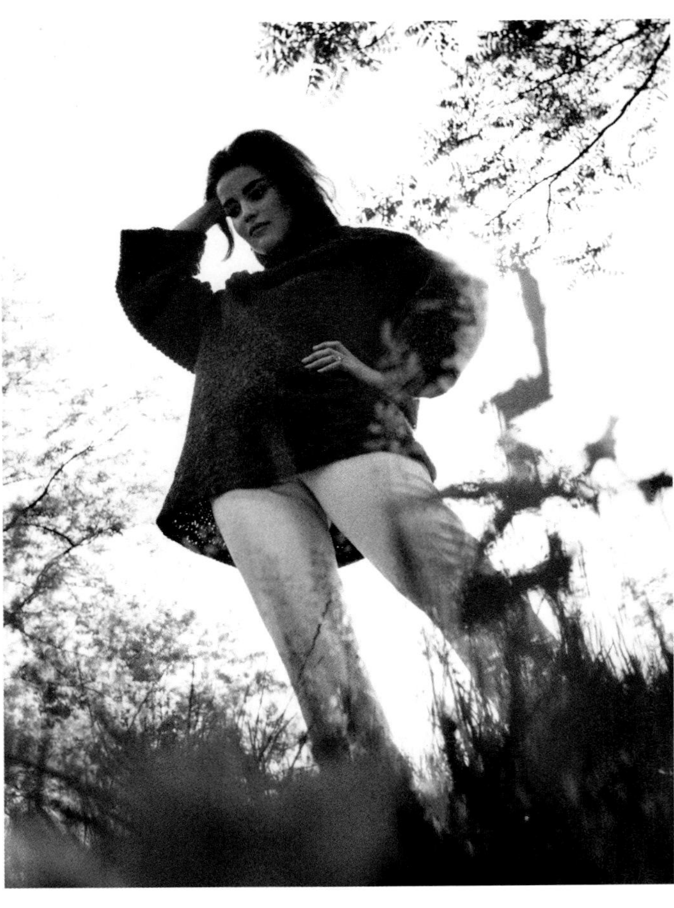

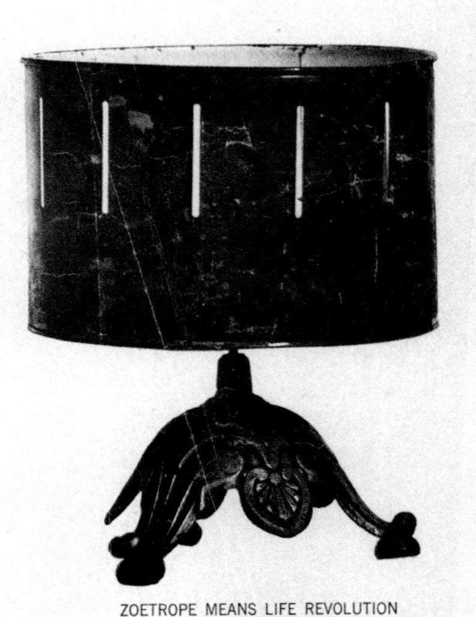

The zoetrope device Mogens Skot-Hansen gifted to Francis Coppola, and which gave Coppola's company its name. Pictures were printed on the inside of the cylinder; looking at them through the moving slits when the cylinder was spun created the illusion of motion. (AMERICAN ZOETROPE)

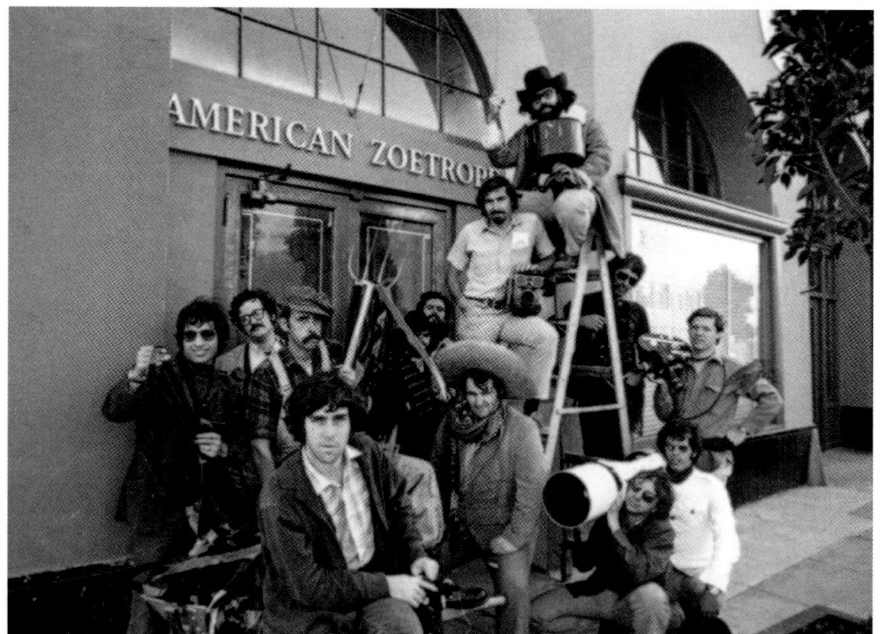

The founders of American Zoetrope, standing on Folsom Street in 1969, including Walter Murch (dressed as a farmer, with pitchfork), John Milius (in sombrero), George (in background, hidden behind a big hat and sunglasses), and Francis, sitting on the ladder, holding the zoetrope gifted to him by Mogens Skot-Hansen. (AMERICAN ZOETROPE)

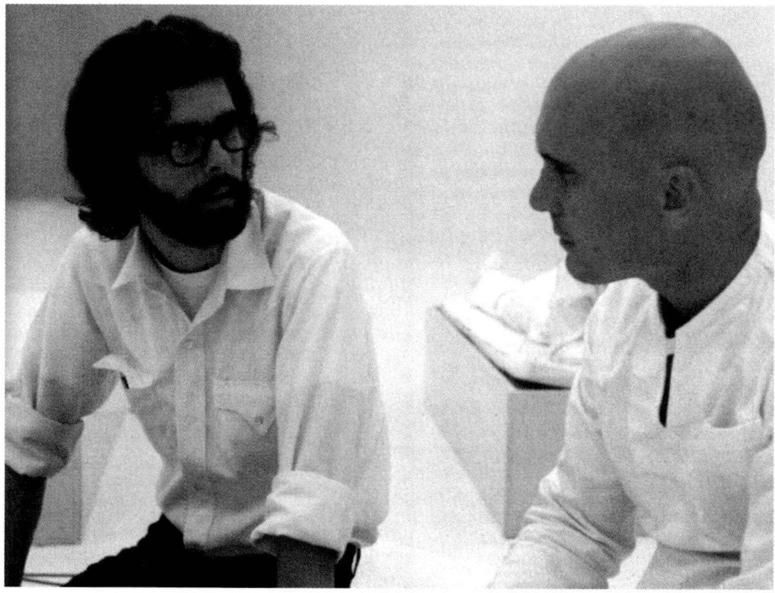

George Lucas directing Robert Duvall on the set of *THX 1138*, his directorial debut—and the only film the original American Zoetrope produced before Warner Bros., financing the company, pulled the plug. (WARNER BROS. / PHOTOFEST)

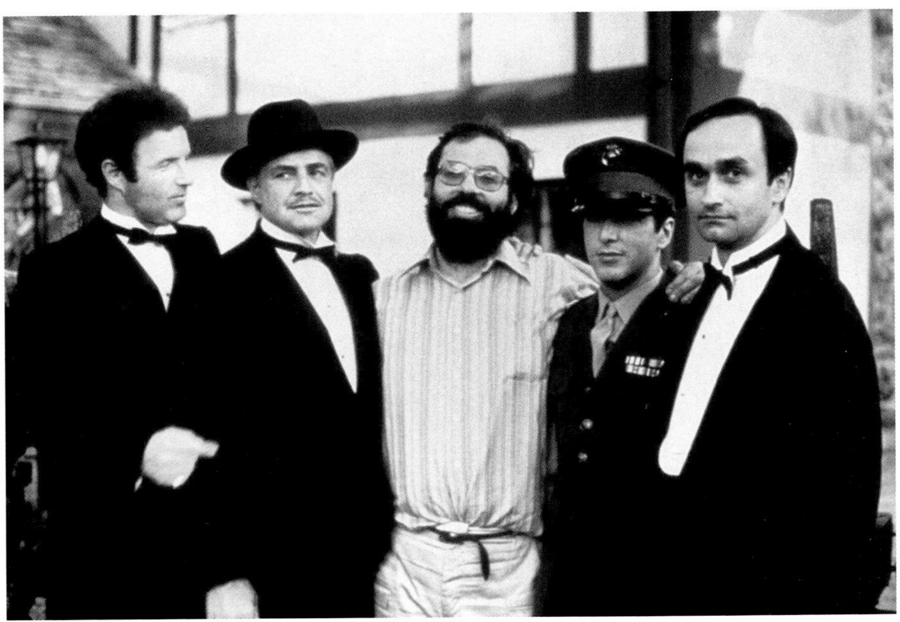

The Godfather family on location in New York City: Francis, James Caan, Marlon Brando, Al Pacino, and John Cazale. (ZOETROPE STUDIOS / PHOTOFEST)

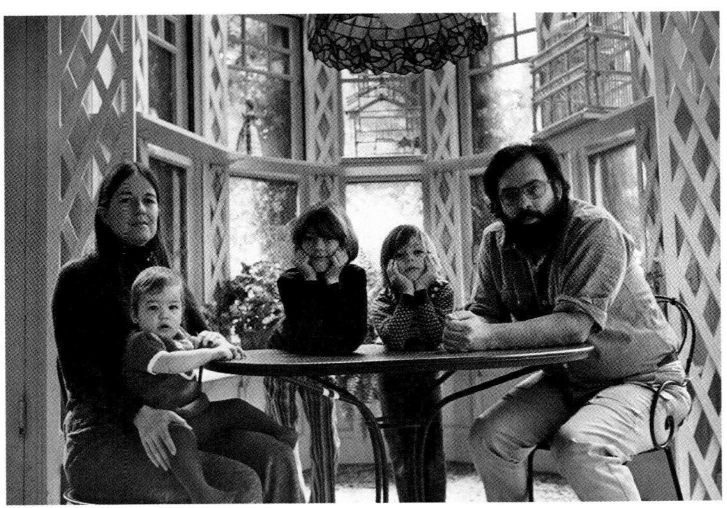

The Coppola family at home in San Francisco, soon after the completion of *The Godfather*: Eleanor, baby Sofia, Gian-Carlo, Roman, and Francis. (TED STRESHINSKY / CORBBIS VIA GETTY IMAGES)

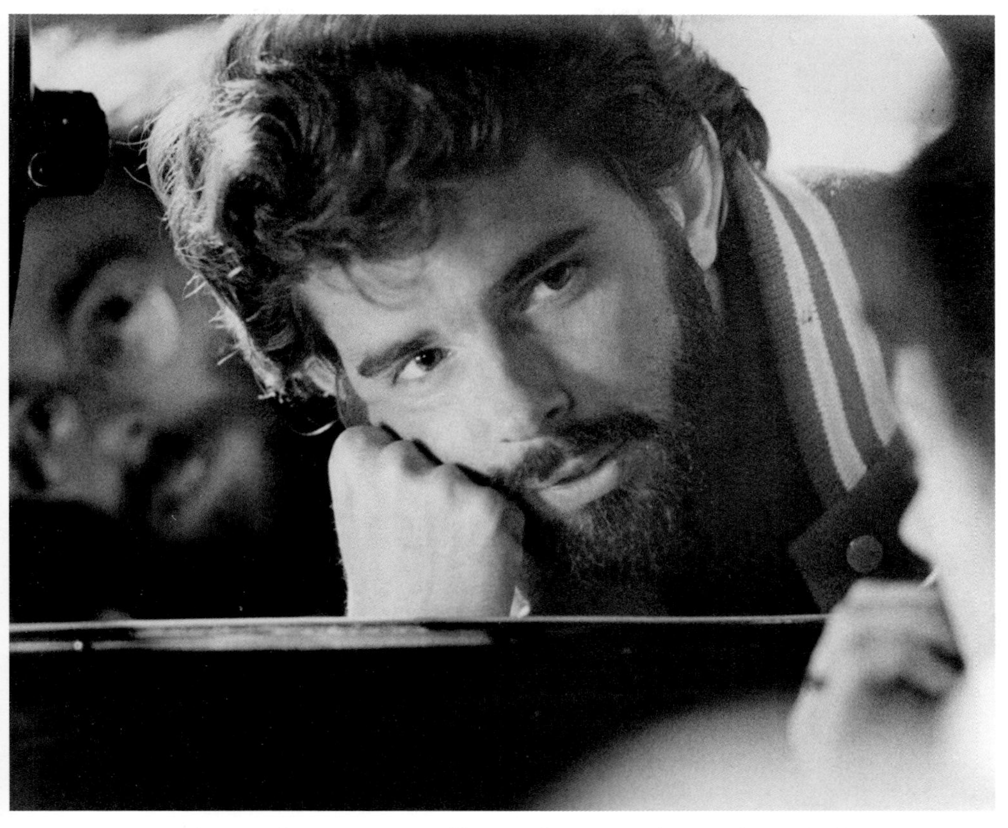

George on the set of *American Graffiti*—with Francis, his producer, looking over his shoulder. The project started as George's reluctant attempt to make something warm and commercial, and became the most profitable independent film ever. Francis regretted passing on the opportunity to own it. (UNIVERSAL PICTURES / PHOTOFEST)

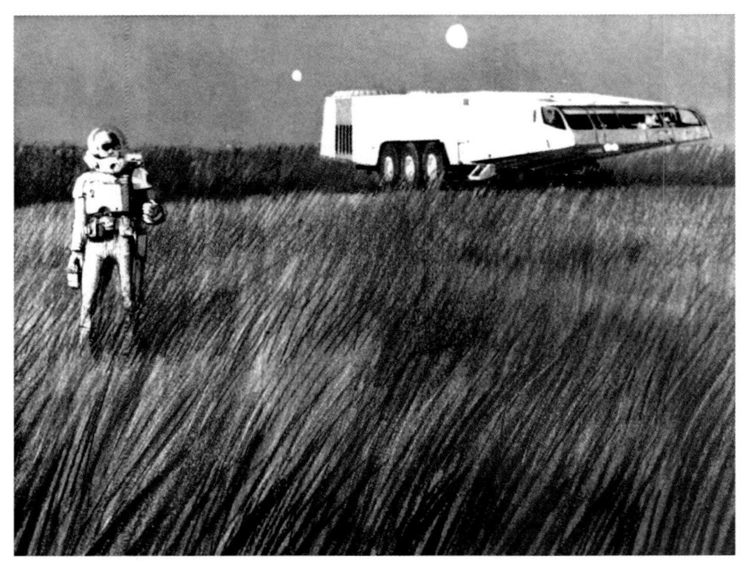

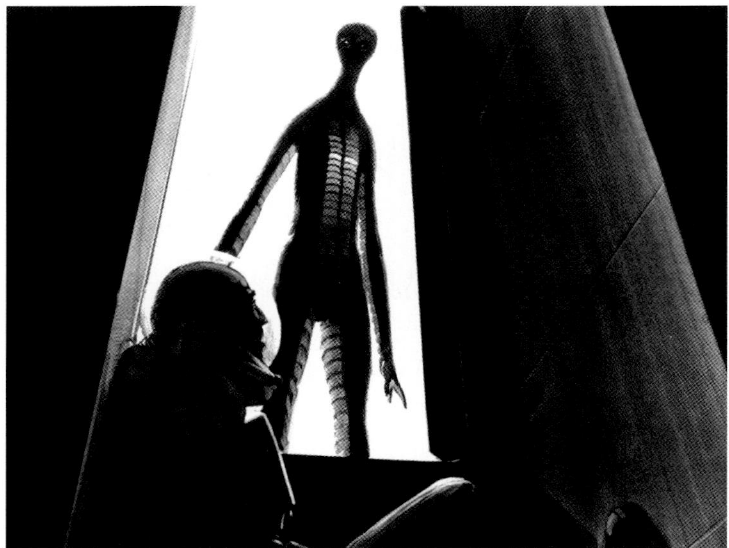

Ralph McQuarrie, an engineer for Boeing, created concept art for a science-fiction film written by Hal Barwood and Matthew Robbins, which Steven Spielberg considered directing. The film was never made, but the art made an impression, and McQuarrie went on to create much of the key concept art for *Star Wars*. (HAL BARWOOD)

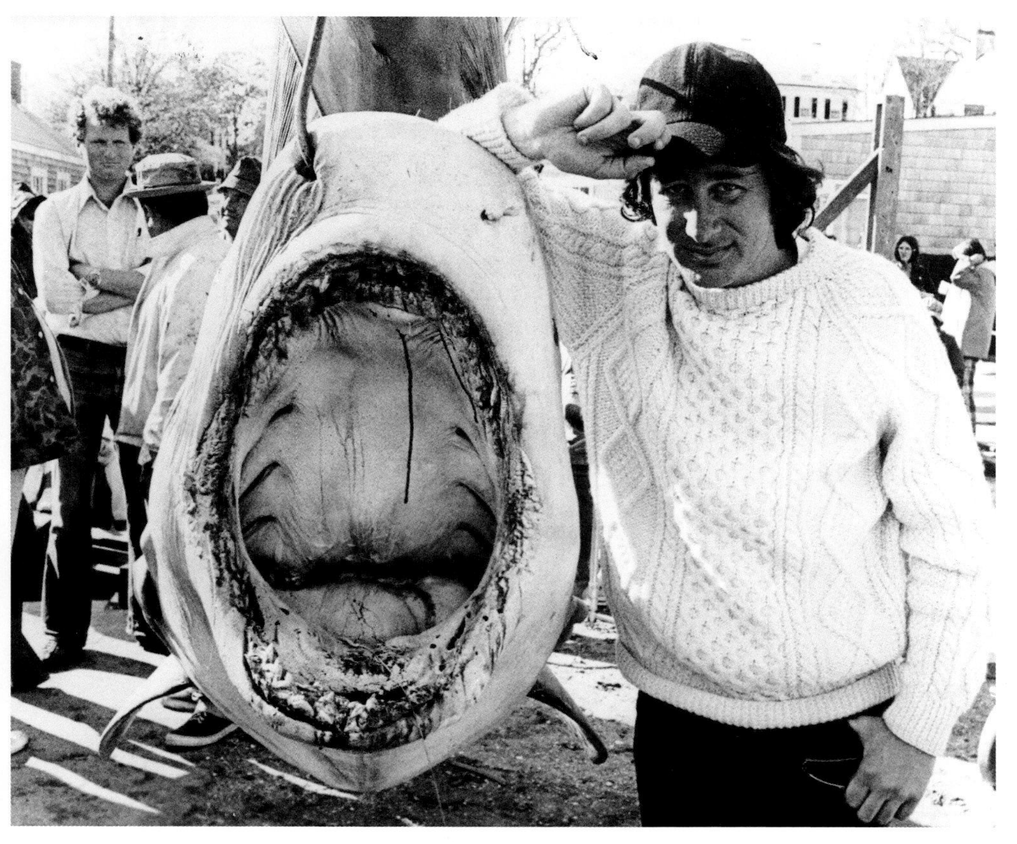

Steven struggling through the making of *Jaws*. (UNIVERSAL PICTURES / PHOTOFEST)

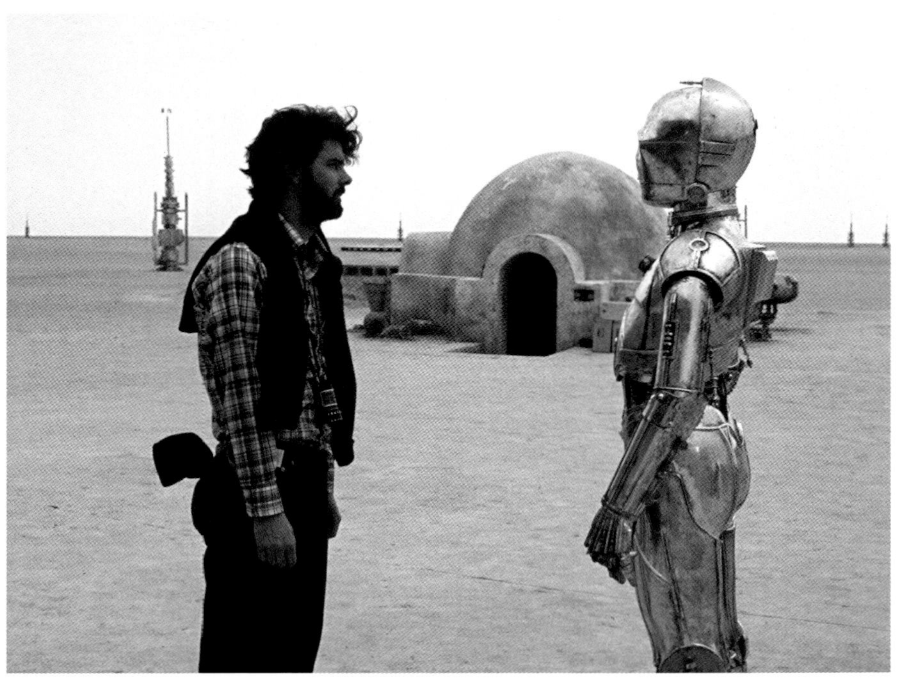

George filming *Star Wars* at Elstree Studios in Tunisia. He found the shoot exhausting and distressing. (LUCASFILM LTD. / TWENTIETH CENTURY FOX FILM CORPORATION / PHOTOFEST)

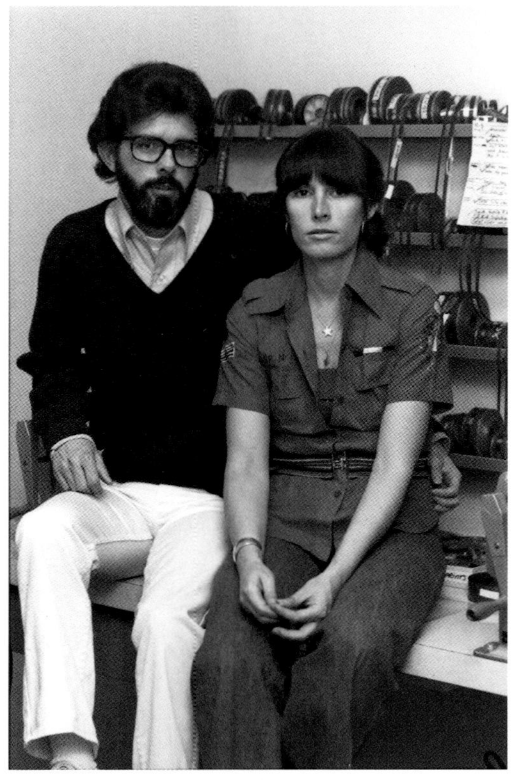

George and Marcia Lucas, who lived such a quiet life Francis called them "country mice." (JULIAN WASSER ESTATE)

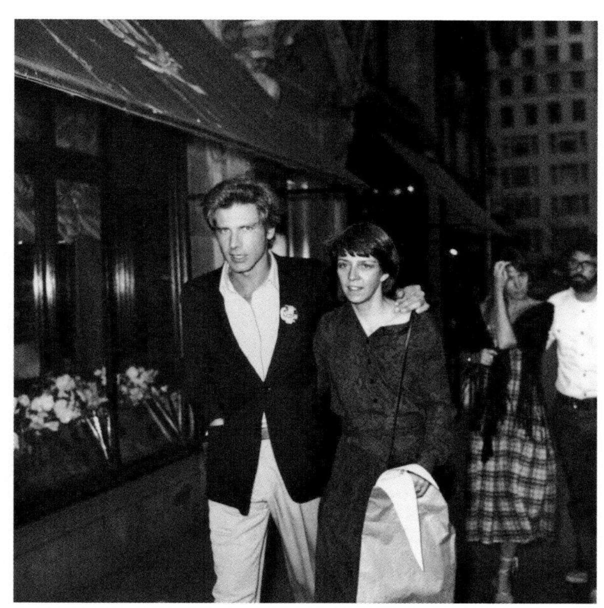

Harrison Ford and first wife, Mary Marquardt, with Marcia and George Lucas in the background, in New York City in early June 1977, just days after the release of *Star Wars*. The film made Ford one of the most recognizable—and desirable—men on planet Earth. Both he and Marquardt blamed celebrity, in part, for the failure of their marriage. (FRANK EDWARDS / FOTOS INTERNATIONAL VIA GETTY IMAGES)

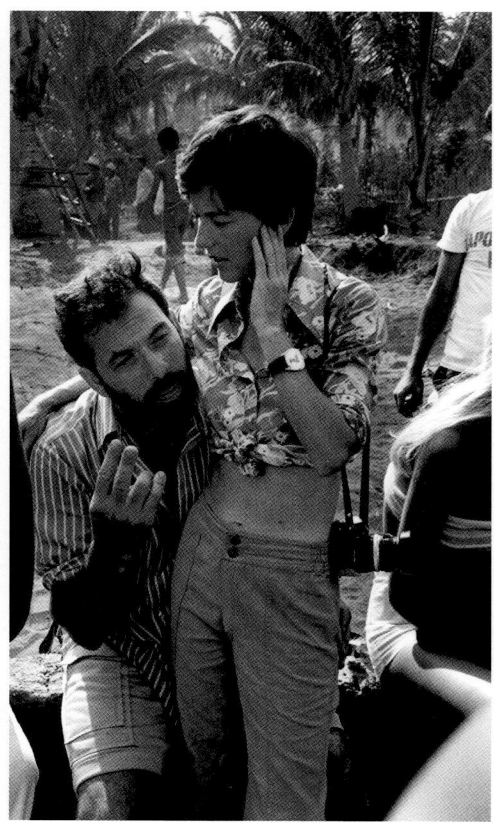

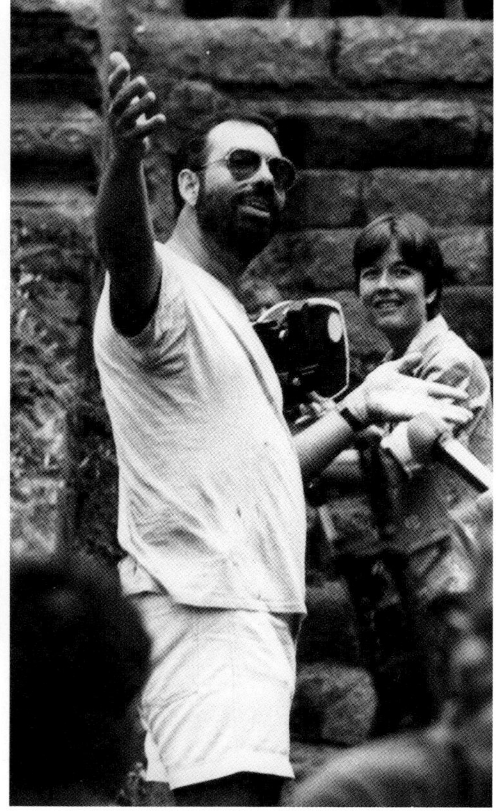

Eleanor Coppola learned about Francis's yearslong affair with Melissa Mathison while in the Philippines, on the set of *Apocalypse Now*. (AMERICAN ZOETROPE)

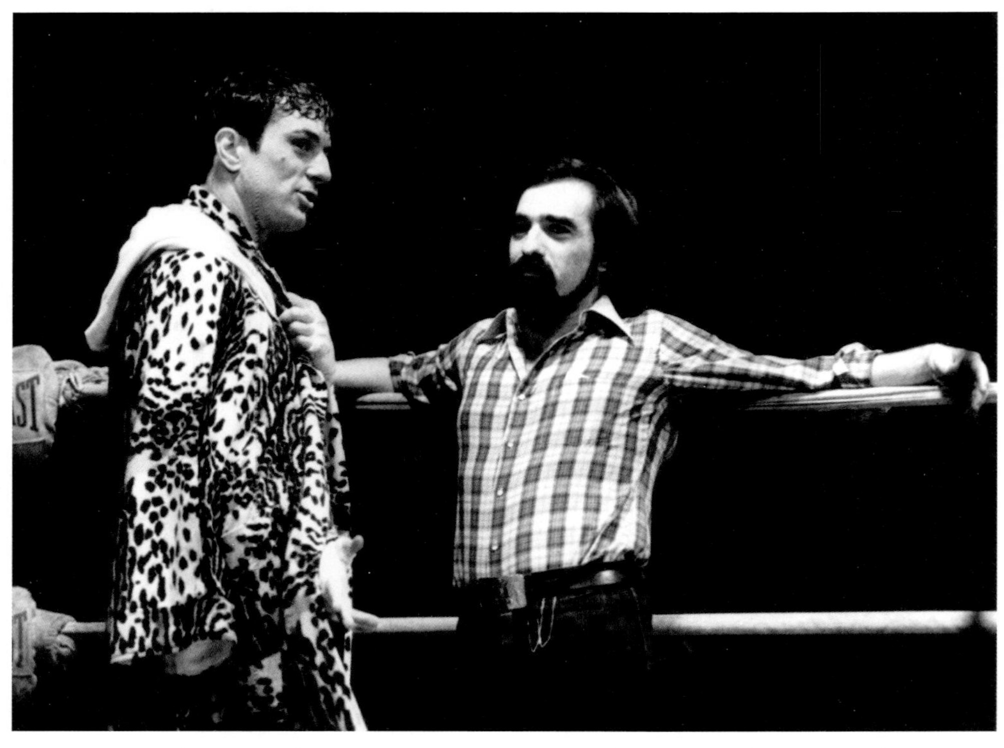

Marty in the ring with Robert De Niro. *Raging Bull* resurrected Scorsese's desire to make films, and live, his way. (UNITED ARTISTS / PHOTOFEST)

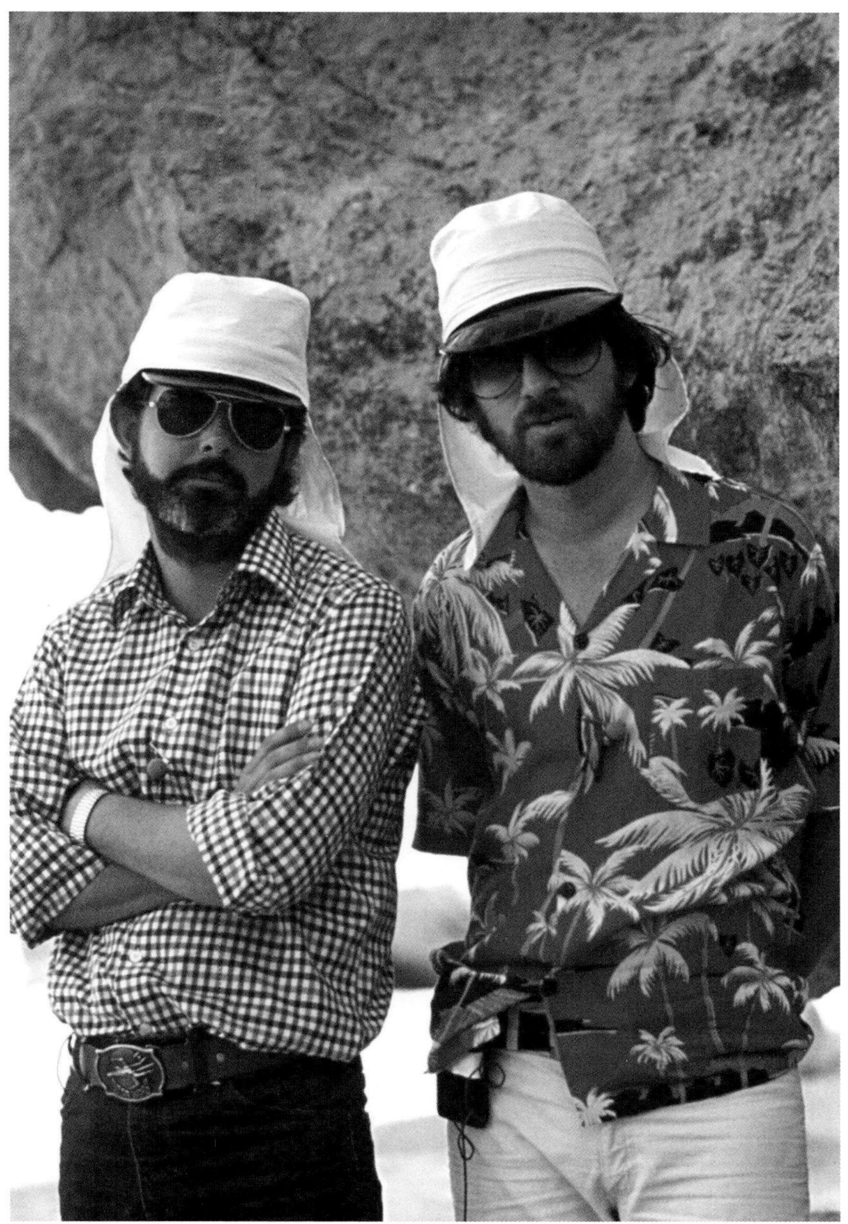

George and Steve on the Tunisian set of *Raiders of the Lost Ark*. Conceived and produced by Lucas, the film, along with *Star Wars*, contributed to Lucasfilm's financial independence—but was also partly responsible for Hollywood's obsession with franchiseable intellectual property. (PHOTOFEST)

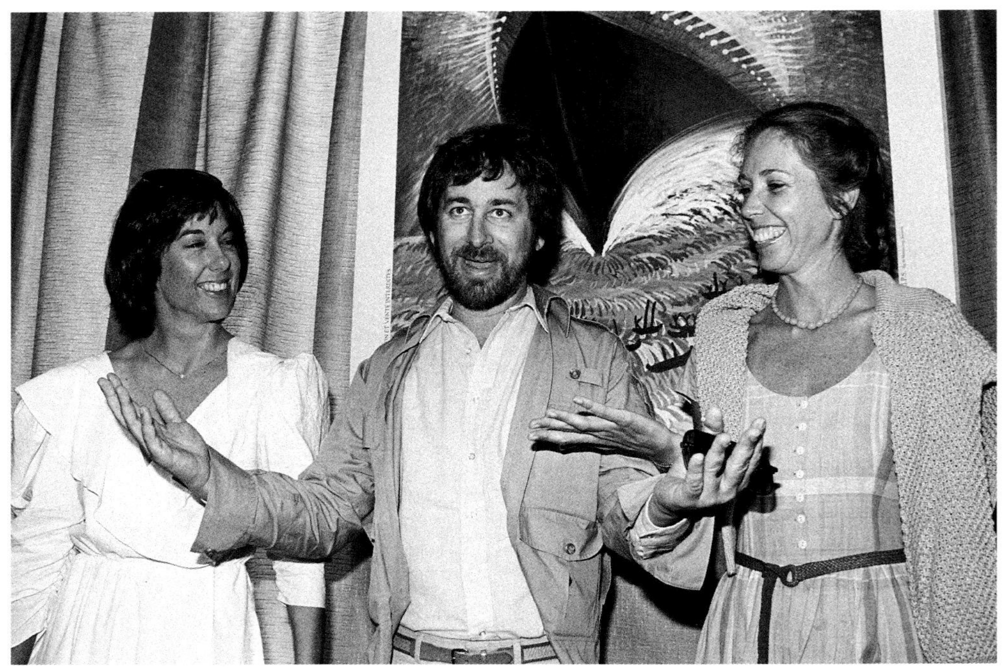

Steven and the women who helped make *E.T.*: producer Kathleen Kennedy (*left*) and screenwriter Melissa Mathison. (PHOTOFEST)

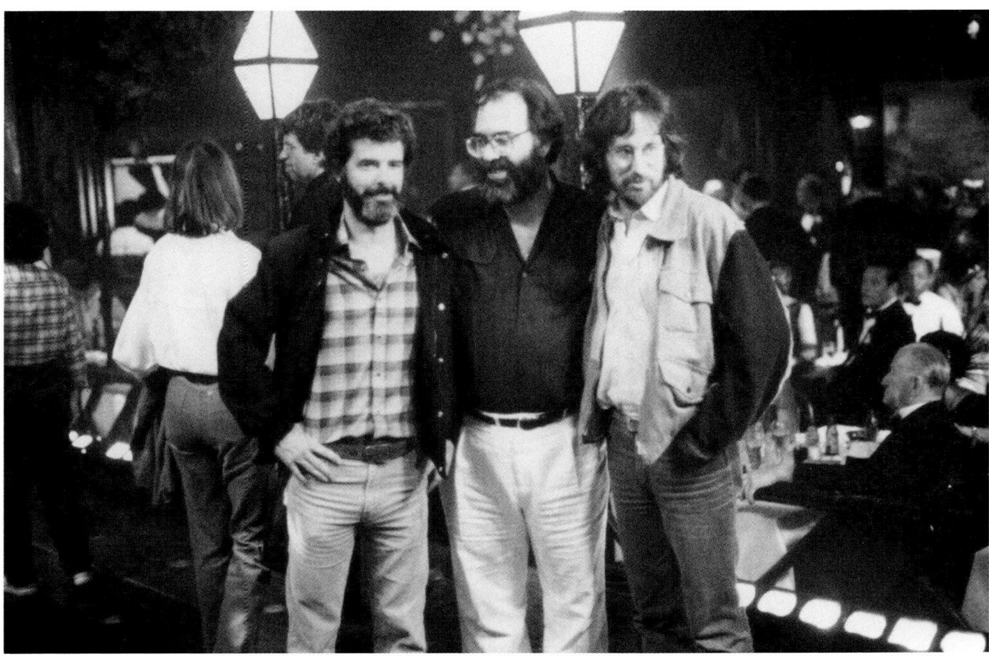

George Lucas, Francis Coppola, and Steven Spielberg in 1983, together on the set of Francis's *The Cotton Club*. (AMERICAN ZOETROPE)

Warren Hellman, a billionaire investment banker who sat on Fox's governing body.

George took a page out of Francis's book. He sent his agent, Jeff Berg, and his lawyer, Tom Pollock, to tell Fox he was making the film, "whether they were in or not."

Alan Ladd pushed for the former.

"I'm a believer in this," he told his board. "We've gotta go ahead with this project. Now's the time we really have to get behind this."

The board green-lit the picture. George was committed to the modest compensation of $150,000 plus 40 percent of the film's net, not gross, profits that Ladd had negotiated for his writing and directing services when Fox had first optioned the treatment in the summer of 1973, before the huge success of *American Graffiti*. But the initial memo had left many other terms undefined, and now George asked to retain the copyright to *Star Wars*, as well as control over any sequels or spin-offs—and to retain the rights to the film's merchandising, including toys, games, apparel, and pressings of the soundtrack.

The copyright request was unexpected but not uncommon—increasingly, studios paid to produce movies but structured the deals so that the ownership of the project, and therefore the responsibility for completing it on time, remained with the film's producers, limiting the studio's exposure to overages.

Merchandising and sequels, on the other hand, were little more than an afterthought, so much so that lawyers sometimes referred to the paragraphs dealing with them as "the garbage clauses."

Fox, gladly, acquiesced to George's requests.

With his green light secured, George's attention turned to casting. He wanted unknowns to play his three leads—young Jedi Luke Skywalker, the space pirate Han Solo, and the captive Princess Leia Organa—and he was reluctant to work with anyone he'd directed before. Fred Roos, back as his casting director, made it his task to convince George that Harrison Ford was Han Solo. He'd known George long enough now to know he liked an idea best when he felt he'd been the one to come up with it. George came into the Zoetrope offices in San Francisco one day to meet Richard Dreyfuss, and Roos arranged for Harrison to be there—as a carpenter.

"I'm not working a fucking door while Lucas is there," Ford said when Roos first brought up the idea, but Roos kept pushing. So here was Ford, kneeling in the hall, tool belt looking not unlike a gun belt on his hip, fixing up the wooden frame in a way not too dissimilar to a space pirate fixing up his broken-down ship. George walked in and said hello, and something clicked.

Here's a possibility, he thought.

"I wanted someone just like Harrison, but not Harrison," George said later, "because he was in *Graffiti*, and I didn't want people thinking of another film while watching *Star Wars*—I wanted it to be new."

He asked Ford if he would read the part of Han Solo during screen tests in Los Angeles. Ford agreed. The sessions took place at the Goldwyn Studios on December 12, 15, and 30. George shared them with De Palma, who was looking for unknowns of roughly the same age as George's characters to play the high schoolers in *Carrie*, an adaptation of Stephen King's novel, which De Palma was directing for United Artists. Women tested for Princess Leia and the two lead roles in De Palma's film, telekinetic Carrie White and remorseful bully Sue Snell. Men tested for the part of Sue's boyfriend Tommy, and for either Luke Skywalker, Han Solo, or both.

Over the three days in the little faux-Spanish building on the lot, Lucas and De Palma saw every hopeful actor in Los Angeles—De Palma easygoing and talkative, George all but mute in a high-backed wicker chair. In came Kurt Russell, Christopher Walken, Perry King, William Katt. Twenty-four-year-old Karen Allen, who had yet to appear in a movie. Twenty-eight-year-old Farrah Fawcett, a year before being cast on television's *Charlie's Angels*. Twenty-five-year-old Sissy Spacek, who had already had her breakthrough in Terrence Malick's *Badlands*. Up-and-coming stage actors Sigourney Weaver and Amy Irving, both around their mid-twenties. On the final day, Roos slipped in television actor Mark Hamill and Debbie Reynold's daughter, Carrie Fisher, who was living in London and studying at the Central School of Speech and Drama. Roos liked Fisher best, but he confessed to her that George pictured Leia as a young teenager and was hoping to hire thirteen-year-old Jodie Foster, who had spent the summer playing a child prostitute in Marty's *Taxi Driver*. Foster was interested but already under contract to star in Disney's *Freaky Friday*, with a shooting schedule set to overlap the one penciled into the calendar for *Star Wars*. George considered fourteen-year-old Terri Nunn, soon to be lead vocalist of the pop band Berlin, before whittling his list down to two nineteen-year-olds: Koo Stark and Fisher. They were strikingly similar: bright, funny, and gorgeous, both from show business families—Stark's father, Wilbur, had produced film and television since the 1940s—and each with limited screen acting experience. Koo had appeared in one of her father's smaller pictures and popped up, uncredited, as a bridesmaid in *The Rocky Horror Picture Show*. Carrie had stolen a couple of scenes earlier that year in Warren Beatty's *Shampoo*.

Fox, eager for star names to protect their investment, offered the part of Han Solo to Al Pacino. Hot off a back-to-back-to-back run of *Serpico*, *The Godfather Part II,* and *Dog Day Afternoon*—three nominations for Best Actor in three commercial and critical successes—Pacino had become American cinema's hottest property. Every script came across his agent's desk, whether he was right or wrong for it; he joked that studios would have given him Queen Elizabeth to play if he'd asked for it. The diminutive kid from the Bronx, already an overthinker, took uneasily to the fame and acclaim he somehow had always known was coming his way. "I always root for the losers, until they start winning," he admitted, "and then I say to myself, Oh man,

I'm not rooting for them anymore." Now he was a winner, and his new status brought not relief, but a sort of dissociation.

"*Star Wars* was mine for the taking," Pacino remembered later, "but I didn't understand the script." The actor was indecisive at the best of times. He turned it down.

George placated the studio when he hired Alec Guinness, an Oscar winner and established name, to play the wise old Jedi Obi-Wan Kenobi, for a fee of £15,000 a week and 2 percent of the net profits. (Nobody who wrote contracts in the Fox legal department expected there would be any net profits.) He weighed the chemistry between the younger actors he'd seen. He liked Christopher Walken—he had a "maniacal" intensity—but Walken seemed too old to banter with a nubile nineteen-year-old princess, even more so if Leia remained fourteen or fifteen, which she might do, as George kept unscratching Terri Nunn back onto his list. She was blond and slight, like a fairy-tale princess, but edgy. George liked Fisher, but she was sweeter, warmer. Mark Hamill was perfect for Luke Skywalker as Luke was described on the page, but he riffed best with Harrison Ford, and George still clung to the idea he wouldn't work with the same actors again . . .

Round and round he went. Across town, Steven was going through the same pains trying to cast *Close Encounters of the Third Kind*. He offered the lead role of Roy Neary to Steve McQueen, who turned him down, apologizing that he couldn't cry on cue. He pursued Dustin Hoffman, who read Steven's screenplay and thought, *That's the best script I ever read and I'm not gonna do it.* Like Pacino, with whom he competed for roles, "I think I had a problem with success," Hoffman said. Steven went to Pacino, too, and to Gene Hackman and Jack Nicholson, walking the same path Francis was treading. They all said no. Slowly, almost by default, he turned to Richard Dreyfuss, in much the same way George was giving in to Harrison Ford. His and George's films were sides of the same coin: both science fiction, but one realistic and taking place on Earth, the other a fantasy set in outer space; both dependent on the credibility of their groundbreaking special effects. The man Steven had hired to design his, Douglas Trumbull, was the man George had first sought to run Industrial Light & Magic. Each of the filmmakers was motivated by the emotions of his childhood. For George, it was the comfort of comic books and Saturday morning television—the warm, aspirational optimism that surrounded a little middle-class white boy in Modesto in the '50s. For Steven, it was "When You Wish Upon a Star," but also the ominous quiet of rural towns and suburban streets, the lurking tension of divorcing parents—the wonder and terror that surrounded a little Jewish boy in Arizona in those same 1950s. George Lucas believed in the goodness of humanity. He thought it needed reinforcing, and that it would be good for children of the '70s to be reminded of it, but deep down, he knew it to be real.

Steven Spielberg wasn't so sure. He could still taste the bloody noses given to him by antisemitic bullies. He never forgot the crooked numbers tattooed on the old people's forearms, or moving from neighborhood to neighborhood, until he and his family were the only Jews, feeling as solitary and forsaken as a boy whose dad had left, or a boy looking up at the vast, cold, unfeeling expanse of the night sky.

Marty, too, ended 1975 driven by impulses branded on his soul in childhood. On December 30, the same day George put Mark Hamill and Carrie Fisher on tape, he ran off and married Julia Cameron in her hometown of Libertyville, Illinois. "I got pregnant on our wedding night," Cameron recalled. "Like a good Catholic girl."

The church had given Marty his own unhealthy expectations. Many of the characters he wrote were infused with that very Catholic "torment" he suffered from himself, he said—"the well-known tendency of some men, especially those raised in the church, to see women either as Madonnas or as whores."

"You're raised to worship women," Scorsese told Roger Ebert in 1976, three months after he married Julia. "But you don't know how to approach them on a human level, on a sexual level." He lived the pattern he wrote into his films: He idealized a woman and then pushed her away.

Taxi Driver came out in February 1976, in the old platform release, starting at the Coronet Theatre in New York. Marty's intransigence paid off; his film was met with universal acclaim and strong box office—no blockbuster, but his biggest success yet.

Steven Spielberg had his trouble with women, too. Julia Phillips, who produced *Close Encounters*, as well as *Taxi Driver*, remembered a day around this time when Steven auditioned, for the same role, both the young and acclaimed theater actress Meryl Streep—and "some bimbo whom he is fucking." He took to fame and success with an awkward, sometimes self-absorbed lack of guile. A week after *Taxi Driver*'s release, Steven welcomed a camera crew into his office at Universal to record his reaction to the televised announcement of the year's Academy Award nominations.

"My name is, uh, Steve Spielberg, and I just directed a movie called, uh, *Jaws*," he told the camera haltingly, with a winsome mixture of awkwardness and self-satisfaction. "And *Jaws* is about to, uh, be nominated in eleven categories. You're about to see a sweep of the nominations. We're very confident this very moment, so you all have a seat, and we'll get on with it." The couple of friends he had with him cheered and clapped. An assistant served coffee and tea. Steven's friend Joe Spinell, an Italian-American actor who had appeared in *Taxi Driver* and both *Godfather* movies, wore a suit over a *Jaws* T-shirt and grinned excitedly.

"Who has the envelope?" he called. "We're ready!"

They assembled around the television as a presenter announced the nominees for Best Achievement in Direction: Federico Fellini, for *Amarcord*. Stanley Kubrick, for *Barry Lyndon*. Sidney Lumet, for *Dog Day Afternoon*. Robert Altman, for *Nashville*. "And Miloš Forman, for *One Flew Over the Cuckoo's Nest . . .*"

Groans and gasps rippled around Steven's office.

"Wow, I didn't get it!" Steven exclaimed. "I didn't get it!"

His head was in his hands.

"I wasn't nominated!" he wailed. "I got beaten out by Fellini!"

Spinell threw his hands in disgust. "That's, that's—I can't believe it."

The presentation moved on to the nominees for Best Actress.

"Wait a second," Steven joshed, unsteadily. "We have—the shark was an actress."

When *Jaws* was nominated for Best Picture—the only film in the category not to also receive a nod for director—Steven cheered half-heartedly.

"That's bullshit," Spinell announced. "You can't have the best picture unless the director is also nominated. Who made the picture? Somebody's mother?" He kept going: "Who made the picture? The shark?"

"All right, all right, enough," Steven said. "I'm suffering enough."

His assistant came in with a tally: The film had only received four nominations, not the expected eleven.

"Four what?" Steven cried, his voice rising higher. "That's it? Not Best Screenplay? Not even Special Effects?"

It was commercial backlash, he said, turning to the camera. Hollywood liked success, but it didn't like domination.

"Everybody loves a winner," he said. "But nobody loves a *winner*."

He looked as sad as a little boy on his birthday opening a gift box and realizing it was empty.

Steven took the rest of the day off, then moved on. He confirmed his cast for *Close Encounters*—Richard Dreyfuss, Teri Garr, Melinda Dillon, and the French filmmaker François Truffaut, who had popularized the auteur theory, in the role of the French government scientist. George settled on his own actors—Mark Hamill as Luke Skywalker, Carrie Fisher as Princess Leia, Harrison Ford as the scoundrel Han Solo.

Francis, after being turned down by Robert De Niro, offered the part of Willard to his *Taxi Driver* co-star Harvey Keitel. Then Brando reconsidered and had his agent call Francis back. Now Kanter told Francis that Brando would play Kurtz for $1 million a week—the same amount McQueen had demanded up front, and which Francis had thought ridiculous—and an added 11 percent of the gross profits. Francis, desperate, yielded. Soon he filled out the rest of his cast. Robert Duvall as the macho, warmongering, cavalry-hat-wearing Lieutenant Colonel Kilgore. The drug-addled and difficult Dennis Hopper, all but unemployable, as an unstable, tripped-out photojournalist who lives as one of Kurtz's disciples. A platoon of talented unknowns and little-knowns to surround Keitel: Sam Bottoms, Scott Glenn, Frederic Forrest, sixteen-year-old Laurence Fishburne. Harrison Ford, whom Francis had always liked, agreed to a small role as one of the army men who sends Willard after Kurtz. As a joke, Francis called the character Colonel G. Lucas, and Ford decided he'd cut his hair short and wear eyeglasses, play him a bit *like* George—the rhythm of his voice, the discomfort with making eye contact.

Everything, finally, was coming together. Francis had spent about $1 million of his own money on preproduction. Now he sold US distribution rights to United Artists for another $10 million, bringing his cash budget up to $18 million. It was a few million short of the budget he and Roos had drawn up, but it was a huge sum—twice what George was working with on *Star Wars*. Francis would find a way to bridge the gap. The key, he had just proved to himself yet again, was not to stop. Money multiplies, he kept saying, if you use it boldly.

He set *Apocalypse Now* a release date of April 7, 1977. Sevens again—and his birthday. As he prepared to leave for Southeast Asia, Francis stepped out of the Sentinel Building and looked up at the Transamerica Pyramid across the street. Transamerica owned United Artists, and the corporation's gleaming, forty-eight-floor skyscraper towered over Francis's little copper headquarters. Francis couldn't resist a defiant bit of showmanship for the journalist accompanying him.

He gestured at his little Tower. “Someday I won’t just own this,” he announced, before turning to the Pyramid and addressing the high-rise, “but I’ll own *you* too.”

· 21 ·

FINAL-CUT DIRECTORS

In early 1976, Kaja Fehr met with Melissa Mathison, the only friend Fehr had kept in touch with after high school. Missy was headed to the Philippines, too. Francis had hired her as an "executive assistant."

"You know," Mathison told Fehr, "he keeps saying he's going to leave Ellie, but if he doesn't leave her after I've been with him seven years, I'm done."

Wow, Fehr thought, *she's hung on for* seven *years.*

Fehr could see Missy and Francis loved each other—"they were just compatible," she says, "both very, very smart, but not intellectual—smart, creative people that enjoyed the hell out of each other, and I don't think for one minute it had anything to do with his fame or his fortune, for Missy. It was the creativity. And I think she brought a lot to the picture, I think she was like—what do they call it?—a muse." Her kindness and joyfulness brought Francis up when he was down. But she wasn't yet twenty-six and had missed out on much of the usual things that fill one's early adulthood.

"I'm almost seven years in here, and I'm done," Missy repeated. "He's not going to leave."

• • •

On March 1, 1976, the same day De Palma began filming *Carrie* on soundstages in Culver City, Francis, Ellie, and the Coppola children boarded their own flight to Manila. George had gone to England in early January. He took a house in Hampstead, in northwest London, writing and rewriting as producer Gary Kurtz staffed the offices and workshops of EMI-Elstree Studios, in nearby Borehamwood. On Saturday, March 20, Francis would begin filming *Apocalypse Now* in the Philippines; two days later, on the Monday, George would be in Tunisia, rolling cameras on *Star Wars*. In May, Steven went to Arizona for principal photography on *Close Encounters*. Marty had entered preproduction on his next film, *New York, New York*, a grandiose, romantic musical starring De Niro and Liza Minnelli. He would shoot it starting in June, at the MGM studio in Culver City, a mile away from De Palma's soundstages on another lot. *New York, New York* was about "the kind of woman I like," Marty said, "driven and ambitious, with a brilliance all her own," and the man who loves her, a male chauvinist who is "trapped and frightened, like a child, and he doesn't know how to reach out." The film ends unhappily. ("The main female character is based on me," Laraine Brennan says today, "and De Niro is definitely a Martin substitute.") It was, Marty confessed, "a very personal movie for me."

A phase of all their careers had ended. Every one of them, in this brief shared moment, was on top of the world. Even De Palma, long on the fringes, finally had, in *Carrie*, his own best-selling novel to adapt. At film school, they had been told it was impossible for a young person with no industry connections to become a studio filmmaker, let alone a successful one, even less a successful filmmaker with a degree of creative freedom. Somehow, and all at the same time, the Trancas Beach gang had achieved the unattainable.

"We were final-cut directors," De Palma says. "And we were not pushovers. We would just say no, no, *no* . . . Each one of us was tough. And we could outlast. Because *they* don't have any convictions. We believe in something that none of these executives believe in, except where the next dinner is coming from and what star they can hang out with. They don't believe in anything. *We* believe in what we're doing. So, you know. We'll just stand there and not be budged, and they can try all kinds of things on us, and we'll just say—no way."

One day, Margot Kidder found herself in the house at Trancas Beach, reading a screenplay, and she was struck by the quiet. The "gang was starting to break up," she said. 1976 was when it shifted. Francis had three kids; Milius had two. Marty's second was on the way. De Palma would soon start going out with Nancy Allen, whom he had cast in *Carrie* and would marry in 1979. Steven was spending more and more time at his own place with his new girlfriend, Allen's co-star Amy Irving, who De Palma had chosen to play Sue Snell.

"Suddenly," says De Palma, "we started to separate, you know. The Northern California people went one direction. Marty went in and out to New York, as I did."

Kidder and Salt moved out of the A-frame house north of Malibu. Sometime in the late '70s, it was bought by a developer. They tore it down and turned it into a parking lot.

Part Three

COMPANY MEN

· 22 ·

THOSE FUCKERS ARE CRAZY

Francis set himself up in the Philippines with all the comforts he expected at home—the best wine, the best food, custom stereo equipment so he could play his favorite music as he cooked meals for the crew after a long day's filming. His cinematographer, Vittorio Storaro, brought his own Italian crew, with their own espresso beans, their own olive oil, their favorite canned tomatoes. For about a month, the shoot proceeded with little trouble. Francis smoked grass and worked shirtless in the sun. Ellie found local schools for the kids. Six hundred Filipino laborers, paid a dollar a day, built the ancient temple used by Kurtz as a home base.

Occasionally, filming was delayed when the helicopters the Filipino army had lent to Francis were called away at the last minute to engage in the civil war the government was waging on Muslim separatists in the south of the country, but Francis found ways to schedule around the delays. In mid-April, he threw himself a profligate birthday party, with all three hundred members of the cast and crew invited, hamburgers and hot dogs flown in from the United States, a cake taller and wider than he was. A bodyguard assigned to him by the government shadowed Francis day and night. Armed guards patrolled the set and the Coppolas' rented house, out of fear the rebels might kidnap the famous American director or his wife and children and hold them for ransom, but the mood remained stubbornly celebratory. Francis had lost weight, traded his glasses for contact lenses. He looked healthier than he had in years.

On April 15, a week after the birthday party, he sat down with producers Fred Roos and Gray Frederickson in the improvised screening room at his house to watch their first batch of dailies. When they were through screening the footage, they trudged to the living room, and Francis sank into the couch.

"Well," he said, finally, "what do you think?"

The three of them agreed: Keitel was all wrong. The character of Willard was an observer, requiring of an actor who could hold the space silently, reactively. Keitel, without wall-to-wall dialogue, was inert. If they shot the whole picture with him, *Apocalypse Now* was dead on arrival.

Few producers ever fire a leading actor a month into filming—it sends a message that a film is struggling, it damages the actor's reputation, it necessitates all the work already shot to be redone. Francis, however, felt he had no choice. He tossed and turned that night, waking up in the darkness to walk to the house's bathroom and shave his beard. He had decided to fly to Los Angeles immediately and recast the part, and he thought that—having lost both weight and his glasses—if he shaved his beard, no one would recognize him.

"Ooooh, Daddy," Sofia laughed when she woke up for breakfast. "You look silly . . . really silly."

She had never seen him without a beard in her life.

Francis worked fast. He dismissed Keitel, who was gracious about the situation, though upset when he learned, years later, that Francis told people he couldn't handle the jungle. (Keitel was a veteran of the US Marine Corps and had served three years in Lebanon, including during Operation Blue Bat, and felt, reasonably enough, that if he had handled that, he could handle a film set anywhere.)

Martin Sheen had just finished filming *The Cassandra Crossing* in Italy—the film that had prevented him being available for the start of *Apocalypse Now*'s shoot—so Francis flew from Manila that morning, April 16, and Sheen boarded a plane in Rome around the same time. They met privately in the VIP lounge at LAX. Francis handed him a copy of the script and offered him the part, then turned around and boarded the first plane back to the Philippines. By April 18, Sheen's agent had agreed on terms with Roos, and the actor was on a flight to Asia himself.

Sheen was a brooding live wire, not unlike Pacino, with whom he'd been friends for years, the two men thinking of one another as creative compatriots. He smoked three packs a day and feared death. His eyes, even when he stood still, were alive with doubt and intensity. The poverty in the Philippines, where local builders dug Francis's backyard pool with their bare hands for three bucks a day while the crew wasted thousands of dollars flying their favorite foods in from halfway around the world, pulled at his heart.

He was much better suited to Willard than Keitel had been. All the same, the situation deepened what Ellie called the "state of anxiety and fear" her husband suddenly found himself in. Francis had asked his wife to film a behind-the-scenes documentary of the making of the movie, partly to keep her occupied and partly so he wouldn't have a United Artists employee on set, putting her in the same role he had given to George, years earlier, on *The Rain People*. She also kept a detailed diary. "He is really going through the most intense struggle to write his way to the end of the script and understand himself on the way," Ellie wrote about Francis on April 28. "Looking back, maybe that is why he has struggled with all his scripts, starting with *The Rain People*. They are about themes he is in the process of working out within himself, rather than from things he has resolved and can be detached and objective about."

Baler, the location chosen by Francis, a six-hour drive from Manila, did funny things to people. Ellie woke up one morning to find

Robert Duvall's girlfriend, who had come for a visit, walking into the sea with tears streaming down her face and suicide on her mind. Two days later, Martin Sheen fainted in the street. As shooting dragged, Francis fired coordinators and assistant directors. Every new hire, found last-minute and aware they might not last long themselves, was paid twice the weekly fee of the person they'd replaced, sending Francis's spending soaring even higher and exacerbating his resentment and anxiety.

On May 18, less than a month after Sheen's arrival and with Francis still behind in making up the scenes shot with Keitel, torrential rains lashed at Baler. Bamboo trees bent almost horizontal in the murky yellow light. The ground turned to soft, swirling mud, up to your knees. After eight days of deluge, Ellie wrote in her diary: "The office called and said that the whole company is coming back to Manila . . . The production is closing down." The typhoon had destroyed sets and all but halted filming for a week. Francis "is so exhausted by everything," Ellie wrote on the 29th. "He is on some brittle edge . . . This morning I noticed a piece of notepaper by the coffee machine with various numbers in red pen. At the bottom it said that the production is now six weeks behind and two million over budget."

Apocalypse Now was shut down for a month and a half. Cast and crew flew back home. Before they could board their own flight, Francis and Ellie were checked into hospital, severely dehydrated and, Ellie wrote, malnourished. They screened some of the dailies, and Francis hated what he saw. He negotiated for United Artists to give him an extra $3 million, but the studio had him agree the investment would become a loan for him to pay back if the film failed to gross at least $40 million at the box office. The Hollywood press went to town: Megalomaniacal Francis Coppola had lost it; he had fired his lead actor and his sets were destroyed; his Vietnam epic was in such disarray he was mortgaging his property to keep going. The words used by Ellie in her diary to describe his mental state over those weeks were bleak: "hopeless," "scared," "miserable," "angry," "trapped." The simple action film he had embarked on to make box-office bank and finally gain true financial independence was turning into the biggest disaster he had ever been a part of.

He could back down or he could double down. Too much money had already been spent, too much of his reputation publicly staked. He spent the early-summer days in California feverishly rewriting, rewriting, rewriting, abandoning as much of Milius's simplistic jingoistic screenplay as he could. He would make a personal film, one about the despair he was going through.

The Coppolas returned to the Philippines with cast and crew in late July. Francis was animated with an almost manic energy; from now on, he would run to the danger rather than run from it. He worked all day and couldn't sleep at night; he crawled into bed at four in the morning, sweat cold and clammy on his skin, the air hot and suffocating all around him, a sickening, paradoxical feeling, like freezing in an oven. He struggled with his moods. His whole life, it had been the same way: He'd lose his temper, and as the anger roared out of him, it left him empty, and he was deflated for days afterward. His energy returned slowly, then all at once, a switch turned on and the voltage raised, and that was exhausting, too.

"The film will not be good," he complained to Ellie.

"So you get a B," she answered.

"I will get an F!" Francis shot back.

"I never felt my wife had any confidence in me," he complained later. He snuck away to spend time with Missy instead. "Her confidence in me made me feel confident . . . She always made me feel like a million dollars, in terms of 'I was talented, and I could do it.'" When Ferdinand Marcos, the brutal, corrupt, authoritarian president of the Philippines, without whose collaboration Francis could not have filmed in the country, invited Coppola to his residence at Malacañang Palace to a formal dinner to screen some footage from *Apocalypse Now*, it was Missy, not Ellie, who Francis took as his date.

Mathison described Marcos's palace as a "den of evil," soulless and obscene. She sat behind Marcos's wife, Imelda, as Vittorio Storaro set up a portable projector. "Every time a handsome actor appeared on the screen," Missy recalled, Mrs. Marcos would turn around and ask, "Is that Marlon Brando?"

At some point, in the tight proximity of the location in Baler, Ellie finally learned about the affair. The revelation devastated her. It did not help when Francis, torn as he was, seemed most concerned about losing the children than he was her. But he asked for forgiveness, swore to end the relationship.

"I'll never do it again," he swore. "I'll never do it again."

The promise was empty. He kept on seeing Mathison. He felt he couldn't do without her. Ellie was torn. Her heart was broken, but she had always been a nonjudgmental, empathetic person. It seemed like Francis couldn't quit the affair for the same reason he couldn't quit the movie, no matter how dangerous either became. How do you quit from yourself?

She was turned on by the self-destructive risks Francis was taking—the extremes to which he was willing to push himself, personally and professionally. She had long thought of herself as the wife—an observer, almost a bystander, to a great artist. Francis lost weight in the Philippines, he sweated through the heat, he had nightmares—but she lost fifteen pounds and her sense of self, too. They were both scared. She realized now that she had always been on the journey, too.

On the evening of August 8, shooting a scene in which a nude Willard is drunk in his hotel room, Francis encouraged Sheen to get drunk himself and pour his own fears and anxieties into an improvised performance. Sheen smashed his fist through a mirror and smeared the blood over his face. Francis called cut, but Sheen "begged" him to keep going.

"Please," he slurred. "I must do this for myself."

Deep down, the actor had known for a long time that he was

an alcoholic—self-loathing, immature, in pain. He'd been in hotel rooms alone and naked and wasted before. He needed to relive it not just as Willard but as himself, publicly, to see himself on film as his wife and friends had seen him. A sort of exorcism, he said later, of the shame and secrecy.

"I don't know if I am going to live through this," he'd told a friend in Los Angeles, during the break from filming. "Those fuckers are crazy."

Something in him told him to match the crazy.

"I don't know who this guy is," he'd once asked Francis. "Who is this Willard?"

"He's you," Francis answered. "Whoever you are."

Sitting naked in the dim light of the hotel room, Sheen let go of the weight he had been carrying, the unhappiness, the feeling he had been killing himself with every sip of liquor, every light of a sour cigarette. The room crackled. Storaro and his assistants held their breaths behind the camera, unsure if Sheen would lunge at them. When it was done, Sheen lay back on the bed, sweating and crying, singing "Amazing Grace" to himself. He held Francis's and Ellie's hands so tight his bandaged hand kept tearing open and bleeding through.

"There was that emotional electricity in the room, anything could happen," Ellie wrote. "They were inside somebody, in his personal territory, with a man alone in his most private moment."

It was exactly—finally—filmmaking as Francis thought was the only way it should be done.

· 23 ·

A WALK IN THE DARK

"When you're directing," George said, "you have to get up at four thirty, have breakfast at five, leave the hotel at six, drive an hour to location, start shooting at eight, and finish shooting around six. Then you wrap, go to your office, and set up the next day's work. You get back to the hotel about eight or nine, hopefully get a bite to eat, then you go to your room and figure out your homework, how you're going to shoot the next day's scenes, and then you go to sleep. The next morning, it starts all over again."

He hated it. London was drab, wet, and cold. Before filming started, George took Hamill, Ford, and Fisher out for dinner at a local Chinese restaurant to bond—Francis's old *Godfather* trick. Only this time, the actors said nothing and nor did George, who was too socially awkward to host. An "embarrassing silence," Hamill remembered, fell over the table.

The shoot was a disaster. George had never shot something this ambitious—sixteen weeks, most of it at Elstree, on forty-five sets across eleven soundstages—and caring for every detail of such a big production exhausted him, particularly because nothing he saw through the camera viewfinder lived up to the images he had pictured in his mind. None of the special effects worked as he hoped. The awe-inspiring world he had invented looked like cheap rubber and plastic. Anthony Daniels—the English actor locked inside the metal body of droid C-3PO—complained that the costume's sharp joints cut into his skin. Peter Mayhew—the seven-foot-three performer who played Chewbacca—complained of the heat inside his own heavy, furry outfit.

No one, other than George, took the picture seriously. The British crews didn't warm to their stiff young American director, in his blue jeans and preppy sweaters. They treated *Star Wars* like it was another cheap episode of *Doctor Who*. They insisted on timely lunch breaks and wrapping at 5:30 PM. George was used to the USC way of making films, the Zoetrope way, where everyone helped everyone—now he had to deal with the most sensitive union rules he'd ever come across. Cinematographer Gil Taylor lost his temper when George moved his lights without asking. Production designer John Barry, fed up with George's micromanaging, sternly told him one day, "I want you to tell me what you see, but I don't want you to tell me how to do my job."

"They don't know what the fuck they're doing, this lot," Taylor boomed, in his thick Sussex accent.

Not that the Americans in the cast backed their director up. Hamill cracked jokes about George's direction—all he said, it seemed, was *faster* or *more intense*. Ford routinely made fun of the screenplay.

"George!" Ford called out one day, in front of the entire crew, as the director sat behind the camera. "You can type this shit, but you sure can't say it! Move your mouth when you're typing!"

George's head hurt. His stomach hurt. He shook with what he had taken to calling his "director's cough." He hated that everything in London was closed on Sundays, hated that you couldn't get a good hamburger anywhere. There was nothing good on the television. Marcia came down with the flu, so bad she was sent to hospital. Thieves broke into the rented cottage in Hampstead and stole her jewelry.

By the time George flew back to America in July 1976, he felt broken. He took an extended layover in New York to visit De Palma, who was in town ahead of the premiere of his newest film, *Obsession*, a Hitchcockian thriller he and Schrader had come up with and which De Palma had shot just before *Carrie*.

George, pallid and muted, "was not well," De Palma says. The two friends went to a café. "You know, he can't eat sugar," De Palma says—Lucas is diabetic—"and we went to a place, and he was, like, having chocolate sundaes. It was suicidal." Lucas told De Palma that the film wasn't what he'd imagined, that the British crews had given him such a hard time. "George is so meticulous, he knows exactly what he wants," De Palma says. "He was very, very depressed about the whole shooting experience."

Next, George stopped in Mobile, Alabama, and dropped in on Steven, still deep into filming *Close Encounters of the Third Kind*. He showed his friend a stack of black-and-white stills from the London shoot, which Steven found beautiful, "but George was so depressed," he remembered. "He was really upset." Steven was so convinced *Star Wars* would be fine that he offered to trade one of his profit points on *Close Encounters* for one of George's on his own film; later, John Milius—who was directing *Big Wednesday*, an autobiographical film about surfing, told around three friends not unlike himself, George, and Francis—would get in on the deal, too. George eagerly made the trades. He predicted profit points on *Star Wars* would be worth nothing.

He flew back to Los Angeles and learned ILM, having spent half of their $2 million budget for the picture, only had three shots to show for it. He and special effects lead John Dykstra screamed at each other. That night, on the plane back to San Francisco, George's chest seized with sharp pain. The doctors at Marin General Hospital diagnosed him with serious hypertension and prescribed a long period of rest. George told them he couldn't take one.

"That's when I really confirmed to myself I was going to change," he said. "I wasn't going to make more films, I wasn't going to direct anymore."

He just had to get rid of *Star Wars* first.

George's English editor, John Jympson, put together a first cut of the movie that played, remembers Richard Chew, "so staid and conventional: master, cut to the two-shot, cut over the shoulder." It had no rhythm or swagger. George put Marcia in charge of recutting the film, and Marcia called Chew.

"George had to let go of our English editor," she said. "He wants me to work on it, but I can't do it all—are you available still?"

"I am," he answered.

"Well, come and join us," said Marcia.

Chew headed up the road to the Lucas house in San Anselmo. He and Marcia got to work breaking down Jympson's cut and putting the footage back together, a process known as reconstituting the reels—"reassemble it into the dailies," explains Chew, "so that we, as editors, get to work with fresh stuff."

George seemed better already. He had always been more at ease editing than shooting. He showed Chew old black-and-white footage of World War II dogfights and explained that they would be cutting some of it into the picture as a placeholder while Industrial Light & Magic built and shot the miniature spaceships that would remain in the final film. He had fired Dykstra, who, he thought, had spent too much time and money developing equipment, rather than completing shots. He told Chew he wanted the film to be dynamic, to have a lot of movement.

The job was gigantic. Marcia took on multiple co-editors and assistant editors to help her and Chew. They had to make sense of the blue- and green-screen shots George had filmed abroad, anticipate how they would cut with the optical effects and miniature effects being shot at ILM, coordinate it all with the otherworldly sounds and alien languages being created by Ben Burtt, a USC graduate with just two credits on low-budget monster movies to his name.

One day, Mike Kitchens—formerly of Zoetrope, now house-sitting Kurtz's house while the producer remained in England—dropped in at the house. Like seemingly everyone in San Francisco's insular film community, Kitchens and Marcia knew each other socially, counting Murch in particular as a common friend. Mike was surprised to find her upset with him the second he walked in the door.

"How come you didn't want to edit with me?" she demanded.

"No one asked," Kitchens said.

"Damn it. I asked Gary."

"No one told me anything," Kitchens repeated. "I don't have any editorial experience."

"I'd rather have someone who's smart than someone with experience," Marcia answered.

Kitchens more or less moved into the editing room, working around the clock. "I loved Marcia," he says. "She had a sense of humor. She's really smart and she's focused. She goes into the editing room and she doesn't come out."

He had a front-row seat to George and Marcia's arguments. They were both opinionated and outspoken, and Marcia's decisive cutting didn't always match the film George had been carrying around in his head. He deferred to her, though perhaps only for show. "When I showed them stuff, she was always the one who spoke up first," says Chew. "George would be much more quiet and wouldn't state his feelings about something. After I left the room, he would talk to her about it."

Marcia shaped scenes around the characters' emotions. She cut her first passes quick and rough, like a writer following her gut, or a painter instinctively flicking her brush at the canvas. George, on the other hand, was motivated by a mixture of cerebral logic and a subjective sense of rhythm. He still held many of the same strong opinions about editing that he had held at film school. He believed in good cuts and bad cuts; every shot needed a point of view and a narrative justification. He asserted that every movie should start with its second-best scene and end with its best, with the third-best somewhere in the middle like the center mast that holds up a circus tent. He insisted dialogue could only be played when the speaker was visible or at least established, and hated scenes that began with a character's voice laid over a shot of a landscape or a building. He'd ask, "Is the building talking?"

If he didn't like a cut, he called it goofy. He trusted Marcia—but he was needled by the growing knowledge his wife looked down on his passion project.

"Marcia didn't want to do fantasy," Kitchens says plainly. Since she and George had last worked together, she had edited *Alice Doesn't Live Here Anymore* and *Taxi Driver* and was committed to cut *New York, New York* when Marty finished filming. She had grown.

Marcia sped the narrative up considerably. She cut a long early sequence of Luke and his friends hanging out on Tatooine that felt like *American Graffiti* in space. She constructed a new scene introducing Luke and cross-cut it with the sequences of C-3PO and R2-D2 adrift on Tatooine and Princess Leia in Imperial captivity, energizing the first third of the picture with a momentum it lacked on the page. She and Chew used the same technique at the film's climax, playing Luke Skywalker in the cockpit of his X-wing against Leia and the rest of the Rebels waiting impotently on the ground, fusing two separate narrative strands—will Luke blow up the Death Star, and will the Empire wipe out the Rebel base—into one: Will Luke blow up the Death Star *before* the Empire can wipe out the Rebel base?

Most challenging was the "gunport sequence" in the middle of the picture, in which Luke and Han, manning the *Millennium Falcon*'s blasters as the ship escapes the Death Star, fight off Imperial fighters pursuing them.

"When I was assigned the gunport sequence," Chew says, "it was all, at that time, green screen behind Harrison Ford and Mark Hamill, and with lines that were just triggers for action or movement. Like—*hey, go get 'em!*—you know." Without music, sound effects, or ILM's wizardry, all he had to work with were the shots of Ford and Hamill, clunking around on their gun seats, firing noiseless weapons at more green screens, and footage of Peter Mayhew in the cockpit in his Chewbacca suit, looking like a big wet dog, the alien's growls and roars not yet dubbed in, with Carrie Fisher in her lip gloss and round hair buns by his side. All four actors moved their heads and spoke their lines in reaction to directions George gave them off-screen, like an absurd game of Simon Says. And in the place of any temporary footage or preliminary animation of the TIE fighters whooshing past the *Falcon*'s guns, Chew and Marcia had their grainy, black-and-white World War II dogfights.

It was virtually impossible to tell if any of it was good, what to fix, or how to fix it. On most films, even a rough assembly gives the editor a sense of whether a scene has a chance to work. In this case, remembered Chew, everything "was a walk in the dark." He focused on the kind of thing he had learned from Murch: keeping the eye activated and engaged, "crossing the screen or crossing through different quadrants of the screen." If he cut from Hamill swinging this way, to a Spitfire diving that way, to Ford's eyeline and gun barrel following, then he had continuity of movement, and he hoped the visual effect artists at ILM would riff off his rhythm. Marcia kept having to rush him along. "Richard, don't fuck around" became one of her mantras.

To cope with the workload, in late September, George hired Paul Hirsch, De Palma's editor on *Carrie*, which had just been released to great reviews and great business. George had admired Hirsch's work on several of De Palma's earlier films, and respected that, when De Palma had briefly left the edit of *Carrie* to attend a film festival and ordered Hirsch not to show the cut to anyone in his absence, Hirsch had staunchly refused the producer and the studio's insistent requests they be allowed to do so, and had been fired for it. (De Palma rehired him the second he came home.) Hirsch confessed to George that he had never worked on any film as big as *Star Wars*.

"Oh, don't worry about that," George said. "No one ever has."

Hirsch finished work on *Carrie* on a Friday night, and had a celebratory dinner with De Palma, his agent Sue Mengers, Marty, and Steven. The next morning, he traveled up to San Anselmo, and though it was a Saturday, he found everyone at work on the property: Marcia, Chew, Kitchens, and two other assistants in the cutting rooms in the carriage house; Ben Burtt, playing with sounds in the basement of the main house; and Robbins and Barwood, writing a separate script in their offices upstairs. George put Hirsch to work on whatever reel Chew wasn't reassembling, while Marcia toiled on the final Death Star battle.

"The fact that Marcia was one of the editors as well as [George's] wife made the working dynamic in the editing room a bit tricky at times," Hirsch wrote in his memoir, remembering discussions about the film that started with all three editors in the room but quickly "evolved into a one-on-one wrangle between George and Marcia." Chew would slip away, uncomfortable; Hirsch would stay and try to break the tension by offering his own opinions, of which he had plenty. He claimed later that he had discouraged George from making Luke Skywalker's lightsaber red and Vader's blue, insisting it was more natural for the colors to be reversed, and he was so proud of *Carrie*'s final shot, a departure from Stephen King's book, in which the dead Carrie's hand bursts through the dirt of her grave, that he brought it up several times a week while working on *Star Wars*.

"You know, I thought of that," Hirsch told Marcia and Kitchens.

"*I thought of that*," Kitchens repeats. "He kept telling everybody: *I thought of that, I thought of that!*"

As a joke, Kitchens slipped into Marcia's office one day and climbed into the trim bin, the barrel in which editors discard cut bits of film they no longer need. He crouched low and had one of the assistants cover him in celluloid scraps. When Marcia and Hirsch walked in, he planned to push his hand into the air, like Carrie's, and scream, *I thought of this!*

But when Kitchens heard the door open, it was George who walked in, already deep into an argument with Marcia about the gunport cuts. He slammed the door behind them.

Fuck, Kitchens thought. He listened to them fight, exchanging harsh words clearly intended to be private. There was evidently a "distance between them beyond" the editing, Kitchens says.

This is none of my business, he thought.

He took a deep breath and rose slowly out of the bin, film strips hanging off his head and shoulders. "It scared the piss out of George, but Marcia cracked up, and that's what saved me, and I managed to get out of the room."

The same scene, minus the prank gone wrong, kept repeating, like footage played and replayed on an editing bed: the slammed doors, the raised voices. Sometimes George, fed up, went upstairs to his own bay and edited a scene himself. More often than not, Marcia ended up giving in, undid her work, and recut as George wanted her to. "He was second-guessing her," Kitchens says. "She was drained by it."

In December, Marcia left for Marty's *New York, New York*. George let Chew and everyone else go as well, retaining only Hirsch. George told Chew he had to cut down on expenses, and besides, all there was left to do now was wait for ILM to complete the final effects to be dropped into the existing cut. Shortly before Christmas, Chew watched the full cut through one last time, with the missing shots slugged, the temporary music cobbled together from bits of Mahler and Holst. When the picture ended, he still had no idea if it was any good or embarrassingly amateurish. He turned to George and mustered the best joke he could.

"George, don't worry," he said. "You can always make toys out of the robots."

He left the screening room and drove back to San Francisco.

Marcia had already gone. When Hirsch returned to work the next day, to tinker with some scenes before George screened a cut for a visiting Alan Ladd, he was the only editor left in the cavernous carriage house—but he wasn't downhearted. The weather had turned bitingly cold, the small towns on his commute to work were strung with joyful Christmas lights, and "a buzz started to go around the community," he recalled. "Francis was coming home for the holidays."

· 24 ·

THIS IS THE WAY THE WORLD ENDS

Francis needed a break. It wasn't a wrap but a pause, to assemble and see what he had. Brando had turned up to set in September overweight and self-conscious and difficult, refusing to shoot anything for several days, insisting he wanted the part to be more like Conrad's Kurtz before finally confessing he had never even read Conrad's book. Prop men put real corpses in prop body bags—"the script says 'a pile of burning bodies,'" they protested, "it doesn't say a pile of burning dummies"—and a carabao buffalo had been ritualistically killed on camera, allegedly to accurately capture local tradition. Francis embraced it all. If Storaro wanted to shoot methodically, every frame a work of art, then that's how they would shoot. If Brando was bald and fat, then Kurtz would no longer be a lean, mean, action-movie Green Beret villain—he would be bald and fat. If Francis himself was a contradictory, indecisive mess, then he would stop fighting to control, to *direct*, as a director was traditionally expected to do. He would be a conceptual artist. Life and collaboration would fill in the blanks.

Ellie came home first, Sofia in tow. The world outside of the *Apocalypse* bubble was like a dream, she wrote in her diary, "all familiar but different." Friends who had missed her didn't understand why she refused to see them. "I was the wife sent home to get the house in order for a family Christmas," she wrote. "I was mad and confused, irritated, stumbling over this big house in my life once again. The freeways and car pools and supermarkets seemed idiotic."

When Francis arrived, right before Christmas, he was manic. He told Ellie everything he had shot without her had been spectacular, that he was happier than he had ever been in his life. Ellie felt shut out and superfluous. Why couldn't she be high, too?

Matthew Robbins threw Francis a welcome party at his home in Inverness, a half hour's drive north of George's house. Everything on the north side of the Golden Gate Bridge was at least a half hour's drive from everything else. Francis drove up late, at the wheel of his collectible red Tucker 48, long and sleek and shiny as a torpedo, the beams of its three headlamps sweeping across the front of Robbins's house. He wandered grandly through the crowd, shaking hands without introducing himself. Then Marcia threw a New Year's Eve party, cramming a hundred people into the house on Park Way to dance to the fast-paced accordion and frottoir of a hired zydeco band. The Coppolas came, as did much of the old Zoetrope gang.

On New Year's Day, Francis returned the favor by hosting lunch at his home on Broadway, in the city. This time he held court in black pajamas that seemed intended both to make him look like one of the Vietcong and to showcase his dramatic weight loss. He screened a Soviet movie. He said he was designing his life to live "magnificently." Four days later, he woke Ellie up in the middle of the night, delirious with energy, "so excited it was like an electrical charge." He had watched a rough first assembly of *Apocalypse Now*.

"It's great, a masterpiece," he exclaimed. "It's all there. I can see it."

He flew back to Philippines before the end of the month. He needed more. Just a little more. He needed an ending.

George, meanwhile, was almost done with *Star Wars*. He scheduled some final pickups to improve on special effects shots that had underwhelmed him during principal photography. On January 12, he planned to go out to Death Valley, in the Mojave Desert in eastern California, and take some new shots of Luke driving his landspeeder—the wheels of the vehicle were visible in the footage taken in Tunisia the year before—and of a bantha, a woolly-mammoth-like desert creature, that would be played by an elephant borrowed from the Marine World/Africa USA animal theme park in Redwood City. George had asked Carroll Ballard to help him out; they would film it run-and-gun, like in the old *THX 1138* days.

At five AM on the morning of the shoot, just as George was stirring, his phone rang. Gary Kurtz was on the line. Mark Hamill had crashed his car and was in the hospital. His face was badly wounded.

George's alter ego had had a life-changing wreck of his own. Hamill had got lost late the night before on his way down State Route 14, speeding, doing seventy miles an hour on an off-ramp. He'd lost control of his BMW and it had flown off the ramp, flipped, rolled thirty feet down the steep hill before coming to a crunching halt. The actor was knocked out. When he woke up, he was at Los Angeles County General Hospital, waiting in a gurney. A nurse held a mirror up to his face. "My nose was off," Hamill remembered. He had broken it, along with his cheekbone; the right side of his face was badly slashed. Surgeons rebuilt his nose using cartilage from his ear. As he recovered, he read stories in gossip magazines telling how he had nearly died, how he had dragged himself out of the wreckage, how he had disfigured himself.

"I was so upset to see how badly I had hurt myself," Hamill said. "I just felt my career was over."

He would heal, though he didn't know it yet; the scars would fade, though the shape of his face had changed, faintly but forever. For now, he lay in his hospital bed, despairing, and George stood in the overbearing heat of Death Valley, filming a landspeeder driven by a body double. Then came the elephant, and it refused to behave. It kept throwing off its heavy hairy costume.

George squinted in the harsh sunlight. "I just wanted," he said, "to get done with the damn movie."

A month later, he felt ready to show "the damn movie" to his friends. He invited Steven, as well as Milius, De Palma, Matthew Robbins, Hal Barwood, his screenwriter friends Willard Huyck and Gloria Katz, and the film critic Jay Cocks up to Northern California to screen the first cut. Marty had been meant to come, but the runway in Los Angeles was wet with fog that morning and he got cold feet on the tarmac, said his asthma was giving him trouble. It wasn't clear if he was afraid of flying in the fog, or afraid of hating the film and having to break George's heart.

Everyone met up at George's house. The screening room there, wrote Paul Hirsch, "was the plushest I have ever seen. Every seat was a large, upholstered armchair, such as you would have in your living room. Down front, there were several couches with ottomans, which allowed viewers to stretch out as if they were at home in bed." Everyone settled in, and they ran the picture. Some of the effects were still missing. The silence afterward made George uneasy. The mood remained awkward as everyone filed out and got in their cars.

They went to the local Chinese restaurant, sat down, and ordered lunch. The film was a bit difficult to follow, someone tentatively offered.

"What was that stuff about a tractor beam, George?" De Palma asked innocently. George told him, and De Palma nodded seriously. "Oh," he said. "You mean the big magnet."

Who were those "stormtroopers"—were they like space Nazis? Were they human? Why were they armored all in white? "Where's the blood when they shoot people?" De Palma asked. Why was Leia's hair in those two stupid buns?

De Palma then launched into making fun of the Force. There was this mystical force binding the whole universe, and George was just calling it that? The force was called the Force?

He kept repeating the word—*the Force, the Force, the Force*—until it lost all meaning.

"I made some cracks about it," De Palma admits. George grew defensive. He mumbled some explanations. Voices rose.

"I don't understand your story!" De Palma yelled. "There's no context! What is this space stuff? Who cares? I'm lost!"

"You never made a commercial movie in your entire life!" George screamed back. "What are you talking about?"

"This won't be commercial. Nobody will get it. It's just a void with stars and some silly ships moving around!"

The rest of the group sat with their eyes down, picking at the fried rice. Eventually, Marcia took De Palma aside. "You're really hurting George's feelings," she said. "He's really affected by what you're saying."

De Palma agreed to tone it down and try to be more constructive. Fundamentally, he told George, the film needed context. "Who are all these people?" he asked. "You've got all these funny names, and this history that nobody could follow." If he was making a *Flash Gordon* movie, then "you gotta set this up like those *Flash Gordon* things," by which De Palma meant using something like the text that crawled up the frame at the beginning of every *Flash Gordon* and *Buck Rodgers* episode, catching viewers up on the events of the previous episode, so they didn't feel confused by the action starting in medias res.

George was stung, less because he was angry at De Palma, but because he trusted him. It was, after all, why he'd held the screening in the first place. "The trouble with the Hollywood system is you're not getting correct feedback," De Palma says. "What was good about our group was, we were very honest with each other, and there was nothing political about it. We just said what we thought, basically, and that's how we had formed such a strong bond." The arguments happened all the time. But George was the most sensitive of the group, and he'd sunk so much time into *Star Wars*, had felt misunderstood for nearly every second of it already. Not just misunderstood, but dismissed, as if the very kind of film he'd chosen to make was a waste of time, even an insult to serious filmmaking.

All the same, De Palma's suggestion felt right. George took a breath and sat back down with De Palma and Cocks, and got to work writing an opening text crawl. As they all left the restaurant, Steven made sure to take George aside.

"George, it's great," he said. "It's gonna make $100 million."

He told Laddie as much in a phone call later that night. George got back to work, cramming the hours in, like being back at film school. The staff at ILM worked around the clock. Marcia took a few days off *New York, New York* to join Hirsch, cutting the negative—the original, foundational physical copy of the film—during the day, while George supervised the sound mix at night. Every morning at seven AM, Hirsch and George met to review each other's work and, if they had time, go for breakfast at Duke's Coffee Shop, in the front of the Tropicana Motel on Santa Monica Boulevard, a West Hollywood staple where the waitresses wore studded flared jeans, the cakes were the diameter of motorcycle wheels, and the club sandwiches were stacked like cinder blocks. Out-of-work actors and musicians passed the time at the communal tables, browsing through copies of *Variety* and the *Hollywood Reporter* as they dug into their omelets, pancakes, and corned beef hash. Touring bands liked to stay upstairs at the Tropicana on their way from the Coast to the Midwest or vice versa, grateful at management's embrace of their drunken brawls and drug-fueled sex fests. In '77, Tom Waits lived in a bungalow round the back of the motel, with his booze bottles and a piano he'd snuck past management and into the kitchenette.

Hirsch loved Duke's, but it was everything George hated about Los Angeles—a mythologized dump full of navel-gazing hustlers, where every patron looked up from their obscenely overfilled plates every time the door clicked open, just in case it was someone famous—or someone who could get them a job—walking over the threshold. One early morning, George took his seat at one of the large tables, only for his neighbor to immediately lean in and ask: "You're George Lucas, aren't you?"

George shook his head. "No," he apologized, "but I wish I were."

Out in the Philippines, Francis kept thinking of the final stanza of T.S. Eliot's poem "The Hollow Men":

This is the way the world ends
This is the way the world ends
This is the way the world ends
Not with a bang but a whimper.

He wanted a bang. He pushed the shoot further and further out of control—deliberately. Walter Murch compares George and Francis in this way: George approached filming as an ordeal to endure: The film had been conceived and incubated in George's mind, and making it was like labor—"now I just have to go through the birth canal of shooting it. It's painful, and I don't like doing it, but I will do it. Whereas the—let's call it the Coppola approach—is that you can go above that. Something can happen that makes you think, *Where did this come from?* Francis does it by giving his heads of department a huge amount of rope to hang themselves with, but paradoxically, he does it in a way, because of his own personality, that makes you even more beholden to him, to protect him. *He's giving us so much rope, we have to protect him!* . . . And that's what happens with Coppola. It comes because he's so—so *skinless*, in a sense, because he's given you so much control. Wonderful things happen that would never otherwise happen as a result."

In late February, Ellie—though she knew it would make him angry, provoking him to accuse her of "negativity, disloyalty or jealousy"—sent Francis a cable from San Francisco. She told him "what no one else was willing to say, that he was setting up his own Vietnam with his supply lines of wine and steaks and air conditioners. Creating the very situation he went there to expose. That with his staff of hundreds of people, carrying out his every request, he was turning into Kurtz—going too far. I called him an asshole." She copied his heads of department on the missive.

As expected, Francis, betrayed, raged. Wasn't he doing his best work? Didn't his own wife understand? How could she say these things?

A few days later, on a Friday night, Francis called the house in San Francisco. He sounded shaken. He needed her to be calm, he said, and get in touch with Tom Sternberg, his producer at Zoetrope, as well as the company's lawyers. He asked her to find out the terms and state of the film production's insurance policy. She should do this as quickly as possible, and in total secrecy.

He said Martin Sheen had been found crawling down the street in pain. He'd had a heart attack, and he was in critical condition.

· 25 ·

LUCKY SANDCASTLES

Word traveled around Baler, from production office to crew meeting to drinking hole: Martin Sheen was dead.

He had been resting in his room, reading, when he suddenly had a feeling like "a hot poker on my chest." He stumbled into the street, looking for help, only to collapse. He tried to drag himself onto a passing bus. He didn't know anyone except members of the crew. Later that morning, production designer Dean Tavoularis, walking through the production compound, was waved down by a Filipino man, who dragged him to one of the wardrobe trucks. Tavoularis stepped into the confined space. At the back of the truck, Sheen, pale and sweating, was lying across a pile of army boots.

"What happened?" Tavoularis asked.

"Get me a priest," Sheen implored.

Tavoularis found a way to call for medical help. As they waited, a local priest was found. He performed the last rites in Tagalog.

The news traveled quickly. It reached Francis, and Francis tried to put a lid on it, not because he was in denial, but because, as the old war posters went: Loose lips sink ships, tittle-tattle lost the battle. His request made things worse.

Marty's had a heart attack, voices said on phone calls back home, *and Francis doesn't want to admit it.*

"What the fuck is that? What the fuck is that?" Francis raged. "This will be all over Hollywood in half an hour. If Marty is so seriously stricken that he must go back, of course he'll go back and we'll eat it, but I talked to the doctor, they didn't know, Marty's a young man, and probably would be up and about in three weeks." He'd asked the doctor if he could get Sheen back to work by then, and the doctor had said possibly. "That's all I need to hear from the doctor . . . That gossip could finish me off, because if UA hears that we've lost eight weeks, then UA with a $27 million investment, if they're gonna force me to complete it with what I've got, then I don't have the movie yet!"

Ellie flew back for support, and it was Ellie's camera that captured Francis ordering, "He's not dead unless I *say* he's dead." It sounded worse than he meant it. He and Sheen had agreed to lie to the press, to say Sheen had collapsed while jogging from heat exhaustion. Neither of them wanted the film shut down. But sound bad it did, like a man playing God. Ellie thought Francis was suffering a nervous breakdown. He told her he had seriously considered suicide.

Sheen's wife of seventeen years, Janet, slept on the floor of the intensive care unit by his bed. She arranged for a psychotherapist from New York to call Sheen daily and talk through his demons.

"I *chose* to have that heart attack. I *needed* to have that heart attack," Sheen said later, "because there was a part of myself that had already died . . . metaphysically and spiritually. I was a dishonest man."

Francis was not ready to live honestly. As Sheen recovered in his hospital bed, he sat in his bathtub in Baler, the water going cold, Ellie weeping on the floor nearby. "We were talking," Ellie wrote in her diary, "about whether to get separated or divorced."

That conversation went on, in bits and pieces, for several weeks. Francis kept filming, coming up with material to shoot around Sheen's absence, counting the days until his leading man could return. In between setups, he and Ellie argued, on and off, never resolving anything. On April 18, at the end of one such row, Francis called their eldest child, Gio, into the bedroom. Gio noticed his mother crying at the table; he looked over as his father sat, exhausted, on the bed.

"We're getting a divorce," Francis announced suddenly, "your mother and I aren't happy together and we're getting a divorce."

He walked out. Ellie disappeared into the bathroom. At length, she emerged. Gio had left the bedroom. Ellie put on her bathing suit, went to find Sofia, and took her for a swim in the pool. Ellie floated. Sofia swam back and forth, showing off her tricks, oblivious to anything. Francis came down the path with Gio and Roman, looking worried, and then surprised, at finding Ellie calm and in the pool.

"We began to realize that we both felt an enormous relief," Ellie recalled.

They made silly faces at each other and jumped around.

"Well, kids," asked Francis, "how do you like us now that we're divorced?"

"What," asked Sofia, "is *avorced*?"

On Wednesday, May 25, 1977, the day *Star Wars* came out, Francis was still in the jungle, and George and Marcia prepared to depart for a holiday. He had been working on *Star Wars* for three years straight without a break—without a day free of the pressure and anxiety—and he didn't want to be in Los Angeles for the opening. He spent the morning supervising the mix of the dubbing tracks for *Star Wars*'s foreign prints, then met Marcia for a burger on Hollywood Boulevard before their flight. They came out of the diner to find a long line of people queuing outside of Mann's Chinese Theatre. When George enquired, he was told they were all there to see *Star Wars*. That was the entirety of his audience, he thought—sci-fi nerds like himself, turning up on day one. It'd dry up within twenty-four hours. He had a bad feeling about it.

George had invited Steven for a weekend break in Hawaii. Spielberg was still working on *Close Encounters*. He was way over schedule and way over budget, partly due to his own indecision, partly due to the cutting-edge nature of the special effects he and Trumbull were putting together and the painstaking processes involved in creating many of the film's sequences. He was often lonely. At the heart of *Close Encounters* was the idea of communicating with aliens using music, a callback, though Steven did not realize it yet, to his mother's past as a composer, his father's work as a computer engineer. He and John Williams had spent a day playing on Williams's piano, looking for a five-note combination that would express the longing Steven so often felt inside him—hopeful and unresolved. "We wanted the last note to beg for a response," Steven said.

He was still looking for someone whose music matched his. He was dating Amy Irving, but they were an ill-fitting match, she well-read and direct and not easily pleased, he still immature and uncomfortable with confrontation. He had dreams about "things" outside his window, "beckoning me to leave the house," "trying to get me to come outdoors, which I refused to do."

As he edited the film, he lived alone in an apartment in Marina del Rey, five minutes from Trumbull's special effects facility. The closest place Steven had to home was a thirty-minute drive across the city: his mother Leah's new restaurant, the Milky Way, just opened on Pico and Oakhurst. Her paintings hung on the walls next to family pictures. She worked from breakfast to close, serving ethnic dishes—Mexican, Italian, Cajun—all strictly kosher. Steven's sisters often huddled together at a corner table over a plate of Leah's cheesecake, asking for their mother's life advice as she sped by, a short-haired blur of patterned tops, denim jeans, and sparkling jewelry.

"Nobody expects one mega-hit, let alone two," Steven remembered of *Close Encounters*. After *Jaws*, he just hoped this one would break even.

He gladly met George at the hotel in Hawaii. As Marcia rested, the two men changed and walked out of the lobby and toward the ocean. They sat on the beach near the shore. George put his hands into the sand. He told Steven he was building a lucky sandcastle, close to the high-tide line. If the castle made it through the night, *Star Wars* would be a hit. If the early morning high tide swept it away, the film would be a flop. It was a metaphor, he felt, for the gamble of filmmaking: You built something close to the edge, and the line between success and failure was so narrow as to feel arbitrary.

Steven leaned forward and helped. George asked him what he was thinking of doing after *Close Encounters*, and Steven answered that he had always wanted to direct a James Bond film, but the producers kept turning him down.

"I got something very similar to what you would like to do," George said. He told Steven about *Raiders of the Lost Ark*: an adventure about Indiana Smith and the lost Ark of the Covenant, the Nazis chasing him, the idea of a movie built like a string of serial episodes, with an action sequence and a mini cliff-hanger every ten or fifteen minutes. It would be the first film in "a series of *Raiders* sagas," a franchise of films "not unlike the Tarzan series or . . . the serials of the '40s and '50s."

"Look, this is a B-movie," George qualified. "They used to make four of them a week, at each studio, for fifteen years from the '30s to the '40s." In other words: Roger Corman territory, but on a higher budget.

Only two years separated George's and Steven's births. Their cultural references were the same. Back in Arizona as a child, Steven had spent countless weekend afternoons at a little art-house cinema called the Kiva in Scottsdale. On Saturdays, the Kiva played an extended double bill, with ten cartoons and a couple of old serials sandwiched in between. Young Steven spent hours in the theater's dark, and the serials stuck with him more than anything else: the escapism, the frenetic pace, the narrow misses, the close calls. They were as close to the films he and his friends made at home as anything else to be taken in on the big screen.

Steven grew more and more interested, and his heart was broken when George casually added that the film was "probably" going to be directed by Philip Kaufman, who had helped him refine some elements of the story. "Hold your breath," though, George said; he had a feeling Kaufman might "give it up for something else."

The sun descended across the sky. The two men rose and made their way back up toward the hotel. The next morning, Steven woke and went to the window. The lucky castle still stood.

Around lunchtime, George spoke to Laddie. Every single 10:30 AM showing of *Star Wars* across the country had sold out. Within days, it became clear *Star Wars* would not just surpass *Jaws*'s box-office record, but smash it.

George called Mark Hamill to cheer him up.

"Hiya, kid," he said. "You famous yet?"

After that, "I broke up with my girlfriend for a while," Hamill admitted. "I was like a kid in a candy store. *Gee! All these groupies.*"

Star Wars, like *The Godfather* and *Jaws* before it, became the rare kind of success that bestowed freedom on its director. It was the top film in America, on and off, for over four months and played in some cinemas for over a year, bringing in over $220 million over its first run in theatres. De Palma's *Carrie*, released a few months earlier in November 1976, had done really well, grossing $33 million against a $1.8 million budget, but "really well" was no longer enough. The only doors the film opened for De Palma afterward led to more horror films about telekinetic teenagers. "I couldn't get the movies I wanted to make off the ground," De Palma says. "You have your own projects, you're trying to get them made, sometimes you're successful, sometimes you're not. And then somebody offers you something and you say, *Well, am I going to sit around here for another year or so, trying to raise the money for this? Or do I just take this job?*"

George had joined Francis and Steven in lifting himself out of that conundrum. The "garbage clauses" he had negotiated away from 20th Century Fox—giving Lucasfilm control of merchandising, and a huge share of the proceeds derived thereof—made him even richer still. Every kid in America wanted a plastic lightsaber, a Luke Skywalker action figure, a Darth Vader lunchbox. George could choose to make virtually anything he wanted to next, and someone, somewhere, be it 20th Century Fox, another studio, or an equity investor, would back him. He would be dependent on that next film's success to remain in that position, however, and dependence was exactly what he wanted to get away from. "George had this whole plan," De Palma says. "He wanted to build a business that had nothing to do with Hollywood." That meant making a sequel, and having it be as or more successful than *Star Wars*—which was, ironically, exactly how the suits George loathed approached their business.

The press surrounding the movie catapulted George to a level of fame and success with which he was not entirely comfortable. Journalists were fascinated by his lifestyle—the fact he ate junk food and wore plaid shirts, jeans, and sneakers; that he still lived in the house in San Anselmo and still drove his silver '67 Camaro. Inevitably, reporters wanted to know about his relationship with Francis. In his answers, George was friendly, though he frequently made a point of underscoring the differences between the two of them. "We are opposites," he told a journalist from *Time*. "If Francis says black, I say white. He is impulsive, always on the edge of trouble. I am inherently conservative. We complement each other." They were, as *Star Wars* raked in money, in a period of antagonism, fueled primarily by Francis's upset that George hadn't given him any profit points.

"Why should he [have any]?" George asked. "He had no connection to the movie."

George also reneged on his trade of a profit point with Milius, after *Big Wednesday* came out and bombed, dismissing the agreement as a "bad investment" he was free to withdraw from. George's sense of superiority stung; he had become "too good for everyone," Milius said, and "very, very distant. George has his entourage around him. Could do no wrong. Everything was for George."

The press was not privy—yet—to the depth of the disputes.

"Instead of showing their friendship by pricking fingers and mixing blood like so many Tom Sawyers," wrote the *Time* journalist interviewing George, "the Big Four directors—Coppola, Scorsese, Spielberg and Lucas—have traded scripts and sometimes even percentage points of the profits from their new films. They are not yet Metro, Goldwyn and Mayer—but they are getting close."

New York, New York came out in theaters a month after *Star Wars*. Marty, by his own admission, had screwed the film up. It was a bigger picture than he had ever tried to wrangle, and he'd been at the worst point in his life in which to wrangle it. Minnelli and De Niro were huge stars; the eventual $9 million budget was bigger than he'd ever had, four times the amount spent on *Taxi Driver*. And he'd become, he confessed, "cocky." He convinced himself he didn't need a script—he'd improvise. He didn't need choreography—he'd shoot it like a documentary. He didn't have to choose between making an homage to the artifice of classical Hollywood filmmaking and making a gritty, personal film about "the impossibility of two creative people in a relationship"—he was Martin Scorsese; he could do both.

Marty had never learned to make a movie "without becoming part of . . . the suffering of the characters." He snorted coke to keep himself going, took prescription lithium to balance out his moods. He started sleeping with Minnelli and living in an apartment on the studio lot. His wife, Julia, would appear on set unannounced, trying to catch her husband with his pants down. As she raged around the lot, often drunkenly, Marty and his leading lady retreated to her trailer. Assistant directors told Julia they were having story meetings and should be left alone.

She gave birth in the fall, to a daughter she and Marty named Domenica. Within days, with the baby bundled on her arm, Julia returned to haunt the set, and Marty and Liza locked themselves in her trailer again. When Marty and Liza weren't having sex, they were getting high, and for the first time, Marty sat in the editing room and was too messed up to turn his footage into a movie. "I was just too drugged out to solve the structure," he confessed. He was exhausted and had lost all perspective. George dropped in to support him and told him that if he wanted the film to be a success, he should give it a happy ending, and Marty knew George was right, at least as far as box-office success went, but he couldn't bring himself to do it.

After all that, the film came out and underperformed, and the reviews felt uniformly dismissive. Even Roger Ebert, always Marty's champion, thought it confusing and only worth watching if your expectations were low. "Marty had this feeling that *New York, New York* was his valentine to Hollywood," Minnelli said, "and then Hollywood rejected it."

"*Star Wars* was in," Marty said. "Spielberg was in. We were finished."

Julia found Minnelli's silk blouses in her own closet and filed for divorce. She tried—and, mostly, failed—to get screenplay assignments. For about a year, she drank and did drugs and self-destructed; the pain and anxiety were so intense she felt like she was coming apart. She asked friends how they managed to write without drinking.

"Try and let the higher power write through you," one suggested.

She couldn't picture herself doing that—hard as it was to shake the habits instilled by a Catholic upbringing, she had rejected God as a child, and found the idea of letting the imaginary man in the sky write through her a little ridiculous. But the title of a Dylan Thomas poem swam into her mind: "The force that through the green fuse drives the flower."

Well, she thought, *I can believe in that.*

She set herself what she considered an achievable goal: She would handwrite at least three pages every morning, no excuses. By 1978, she was sober and working for Paramount. She had found a way to "creatively unblock" herself by writing her fears and self-judgment down, accepting them as a part of her craft rather than an obstacle to it. Encouraged by friends, she taught the method at ad hoc workshops, wrote its steps out in a book she called *The Artist's Way*, and sold photocopied, self-published copies.

Marty, for his part, didn't find a path to peace. The affair with Minnelli ended. His second marriage was over; he had a second young daughter to co-parent. As a sickly child in church, he had wondered, "What's the sense of hanging around here? If you die, you can go to heaven. So why be here?"

Though he wouldn't put it in those exact words, Marty felt something akin to a death wish. His drug consumption increased.

"I have very little time left," he told journalists.

"I took chances," he confessed. "[I was] out of time and out of place and also in turmoil in my own life and embracing the other world, so to speak, with a kind of attraction to the dangerous side of existence."

He shot music documentaries and partied with the rock groups. Loneliness overwhelmed him. Robbie Robertson, the Canadian singer and guitarist for the Band, moved in with him as his own marriage fell apart. The two men listened to music and watched movies around the clock, never sleeping. Robertson liked the films for the stories, but Marty always responded strongest to pictures about guilt.

The same guilt, Robertson thought, driving him to destroy himself.

George called Steven in the fall. Philip Kaufman had signed on to direct a remake of *Invasion of the Body Snatchers*.

"Are you still interested in that movie I told you about in Hawaii, because Phil isn't going to do it now?" George asked.

"Yes, I am," Steven answered, "certainly."

· 26 ·

THE HORSE MAY TALK

Francis returned to San Francisco in the middle of June 1977, trailing with him over a million feet of film. Nominally, Richard Marks, one of the editors of *The Godfather Part II*, supervised the picture cut, and Murch designed the film's soundtrack, but the sheer mass of film, and the chaos of Francis's indecision over the shape the film should take, quickly blurred the lines of duty. Francis would ask one editor to cut a sequence, watched it, and then had assistants reconstitute the reels so he could pass them on to another editor and ask them to cut it their way. When they were done, he'd sit in the screening room at the Tower and run it, maybe mumble "That's good" or "I like this," and leave, before starting the process all over again. Murch described the process as watching the river to see which fish gets upstream. The film's premiere, scheduled for December, was pushed back to May 1978.

Francis wanted to lay a soundtrack ranging from the Doors to Richard Wagner's "Ride of the Valkyries" over Storaro's images of astonishing beauty, each frame a work of art; he wanted the film's pace, and its sound mix, as immersive and ambiguous and hypnotic as the performances. But he was unclear how to make it all work, and many at Zoetrope felt it was Murch who held the picture from falling apart. It was hard to tell, as Francis spent days and nights in the penthouse, whether he was avoiding his problems or stoking a fire until his own inspiration caught.

"Is this ever going to work?" he asked.

"The horse *may* talk," Murch reminded him.

Paramount called regularly, asking Francis to direct *The Godfather Part III*, saying Puzo had written a draft already and John Travolta, the hottest name in town coming off *Saturday Night Fever* and *Grease*, was interested in starring. Francis couldn't help making fun of the idea, especially after dinner in Napa, with an audience around him and a hot espresso in his hand. "What I'd really like to do is *Laverne and Shirley Meet the Godfather*," he said. "Or how about *Abbott and Costello Meet the Godfather*? With John Belushi as the Godfather?" Tony Chiu, a reporter present, listened to the laughter build, feeding Francis's routine. "Francis Coppola puffs out his cheeks," Chiu wrote, "furrows his brows and pops his eyes in a dead-on Belushi imitation then, in Lou Costello's rising wail, he hollers, *Heyyy, Aaaabbbboottt!*"

He was almost too unserious to cope with the day-to-day running of business. Kitchens had left to work on *Star Wars*, and Francis replaced him with a series of managers, none of whom lasted more than six months. Every time, Francis would call all the employees together to introduce the new hire, and every time he would sing the same song. "You're the manager," he told them. "I'm just one of your employees. You're in control. I'm terrible at these things; you call the shots." Inevitably, Francis and the manager would butt heads, it became clear who really called the shots, and Francis hired somebody else.

He distracted himself with other projects—and with Missy. One of the films he and Fred Roos were producing for Zoetrope was an adaptation of Walter Farley's *The Black Stallion*, a novel about a teenager, Alec, stranded on a desert island with a horse after the ship on which they were both traveling sinks. Alec and the horse survive together and, after they are rescued, team up to enter into a race against established champions. The film was a family affair crewed with familiar faces: Carroll Ballard would direct the film, his first fiction feature; Caleb Deschanel was the cinematographer, Robert Dalva the editor, Francis's father, Carmine, the composer.

Francis, however, couldn't quite crack the script. Ballard took a run at it. Murch had a crack, as did the Texan writer William Wittliff. The drafts got more and more mystical. Francis grew exasperated.

The idea emerged that, maybe, Missy could write it.

It was unclear whose idea it had been, Francis's or hers. But it was an opportunity for Missy, who had never written a screenplay before, to become a produced writer. Intentional or not, it became Francis's parting gift to her.

Missy traveled to Canada to meet Ballard and start work on the film, collaborating with Jeanne Rosenberg, a USC graduate Ballard trusted. Neither Jeanne nor Missy had a credit between them, and Francis's partners, Fred Roos and Tom Sternberg, expressed concerns. "They were thinking, *Oh my God, we're going to have these two* girls*, and it's going to be a catfight*," Rosenberg remembers. (Roos, in particular, was so obtrusively macho that his ex-girlfriend, the writer Eve Babitz, described him, in one of her trademark cryptic expressions, as one of those men who "liked baseball too much.")

"Meanwhile," Rosenberg says, "Melissa was the most generous, the most open, the most fantastic storyteller, always even-keeled and imaginative and creative, so easy to be with." They wrote and rewrote throughout filming, trying to find scenes Ballard would like, even though Ballard preferred "everything open-ended, all of the time." They tore handwritten sheets out of their pads and handed them to the actors, the ink still wet, minutes before the camera rolled. As first screenwriting gigs went, this was a baptism by fire. "I think Francis—however they met and whatever was going on—I think he really, really respected Melissa's intelligence, her mind, her creativity, her storytelling ability," says Rosenberg. She wasn't there as a favor.

Early in the shoot, Harrison Ford happened to pass through Toronto. He'd been on the *Star Wars* press tour, on and off, for about six weeks, hitting premieres, press junkets, and television sets with Carrie Fisher and Mark Hamill, and all three were feeling the whiplash of sudden, dramatic celebrity. Months earlier, Ford had been a stoner-carpenter dad who could barely get an acting job. Michelle Phillips, of the Mamas & Papas, went to see *Star Wars* and leapt out of her seat when Han Solo appeared on-screen.

"That's my pot dealer!" she yelled out.

Now he was one of the most recognizable and desirable men on earth. In New York, right before flying to Canada, he realized he would no longer be able to walk around in public unmolested—not for weeks, and maybe not ever again. Whenever he left the Sherry-Netherland, it was to run to a waiting car, the screech of hysterical fans ringing in his ears.

The three leads dealt with the attention in their own ways, and Ford seemed to wear his new status least comfortably. Hamill was often excited as a puppy, and Fisher—as suffocating as Princess Leia would sometimes come to be—was the daughter of Hollywood royalty, and had grown, at least, the illusion of thick skin. Harrison learned in the public eye. He spoke slowly, thoughtfully. He wasn't always the most interesting interview. As the promotional tour dragged on and the three stars were asked the same questions, day after day, he seemed the least able to feign enthusiasm for answering them.

His wife, Mary, was even more alienated by the new reality. She had met and fallen for "Harry" at little liberal arts Ripon College in Ripon, Wisconsin, had never cared for Hollywood, and now it was everywhere, like a miasma seeping through the cracks under her home's doors and windows. Harrison was away all the time. The press took a keen interest in everything he did. There were thinly veiled suggestions of extramarital flirtations. There was the palpable morning-after self-consciousness between her husband and his gorgeous twenty-year-old co-star, plainly visible when they sat together on every talk show couch. Ford and Fisher had, in fact, consummated a fling on location while filming *Star Wars*, an affair Fisher only admitted to publicly after forty years of open speculation from fans and the media. For Harrison, fourteen years older, it had been a casual carry-on, but Carrie had fallen hard, and it marked her, exacerbated all of her raw, youthful insecurities. And though it was over, it made Mary Ford, at home caring for Harrison's two young sons, feel like a background extra in her own life.

By the time he landed in Toronto, Ford's life was in awkward, difficult transition, just as Melissa Mathison's was, though the parallels were not on Fred Roos's mind when he invited them both to dinner one night after *Black Stallion* wrapped for the day. He was just going out to eat with two old friends.

Harrison and Missy hit it off. She was smart, sensitive, had a way of making people feel understood. She wasn't daunted by celebrity, could see the silliness in it. She'd been around it her whole life.

They kept in touch. Soon after Ford returned to Los Angeles, he moved out of the family home and took a pad in West Hollywood. In the fall, he flew to Yugoslavia for nine weeks, to film the war movie *Force 10 from Navarone*, continuing on from there for another month in England and three weeks in Malta. The picture didn't even sound good on the page, and Ford had no real reason to be in it except to make some extra money, maybe get a film in the can quick to help people remember he wasn't *just* Han Solo. He flew Mary and the boys to Yugoslavia for a brief family holiday, the kind that brings families further apart. At the same time, Mathison was still in Canada, and Francis paid her a desperate visit. "Francis promised me he wouldn't go see her," Ellie wrote in her diary on October 12. "I just found out he is there. It feels like [a] ball hit me right in the stomach." By November, Francis was back in San Francisco, and Melissa had followed the *Black Stallion* crew to Europe—first to Sardinia, then Rome. It was good for her to be away. Friends of the filmmakers dropped in for a visit, including Marty. According to several crew members, Harrison Ford, too, came—to see Missy.

Two years later, Ford would ruefully joke to an interviewer that he couldn't remember where in Eastern Europe *Force 10* had been shot. "That was a difficult film to make," he said. When asked why, he stumbled. "That's just . . . a whole area I don't, uh, don't want to talk about." Relationships ruptured—shabbily, painfully. New ones burgeoned.

Ellie looked up the word *apocalypse* in the dictionary. "One of the definitions," she wrote in her journal, "was, 'revelation of hidden knowledge.'"

Back in San Francisco, the sound designer for *The Black Stallion*, Alan Splet, strapped a microphone to a horse's barrel to record it galloping, and another to its muzzle to capture its snorting and breathing. A beautiful, blond, blue-eyed twenty-two-year-old named Valerie O'Conor—"naturally manic and stupid," she says of herself, and professionally trained with horses—was hired to assist him. She stayed on at Zoetrope, as a sort of general assistant. Every day on Pacific Avenue was fast-paced and surprising, with none of the corporate hierarchy and stiff division of labor that had made O'Conor's previous jobs feel dull and routine. She began dating Tony Dingman, a San Francisco poet and bon vivant who worked as Francis's jack-of-all-trades aide. Dingman enjoyed a good drink and a good adventure. Valerie did, too.

Francis, when he was around, was larger-than-life and charismatic. "There are plenty of people who quite rightly talk about how much they love him," O'Conor says. "He made you feel like he was interested in your opinion, like it really mattered." He hired her as his script typist, set her up with a desk in the penthouse at the Sentinel. She worked directly for him for eight months, during which he seemed to her to be in the midst of a serious breakdown. Up there, at the top of the Tower, O'Conor experienced what she calls "heavy, pure Francis." The apartment wasn't big—the living space and office, a tiny bedroom with a tiny en suite bathroom, barely bigger than an airplane toilet. He wanted her around almost around the clock, transcribing everything he said. He seemed to feel that the solution to *Apocalypse Now*'s structure lurked in his subconscious and might emerge at any time. Much of what O'Conor had to write down, however, was manic procrastination.

"Almost none of it had to do with finishing the film. Not one damn thing," she says. "He would find anything to be distracted by—anything that wasn't the picture." He complained about growing up a "fat kid" none of the girls liked, about their desiring the more-handsome Augie instead, about a lifetime of unrequited love and lust. He spun a plan to establish a story development department and produce a slate of films. Sometimes, with O'Conor hammering at the keyboard, Francis would write a whole scene out of nowhere, seemingly on the fly; she would learn later it was inspired by real-life pain being experienced by people he knew. Once, at a party, she watched as Francis noticed a married couple—close friends of his—on the brink of an argument. He was fascinated. "Maybe it was about a divorce, or maybe not," O'Conor remembers, "but in any case, there was some huge conflict, with three or four people there, and someone was definitely crying. And he started goading them. Cleverly goading them—they didn't know they were being goaded. He was poking them to create this . . . orgasm of them topping out on the other side. It was a social event, and they didn't want to lose it right there and then in front of everybody, but he *wanted* them to lose it right there and then. And when they did, he stood back and watched it, and then he had me type it up the next day. He created it in the first place. That's what got me—that he would sacrifice personal things you had with people in the pursuit of drama."

He encouraged her to trust her talents as a writer and story editor, and she once wrote a scene for him, showed it to him. Soon after, at another party—there were a lot of parties—she overheard him telling other people about it as if he'd written it himself. He looked at her as he did so, knew she was standing by, listening. "It was so unimportant," O'Conor says. "Was it a test of my loyalty? Was I going to bust him? What neediness caused him to do that odd little thing?"

When he did turn his attention to *Apocalypse*, it was almost always about the voice-over narration. Murch wrote several versions, Richard Marks wrote several versions, the novelist and poet Richard Brautigan tried a pass. Michael Herr, who had been *Esquire*'s correspondent in Vietnam, had a little desk at the back of the penthouse, and he and Francis rewrote draft after draft. Late one night, Francis dragged upstairs a drunk, houseless veteran, who he'd found in the alley behind the City Lights bookstore, his veins thick with cheap booze, his feet wrapped in blood-soaked rags. Francis planted him in the middle of the room and let him rant and rave and asked O'Conor to transcribe every word, in case they could make something out of it.

It all made Milius furious. O'Conor was one of the women on whom Milius's meager charms didn't work—"He was a screaming, misogynistic, shoot-your-gun-through-the-ceiling-in-meetings asshole," she says—and she hated when he came to the penthouse, packing a handgun in an armpit holster, wearing a jacket that seemed chosen to emphasize the bulge made by the weapon. He was insistent no one else could have writing credit on the movie. "He kept making aggressive sounds towards Michael Herr, who wouldn't hurt a fly—and had actually *been there*," O'Conor says. Milius seemed particularly insecure around Herr, who had spent much of two years in Vietnam and later suffered a breakdown from the trauma of what he had witnessed during the conflict. His presence made Milius eager to justify himself, and he kept reminding everyone in the building he'd have gone to Vietnam himself if he hadn't had asthma. "Oh, it was his asthma, it was his asthma," O'Conor intones derisively. As if it were a given Milius would have gone and been a war hero if not for this Achilles' heel.

After rejecting Milius's original ending, Francis considered replacing it with the same framing device as in Conrad's book, which would have seen Willard working on a rich man's pleasure boat and telling the story in flashback. He ditched that, too, and Milius wrote a new ending, in which Kurtz dies and Willard visits Kurtz's wife back on home soil, a scene he thought was "very good," but which didn't excite Francis. Milius still thought he was writing a film about war, but, says Mike Kitchens, Francis was making a film "about filmmaking. About ego. Not about Vietnam."

Francis settled on a final scene in which Willard, having killed Kurtz, stands uncertain on the steps of his temple, realizing he has not eliminated him but replaced him. "I was trying to say that morality is an issue that we have to take as it comes," he said.

And then, using the first example relating to his own life that came to mind, he added: "One day you lie to your wife, and one day you don't."

· 27 ·

DO YOU WANT TO LIVE OR DIE?

Ellie didn't know how to deal with Francis's dishonesty. She thought the two of them had agreed to face the complications of life together, honestly and without trying to change each other, but now she felt simply suspended, prey to someone else's whims. "Part of me has always believed that my prince, an artist, would make my life happen for me," she wrote. "I realized that I have always been waiting. Waiting to be old enough to drive, waiting to go away to college, waiting to fall in love, waiting to lose my virginity, waiting to finish college, waiting to get a job, waiting to get married, waiting to have a baby, waiting for Francis to get a chance to direct, waiting for him to finish his film, waiting for the next one, waiting to go on location, waiting to go home. Waiting for the rough cut, waiting for the fine cut."

She felt both wronged and responsible. Francis was full of contradictions and so was she. What pulled them apart was also, she later told Francis's biographer Peter Cowie, "the dynamic that has kept us together."

In early November, United Artists agreed to postpone the release of *Apocalypse Now* once more, all the way back to October 1978.

Ellie hoped some pressure would be relieved. On November 16, she and Francis took a break to fly to Washington, DC, for a reception given by President Jimmy Carter to celebrate the film industry.

George and Steven were aboard the same private plane. Up in the air, staring at the crab-leg cocktail on the fold-out plastic table in front of her, the aircraft's engines humming a monotone, Ellie felt almost alienated from physical reality.

Close Encounters was opening in cinemas across America as they flew. George knelt in his seat in front of Francis, and turned toward him over the headrest. *Jaws* was still the biggest film in history, for ten more days.

"*Star Wars* will be number one at 7:05 next Saturday night," George said. He'd done the math.

Steven turned to them from across the aisle. The three men started talking about the depression that hit each of them after their successes.

"After *Jaws* opened," Steven said, "I wanted to get away. I went around the world, and there was no place but India and Russia where there weren't *Jaws* billboards and t-shirts."

"You have to use success to stretch the bounds of filmmaking," Francis said. "Stretch the form, make the films you want, make a forty-minute film, a six-minute film. Make the films you really want to make."

"I want to do a live TV show," Steven said.

"Do a daytime soap if you want to. Take a chance, be risky."

"You, too, Francis," George said.

"Yes, but I no longer have the financial base."

"Ah, come on," George said. "You'll always have the money."

"You just have to make something beautiful," Francis said, "you can't worry about if anybody will see it. You can distribute it. Success is a drug. It's like a woman: if you chase it, you won't get it."

Ellie did not record in her diary how the talk of chasing women made her feel.

"Success is a drudge"—George smiled—"like chasing girls."

The rest of the trip was equally surreal. They dined at the White House, stayed at the Watergate Hotel. A *New York Times* photographer staged Francis, George, and Steven for a photograph outside the hotel, "the three hotshot directors." Over tasteless room service breakfast, George predicted that laser discs and cassettes would soon destroy the feature film, enable the audience to watch just short scenes, whatever suited their mood for a moment, like choosing a song or a piece of music.

"It's as if the core of me is trying to cut through the illusion and look at the structure," Ellie wrote. "Francis wants to cover over the seams and wrinkles of life and maintain the illusion. That is the basis of filmmaking."

Close Encounters of the Third Kind hit cinemas in mid-December 1977. The media was quick to compare Steven's work of "science fact," as the director called it, to George's escapist science fiction, and not always favorably. Writing for *Variety*, the critic Arthur Murphy—who had studied mathematics, not film, and who, in the publication's own words, "pioneered the field of box-office reporting," prioritizing "financial and economic analyses" of a film's earning potential over its artistic merit—found Steven's film spectacular, but also "misanthropic" and "irritating," "unusual" for a film "designed to reach a very broad, blockbuster-type mass audience," and painfully lacking in "the warmth and humanity of George Lucas's *Star Wars*."

This time, at least, the pioneering Murphy misread the mood of the American public. Many of his peers celebrated *Close Encounters* as one of the great genre films ever made, and though it wasn't as big as *Star Wars*, it set house records and became the biggest box-office hit Columbia Pictures had ever had. When Academy Award nominations were announced the following February, both Steven and George were among the nominees for Best Director, both films were nominated for their special effects and their editing, and John

Williams was nominated twice—for his score for each of the films. In total, *Star Wars* was nominated ten times, including Best Picture, and *Close Encounters* eight. At the ceremony in early April, Marcia won her Oscar, shared with Richard Chew and Paul Hirsch; George and Steven went home empty-handed. Steven's film was great—but to many, it was, like *The Sugarland Express* and *Jaws*, just a little too dark. It gave the audience pleasure, but, to paraphrase Alfred Hitchcock, it was the kind of pleasure one feels when they wake up not from a dream, but from a nightmare.

Francis, who had become a staple at Oscar ceremonies in years past, was hard at work on his own pleasurable nightmare. That spring, he showed a rough cut of *Apocalypse Now* to cinema exhibitors, who received it with muted enthusiasm—not the kind of reaction that suggested he might make the gigantic profit he needed to open his own movie studio. He set up more screenings, inviting random audiences plucked from the public, handing them questionnaires, workshopping what changes he should implement. The film's scheduled release date was pushed back a third time, nearly another year, to August 1979. United Artists couldn't take away the film, as executives usually did with difficult directors—*Apocalypse Now* belonged to Francis, not them—but there was talk of the studio taking legal recourse to repossess the Coppola home in San Francisco, the vineyard in Napa, anything Francis owned that wasn't nailed to the ground.

Francis had thought of the film—an ambitious project he paid for himself, putting his money where his mouth was, serving as the director, the writer, the producer, the financier—as a "heroic" venture, yet the press kept making fun of him for his ambition, his perceived self-indulgence, all the while treating films like Columbia's *Superman*, released in 1978, as commonsense business. The culture shift away from celebrating risk-taking art and toward promoting pure entertainment, and the moral assumptions underlying that shift, frustrated Francis no end. "Why was *Superman* a prudent film to make," Francis bemoaned, "and *Apocalypse Now* the effort of a lunatic?"

In early September 1978, Marty flew to Telluride, Colorado, for a film festival co-founded by a friend of Francis's, the curator of the Pacific Film Archive, Tom Luddy. By now Marty was down to under 110 pounds. Drug use, mainly a combination of Quaaludes and cocaine, made his asthma worse, his breathing labored. A doctor had put him on lithium to stabilize his moods. He mixed and matched legal, prescribed medications in combinations that made his body feel even weaker. His soul was profoundly depressed. He couldn't even bother to hide it anymore; back in May, while in Cannes, he'd only managed to answer questions at a press junket by snorting snow between five-minute interviews, and cut short the event when he ran out of drugs, telling the journalist entering the room for his time: "No more coke, no more interviews!"

While in Telluride, where he didn't know any dealers, Marty scored what turned out to be some bad blow. Soon he was coughing up blood. He lost consciousness and woke up in a New York hospital, "surprised that I was near death." He was bleeding internally, at imminent risk of a brain hemorrhage.

It had been less than five years since the release of *Mean Streets*, and Marty—instead of being halfway to being Fellini—was an addict in a hospital bed. "I almost died," he told Ebert. His desire to make movies was gone, as swiftly and surely as an apostate's faith.

One day, Marty looked up from his hospital bed and there was De Niro walking through the door, a book in hand.

"Do you want to live or die?" De Niro asked. He seemed heartbroken and furious. "What's the matter with you, Marty? Don't you wanna live to see if your daughter is gonna grow up and get married? Are you gonna be one of those flash-in-the-pan directors who does a couple of good movies and it's over for them?"

The actor threw the book onto the bed. A hardback with a red dust jacket and pulpy cover illustration of a square-jawed man smoking a cigar, against a smaller picture of the same man in boxer's gloves and shorts. The title *Raging Bull: My Story*, by Jake La Motta.

"Now, do you wanna shoot it?" De Niro asked. He'd got Schrader to write a version of the screenplay, but it wasn't right—not yet.

Marty was in hospital for ten days and ten nights. He prayed. He read La Motta's book again. He felt humbled by the love in his doctors' and nurses' careful care. The time they took to mend him.

Robbie Robertson dropped in while Marty was considering *Raging Bull* again, and dithering still.

"Let's get off the fence on this thing," Robertson said. "Are you passionate about this? Do you have to do this movie? Because if you don't have to do it, don't do it. And I don't mean *obliged*, as in have to, I mean *passionately* have to. Can you go on with your life without doing this?"

Whether he should go on with his life at all was the question on Marty's mind. Lying in that foreign bed, alone—loneliness always terrified him—he thought back to the churches of his childhood, the cold mornings when he couldn't make it to Mass on time, his early dreams of being a priest. He thought of the Sicilian culture in which he'd grown up: the fear of betrayal, the pressure on men to become hard, to put their pride over their peace. He felt he had lived his life in "naivety and denial." He had tried to destroy himself, and something had saved him, and "I felt it was for some reason," he said. "And even if it wasn't for a reason, I had to make good use of it."

He thought of a passage in the Gospel of John, in which Jesus makes a blind man see, and the Pharisees call the once-blind man to testify so they can decide whether Christ, performer of miracles but also friend to the poor, the destitute, the sex workers and the tax collectors, is a prophet or a sinner. The once-blind man answers, "Whether He is a sinner or not I do not know. One thing I know: that though I was blind, now I see."

He thought of himself and he thought of Jake La Motta. Maybe the distinction between the sinners and the saints was not as clear, or as meaningful, as he worried about. Keitel had said this once, about the pimp he played in *Taxi Driver*: "There is a great humanity in a pimp," he said. "I don't mean humanity in its benevolent sense, I mean humanity in its suffering sense."

Marty had spent his life torn between goodness and sin, depressed by a world that was anything but divine, flagellating himself for his own inability to transcend, his own failures to believe. For too long, he had been ashamed, "silent about where I came from or hiding certain things," he said. Finally, he thought, "it didn't matter. It's who we are."

Marty began to see what had drawn De Niro to *Raging Bull* for all these years—the humanity in the suffering. Not a boxing story, but the story of a man—who happened to be a boxer—who put himself through pain, and put the people he loved through worse pain; a compulsive man with base instincts always getting in the way of dignity.

"Yes," Marty told Robertson when he saw him, "if I don't do this movie, I have no reason to live."

"There you go," said Robertson. "Do it and do it really good."

· 28 ·

EMPIRE

In March 1979, cameras rolled on *The Empire Strikes Back*, George's follow-up to *Star Wars*. He and Kurtz cast around for someone who could direct it for him, and George chose Irvin Kershner, his former instructor at USC. He still remembered Kersh vouching for him when Warner Bros. wanted to cancel *THX 1138*.

Kurtz called Kershner, who wasn't convinced about the value of sequels and was wary of the expectations but agreed to meet George anyway. Over lunch in the Universal commissary, the younger man only added to the pressure. The second *Star Wars* movie, he told Kershner, was not just a movie.

"If the second one works," George said, "then I can make more. If the second one doesn't work, then that's the end of *Star Wars*."

"Well, why do you want me?" Kershner asked. "Of all the younger guys around, all the hot-shots, why me?"

"Because you know everything a Hollywood director is supposed to know but you're not Hollywood," George answered.

When Kershner finally agreed to take on the job, he flew up to San Rafael, where he and George shook on it, and George showed him plans for a complex he called Skywalker Ranch. He had bought land in the woods north of the Golden Gate Bridge, and wanted to build a campus for filmmakers, with everything they needed in an idyllic setting. Like Zoetrope, but bigger and better. A Disney Imagineer was drawing up the architectural plans, and Marcia would help design and decorate the details.

"This is what this film will pay for," he said. "This will only happen if *Empire* works."

Kershner was fired up. "It's not like saying, 'Look, we're going to make a lot of money!'" he remembered. "It's saying, 'We're going to build something.' And that was the difference for me . . . Money itself means nothing. It's what done with it that matters."

While Kershner shot the movie at Elstree under Kurtz's supervision, George would supervise ILM's move away from Los Angeles and into the new facilities outside San Francisco. George had negotiated unprecedented terms with 20th Century Fox: He would pay for the film himself, and the studio would act solely as a distributor—with no right to any creative or financial input, "no access to set or locations or post-production facilities," and "no right to view dailies, rough cuts or any other portion of the Film until delivery thereof." Fox could not organize test screenings, though they would have to pay for any George chose to hold. They could not change the film's title. Lucasfilm committed only to making a picture set in the *Star Wars* continuity, with a budget of at least $8 million, rated no higher than PG, running no fewer than 90 minutes and no longer than 150, and starring at least two of Hamill, Ford, and Fisher. Fox would pay Lucasfilm $10 million upon delivery of the final cut—and then pay George's company 52.5 percent of *Empire*'s profits up to $20 million, 72.5 percent up to $100 million, and 77.5 percent thereafter, in perpetuity.

If *Empire* was a success anywhere near the scale of the first *Star Wars* film, George would finally be truly, and wholly, independent. He would produce the third film in the Skywalker trilogy immediately after that, consolidate his financial stability, and he would never have to deal with a Hollywood studio again. He'd go back to making films like *THX* without worrying that anyone else found them cold or abstract. He could give his friends, from Korty to Robbins, the means to make films cheaper, without begging hat in hand.

George sat down and told ILM supervisor Jim Bloom that they would be making twelve *Star Wars* movies, of which this one, *The Empire Strikes Back*, was the second, even though, in the narrative, it took place fifth. They would then make a third film, which was chronologically the sixth, before moving on to a prequel trilogy, and then the final Skywalker trilogy. The tenth, eleventh, and twelfth films, as Bloom remembers, would expand the universe: George planned one to focus on the Wookiees, another on the droids. (Bloom doesn't recall the pitch for the last one.)

George hired Charlie Weber, an East Coast businessman, to serve as Lucasfilm's CEO, and tasked him with using the money coming in from *Star Wars* licensing deals to grow the company into something bigger than a film production business. On Francis's recommendation, George hired Sid Ganis—one of the young sales executives from the old Warner Bros.–Seven Arts days—to head Lucasfilm's marketing department.

A young writer named Lawrence Kasdan, recommended by Steven, had written most of the script for *The Empire Strikes Back*, after science-fiction author Leigh Brackett had worked on an early draft before suddenly passing away; the result was darker and more romantic than the original, with an open-ended cliff-hanger at the end to motivate audiences to return. Part of the cliff-hanger had been thrust upon George, however, by Harrison Ford. Neither the filmmaker nor the actor had foreseen Han Solo's popularity, and he didn't really fit in George's master plan. Solo was a narrative device. But then Huyck and Katz had given him all the hip banter, and Harrison Ford had got up on that screen and stolen the show, and now George had a dilemma: Before *Star Wars* had ever started shooting, he'd managed to sign Mark Hamill and Carrie Fisher to a three-picture contract—but Ford had only agreed to two. What if he refused to come back for a third and undid all of George's careful world-building?

Lucas and Kurtz tried to get Ford to agree to an extra film so George could at least finish his trilogy unfettered. Ford refused. He didn't want to be defined by *Star Wars*, or forced to turn down something better because the franchise had dibs on him. *Wait and see*, he suggested. *Cross that bridge when we get to it.*

George, who had publicly committed to at least three films, felt very much on the bridge now. He was reluctant to kill Han Solo off, especially with *Empire* shaping up to be much more somber than *Star Wars* already. In the end, he decided to do to the character what Ford had forced him to do to the contract negotiations: He put him on ice. The end of *The Empire Strikes Back* would see Han Solo frozen in carbonite, somewhere between life and death. A second cliff-hanger on top of the main one, about Luke coming face-to-face with Darth Vader and his own fate. Another reason for the kids to come back for another picture.

The *Empire* shoot began in Norway, standing in for the frozen planet Hoth, to which the Rebel Alliance has retreated in the face of a vengeful counterattack by the Empire, stung by the destruction of the Death Star. From the first week, the film ran over schedule and over budget. Kershner, unused to working with computer effects, liked to move the camera around the blocking that grew organically every day, without realizing that every time he changed an angle, or the lighting, it would no longer match the work ILM was creating, following the storyboards, to be optically inserted later. Kershner was under the impression he had free rein. As he remembered it, George told him, "Don't worry about the fact that you don't know special effects. What I want you to do is think up the shots . . . Then we'll let the boys figure out a way to do it. That way it's a challenge for them, and we'll do stuff that hasn't been seen." But sometimes Kershner chose a perspective that was impossible to work with at all. He resorted to fast-moving handheld shots when an idea struck him. His director of photography, Peter Suschitzky, shot beautiful work, much more artful than the first picture, but he was expensive and exacting, too. When shooting the battle on Hoth, Suschitzky would frame his shots in a beautiful composition, aimed squarely at the foreground action. Jim Bloom, representing ILM, would tell him he had to tilt his camera upward, and Suschitzky would explode, "What do I want to go up there for? It's empty sky!"

"Because there's meant to be snow walkers up there, coming towards you," Bloom explained. "They're firing the stuff into the snow, and you've got to see these explosions going off."

Suschitzky would frown, shake his head, and readjust, but he never got accustomed to framing half the shot in his imagination. Bloom returned to California, the rest of the crew carried on to Elstree, and the trouble continued. As intelligent and creative as Kershner was, it became apparent that, even when the sets were built and the actors were in costume and the cameras were ready to roll, so much of a *Star Wars* film existed only in George's head. And George, stretched thin by the multiple challenges of making the film and establishing ILM, was not in England. He trusted his producer, Gary Kurtz, to keep the train on its tracks.

"There was a communication problem on *Empire*," says Bloom. "It wasn't communicated back to LA that they were running out of money. And George must have trusted Charlie [Weber], but Charlie knew fuck all about the movie business. The people in England must have thought, well, we're telling Gary, and Gary's the one who's responsible for getting money in the bank account. And for some reason, it came as a big surprise that they were going millions of dollars over budget."

Part of the miscommunication might have stemmed from the volatility of the pound—the same dollar amount got you more, or less, on the ground in London depending on the month—and Kurtz insisted the overages were not a problem. It was "typical movie stuff," he said. *There's no way this is ever going to lose money*, he told George. The studio would cover the costs; the box office and the merchandising would easily make up the added expense. His attitude outraged George.

In England, Kershner himself felt "behind before we even started," he remembered, because Stage 3, one of the eight stages booked by Lucasfilm at Elstree, had burned to the ground on the night of January 24, most likely after a crew member on Stanley Kubrick's *The Shining*, then still using the stage, had carelessly flicked a cigarette down without properly putting it out. Editor Paul Hirsch, who had relocated to London with his wife and young child for the picture, remembered Gary Kurtz telling them the production was a week behind schedule—after the first week of shooting. Kurtz otherwise kept the news to himself, thinking he could make up time, but he was wrong. By the end of the second week of filming, he told Hirsch they were now *two* weeks behind.

The replacement stage was only ready in May—six weeks late. The delay was intolerable, particularly because Kurtz had already scheduled the shoot so tight it left no room for contingency. Then tragedy compounded the film's troubles: On May 31, second unit director John Barry, who had been the set designer on the original *Star Wars*, collapsed on set, burning with fever, and died of meningitis the next day. He was only forty-three.

The production could not afford to stop, so Kurtz hired Harley Cokeliss, a young director who had made a sci-fi fantasy a couple of years earlier for the Children's Film Foundation. As Cokeliss remembered it, *Empire* was ten weeks behind schedule when he came on board. Kershner shot the bare minimum he needed with the principal cast on each set, and then Cokeliss took over, filming every green screen and explosion, with a second unit crew laboring to match the lighting and camera movements of Kershner's first unit work. Shooting inside the forty-ton *Millennium Falcon*, Cokeliss had an editing machine brought onto set so he could watch Kershner's preliminary assembly of the scene and instruct his stagehands on how to rock the gimbal on which the spaceship was built: "Okay, it's flash, down on the right—okay, flash, flash, and down on the left . . ."

Hundreds of construction crew worked around the clock. Kershner arrived in the morning and blocked and rehearsed scenes while the paint on a new set dried; the second he called "print" on the last shot of any given scene, the workers descended to tear the set down and replace it with one scheduled to be used a few days later. Filming the scenes on Dagobah, the swamp planet to which Luke Skywalker travels to complete his training, was most complicated, because making Frank Oz's puppet of the alien Jedi Master Yoda believable was "the most difficult thing," Kershner remembered, "like pulling teeth," a process of fits and starts and fragments made even slower by the knock-on effect of all the delays. "I had to start shooting many sequences from the last shot and work backwards because the set wasn't completed when I had to start shooting. I would do the shot and everyone would stop building. After the shot was completed, you would hear banging all around the place and see trees going up." Hamill couldn't hear Oz speaking Yoda's lines from under the set, where he hid from the cameras, and no one could clearly hear Kershner, because he had to wear a gas mask to protect his lungs from the smoke pumped across the bog and the fumes and dust floating up from construction. Like the shark in *Jaws*, Yoda was the kind of trick that sounded simple, but had never really been done before, and like Steven's mechanical sharks, none of the Yodas—there were three—worked reliably. Their eyes misbehaved particularly, refusing to focus and blink. Kershner stayed relaxed—a good quality to have as far as the work was concerned, though less so in terms of making up for lost time. He would improvise with the cast—Ford, especially, enjoyed being free of George's strictures, and he and Kershner developed such a close working relationship that Carrie Fisher—whose chemistry with Ford now crackled with pining, post-break-up recrimination—grew frustrated when her former lover talked down to her, telling her about scene rewrites as if he were not a peer, but a sort of second director. Kershner let the unfulfilled sexual tension smolder. It suited the bickering dialogue Lawrence Kasdan had written for Han Solo and Princess Leia this time around, though it slowed work further still. Every time Fisher stormed back to her trailer, or skipped a day's work, begging illness, Kurtz hovered by the camera, sweating bullets.

In truth, Kurtz thought, George's inconsistencies sat at the root of all of *Empire*'s difficulties. He wanted the film to be his exact vision, but he wouldn't go through the ordeal of directing it. He wanted the film to be better than its predecessor, but he was so concerned with the cost he increasingly told the people who *were* on set every day to stop wasting time on subtleties. He wanted a story that captivated audiences, but he was also so obsessed with secrecy, so fearful a tabloid journalist would sneak into Elstree or a crew member would leak a plot point, that he refused to give most actors a full script to work from. The performers in smaller parts received only their own lines; David Prowse, who played Darth Vader inside the suit, didn't even know his own, since George knew he could have James Earl Jones dub whatever lines he chose into the soundtrack in postproduction. No one but Kershner knew Darth Vader was Luke Skywalker's father; Mark Hamill only found out the morning they shot the scene, and was sworn to secrecy. The line was printed in the shooting script not as "I am your father," but as "Obi-Wan killed your father," and that was how Prowse read it on the day. George hadn't even told Kurtz. "Sometimes he would want to control everything," Kurtz said of his friend, "and then other times he would go away and you wouldn't hear from him for a long time. He blamed me for all the things that were difficult on *Empire*."

Eventually, George flew in. Irving Kershner turned away from the camera, and there he was, watching silently. Kershner, oblivious, lit up.

"George! Come over here!" He brought the younger man closer, misreading the look on his face for embarrassment, and made him watch as "we shot a scene that ended up about six seconds on film and took us 10 hours to shoot!" Kershner laughed. "Everything kept breaking! Nothing worked! And George just stood there and never said a word."

Eventually, Kershner offered to cut a sequence or two from the script, in an attempt to speed the schedule up.

"Don't change a thing!" George shot back. "Keep going as you're going."

Privately, he seethed. As he watched Kershner play around on the Dagobah set, coming up with ideas that sounded as expensive as they were wonderful, George turned to Kurtz.

"You tell him to get this done fast," he said, "or I'm going to plunk that puppet down in one spot and shoot all his lines in close-up!"

In front of the lens, Luke Skywalker struggled, dejected, with his training in the Dagobah swamp. Behind the camera, the making of *Empire* mirrored the mood of the picture: It was a long, slow ordeal, a Sisyphean attempt to fulfill earlier promise. At times, George was Yoda; more often, he was the alter ego he had invented, Luke, with what felt like the pressure of a whole world weighing down on his shoulders, alone and away from his friends and comforts, laboring day after day in a wet and foggy hinterland.

Kershner felt "humiliated" when he learned George had started editing the first half hour of the film without his input or consultation. This time, there were no impassioned speeches from George about the auteur theory and the supremacy of a director's vision. No more pained cries about nitpicking over budgets or interfering producers cutting fingers off his baby. As far as *Star Wars* went, the vision would always be his—because so was the money.

In mid-July, the production ran out of it.

George scrambled. He risked losing everything.

Charlie Weber came up with some accounting ingenuity so Lucasfilm could lend *Empire* some cash from its merchandising division—just enough to keep the film going while he and George arranged a better solution. George didn't want to go to Fox and surrender ownership of the film, but he gave the studio the chance to give him some extra money, which he pledged to pay back. Weber flew down to Los Angeles to meet Fox's new chairman, Dennis Stanfill, who wasn't a movie guy but a finance guy. Stanfill refused to extend Lucasfilm a loan. When Weber suggested that George had made the studio a fortune, that *The Empire Strikes Back* would rake in even more money, that at least one more *Star Wars* film was virtually guaranteed to do the same, and that George would soon be looking for a partner on *Raiders of the Lost Ark*, Stanfill appeared unmoved.

"I've got you," he told Weber, "and I'm going to squeeze you."

Weber sprung to his feet. "You just lost *Raiders*," he said, and stormed out.

Stanfill's manner upset Laddie, too, who left Fox for Warner Bros. as *Empire* was halfway through filming. Stanfill doubled down and threatened to buy out the completion bond on *Empire*, meaning the studio would take over the production, replacing Kershner, Kurtz—*and* George. At the eleventh hour, Weber played on his contacts back East, and convinced the Bank of Boston to lend Lucasfilm $27.7 million. Only then did Stanfill, realizing he had been circumvented, agree to inject a further $3 million into the film's running budget, in exchange for a small increase in Fox's share of the film's eventual box-office and merchandising receipts.

Empire had come dangerously close to being shut down, bringing down with it all of Lucasfilm and George's careful plan for long-term independence.

"It was excruciating," George said. "A movie company operates on the split second, like a football game. If you are not there when the decision has to be made, you lose the moment. Soon those moments add up to hours, days, weeks."

He quietly removed Kurtz from the movie and sent a new producer, his old friend Howard Kazanjian, to London for the last two weeks of filming at Elstree.

As Kurtz felt it, it was George who had changed. "He was very different," he remembered. "He became convinced that all the audience was interested in was the roller-coaster ride, and so the story and the script didn't matter anymore . . . One of the arguments that I had with George about *Empire* was the fact that he felt in the end, he said, we could have made just as much money if the film hadn't been quite so good, and you hadn't spent so much time. And I said, 'But it was worth it!' "

George would bring up the old Howard Hawks adage: All a film needed, over the course of ninety minutes, was three good scenes and no bad ones. Kurtz hadn't thought that way since the low-budget Roger Corman days. As *Empire* was filming, the two men had been discussing the third installment in the trilogy, *Revenge of the Jedi*, and the mythological note on which they had always agreed the trilogy should end—Han Solo would sacrifice himself, Princess Leia would become queen of what remained of her decimated people, Luke would strike out on his own—was progressively discarded. George decided to bring back the Death Star, because it was recognizable from the first movie. Cuddly alien creatures called Ewoks—little more than teddy bears Lucasfilm could sell replicas of to the kids—became central to the plot. Almost losing *Empire* and thrusting himself into bankruptcy made George only more convinced the main thing a *Star Wars* movie had to do was make money. Once a young director who valued a film's quality and integrity above all—he had made *THX 1138*, after all, without a thought for its box-office potential—he had slipped into the thinking he and Francis deplored in film executives. Here he was, making a movie to make money—so he could make the next movie, yes, but also so he could grow Lucasfilm and build Skywalker Ranch. The bottom line had become as much a concern to him as the quality of the film on the screen.

For now, Kershner's integrity kept *Empire* on track. He made the most of Kasdan and Brackett's work, and his devotion to character detail paid off in the subtle moments that made the film more complex than the first movie had been. Late in the story, as Han Solo is about to be frozen in carbonite, Kasdan's script called for Solo to kiss Princess Leia.

"I love you," Leia's dialogue reads. "I couldn't tell you before, but it's true."

"Just remember that," Solo's dialogue responds, "'cause I'll be back."

Neither Kershner nor Harrison Ford liked the exchange. They shot the scene as written, then retreated for lunch.

"I think she ought to just say 'I love you' as I'm passing by," Ford suggested. Kershner liked that. What about Ford's own line? Telling Leia he'd be back took all the jeopardy out of the situation, he thought. The audience would hear that and assume Han Solo survived, which was also not a sure thing, given Ford's reluctance to sign on for a third movie. Ford said, "If she says, 'I love you,' and I say, 'I know,' it's beautiful and it's acceptable and it's funny."

Not being part of the conversation pissed Fisher off, but her anger fed into her performance as Leia loses the man she loves. George, unsurprisingly, also resented the change.

"Wait a minute, wait a minute," he said when he saw Kershner's first cut of the film. "That's not the line in the script."

"'I love you, too' is not Han Solo," Kershner said.

"The audience will laugh," George complained.

"That's wonderful," Kershner said.

George only kept it in the picture after the first preview, when the audience did laugh—and then lined up afterward to tell him what a wonderful line it was.

Kershner inserted another small addition even later in the film, when Luke has a mechanical hand attached to replace the one lopped off by Darth Vader. In a brief close-up shot, the medical droid pricks Luke's prosthetic finger and it twitches, showing that he feels touch through the synthetic skin. Kershner didn't know what George's third and final film would be like, but he felt "it would attempt to be a love story, and [for Luke] to feel that he's got a rubber hand there, touching a woman, would have been horrible. So I gave him feeling." It was the kind of sensual detail George never would have conceived of, and it anchored his fairy-tale galaxy with real humanity.

The Empire Strikes Back came out on May 21, 1980. It made more money its first week than *Star Wars* had, and ended its run with a $200 million gross. The Directors Guild of America, the union of which George was a member, spoiled the party by opening proceedings against him for breach of their rules on credit. The Lucasfilm logo that opened the picture was a proprietary credit, they said—after all, the company contained Lucas's name—and having it at the front of the film, while Kershner's credit as the director appeared only in the end credits, broke the union's rules.

George refused to change anything. Kershner protested that he didn't have a problem with it. In the end, George simply quit the union. It didn't matter. He didn't plan on working within the system the guild propped up, and Kershner had already done his job. George gave the go-ahead for construction at Skywalker Ranch.

Charlie Weber left Lucasfilm soon after. It wasn't all to do with the debacle on *Empire*. Fundamentally, Weber was a boardroom suit and conditioned to prioritize short-term, year-on-year profits—the exact sort of executive with whom George, even though he had hired him, had spent his entire career in conflict. Weber had urged George to keep his ambitions "sensible," and pushed back on all the money being—as he saw it—wasted on the Ranch.

"The ranch is the only thing that matters," George protested.

Weber's outlook clashed with George's ironclad conviction that Lucasfilm should stand for something more than the bottom line. And yet he replaced Weber with more corporate suits, one after the other, the first sign that he was drifting away from the painful, stressful, uncertain experience of making movies. Bloom says, "He ran into trouble with *Empire* and probably decided, with that point of view, that, *I'm not spending my own money anymore. I'll spend my money on other things, but not that. I'm gonna make my money where all the money came from,*" which was toys, T-shirts, games.

"He set Lucasfilm up as a business to be run by businesspeople," Bloom adds, "whose backgrounds were in business and licensing and merchandising and marketing and investing money. But none of them were movie people," whom George distrusted. But also, "I know that George didn't want to be like Francis. Francis didn't care if he made a billion and lost a billion and made a billion. That's how Francis rolls. He doesn't care if he's up or down. And George didn't want to have a life like Francis."

· 29 ·

WHAT IF HE GOT THE DOG?

Steven, tired of being too dark, desperate to be hip, returned to Universal to direct *1941*, a chaotic, madcap comedy about a mass panic across Los Angeles in the wake of Pearl Harbor. Milius had developed the story with two young USC graduates, Robert Zemeckis and Bob Gale, and part of Steven longed to be more like Milius—more arrogant and showy and *fun*—and he urged them to include as many self-referential, clunky gags as they could come up with. He cast drug-addled *SNL* comedians John Belushi and Dan Aykroyd, British horror legend Christopher Lee, and Japanese icon Toshiro Mifune. He packed the shoot with expensive and complicated set pieces. The whole thing had a gluttonous, quantity-over-quality recklessness. Everything he had made in his career had been hard; he wanted to let loose.

The Steven who directed *1941* was, perhaps, the closest he had been in years to the kid who had fallen in love with movies, experimenting, delighting in mayhem. As soon as the film wrapped in May 1979, Steven snapped to, as if returning home from a high school joyride and sheepishly having to inform his father he'd crashed the family car. The film came out and did okay business, though reviewers sneered at it. Steven, just a grown version of the boy desperate to fit in and be accepted, had always been the kind of filmmaker who judges how good his films are by how much money they make. He felt embarrassed in front of Sheinberg.

Milius loved the whole thing. The degree to which he felt responsibility for spending Universal's money or upsetting film critics could have been summed up in one of the most famous lines from the previous year's *Animal House*, which had contributed to making John Belushi a star: "You fucked up! You trusted us!"

One good thing came out of *1941*, though. Steven took note of Milius's assistant, a twenty-five-year-old former television producer named Kathleen Kennedy.

Kathy, as everyone called her, was bright, cheerful, and incredibly organized, a quality that stood out all the more in the midst of Steven and Milius's deliberately over-the-top zaniness. She was even impressive at the part of her job she didn't do well: taking transcription. Steven, Milius, Zemeckis, and Gale would sit in story conferences, or Steven and Milius would throw ideas for gags and set pieces back and forth, and Kathy would sit to the side of the room, steno pad and pencil in front of her. "She was terrible, and didn't know how to do it very well," Steven remembered. "But what she did know how to do was interrupt somebody in mid-sentence. We'd be pitching ideas back and forth, and Kathy—who was supposed to be writing these ideas down—suddenly put her pencil down and would say something like, 'And what if he didn't get the girl, but instead he got the dog?'"

Steven was never one to put someone back in their place, especially if their ideas were good—and Kathy's were. Her taste was sharp and her questions were unabashed, as if she had a nose for the untouched potential in a scene or setup, and no embarrassment about feeling around in the dark if it helped uncover it.

Born in Berkeley, one half of a pair of twins, to attorney Donald Kennedy and homemaker Dede, Kathy had always been driven. She was the starting quarterback on her middle school football team—the *boys'* team. In high school, she was the kid who was always on the student council, always one of the attorneys in mock trial, always volunteering for things. Her life had changed in her senior year at San Diego State University, where she was majoring in telecommunications. She got a part-time job working for a local television station, KCST, where she was surrounded almost entirely by men. And she stood in line with friends for hours, one warm day in late May, to see *Star Wars*. It was like a party outside the picture house, before the show even started. She had never experienced anything like this.

A few months later, she sat in a cinema and watched *Close Encounters*. The queues to get in hadn't been quite as long this time, but the experience was equally powerful. She decided, as she left the movie house, that she wanted to work in Hollywood, preferably for the man who had made *that* picture. She called up her old college roommate, Mary Ellen Trainor, who had already made the move to Los Angeles. "Mare," as her friends called her, had got a job on Milius's *Big Wednesday*, working as producer Buzz Feitshans's assistant. As it turned out, she had heard through her boyfriend, screenwriter Robert Zemeckis, that Feitshans's business partner, John Milius, needed a production assistant of his own, a sort of receptionist and gal Friday, to cover the new film he and Feitshans were preparing, *1941*. The film was going to be directed by Steven Spielberg.

"It sounds made up," Kennedy said later of the start of her career, "but it's true." She packed up, drove up to LA, and claimed the position. The first job Milius gave her was cataloguing his gun collection.

Is this really what I want to do with my life? she thought.

She stuck with it. In their spare time, she and her friend Martin Casella, who also worked in the office, went to see hundreds of movies. They yelled quotes from Terrence Malick's *Days of Heaven* at each other across the office. Kathy sat in on meetings, and "Kathy," says Casella, "was the only person who would ever say no to Steven. Everyone else would always go, *Yeah, sure, we can do that*, and Kathy would actually laugh out loud and go, *Steven! That's the silliest thing I've ever heard.* And all of a sudden he would go, *Yeah, yeah, let's—okay. Let's not do that.*"

Steven noticed that, even though Kathy worked for Milius, she always seemed to be floating around his office, eavesdropping, looking for an opportunity. One evening, he handed her a messy stack of his notes and asked her if she had the time to put them in order. Kathy went home and stayed up all night organizing them into tidy booklets. When she showed up at work the next morning with the job already done—in *booklets*—Steven looked blown away.

"I thought that's what was expected," Kathy said.

"She's not intimidated," Steven said. By anything. She was tough. One day, he walked past her workspace and placed a screenplay down on her desk.

"This is my next movie," Steven said. "Read it, I want to know what you think. Don't tell anybody anything about it."

The title on the cover read: "Raiders of the Lost Ark."

When Marty was well enough and discharged from the hospital, he and De Niro took a trip to Saint Martin, an island in the Caribbean, and rented a house for three or four weeks. De Niro woke early, took a run on the beach, then made coffee and dragged Marty out of bed. They sat at the little patio table and went through Schrader's script of *Raging Bull* scene by scene, cutting the writer's more over-the-top contributions—in particular a long soliloquy in which a self-loathing La Motta harangues himself while masturbating and finally blames his hand for being unable to come—and adding scenes from details they found in the scrapbooks La Motta had saved over the years. De Niro acted moments out, with such commitment Marty wished he could film them. They rewrote the dialogue. They turned the character less theatrical and more primal. They were committed to loving La Motta, for all his horrible flaws. Before they left for Saint Martin, they'd been coaxed into meeting United Artists executives at Marty's apartment on East 57th Street in New York, where the suits berated them about the depressing script, the graphic imagery, the repugnant main character. Production executive David Field had referred to La Motta as "a cockroach."

"He is not a cockroach," De Niro interrupted, in a whisper full of fury. "He is *not* a cockroach."

He insisted on even a monster's humanity. He and Marty finished writing on the beach and returned to New York and De Niro went to work, training with La Motta, painstakingly rehearsing every one of the nine choreographed fights the script called for him to put on film. No compromises. Marty went down to Gleason's Gym on 14th Street and watched De Niro go through them. He breathed in the funk of sweat and hot leather, the chemical sweetness of the antiseptic used to clean the ring and the mats.

"Are you watching?" De Niro called out.

We can't shoot this from my angle, Marty thought. He had already decided to shoot the picture in black and white, make it look like one of those old Weegee crime scene photographs, but he decided now he would also have to get in the ring. Choreograph the camera as if to a piece of music, punches and slips for notes, in rich period black and white.

He went to a couple of fights, one at Madison Square Garden, with Brian De Palma for company. He looked out for details. Blood dripping off the ropes. A trainer dunking a sponge into a pail of cold water and wringing it over the fighter's back, and the water, mixed with blood, running pink.

De Niro found old videotape of an actor called Joe Pesci, who was retired and running a restaurant in the Bronx; he called him up and set up a meeting, and they cast him as La Motta's brother. Pesci was in a club one night soon after and watched nineteen-year-old Cathy Moriarty win a swimsuit beauty pageant and thought she looked like La Motta's wife, Vikki, and Marty agreed, so they cast her, too. Neither of them were names, but Marty no longer cared. No compromises. On the first day of filming, Marty received a telegram from Schrader, who knew what was on his mind. It read, "I did it my way, Jake did it his way, you do it your way."

They filmed the boxing scenes first, ten grueling weeks, and then ten more weeks of non-fight scenes.

"He's the most risk-taking director I've ever met," the film's producer, Irwin Winkler, says of Scorsese. "He's brilliant, but he's brave, too."

"This is going to be my last film," Marty kept saying on set. Why not leave everything he had out on the ring? It felt good, he thought—working again, as he put it, "without a net."

"It wasn't even good or bad," he recalled of the process, "it was *experienced*. For me, it was a culmination of everything I desired to do, and I made it as if it was pretty much the end of my life . . . a suicide film. I didn't care what happened to it. I didn't care if I made another movie." Every day on set, he told himself, *This is the last one, and we're going for it.*

"Marty does [it] all on his own terms," Steven wrote a few years later. "He doesn't fret about what's going to 'work,' or 'not work,' for an audience. His concern is what's true to his characters and what's right for their feelings. If he can work that out—and he always does—then he goes right ahead and lets the audience catch up with him. And if they don't, Marty doesn't wait around for them. I admire that, too. Maybe I even envy it a little. Francis Coppola also takes those big chances. He goes his own way."

Production paused so De Niro could go to France and Italy and eat bread and pasta and ice cream all day, to put on the weight he needed to play the older Jake La Motta. He tackled the eating with the commitment he brought to everything, and found it more painful than sparring in the ring. Then he came back for a few weeks, filmed the stuff with the retired La Motta.

When filming was done, Marty hired another old NYU classmate, Thelma Schoonmaker, to cut the picture. It was her first fiction feature. She had won an Oscar over a decade earlier, for cutting the documentary *Woodstock*, but the editors' union wouldn't let her in unless she had worked five years as an apprentice and an additional three as an assistant, an absurd requirement by which she refused to abide. Instead, for over a decade, she had worked only on nonfiction projects. She and Marty cut *Raging Bull* in the director's apartment at night, Marty in a kimono on the couch, watching movies on a little television while she prepared scenes for him. Their old university teacher, Haig Manoogian, the man who had turned Marty on to filmmaking, died in May, as they were cutting, renewing Marty's commitment to finish the movie in a way that would've made him proud. When the final picture was locked, Marty went to LA to finish postproduction, and spent another sixteen weeks just mixing the sound, "inch by inch."

"I've got to show them something," producer Irwin Winkler complained one day after a meeting with United Artists. "I keep going to the[m] for more money, and they haven't seen anything."

Marty told him to calm down. "What's the worst that can happen? It doesn't open."

"Right," Winkler exclaimed. "That's terrible!"

"It isn't worth getting a heart attack about," Marty said. He'd do it right, or there was no point in doing it anyway. No compromises. No concessions.

He locked the reels two days before the film opened on November 14, 1980, flying back to New York with one of three prints of the film in his bag and delivering it himself to the Sutton and Cinerama 1, where it would premiere, two blocks away from his own apartment. *The Empire Strikes Back* had come out in May and easily become the biggest picture of the year, clearing George's debts and enabling him to pay a cumulative $5 million in bonuses to Lucasfilm and ILM employees. But Marty felt none of the dread he had felt when *New York, New York* had come out weeks after the original *Star Wars* and been wiped out. The box office didn't matter. The reviews didn't matter. He had made it for himself.

Marty and De Niro had written a closing scene for the movie, one that neither Madrik Martin nor Paul Schrader had imagined. It shows La Motta, middle-aged and bloated, standing in his dressing room, delivering lines from the one-man show he performs to make a living as a retired boxer. He stumbles over the memorized, sing-songy words, and they come thick through his lips, as if from jaws freshly wired back together. "I remember those cheers, they still ring in my ears, and for years they remained in my thoughts," he says. He turns the page on the ring and looks to the future. "Though I'm no Olivier, if he fought Sugar Ray, he would say that the thing ain't the ring, it's the play. So give me a stage, where this bull here can rage, and though I can fight, I'd much rather recite"—he pops his arms wide—"that's entertainment." He pauses, swirls his tongue around his cigar, nods to himself. "That's entertainment."

"I want to feel like Jake does at the end of *Raging Bull*, a stage I've never gotten to," Marty said later. "He's at peace with himself, by the end . . . I knew when I was doing it that I wasn't there. Up to that point I was with him, but I couldn't get beyond that point."

He still thought he could find a way to live a spiritual life. He still raged and agonized over the ways he fell short. Self-acceptance remained, for now, out of his reach. He went back to New York. He rented a little apartment not far from where he had grown up, furnished it with cheap furniture, as sparse as a room in a rectory. He watched movies. He spoke to his therapist every day.

Raging Bull was not his last film. He was back on set less than a year later, again with De Niro by his side, making another film about an obsessive psychopath. Most of Marty's movies revolved around men with unrealized or fantastical self-images, idealized lives they could pursue, maybe even, briefly, falsify, and *The King of Comedy*, about an aspiring comedian who kidnaps a famous talk show host and demands a spot on his nationally televised show as ransom, was no different. As a takedown of American culture's obsession with celebrity and public recognition, it was sincere, unflinching, almost purposefully unpleasant. Its entire point seemed to be the denial of catharsis.

Marty was not at peace with himself yet. There were wounds left to pick.

· 30 ·

THE DREAM

Apocalypse Now finally premiered at the Cannes Film Festival in the spring of 1979. Members of the press booed and jeered when writer Françoise Sagan, president of the jury, announced it as the joint winner of the Palme d'Or, making Francis one of only two directors, at that time, ever to win the most prestigious award in world cinema twice.

A majority of critics seemed thrilled by the movie's first two-thirds but disappointed by the muted ending. They expected explosions, blood, battle. At his press conference, Francis berated them. He attacked American journalists as "the most decadent, lying, deceitful, corrupt press in the world." Behind the scenes, Francis's entourage offended many industry players present at the festival. A cloud of arrogance traveled with them across the Croisette. "It was terrible, the way they behaved," one filmmaker said. "They acted like their shit doesn't stink."

In August, the film finally opened in America, though only in three theaters, the ones with equipment Francis judged sufficiently sophisticated. United Artists charged a premium ticket price of five dollars. It went wide in October, showing in three hundred cinemas, and slowly built its business, eventually grossing $80 million, double its production and marketing budget. Francis would not go bankrupt. He would, in fact, be wealthy again.

Much of the press made fun of the movie or dismissed it. Was it an anti-war film? Was it meant to be realistic? Was it satire? Was the film right-wing, like Milius, or progressive, as Coppola presented himself?

To De Palma, those were the wrong questions to ask. Francis turned everything into either theater or myth. "I don't think politics constitute Francis's strong suit," he said. "Fundamentally, that doesn't interest him."

Kanaly, when he finally saw the film he had been discussing with John Milius for a decade, felt the same way but took the opposite conclusion. He and many of the vets he knew were tired of Vietnam films straining to be political. "I liked *Apocalypse Now* because it wasn't trying to be something else," he says. "It's a story. And you can take away from it what you want."

To coincide with the release of the film, Simon & Schuster published *Notes on the Making of "Apocalypse Now,"* crafted out of a selection of Ellie's diary entries during the film's production. The book did not name Melissa Mathison, but plainly admitted Francis's infidelity; it was candid about Ellie's occasional self-pity. The press mocked her for it. Christopher Lehmann-Haupt, writing for the *New York Times*, found in the diary "evidence of her superficiality, her bad grammar and syntax, and her astonishing lack of memory and roots," an essentially "meaningless" project in which she cast herself as a candidate for "the year's Understanding Wife Award." The critic Harriet Van Horne, writing in her column for the *Los Angeles Times* syndicate, called the book "bitter."

Ellie was stung by the criticism. Francis did not rush to her defense. Journalists were predictably eager to ask him about his wife's book—which portrayed him as erratic, adulterous, and self-involved—and he did not appear to have prepared a response. When the *San Francisco Examiner* writer Jeanne Miller asked him, "Were you comfortable with your wife's rather frank journal?" Francis snapped, "That's my business."

In private, he echoed the press's snide assessment of Ellie's talents. Valerie O'Conor was at her typing desk in the penthouse that August as Francis, holding a copy of *Notes on the Making of "Apocalypse Now,"* vented to Ron Colby. "He was saying—I'm paraphrasing—that the book so clearly revealed her naivete and her lack of intellectual capabilities, it would only make it perfectly clear why he needed the companionship of other women who were smarter. He felt publicly exonerated. He was so fucking pleased with himself," O'Conor says. "I was sitting five feet away at my little word processing station. They *did* slightly lower their voices, but again: They were five fucking feet away."

Ellie's book was an act of public shaming that was somehow confession, revenge, and catharsis, all at once, and revolutionary in its honesty. It embarrassed Francis. By his own admission, he was easily embarrassed—and Ellie admitted she knew embarrassment was his greatest fear. In that sense, *Notes* was like a bloodletting necessary to heal her marriage. If Francis could risk their relationship to face himself, then she could risk it for the same reason. The book reclaimed some of the agency of Ellie's life for herself. The pound of flesh it claimed in the process was fairly owed her.

Kaja Fehr read *Notes* as soon as it was published, and had no doubt that the unnamed other woman was Missy. She felt sad for her friend, and sad for Ellie, too—"how could she move through all that," she says, "knowing what was going on?"

O'Conor, too, knew about Missy. Everyone involved in *Apocalypse*, anyone who had ever been around Zoetrope, knew. "I don't remember Francis talking much about Melissa," O'Conor recalls, "but then again, he was sleeping with me, too."

They had started fucking soon after O'Conor started taking down Francis's every thought—a charged, intimate process in the claustrophobic penthouse. Maybe she was a rebound, to help him get over Missy; maybe there had always been others. "I had no illusions either that I loved him or that he loved me," O'Conor says. She assumed she wasn't his only extramarital relationship—what did people think the penthouse bedroom was for, when he had a house a ten-minute drive away?

Once, Dingman—who often ran errands for Francis, and often had O'Conor tag along—drove her across the Golden Gate Bridge to Wolf Ridge, in the hills above the Marin headlands, to Missy's house. Dingman unlocked the door, and as they walked in, O'Conor noticed blankets and drapes along the entryway, pinned up to the molding, stained with what looked like bird shit. In fact, there were bird droppings everywhere: on the furniture, on piles of laundry waiting to be folded. Mathison owned ten or twelve pet birds, which lived loose inside the house, and not many people visited her at home, in part because she was nervous about the birds escaping. Dingman had been asked to check on the birds while Mathison was out of town.

O'Conor had only met Missy a couple of times, during the making of *The Black Stallion*. She had found her "very, very soft-spoken, extremely quiet." She knew Francis paid for the Wolf Ridge house.

She and Dingman, high on acid, took a walk. The birds were trippy. The setting sun dripped over the house, orange as an egg yolk. They wanted to get a better view of the bay, and somehow they ended up climbing out an upper-story window and crawling up onto the roof. They sat close together as the temperature dropped. A low fog was coming in over the headland, all around them, in undulating waves shaped by the landscape. "We watched the fog rolling over the bay, straight from the ocean, like cotton, at thirty miles an hour right over our heads," O'Conor says. "That's what I remember when I think of Melissa. Bird shit and fog."

• • •

Francis's first plan for all his *Apocalypse Now* money, according to Murch, was to put together "a whole studio in San Francisco. He was going to take over North Beach and make it a cultural protected zone. And he needed money."

He went to George first. "And George thought about it," Murch says, "and George wouldn't give him the money, even though *Star Wars* had made him a multimillionaire."

"I made you!" Francis protested. "You wouldn't be rich if it wasn't for me! And now I'm trying to do something great. It's an investment, George! It'll be a huge success!"

George tried to explain his position. "It's a financial risk to do this," he said.

That was when Francis started looking for land in Los Angeles. It harked back to his admiration for the old Hollywood moguls, and the idea of rolling back into Los Angeles, triumphant, the owner of his very own studio, after everyone had made fun of *Apocalypse Now* for three years, appealed to his sense of showmanship.

"George was now bigger than Francis, because of *Star Wars*," Murch says, and Francis's feeling was "*This town's not big enough for the two of us. This is the real Zoetrope. George can have his Skywalker Ranch. He's the country mouse, and I'm the city mouse.* You know." Murch pauses. "And then it all went belly up."

"I dream of being part of a really scintillating world cinema," Francis told the *New York Times*. "If I ever got the bucks that, say, George Lucas got from *Star Wars*, I'd put every penny into changing the rules. Those people in Hollywood respect my ability, but they think I'm a little crazy. They would like me to be taught a lesson; you know, play ball." Little did they know, he said, that he planned to "turn the studios into dinosaurs. I believe in ten years, half of them will be gone, and there will be new companies."

He wanted Zoetrope to lead the way into the new era. He'd produce one film a month, directing some himself, using "the full magic of technology. We won't shoot on film or even on tape, it'll be on some other memory—call it electronic memory. And then there's the possibility of synthesizing images on computers, of having an electronic facsimile of Napoleon playing the life of Napoleon. It's almost do-able right now; it just takes the wisdom and the guts to invest in the future."

That was what George was already hoping to do at Skywalker Ranch. Privately, his paradise was mired in the mud, too. One of the first people he'd hoped to convince to join him at the Ranch was John Korty, so one day he got into his Camaro and drove out to Stinson Beach to show him the plans. Since the failure of the original Zoetrope, Korty had won Emmys directing acclaimed television movies, as well as an Academy Award for the feature documentary *Who Are the DeBolts? And Where Did They Get Nineteen Kids?*, but he was still perpetually broke. He took on a couple of Hollywood pictures, including a sequel to the smash hit *Love Story*, but they were failures, and each time Korty returned to Stinson Beach burned and dispirited by the cutthroat materialism of studio filmmaking. He was a workaholic with firm moral principles, and it had yielded no reward. He had missed his sons growing up. His marriage was falling apart; his wife, the designer Beulah Chang, says the stress and self-involvement made him verbally abusive. When George turned up and spread out the architect's blueprints and conceptual sketches for Skywalker Ranch, he expected Korty to react with excitement. Instead, he was bemused and reticent.

"Gee, George," he said. "This is kinda far out."

George went into the details: The compound would be just an hour north of Stinson Beach in Novato, and after years of working out of a barn, Korty could work in a state-of-the-art facility, with his filmmaker friends just a walk across the grounds away. It meant continued independence, but in comfort. He was going to build Korty his own building, he said, name it after him, and he wanted him to move his production company there. Korty listened, noncommittal. Once George had left, one of his employees asked him what he was going to do.

"Why would I want to go work up there?" Korty growled. "I'm already working here."

De Palma went to take a walk around the property, he says, "before the Ranch was the Ranch." As they ambled, George explained the vision, "this idea it was going to be some kind of intellectual, aesthetic university out here in the woods somewhere."

"Who's going to come and stay here, when you get to go to San Francisco, or LA, or New York?" De Palma asked him, laughing. "Why? Why would we be up here in the woods?"

George just shook his head.

"It never really worked," Mike Kitchens says. The editors and sound mixers who traveled up to the Ranch for work complained of feeling "trapped. You can't walk out and have coffee or lunch." If you were stuck on a scene, you couldn't go for a walk among other humans, break off from the claustrophobia of the suite, and come back refreshed, although George had never thought of being around other people as a means of relaxing. "So they ended up building these four restaurants," with organic fruits and vegetables grown on the grounds, "and the editors all would've probably preferred to be able to find a Chinese place instead."

Many friends saw the location of the Ranch as a concession from George that, after a decade, San Francisco itself had become Francis's territory. "He based his operations across the Golden Gate Bridge as if to get away from Francis's enormous influence," says Richard Chew, "because if you're around Francis, you can't help but buy into whatever he's trying to sell you."

When the Ranch was finally finished, Francis had an espresso machine sent up to Marin County from Thomas Cara, the San Francisco retailer of Italian coffee makers. A reminder of the lounge on Folsom Street, where their dreams, however imperfectly, had first come true.

· 31 ·

HIGH CONCEPT

George had told Steven he could choose the screenwriter who would tackle *Raiders* for them, and Steven happened to have someone in mind: a young, struggling writer called Lawrence Kasdan, who, after years of trying and failing to get jobs, had just sold his first spec script, *The Bodyguard*, to Warner Bros. Kasdan had followed that up with another script, *Continental Divide*, a romantic comedy in the Spencer Tracy–Katharine Hepburn mode, and his agent had managed to get that one to Steven while he was in postproduction on *Close Encounters*. Steven had asked Universal to buy *Continental Divide* for him to direct, before sliding it to the back burner so he could make *1941* instead. He still loved Kasdan's writing, and *Continental Divide* thrummed with wit and Hawksian charm—exactly the nostalgic, old-fashioned feel Steven thought *Raiders* should have. He gave George the *Continental Divide* screenplay on a Friday, George read it over the weekend, and by Monday, Steven asked Kasdan back into his office.

"I'm gonna do a movie with George Lucas and I want you to write it," he said. "You gotta meet George." The three of them got together, and George gave the writer an even simpler pitch than he'd given Steven in Hawaii.

"I want to do this thing, the hero's named after my dog, he has a whip, it's like the old serials."

In January 1978, George, Steven, and Kasdan met for four days at the house of George's assistant Jane Bay in Sherman Oaks, and talked through the film, idea by idea, beat by beat. Kasdan was nervous, but he relaxed as the first day wound down. He realized George and Steven, for all their creativity, didn't know how to connect the set pieces, gags, visuals, and references pouring out of them. That was where he came in. His job was to stitch the showpiece sequences together, make the characters whole and believable, and find a coherent narrative to bind the whole thing together.

Some ideas were brought up and discarded. Steven suggested the Nazi thug, Toht, should have one prosthetic hand that was a combination flamethrower and machine gun, but George felt that was *too* pulpy. They both imagined a traditional love triangle between Indy, Marion, and Belloq, a concept eventually discarded because it slowed the action down.

Steven went off to shoot *1941*, and turned his office over to Kasdan. It was time for him to write. He completed a draft by midsummer, and George was impressed enough to offer Kasdan *The Empire Strikes Back*, after the original screenwriter, Leigh Brackett, had passed away in March. Not everyone was sure Kasdan had the tone right just yet, though. When that first draft came in, "Indy drank and smoked," remembered Lucas's producer Howard Kazanjian. "I fought hard to get that removed."

George and Steven guided the writer through several more drafts, picking up unused material, discarding what they felt didn't work. Kazanjian sourced old adventure serials on 35mm, and he and Lucas sat and watched them in the Lucasfilm screening room on the Universal lot. They took note of the most interesting cliff-hanger endings for George to feed back into the *Raiders* screenplay. Like George and Steven, Kazanjian had grown up on serials—still remembered the stories that had been his favorite as a child, still held on to 8mm home-screening copies of *Flash Gordon* and *Captain Midnight* to one day show his grandkids. By October 1979, with filming completed on *Empire* and *1941* weeks away from release, everyone felt ready to move into preproduction.

For all his hatred of the studios, George had become the closest thing American cinema then had to early studio producers like Irving Thalberg or David Selznick: a hands-on creative producer who was the originator of the material, responsible for the budget, and the representative of the company that owned the film. He had gone into USC fifteen years earlier wanting to be a cameraman and had graduated as a possessive director who fervently believed in the auteur theory and denounced interfering producers and executives. *Star Wars* appeared to vindicate that philosophy—no one but he could have made that film; no one but he even *understood* it until they saw it—only for George to immediately reject it, and become the very thing he had often scorned: the producer as author.

It was a unique situation, without a doubt, in that he had created the intellectual property. It also was born, by George's own admission, of his limitations as a filmmaker. "I think I'm a *terrible* writer," he said. "I can barely spell my own name, let alone form a sentence." And at the same time, "I've never really liked directing," he added. "I became a director because I didn't like directors telling me how to edit, and I became a writer because I had to write something in order to be able to direct something."

It was vital that he own Indiana Jones—his new name for Indiana Smith—as he owned *Star Wars*. He briefly considered financing *Raiders of the Lost Ark* himself, but the dreadful experience of *Empire* still weighed heavy on him, and he still had the final installment in the Luke Skywalker saga, *Revenge of the Jedi*, to see written, shot, and completed. He didn't want any more loans, and he would never consider taking an equity partner, which meant he still needed a studio.

First, however, George needed to round out his package by finding the actor who would play Indiana Jones. His casting director, Mike Fenton, pushed hard for thirty-year-old Jeff Bridges, an established star. Kazanjian thought they should hire Harrison Ford, who, to his mind, had proven his leading man potential as Han Solo, but George was wary of being associated with the same actor over and over, as Marty was with Robert De Niro or Steven was with Richard Dreyfuss. Besides, Ford was no sure bet. The only success he'd had as a leading man, in the fifteen years since his first movie role, was Han Solo. None of the three films he had chosen since *Star Wars* had worked. *Force 10 from Navarone* was a disappointing sequel to a seventeen-year-old war classic, *Hanover Street* a World War II melodrama that would have felt dated had it been made when the war was still on, *The Frisco Kid* a well-intended and forgettable gentle comedy. None of them made much money. Fred Roos still spoke to producers who asserted confidently that Harrison Ford was not attractive to women. Passersby who stopped the actor on the street often asked him if he had "done anything since *Star Wars*."

His inability to establish any respect for himself weighed heavily on the actor. Lucasfilm employee Laurel Ladevich remembers crossing paths with Ford in London during the filming of *The Empire Strikes Back*, and asking him why he looked so downbeat.

"I can't get a job," he growled. "No one's offering me anything."

George, Steven, and Marcia all preferred TV Western star Tom Selleck, who was older and more grizzled than Bridges, less laid-back, and carried himself like a man who knew how to shoot a gun and hike through a jungle—because he did. He was not yet well-known, and would not bring any preexisting character baggage to the role, as Ford might with Han Solo.

Selleck met with George and Steven, auditioned, taped a screen test in full wardrobe, and was offered the role—all *before* Steven's assistant, Martin Casella, was given the green light to drive a serial-numbered and watermarked copy of the secretive script to the actor's house for him to read.

Oh, shit, Selleck thought. *This is terrific.*

He told Steven and George that he had just shot a pilot in Hawaii, for a CBS crime series titled *Magnum P.I.*, and confessed that if the network picked the show up, he was contractually bound to prioritize that job. Steven and George waved his concerns away.

"Let us worry about that," they said.

Tom Selleck was Indiana Jones.

With his leading actor set, George sent more watermarked copies of the script out to every studio in town, along with an outline of the nonnegotiable deal he expected: a package of himself executive producing, Steven Spielberg directing, and Tom Selleck starring; a $20 million budget, full creative control, and a hefty share of the film's profits. The studio would pay every penny of the budget. Lucasfilm would own the film and retain all merchandising, licensing, and sequel rights, as well as oversee the film's theatrical bookings and promotional materials. "It was outrageous," admitted George's lawyer, Tom Pollock.

Mike Medavoy now ran Orion Pictures, a new film financing company with a distribution pact at Warner Bros. In the outfit's first year or two, he'd green-lit pictures from several of his former clients, including Francis and Milius, but even for him, "the deal was too rich."

George was unwilling to compromise on any aspect of his proposal. Had he been able to finance *Raiders* himself, he would have, but he was already taking that gamble on *Empire*, and wasn't yet in a position to place two such large wagers at the same time. He was open to working with any studio except Warner Bros., which he still resented for their treatment of *THX 1138* nearly a decade earlier. He sent them the script, sure—but even after nearly every studio in town passed, and Warner's Ted Ashley was the only executive to express interest, George, who could be as petty as the next man, turned him down. Nor did he ever go to 20th Century Fox, still smarting over their abandoning him when *Empire* had gone over budget.

The only studio willing to consider George's terms was Paramount, run by a new president, Michael Eisner, who had cut his teeth in television. Eisner thought George's proposal was worth considering, even against the advice of his chairman, Barry Diller—the man many filmmakers charged with ending the golden age of freedom they had enjoyed in the 1970s.

"The moment things changed was when Barry Diller joined Paramount," Paul Schrader says. Diller and his "Killers"—president and chief operating officer Michael Eisner, president of production Don Simpson, vice president of production Dawn Steel, and Diller's former assistant Jeffrey Katzenberg—were ruthless and profit-oriented, with backgrounds primarily in distribution, television, and merchandising. "Their attitude," Schrader says, "was *We know how to make money—can* you *fit into* our *model?*" Emblematic of this, Schrader felt, was Diller's close relationship with Frank Mancuso, the studio's head of distribution. Mancuso had been at Paramount since 1962, and distribution's offices had traditionally been a ten-minute walk across the backlot from the main executive suites, with creatives, filmmakers, and development staff in closer proximity. But "the day Barry Diller came in," Schrader says, "he moved Frank's office right next door to his." Diller, Eisner, and Mancuso developed a strategy for Paramount that Diller's assistant Katzenberg later described as getting into "the annuity business," by creating "tent-pole assets": In other words, rather than build their film slate around stars, as the old studios had done, or around directors, as Robert Evans had done, or around material, as executives like John Calley did, the new Paramount brass looked for successful properties they could turn into franchises. Every year, they hoped, they could have an event film on the release schedule, based on material the public already knew, virtually guaranteeing an income—in other words, countless *Empire Strikes Back*s and *Revenge of the Jedi*s.

This business model led Eisner to doggedly pursue Francis about a possible third *Godfather* picture, alongside similar efforts to lure John Travolta to sequels for both *Saturday Night Fever* and *Grease*. It was also the model on which George had grown Lucasfilm. Eisner wanted to be in the Steven Spielberg and George Lucas business—bad. *Star Wars* was the most successful film franchise in the medium's history, and Steven's *Jaws* had already spawned a *Jaws 2*, which, even without Spielberg's involvement, gave Universal the highest-grossing film sequel ever.

The new Paramount C-suite was made of a fresh breed of film executive, one who didn't believe in films but in "properties," not in "creative teams" but in "packages." Scripts were secondary to log-lines. Don Simpson was a screamer and pathological liar, addicted to the nightlife, who wore his low-brow taste proudly—"I have a cheeseburger heart," went his favorite saying about himself—and told journalists his idol was Warren Beatty, mainly because Beatty was the guy he'd have slept with if he'd been a girl. That was what every relationship boiled down to, for Simpson: fuck or get fucked. Dawn Steel, who had started at Paramount as Simpson's assistant, was hard as nails herself. She didn't believe in glass ceilings then—she was just one of the boys, though one with a leonine mane of tawny hair, wearing hoop earrings and Armani pantsuits. She and Simpson were a revealing professional duo: the man whose abhorrent behavior was forgiven, no matter how offensive, and the woman who was treated like a second-class employee, even if she never set a foot wrong. She had recently rescued *Flashdance* from the slush pile after it was put in turnaround—it would become a huge hit for the studio—but she wasn't allowed to watch the screen tests for the female lead part: Only men, she was told, needed to watch them, because they'd pick the right girl based on how fuckable she was on their "peter-meter." Steel matched her peers in work ethic and intensity, but she suffered from her balls only being metaphorical. She was paid less than the men, she was not invited to all the meetings, she wasn't allowed on the company plane. When she asked to join in on Katzenberg's annual whitewater rafting trip, an event attended by executives from multiple studios and agencies and at which "enormous amounts of business got done," Katzenberg just shook his head. "No girls," he said. "Noooooo girls."

Diller and Eisner ran the studio, but Katzenberg—dogged, relentless, abrasive, chauvinistic—best embodied its new ethos. "Katzenberg," wrote the *New York Times*'s film correspondent Aljean Harmetz, "doesn't have dreams. He has goals." Stories about the short, balding, live-wire young executive quickly grew legendary: how he turned up to work at six in the morning or earlier every day; how he made hundreds of phone calls a week; how he liked to tell colleagues that if they didn't come in on Saturday, then they shouldn't bother showing up on Sunday. On weekdays, he had two breakfasts and two dinners so he could double the number of meetings he had with directors and producers out of office hours. On weekends, he carried a script bag stuffed with two dozen screenplays, all of which he'd have read by Monday morning. He talked fast and colorful and hyperbolic. He couldn't have named any studio heads of the golden age or told you how many Warner brothers there'd been, but ever since he'd dropped out of NYU and got a job as an assistant at United Artists as a twenty-two-year-old, he'd had his eye on two things: an Academy Award and a beach house in Malibu. He was so eager to get scripts to his boss before anyone else could read them that he ran first drafts over to Eisner and Diller with the ink still wet and the paper still warm from the photocopier. Whatever he did, he had to give 110 percent; anything short of exceeding expectation was tantamount to failure.

His direct boss, Eisner, an English graduate from liberal arts college Denison University, prided himself on his ability to spot talent and choose material, and he and Katzenberg made a particularly energetic team. Eisner liked to say Katzenberg, like a terrier with a keen nose and sharp instincts, went out and bought home the meat, but it was he, Eisner, who knew how to cook it. In fact, coworkers frequently compared them both to dogs, emotionally simple and brimming with boundless enthusiasm and energy. Eisner didn't mince his words, and he didn't bother with massaging creative egos. Directors and stars were only as good as their projected box-office dollar value. Across Hollywood, there were filmmakers who loved Alan Ladd and John Calley, even many who defended Ned Tanen, but one was hard-pressed to find any who spoke up for Michael Eisner. The boardroom loved him. The word most used to describe him in private conversation, on the other hand, was *asshole*.

These Paramount executives were like a fun house mirror reflection of the group of Trancas Beach filmmakers—their '80s ethos, flash suits, and race cars in contrast to the directors' late-'60s camaraderie, drug-taking, and creative ambition. The younger breed—Katzenberg, Simpson, colleague Craig Baumgarten—went skiing together, ate breakfast at the Polo Lounge together, raced their matching Porsche 911s to the Palm for lunch. They, too, were friends as well as peers. They, too, had come up through the ranks together, and hung out as a group after hours. Only they didn't want to make great films, as Francis, George, Steven, Marty, and Brian had. They wanted to be rich, famous, and powerful. They wanted to win.

"This was a period in which studios took charge of their movies," said Baumgarten. "It wasn't like, 'Gee, we like it, or we don't like it, or why don't you try this or why don't you try that?' We began to issue blueprints."

Reclaiming initiative in development was one way for the studio to wrest power back from filmmakers they saw as out of control—like Michael Cimino, whose troubled and bloated Western *Heaven's Gate* was threatening United Artists' very existence as an independent entity, but especially Francis, who didn't seem to care about the financiers' bottom line—and also from their increasingly powerful agents, especially those at the new outfit on the block, the Creative Artists Agency, founded in January 1976 by five hungry defectors from William Morris. The founders of CAA had set the company up in a tiny rented office, with a twenty-grand bank loan as starting capital and their wives as receptionists, and within months were making bookings in the millions of dollars. Foremost among the five partners was a twenty-seven-year-old former UCLA med student, Michael Ovitz, who rivaled Katzenberg for indefatigability. Ovitz, more than anyone, had seen the profit potential in the popularity of freelance film directors—the very "unicorns" studios had first courted, and were now wary of. In the old days, when studios had filmmakers and actors under contract, audiences went to pictures on the strength of a studio's roster and reputation—Warner Bros. was known for its gangster films, for instance, or MGM its musicals. Now the moviegoing public was drawn to movie stars they loved and filmmakers they knew and invested in, like Francis, George, and Steven, and those stars and filmmakers could shape their own fortunes picture by picture, renegotiating their going rate with every success and failure. Ovitz popularized the new agency practice known as "packaging," whereby he would bundle several of his clients—a writer, a director, and actors—and sell them to the highest bidder as a take-it-or-leave-it combination. In this way, CAA made its customary 10 percent fee from every in-demand client's deal, smuggled less-in-demand talent on packages with more desirable clients, and even, sometimes, negotiated itself a producer's fee—and the agency made itself the driving power behind project development into the bargain. Studios no longer hired talent. Ovitz, when the stars aligned, gave the talent leverage to shop for a studio.

Diller tasked his Paramount executives with exploiting the one asset agencies like CAA did not control, and which studios had accumulated since the beginning of motion pictures: the intellectual properties to which they held the copyright. The most marketable ones were simple and evocative; Diller had learned in television that if you couldn't get an audience excited within the window afforded you by a thirty-second commercial, you wouldn't get an audience excited at all. He and Eisner transposed the approach to feature films. Thirty seconds wasn't long enough to sell a story or its execution—it was all about an *idea*. The philosophy became known as "high concept," a term Katzenberg attributed to Eisner. Steel later wrote in her autobiography that "Eisner, especially, believed that the idea was the thing. That if it was good—and, most importantly, clear to the public—the movie could work."

A high-concept picture could be pitched in a single sentence, the format in which Eisner's TV movies were described in *TV Guide*. It must be easily summarized, novel enough to catch the eye yet familiar enough to be instantly understood. It should generate excitement, and that excitement should be measurable by the number of filmgoers who turned up to see the film as soon as it was released. The box office made on opening weekend became a more important metric than whether a film had lasting power, which meant, in turn, that Mancuso and his marketing department benefitted from replicating the release model Universal had chanced upon with *Jaws*, releasing every film in thousands of theaters all at once rather than opening in a handful of New York and Los Angeles cinemas before deciding whether to go wide. This made films themselves more expensive—audiences showed up for events, and events cost money. It raised the stakes for every success and failure, but it also pushed aside smaller, more independent, more personal films, which didn't have the financial might of a studio to bring to bear on marketing budgets and nationwide theater bookings. And it made most of the studio's films, as Dawn Steel put it, "critic-proof." By the time the public read reviews in the weekend paper, they would have, hopefully, already bought their tickets. High concept changed Hollywood's entire way of thinking about movies. Film was no longer a business of word of mouth. It had become a business of advance hype.

"Michael wanted to be in control of everything," Baumgarten says of Eisner. He wanted the public to turn up that first weekend, but he also wanted them sufficiently satisfied when they left the cinema that they'd line up again for the sequels. *Star Trek: The Motion Picture* should feel like *Star Trek* the TV show, while reminding audiences of the wonder they had felt two years earlier watching *Star Wars*. *Flashdance* was *Rocky* for women. Sometimes the point of reference was a star: *Urban Cowboy* was John Travolta with country music. *Escape from Alcatraz* was Clint Eastwood in a crime thriller, only this time he was busting out of prison instead of putting punks in it. Perceived as the safest bets were adaptations of preexisting properties. Between 1977 and 1982, in addition to the first *Star Trek* adaptation, Paramount put out a raft of sequels and spin-offs, including *Race for Your Life, Charlie Brown!*, *The Bad News Bears Go to Japan*, *Oliver's Story*, *Bon Voyage, Charlie Brown (And Don't Come Back!)*, *Friday the 13th Part 2*, *Friday the 13th Part 3*, *Grease 2*, *Star Trek II: The Wrath of Khan*, and *Airplane II: The Sequel*.

Paramount wanted the money unicorn filmmakers generated without ceding the control most of them demanded. Its executives expected to "shape the movie," Baumgarten says. "We weren't after the auteurs of the world."

Or, as Simpson was known to tell filmmakers: He wanted *his* ideas in the movie, not theirs.

Eisner summarized his vision for the studio in an internal memo distributed around the Paramount board in 1982. "We have no obligation to make history," he wrote. "We have no obligation to make art. We have no obligation to make a statement. To make money is our only objective."

Familiar, satisfying, and replicable—those were the tenets of high concept, and make money it did. But it didn't help Eisner and Diller's reputation with filmmakers that those principles had little to do with art. They were, however, exactly how McDonald's sold a Big Mac.

• • •

Raiders of the Lost Ark, when it was presented to Eisner, ticked nearly every box. George Lucas and Steven Spielberg had become synonymous with adventure blockbusters. The nuances of the script—the Bible artifact as a MacGuffin, the complicated grave-robbing hero who is also a professor and whose weapon of choice is a whip—could be buried under the simple, propulsive logline "adventurer races Nazis around the globe for possession of mystical relic." The film could be sold both on novelty—an unusual adventure for young audiences—and nostalgia, drawing on older audiences' memories of Saturday serials. (*Star Wars*, of course, hit both targets in the same way.)

At first, Eisner was relentless in his pursuit of the film. "He was a heat-seeking missile," Baumgarten says. "He was obsessed. He was going to get that movie, whatever it cost, whatever the deal was. He just knew it was a massive franchise." It was the kind of film Eisner had taken to calling a "tentpole," because, like *Star Wars*, it had the potential to support a whole edifice of income streams, or make up for a whole slate of smaller failures. He made a quick deal in principle with Lucasfilm, in part out of fear Warner Bros. would claim the film first. And then, as was becoming his reputation, he began reneging on point after point, testing George's willingness to stand firm. The financial terms were too much. Lucasfilm's request to control publicity materials was suddenly a nonstarter.

"I broke a lot of precedents that no-one wanted to break," George remembered. "Its definition of profits upset their apple cart. The other part was I would develop it and turn it over to them, which gave them little control. They didn't like that. I had licensing. I controlled sequel rights. Things that fed off what I did with *Star Wars*."

Eisner didn't buy the budget George, Kazanjian, and Frank Marshall had drawn up, which put the cost of the film at $20 million—"the first ten pages are going to cost $20 million!" he predicted—and estimated that *Raiders* would have to gross at least twice that at the box office, $40 million, to break even, about the same business as *Friday the 13th*. Diller wasn't sure there were that many tickets to be sold for a feature-length adaptation of old-timey movie serials. And then there was Steven, who had gone far enough over schedule and budget on *1941*, only for the film to struggle at the box office, to give studios pause. What if the boy wonder was a two-hit wonder, and no more? Eisner had occasional flashbacks to filming *Popeye*, a picture Robert Evans had got Paramount to green-light for him as an independent producer, with Robin Williams as the comic strip sailor and Bob Altman, of all people, directing. Evans had somehow managed to get the picture out of Eisner's omnipresent control. For weeks, every morning, Eisner would sit in his office in Los Angeles at nine AM, with Katzenberg, Simpson, and Baumgarten, and they'd put in a call to Malta, where the clock showed six in the evening, and Altman was expected to have finished shooting for the day. And every day, Baumgarten remembers with a laugh, "Eisner would just go crazy. He would just rail away at Evans, and Evans would hand the phone to Altman, and I'm sure they were getting high and laughing their ass off at Michael, because they were in Malta, what the fuck could we do?"

Did Eisner want to send George and Steven to Tunisia, and repeat the same mistake? George notoriously held film executives in the lowest of regards, and even Steven had stolen Francis's analogy and begun to occasionally compare his own loss of control on *1941* to being like Colonel Kurtz, though it paled in comparison to Francis's ordeal in the Philippines. While Francis made the joke for self-aggrandizement, Steven used it to reassure the suits: He understood if the establishment had considered "dispatch[ing] Martin Sheen to terminate my command with extreme prejudice," he said, but he was back on saner ground now, and eager for a second chance.

Eisner wasn't sure he bought it. If he did and it backfired, it would be like *Popeye*. It would be the old *Animal House* line again: "You fucked up! You trusted us!"

Paramount sent word to George: *If we can agree on another director we have more confidence in, we might have a deal.*

George replied that he was committed to Steven.

Across the industry, Eisner had developed a reputation for doing whatever it took to gain the upper hand. He liked to say yes to everything, so filmmakers warmed to him, only to send someone from legal or business affairs to say no for him. He routinely bypassed agents and producers to go straight to the talent, who he felt were more likely to let themselves be strong-armed. He disowned his own decisions so often, shifting blame onto others, that Don Simpson and others agreed among themselves to bring a colleague as "a chaperone" to every meeting with Eisner "so there would be a witness" to everything Eisner said.

In many ways, George thought like a small-business owner: a good, honorable deal was one in which both parties won. Eisner, on the other hand, was famous for his need to be *the* winner of any negotiation. As a senior executive at a public corporation, where the slimmest lost margin of profit could save or lose your job, Eisner seemed to take the position that if his opposite number felt like he was winning, then he had something Eisner should have held onto. Every time a filmmaker sat down with Eisner, it felt like a battle of philosophies: mutual gains against zero sum.

Only when Lucasfilm threatened to walk away did Eisner agree to honor his word. George made some concessions: Lucasfilm would control any possible sequels, but Paramount would have an exclusive first opportunity to finance and distribute them, and though George and Steven could retain total creative freedom, they would pay out of their own pockets for any costs incurred by the picture going either over schedule or over budget. In every other essential way, the terms were as George had originally drawn them up.

On the day the agreement was signed, every one of the competitive Paramount executives gathered with Eisner—not to celebrate, but to be there if this was the day he put his own head in the guillotine's pillory. Charlie Bluhdorn flew in from the Dominican Republic, where he was investing heavily and had taken to holding court, with dreams of turning the island into a paradise for filmmakers. He hovered over the room.

"You sure you want to make this deal, Michael?" Diller asked. "This is going to be a great movie, right? We really have to do this, right?"

Eisner's gaze flicked to Bluhdorn. The Gulf+Western boss had to rubber-stamp the deal, and he'd claim some of the credit if the film was a success—hell, so would Diller, that was the way the game worked—but the mood in the room was clear: If *Raiders* was a failure, the blame would fall on Eisner, and on Eisner alone.

He picked up the pen.

Both Baumgarten and Katzenberg, who had read Kasdan's draft, thought it was one of the best scripts they'd ever read. All the same, Baumgarten says, "everybody thought Michael had lost his mind." He had agreed to give George "a massive amount of the first-dollar gross—I've heard different numbers, as high as 35 percent of the first-dollar gross. I don't know that that was true, but we gave away somewhere between 25 percent and 35 percent of the first-dollar gross. It was just massive."

Symbolically, the deal disappointed Steven's film industry father, Sid Sheinberg. Studios couldn't let filmmakers own their films *and* take a chunk out of the net profits. It set an unacceptable precedent. It would destroy the film business, Sheinberg warned publicly.

When all was said and done, the deal with Paramount had the potential to net Lucasfilm the majority of the profits made by any Indiana Jones movie. Up to 77 percent, in fact.

A coincidence, maybe—but sevens were Francis's lucky numbers.

· 32 ·

LIKE THE OLD SERIALS

If they were going to make the schedule and budget they'd promised Paramount, George and Steven would need a strict, disciplined, hardworking producer. Kurtz wasn't the guy. Kazanjian was more a supervisor at Lucasfilm now than a nuts-and-bolts guy. Steven's last producer, Buzz Feitshans, was Milius's business partner, and it wasn't like *1941* had been an uneventful, controlled production, anyway. *Close Encounters* had ended somewhat acrimoniously.

"We need a guy like Frank Marshall to produce it," Steven spitballed.

"Who the hell is Frank Marshall?" George asked.

Well, Steven said, back in 1976, he'd visited the set of Peter Bogdanovich's *Nickelodeon*. It was a Columbia picture, like *Close Encounters*, and both movies were shooting in Burbank at the same time, so Steven had dropped by to say hi to Bogdanovich over lunch. As the two directors spoke, Steven spotted a dark-haired, square-jawed man, of average height and athletic build, running from table to table with a plate of spaghetti in his hand, eating and checking in with crew members at the same time. When the man raced past them, Bogdanovich stuck his arm out and introduced him as his producer, Frank Marshall. The man cursorily shook Steven's hand, turned away from him, and began barraging Bogdanovich with information about the afternoon's work.

"I don't know," Steven told George now. "But I watched that guy and he doesn't even sit down to eat. He doesn't stop."

Though barely thirty-four, Marshall had been in the business longer than either of them. In many ways, he'd been born to the industry. His father, Jack, a composer, had created the theme tune for *The Munsters*, arranged hits for Peggy Lee, and played in the MGM orchestra on scores for pictures like *High Society* and *An American in Paris*. In 1966, Frank Marshall was a political science student at UCLA, where his roommate was a twenty-year-old fellow Californian obsessed with movies named Michael Ovitz, when he met Bogdanovich, then a film critic, at a party thrown by John Ford, and the two hit it off. A few weeks later, Bogdanovich called Marshall, told him Roger Corman had hired him to direct his first movie, *Targets*.

"Would you be interested in working on it?" Bogdanovich asked.

"Can I start in an hour?" Marshall shot back. "What would you want me to do?"

"I don't know," Bogdanovich admitted. "I've never made a movie before."

Together, they learned how. Marshall became a frequent collaborator, working with Bogdanovich on *The Last Picture Show*, *What's Up, Doc?*, *Paper Moon*, *Daisy Miller*, *At Long Last Love*, and *Nickelodeon*, even tagging along to the making of Orson Welles's self-referential and unfinished final film, *The Other Side of the Wind*. Soon Marshall moved into producing.

Steven had poached Kathy Kennedy away from Milius and made her his own assistant; now, with *Raiders* moving ahead, he hired Kathy her own assistant and bumped Kathy up to associate producer.

"Call the producer, Frank Marshall," he said, telling her to introduce herself. She rang Lucasfilm, asked for the producer, and addressed him, politely but repeatedly, as Mr. Marshall.

"Could you please stop calling me Mr. Marshall?" the voice on the phone said finally. "I'm Frank. I'm going to come over and meet."

Within the hour, a greenish-blue Porsche hummed to a stop outside the window. Kathy looked out, expecting a white-haired producer in his fifties or sixties—but then "this really cute guy in a cable-knit sweater jumps out," she remembered.

Well, hell-o, Mr. Marshall, she thought.

She told Marshall that Steven had tasked her with having models built for the truck chase sequence. "I haven't done much model-building," she confessed.

His eyes lit up. He'd be happy to help. He *loved* building models.

They spent the weekend together crafting little trucks, jeeps, and tanks.

Huh, Kennedy thought. *I think I'm in love!*

Marshall thought Steven's assistant was pretty cute, too. Her passion for filmmaking seemed to match his. But this was his first full producer credit, on a film made by the guys with the two biggest movies in the history of movies. He thought, *There's no way I'm screwing this up by hitting on Steven's assistant.*

They both strove to keep their feelings private. As preproduction bore on, they found they made a good professional pair. She liked story and talent; he was a great big-picture thinker and knew how to keep a set ticking over. She was plainspoken and focused; he was a ball of energy—a long-distance runner, an amateur DJ. They were both doers. They both, separately, had a habit Steven and George valued: They never brought their bosses a problem without also bringing them several possible solutions. They never said no without suggesting alternatives. They were decent, down-to-earth, funny, and sufficiently smart and well prepared that when either of them did give a crew member a dressing-down, the authority to do so felt earned, rather than claimed.

They started seeing each other romantically, too, but they kept it quiet. Kathy deserved to become a producer herself, but if people knew they were together, they'd say he'd just handed his girlfriend an opportunity.

"It was the early '80s," Marshall remembered, "and I knew the business."

George, in particular, wanted Tom Selleck as Indiana Jones because the actor was "a new face," not well-known to the moviegoing public. Unfortunately, Bob Daly, the vice president of CBS, had cast Selleck in *Magnum P.I.* in part for the same reason. When the network picked the pilot up for a series, he also refused to adjust the shooting schedule so his leading man could do *Raiders*, too. A month after Steven and George chose him, Selleck dropped out of the movie. A new Indiana Jones had to be found, and fast.

Kazanjian suggested Harrison Ford again. Sid Ganis, now Lucasfilm president, agreed. "It was hometown," he explains. George still resisted.

Steven watched an early cut of *Empire* shortly before its release—George had wanted Selleck as late as mid-April, but he was out of the running by the first week of May, just over two weeks before *Empire* hit cinemas—and as he watched Harrison Ford, he turned to George and asked playfully, as if the thought had just occurred to him: "What about that guy for Indiana Jones?"

George gave in. British character actors Paul Freeman and John Rhys-Davies were hired to play the villain Belloq and the sidekick Sallah, respectively. Karen Allen, who had missed out on Princess Leia, was cast as Indy's love interest, Marion Ravenwood, after a long search throughout which Steven met with every actress in California, even tasked Casella with tracking down models he liked the look of in magazines. But "she came in and she was Marion," Casella says. "It was clear from the moment she walked in." Allen hesitated after her first costume fitting, when she found out George and Steven planned to have her in skimpy eye-candy outfits for most of the picture. The session left her in tears; it wasn't the Marion Ravenwood she'd seen on the page. "It's stuff I don't want to wear," she said. "I don't think it's right for her." Steven, immediately, changed it all around until she was happy.

They shot it like kids. Steven, George, Kazanjian, and Marshall came up with a secret shorter schedule—over seventy-three days, compared to the eighty-seven Paramount would hold them to—and they raced to meet it. Even Doug Slocombe, the English cinematographer in his late sixties, enthusiastically ran around setting up shots and choreographing his two, sometimes three cameras, trilling with the excitement of playing with a gigantic train set. Steven's joy and openness, too, was childlike and infectious. He marveled at Slocombe's ability to use the sun as a key light—he'd never really thought about it himself, he'd chuckle, wasn't the sun just . . . there?—and delighted in learning that his second unit, filming the wide shots of the truck chase, staged everything along slopes in the road, so when stuntmen flew out of the vehicles, they landed on an incline and kept rolling, rather than have their momentum—and bones—abruptly interrupted by hard, flat ground, just as Yakima Canutt, the mythologized first stuntman, had designed it in the '20s. He had the set designers slip sketches of R2-D2 and C-3PO in among the hieroglyphs on the wall of the Well of the Souls, and he had Frank Marshall suit up as a Nazi pilot for a cameo. He ate his mac and cheese and his SpaghettiOs and reminded everyone that when David Lean shot *Lawrence of Arabia*, he'd had to sleep in tents, and they had air-conditioned hotel rooms—what did they have to complain about?

He loved getting ideas, from anyone and everyone. Sometimes the suggestion was so great he embraced it right away—like stunt coordinator Glenn Randall's idea that Indy should slide hand over hand under the Nazi truck, instead of simply rolling out of the way and snapping his whip around the tailpipe so he could climb back on, or Harrison Ford's idea, when he was ill in Tunisia, that he should just pull out his gun and shoot a sword-wielding bad guy dead instead of engaging in the whole whip-versus-scimitar battle Steven had storyboarded. What set Steven apart from many directors, however, was his desire to hear even the stuff that wouldn't work. He would notice a crew member biting their tongue and push them to speak up.

"What is it?" he asked one crew member in one of those situations.

"It's probably a bad idea," she answered.

"Well, tell me," Steven said, "and I'll decide if it's a bad idea."

She told him.

"You're right." He smiled. "That *is* a bad idea."

But he always wanted to hear it.

At Elstree, *Raiders* sprawled and took over. You could walk from soundstage to soundstage and travel from a South American temple to the Egyptian desert Well of the Souls, then on to Marion's bar in Nepal, and in each cavernous building, you would be transported, imagine the heat of the sun baking the sand or the whistling sandstorm buffeting the tavern windows, craftsmanship and illusion so precise and detailed the whipping English rain along the Elstree paths faded away as if dimmed down on one of Walter Murch's mixing dials. During breaks in work, everyone dropped in to Steven's office to play on the *Asteroids* arcade game he'd had installed there, Kathy Kennedy and Karen Allen running up the highest scores.

Everything revolved around George and Steven's relationship. Spielberg, clean-shaven his whole life, grew a beard to match George's. They were about the same height. They wore similar-shaped sunglasses. "They were, they are, such good—name the word—friends, pals, buddies," Sid Ganis says. "Believers in each other. It was perfect. They knew each other, they understood each other, they played around with each other, and they trusted each other. It was good for George."

You could tell they were close, Ganis jokes, because George called Steven "Steve." No one else—except his sisters—got away with that.

Soon after the *Raiders* crew started work in Tunisia, Harrison Ford pulled Martin Casella aside.

"A friend of mine is showing up," he said casually. "We're having dinner, and Steven wants to meet her."

Missy arrived later that day. Casella was carrying her luggage from the car to Ford's room when he came across the three of them—Ford, Mathison, and Spielberg—walking the other way down the hallway.

"—new idea," Steven was telling Missy. "It's gonna be about a little boy, and the alien that he meets . . ."

"That sounds interesting," Melissa said politely.

Steven and Kathy Kennedy had been working on a sort-of-sequel to *Close Encounters* for a while, which transformed into a standalone picture called *Night Skies*. They had hired the independent filmmaker John Sayles to write a first draft. Sayles, following Steven's guidance, had delivered a horror yarn, inspired by real events of a family in rural Kentucky who claimed they had been terrorized by goblin-like extraterrestrials. It was what Steven had asked for, but reading it while filming *Raiders* in Tunisia left him cold. Only two things in the draft moved him: the opening visual, in which one of the aliens kills farm animals with the touch of a long finger, the tip lit from the inside with a glowing orange light, and the final shot, after the aliens return to their planet, which revealed one of them left behind on a grassy knoll, looking up into the night sky as the spaceship disappears without him.

"*That*," Steven said, "is the movie I want to make."

Kathy remembered her early days at that San Diego TV station, how few women were around then; there were more women around on *Raiders*, but she was plainly aware there weren't enough. Years later, looking back on her career, Kathy would talk about "the responsibility to bring other women along," and her disappointment that not enough women took initiative and went after jobs they wanted. The system, probably, had taught them there was no point. She knew Melissa Mathison was coming to visit; both she and Steven loved *The Black Stallion*. Why not ask her?

Missy, as it happened, was in a rut. Soon after *The Black Stallion*, she had written another script for Francis, which became Caleb Deschanel's directorial debut, *The Escape Artist*, but that was mired in editorial limbo as Deschanel and his producers tried to reshape the idiosyncratic story, about a young magician and escape artist living in the shadow of his late father. She had started a few more screenplays since, but hadn't liked anything that was coming out of her. She had agreed to accompany Ford to Tunisia because she wasn't getting anywhere at home.

When Steven first met her, he introduced himself and asked her what she did. She was just a "failed screenwriter," she said. She hadn't seemed engaged with his first attempt at pitching his movie, so the next day, as the crew prepared a setup, Steven and Missy wandered a little away from the activity and into the sand. Steven told her it was fun to look for scorpions.

"I have an idea for a new movie I want you to write," he said suddenly, trying his luck again.

"Sure," Melissa replied, distractedly. She hadn't heeded the crew's warnings about watching what she ate and drinking only water bottled or previously boiled, and her stomach ached with the cramps of dysentery. "What is it?"

"It's about a man from outer space who gets lost on Earth," Steven said.

"I don't like science fiction," Missy said. "I'm also down on myself. I don't think I'm a good writer. I thought *Black Stallion* could have been better."

"How could that movie have been any better? That's already an American classic!"

"Thank you very much," Melissa said, "but I've decided never to write again."

She wanted to take the words back as soon as they'd left her lips. Thankfully, Steven kept nagging her. He told Kathy to try and convince her; he asked Harrison to soften her up. He told her more about what was in his head anytime he had the chance. It wasn't just about the space man, he explained; it was about the children who find him and take him in. The writers of *1941*, Zemeckis and Gale, had been writing a script entitled *Growing Up*, loosely inspired by Steven's experience as a child of divorce in Phoenix. It wasn't going anywhere. But talking to Kathy Kennedy, whose mind was always racing—nearly as fast as Steven's own—he'd recently been hit by a lightning bolt: He should blend *Growing Up* and *Night Skies* into one picture. He saw the small, "squishy" alien glimpsed at the end of *Close Encounters*, "Puck," and imagined *it* as a young being feeling abandoned.

"What if that little creature never went back to the ship?" he asked. Being a stranded alien—that was how he'd felt, as a kid. What if he still did the divorce movie, but as a fantasy?

This time, Missy was so touched she burst into tears.

They threw ideas back and forth. She understood loneliness. She wrote easily about absent fathers, substitute fathers, proxies for fathers. She had an understanding of childhood, it turned out, that rivaled Steven's own. And like Steven, she didn't just seem to understand children, but to remember what it was like to have a child's perspective.

Once *Raiders* wrapped, and after a brief bout of cold feet, Melissa agreed to write at least one draft of Steven's movie. They met once a week for eight weeks in the fall of 1981 as she made her way through a first pass. *E.T.*, like *The Black Stallion*, centered on a preteen boy as its protagonist. "That's who we babysat in the Hollywood Hills," says Mathison's sister Melinda. "She knew these kids. She knew kids of divorce, kids with imagination, bright but not entirely compliant. Like Bart Patton's second son, Tyler." In fact, Missy named one of the older kids in the *E.T.* script Tyler, as an homage; Elliott's memorable insult hurled at his older brother, when he calls him "penis breath," was something Missy had heard Tyler Patton say as a boy.

She was good, too, at making Steven pause, because she was assertive without aggression, as Kennedy was. A bit like an older sister, if not a mother. She would glance at him as they prepared *E.T.* and say, "Steven, stop looking at the whole storyboard. Just be right here, in this moment, now."

As a writer, Missy had become disciplined and no-nonsense, able to crank pages out like every day was a deadline. She put up bulletin boards and mapped structure and character out in cryptic scribbles on colored index cards. When she handed over her first draft, Steven read it in an hour, without stopping, and "I was just knocked out. It was a script that I was willing to shoot the next day." He went to find Kathy Kennedy in the commissary and asked her to cancel all her afternoon meetings, read the draft straightaway, and tell him if he was crazy. She came to find him in his office at the end of the day.

"You're not crazy," she said. "I love it, too."

"You know what?" he asked her. "I think you're ready—why don't you produce this?"

Kennedy was twenty-six. She had been in Los Angeles less than five years.

Steven took all the scary stuff out of *Night Skies* and transplanted it into a film he'd wanted to make about a haunting, which was now called *Poltergeist*, and which he gave to Marshall to produce.

"Don't tell anyone we're going out," Marshall advised her when she told him the news. "They'll think that's why you got the job."

Kathy followed his advice, though it didn't matter. George spotted them at dinner one night and told everybody—except Steven.

Self-possessed as she was, Kennedy still felt overwhelmed. *E.T.*'s budget was half that of *Raiders*, with completely different challenges, not least a cast of children and a lead played by a rubber puppet. She didn't have to oversee a globe-trotting shoot like Marshall had on *Raiders*, but she did have to adapt to Steven's new process: He wanted to shoot the film in chronological order, or as close as possible, to help his young actors feel the emotions of the story, and he had chosen not to storyboard the film, to keep himself responsive to their moods and contributions.

She threw up every weekend of the shoot, but she saw it through.

Raiders came out in June 1981, becoming the biggest film of the year and rewarding Michael Eisner with a $212 million gross. Negotiations over a sequel were opened immediately. Han Solo had made Harrison Ford a household name, but Indiana Jones made him a superstar. In agreeing to return for a sequel to *Raiders*, Ford, in turn, transformed his industry. *Time* magazine had described the most popular actors of the '70s—performers like Pacino, Hoffman, De Niro, Sheen—as "anti-stars," eager to disappear behind every role, obsessive over the purity of the performance. Ford, to the shock of the aging Columbia executives who had cut him from their roster fifteen years earlier, was "a real movie star in the old-fashioned sense," in the words of *New York* magazine's David Denby: charismatic, reliable, "interesting no matter what he's doing"—and an actor with brand promise, conscious of his responsibility to give the audience good value for the ticket price. In the boardroom, Craig Baumgarten says, "we all wanted to make sequels. We were all obsessed with sequels. But in those days, actors looked down on them . . . When actors started to validate that they were willing to stick with movies, Harrison was one of the first." Following George's example, Paramount began drafting contracts to tie stars down for multiple potential movies in a franchise, were it to be required—and, following Ford's lead, actors began to acquiesce.

By September, Steven was already filming *E.T.*, with a cast of children who reminded him and Missy both of their childhoods, and made them both long to be parents. They finished the film in time for it to open a year, to the day, after *Raiders*. Much of Steven's career had been driven by a search for his identity as a filmmaker. He made short films as a child looking to fit in. George's *Electronic Labyrinth: THX 1138 4EB* had made him sick with jealousy, as had Francis's *The Godfather*. *Sugarland Express* had come from a longing to be hip to the times, more than the competent journeyman all those Universal TV executives and his first agent, Mike Medavoy, saw in him. With *1941*, he tried to be more like Milius. *Close Encounters* and, especially, *E.T.* were realizations of what was in him, what made him unique, fruits of a lesson he would pass on later: "In order for you to know where you are," Steven learned, "you have to know where you came from."

E.T. broke every box-office record—again. It earned Melissa her first, and only, Academy Award nomination, and within a year, the movie overtook *Star Wars* as the biggest film of all time. George took ads out in the papers to congratulate his friend. It was the first time a filmmaker had made the biggest film ever twice.

Kaja Fehr was first in line at her local cinema on June 11, 1982, when *E.T.* came out. She called Missy from home afterward to congratulate her.

"Why did you use Reese's instead of M&M's?" she asked, and Missy laughed.

"Well, M&M's . . . they fucked up," she tittered.

"They did, big time!" Fehr agreed.

It felt like the old days at Providence High, passing notes and giggling.

It was a long time before they spoke again.

"After that," says Fehr, "the curtain came down. And I couldn't call her anymore."

Missy did not have another screenplay produced for years. She married Harrison Ford in 1983, and a few years later gave birth to a son, then a daughter. She read the scripts her husband was considering starring in and gave him advice; she doctored the odd scene.

She remained, as she had often been and not unwillingly, the quiet background to a more famous man. “I know just how far back to lean,” she joked, “to get out of the picture.”

Her older child, years later, would remember that there hadn’t been much music in the house as he grew up, except for one composer who reminded Missy of something private and special. Sometimes, her son said—just sometimes—“my mom would have Wagner on.”

· 33 ·

SHANGRI-COPPOLA

Aspiring actress Rebecca De Mornay was barely twenty years old when, one day after a class at the Lee Strasberg Institute on Sunset Boulevard, her eye was caught by a piece of paper taped up to the hallway wall. The note invited actors to visit an address on Santa Monica Boulevard that Saturday, along with the simple announcement: "Zoetrope Seeks Unusual People."

"I had no idea what that was," De Mornay remembers, "but I liked the name."

De Mornay—five foot four, blond, with elfin ears and big, limpid blue eyes—had grown up bouncing around European private schools and, though born in California, thought of herself as "new in town," and new to the business. She followed directions to the address that Saturday and arrived at a crowded warehouse, where casting associates behind a video camera on a tripod were conducting a cattle call. De Mornay joined the line, behind young actors who looked like her but also, as she remembers it, everyday people and entire Mexican families. When her turn came, she stood in front of the camera and was asked to state her name and phone number, then thanked for her time and sent on her way.

The call from Fred Roos came a few days later. He was producing a film for Francis Coppola, he said, and they were interested in auditioning De Mornay to understudy the film's lead, twenty-year-old Nastassja Kinski.

"How can you be an understudy?" De Mornay's friends asked. "This is a movie."

"I don't care," she answered. "This is *Coppola*."

She met Francis at his house. This was how it would work, he explained: He was not just making a movie, but starting a repertory company, and he wanted his six understudies—one for each of the main parts—to perform the entirety of a film, *One from the Heart*, on video, first, "to see if it works." He would pay them $250 a week.

And then the Screen Actors Guild intervened. The union sent Francis notice that, since he was putting actors on video in relation to a union project, he would need to pay them guild minimum—over a thousand dollars a week—regardless of his cockamamie repertory company framing.

"You're here." Francis shrugged. "We'll keep you on as interns. It's a five-month shoot. I want you sent the entire day. Ask as many questions as you can to everyone."

"That was my film school," De Mornay remembers.

Francis purchased Hollywood General, a ten-and-a-half-acre movie studio on Santa Monica Boulevard and Las Palmas, on March 25, 1980, for $6.7 million. He put the profits he had earned from the *Godfather* movies and *Apocalypse Now* into his down payment, with two further payments due, and announced he would be producing several films, the profits from which would be injected back into the company. In time, he expected, he would be self-sufficient, a mini-major in his own right—in the heart of Hollywood, but independent from it.

His production slate was daring and internationalist. German auteur Wim Wenders—fresh off his English-language breakout, the

Patricia Highsmith adaptation *The American Friend*, starring Dennis Hopper—would direct a noir about mystery author Dashiell Hammett. Longtime friend Caleb Deschanel would make his directorial debut with the drama *The Escape Artist*, co-written by Missy. Award-winning documentary maker Martha Coolidge, who had just one fiction film under her belt, would direct a film of her own conception entitled *Photoplay*. David Lynch, having just turned down George's *Revenge of the Jedi*, was in talks with Zoetrope to finance his passion project *Ronnie Rocket*, about a detective who can access a parallel dimension and a three-foot-tall teenage rock star who needs to regularly plug himself in to an electrical outlet to survive. Money was being advanced to Jean-Luc Godard for the writing and development of his next picture. Francis himself planned to direct *One from the Heart* and then follow it up with an adaptation of journalist Gay Talese's *Thy Neighbor's Wife*, a nonfiction study of post–World War II American sexuality.

Francis's own film, *One from the Heart*, a romantic musical set in Chicago, would be used as a prototype of what he called "electronic cinema," a new technological process Francis promised would make filmmaking, starting with his ambitious slate of films, more affordable. The entirety of *One from the Heart* would be pre-visualized in animated storyboard form, then rehearsed on video by De Mornay and the other understudies so that the crew could build exactly what was needed for every shot, and Francis could shoot only what he needed, without waste. When the time came to film the actual movie with the main cast, Francis would direct not on set, but from a customized Airstream trailer he called the Silverfish, its insides loaded with all the monitors and video feeds required to make sure the takes matched the pre-visualized footage. Editing could be carried out virtually simultaneously to filming. It was Francis's dream, finally made real: "a company along studio lines," he said—not one run by accountants and governed by bullies, but one "that is full of creative opportunities and develops talent." *Newsweek* film critic Jack Kroll described the project as a re-creation of "the Golden Age of Hollywood, with [Coppola] as the studio mogul and resident artist—Zanuck and Welles rolled into one."

When Paul Schrader first heard that Francis was coming back to Los Angeles and buying his own studio, "I thought it was a terrific idea"—though the more details he heard, the less terrific it sounded. "It seemed to me a little fishy," he says. "Francis was, uh, and still is—you have to be a little careful. Some of the things he says are true, and some of them aren't." And then he read about Francis's "cockamamie idea of making a film from a video truck," and he knew disaster was coming.

George eyed Francis's new venture with suspicion. As he saw it, it made no financial sense to own a studio. Editing and postproduction equipment, yes, but filming space—that, you rented for the time you needed it and avoided the overhead.

"I disagreed with Francis when he said he was moving to Los Angeles," George told the magazine *Film Comment*. "Being down there in Hollywood, you're just asking for trouble, because you're trying to change a system that will never change."

Francis called the company Zoetrope Studios. Steven, playfully, referred to it as "Shangri-Coppola."

It went wrong from the start. Having spent every penny he had available to buy the studio, Francis had no money left over to self-finance *One from the Heart*, as George was paying for the *Star Wars* films, so, for all his talk of independence, he immediately had to return to the studios for cash. Barry Diller took a flier on the movie, agreeing to pay the $23 million Roos and Zoetrope president Robert Spiotta had budgeted, but, wary of another chaotic shoot, did so only in the form of a "back-end deal," whereby the studio only paid out once the film was completed and ready for release. Spiotta recommended holding off, but Francis was impatient.

"Lookit," he said, "I got this movie and if I can bluff my way through two weeks I'm going to have so much movie done the question will be, who will step forward to stop me?"

It had always worked before, and for a time, it seemed it would again. Francis started shooting, and within weeks, Chase Manhattan Bank lent Zoetrope Studios $19 million against the Paramount commitment. The Security Pacific National Bank put up another several million. Jack Singer, a Canadian real estate millionaire desperate for an entry into the film business, loaned Francis a further $3 million. Singer wore gold chains and open-necked shirts. He chain-smoked cigars and played golf in Palm Springs, threw himself birthday parties with burlesque dancers as entertainment. He had the leathery tan of a man who moved to California and couldn't get enough of the sun after growing up with five-month, Arctic-temperature winters. He owned racehorses, promoted boxing bouts, and loved motion pictures, so much that he claimed he'd only come across Francis because he'd been offered a tour of Hollywood General and wanted to get Coppola's autograph. When Francis signed the papers, he put the studio itself into a deed of trust, as security against Singer's loan.

Francis pushed his luck. He added another month to the film's shooting schedule. He paid himself a $3 million fee. And—even though he was now dependent on *One from the Heart* being a huge box-office success, if he wanted it to generate sufficient profits to make the studio self-sufficient—he took steps to make the picture more and more esoteric. *One from the Heart* had been intended as a low-budget first picture, "to flush out the pipes," says Walter Murch: black and white, set in Chicago, directed by Francis from a screenplay by Armyan Bernstein. "And then the other Francis took over," Murch continues.

"Get rid of Chicago," Francis told Bernstein. "Let's make it Las Vegas." He got rid of the black and white, decided to shoot the film in color; then he decided it should be a musical. He stuck with Frederic Forrest, Teri Garr, and Raul Julia as his lead actors, none of them bankable, and signed them all to long, multipicture, multiyear deals, as if he were Jack Warner back from the dead. He had production designer Dean Tavoularis build a false-perspective replica of Las Vegas across the backlot, another $4 million expense. He decided to film the movie with a pointed, artificial theatricality, "like a Kabuki play set in Las Vegas."

"Francis's problem," De Palma said, "is that everything has to be a masterpiece, in a way . . . There are no limits, no boundaries. It leads to excess—like the incredible castles built by mad emperors." He was glad he never had Francis's success. He saw the isolation, the absence of moderation. It scared him. It could happen to anyone.

Francis told journalists he was going to change Hollywood "by any means necessary"; he refused to "be directed, controlled, maneuvered by people I do not respect, and for whom I hold no admiration."

His defiance was contagious. "He had a wrap party every single Friday," De Mornay says. "It was fantastic." The party spread across the entire lot, and people would come from all over to drink and gossip and see Francis's Folly—some hopeful it would succeed, many rubbernecking already. Everyone in Hollywood turned up. Francis walked through the crowd arm in arm with Brando, as corpulent and charismatic as an aging Henry VIII. Jerry Garcia and members of the Grateful Dead sipped from plastic cups. There was something euphoric about celebrating as the accountants sharpened their abacuses.

"I want everyone to come see this," Francis announced, "and spread the word!"

"It was very lavish," De Mornay says. *I guess this is what Hollywood is like,* she thought—but of course, she remembers, "it was never like that again."

"It was the most wonderful place on earth," says the actress Lainie Kazan, who Francis, two decades after their time together at Hofstra, had called up to cast in a small part. "He gave us all the opportunity to do whatever we wanted to do." Francis invited the actors to watch the dailies, to sit in the editing room. When they weren't required on set, the understudies went off with Gian-Carlo and Roman and filmed little short films the boys conceived together. Gio, charming and handsome, told everyone he was going to be a film director, just like his dad. Roman trotted behind him, taking down dialogue as the understudies improvised it. Sofia, soon to be ten years old, ran around the studio, handing out a typed and printed comedy newsletter she made about the goings-on on the lot.

"Lainie," Francis shouted over the music at one party, "dream the impossible dream!"

Those who knew Francis better, who had been through the Zoetrope experience or had been around for *Apocalypse Now*, saw the writing on the wall even then.

"It went wrong straight off the bat," publicist Beverly Walker says. Francis's eyes were always bigger than his stomach. He couldn't adhere to his own shooting schedule. He indulged every whim expressed by his cinematographer, Vittorio Storaro. "Bobby," the Italian would say to his grip as he walked onto set, fluttering his fingers in the direction of Tavoularis's set, "I don't like the wall"—and work for the day would have to be rearranged so the production designers could adjust their work to Storaro's liking. The experienced prop and grip men grumbled at the treatment. Some in the cast bristled when they watched younger, less accomplished actors do their scenes for them, before they had a chance to find the performance themselves.

"Well," drawled a frustrated Teri Garr one day, after watching her understudy, Cindy Kania, block out a scene for her, "do I *have* to do it *like that*?"

The same patterns that Francis had slipped into in San Francisco repeated, not just writ large but, in Murch's expression, "writ in skywriting." He ran out of money and could no longer go to a Robert Evans, or a Charlie Bluhdorn, to bail him out—he was the head of the studio now. When he tried, shooting an expensive $4 million opening sequence musical number without approval and then sending Paramount the bill, Diller and Eisner flat out refused to pay.

With the movie still shooting, a memo went around the company: Zoetrope was not able to meet payroll. Those who could afford to work for free for a while could stay.

"Parts of the studio just started emptying out," says Anahid Nazarian, who worked as an intern in the research library, and is now one of Francis's executives. The security guard at the gate waved the interns in and told them to park wherever they wanted, even the reserved executive spaces—no one was using them anymore. "All the higher-paid people, they all got let go," Nazarian says, "but people in my position, production assistants and so on, because we made four dollars an hour, or five dollars an hour, we stayed on, just to try and keep the company going." The company spokesperson, Beverly Walker, came to work one day to find adhesive tags on her typewriter, her desk, her chair—everything was to be sold off. Someone came in to remove the water coolers in every office.

As in the aftermath of *Apocalypse Now*, Francis gravitated toward his more inexperienced employees, thrived on the energy of the young people who had yet to burn out, and leaned on those who showed a talent and willingness to help him stay afloat. It took Nazarian a little while to get used to the way his brain functioned. "He doesn't think in the order other people think," she says. "He couldn't tell you the alphabet in the right order if you asked him to. His brain works spatially, and that's how he writes and edits, too. There's no sense in the continuity of things. It does cause . . . complications, but it also makes room for possibilities."

"Everybody loved him," Kaja Fehr says. "So when they couldn't pay you right away, nobody cared. We were all in it together." That *we*, however, were not the experienced crew Francis needed to help pull him out of the mess. They were "just ambitious kids," says Beverly Walker, "who came from well-to-do families. They were living on trust funds." There were too many of them, doing the same jobs none of them knew how to do, bumping into each other as they tried to tick tasks off the to-do list. It left a vacuum of authority, into which publicist Beverly Walker saw yes-men and hangers-on jostle for position. Francis liked to work with women, but the top of the hierarchy, such as it was, remained "a very male-centric, heterosexual male kind of group. That's the kind of place it was. And very treacherous."

Roos and his producing partner, Gray Frederickson, hounded Francis about the spiraling budget. Jack Singer showed his face more often, demanding access to dailies and striking up conversations with the actresses, particularly Garr, to whom he was, in the words of Garr's stand-in, Cindy Kania, "really gross and forward—he'd probably be MeToo'd now."

Francis hid in the Silverfish. Out on the set, the *One from the Heart* assistant directors blocked and staged the cast for him. "ACTION!" would come from the loudspeakers around the lot. They would do a take. "CUT!" the loudspeakers said. There would be silence—everyone "looking up in the air," De Mornay remembers, "like looking to God"—and then God would boom, or mutter, "Okay. We're going again."

Kazan, like others, found her character stopped making sense. She felt like she was watching an attempt at making high art crumble, in real time, in the name of money and conservatism.

Yet, just as Francis complained about Diller and Eisner's meddling, he was interfering in the only other Zoetrope film in production, Wenders's *Hammett*, hiring and firing writers, then shutting the movie down when it was 90 percent finished and refusing to let Wenders complete it until he took Francis's script notes.

"It was atrocious—it was horrendous, the way Wim was treated," says Beverly Walker. "This whole phalanx of people, coming down and telling him how he had to shoot a certain scene, telling him he had to show them anything he wrote the night before because they had to approve it." Francis complained, hypocritically, that Wenders "didn't want to follow the screenplay, he wanted to improvise, he wanted to work with his wife . . . We decided to interrupt the experiment." Coppola, said one Zoetrope employee, was "more intrusive in the creative process than Zanuck or Thalberg"—or Jack Warner—"ever dreamed of being."

As the money ran out, Francis canceled the studio's other projects. No longer was there talk of films by Jean-Luc Godard and David Lynch. Jacques Demy came in to meet about a project and sat in a hallway for an hour without anyone speaking to him. The filmmaker Martha Coolidge, who had spent years developing a project with Francis, was told there was no money to make the picture—news that was so sudden and upsetting she packed up and moved to Canada to start again. Wenders hovered in limbo, waiting for Francis's approval to start shooting again.

"It was very, very stressful to come to work," Lainie Kazan says. "Knowing your whole life is going to be a failure—that's what it felt like. What I thought was going to be joyous was really . . . hideous." It was like the party had ended and the house lights had come on, shining a harsh and bare light on the remaining befuddled guests and the mess that was left to clear.

In August 1981, seven months after the first day of filming on *One from the Heart*, Paramount invited exhibitors to a test screening of the movie, without Francis's blessing, to gauge its commercial potential. The response was more scathing than Diller and Eisner had feared: The movie, cinema owners told them, was unreleasable.

Paramount pulled out of releasing the picture, leaving Francis on the hook for the $27 million he had spent—not counting the payments he still owed on the studio property itself. The banks would want to be repaid. Jack Singer, like a buzzard, circled. Francis convinced himself the Canadian developer had only ever lent him money as a way to steal the lot from under him. He convinced himself Diller had called the surprise screening as a ploy to divest himself from a film that was far from "unreleasable," just experimental and new, harder to sell than Paramount's regular sequels-and-remakes slop. With every tick of the clock, the interest accrued on his loans. Here was disaster. It was everyone's fault but his own.

Francis made a quick deal with Columbia Pictures to step in for Paramount, and they rushed *One from the Heart* into theaters for Valentine's Day. The public, by now, was tired of hearing about Francis Coppola's far-fetched dreams. The movie sold $636,000 worth of tickets, the smallest audience of any film Francis had made in his life.

In January 1983, the banks moved to take away the studio. He fought them off, spent eleven months trying to find a buyer to cover his debt. Three times he came close, and three times the sale fell through at the last moment. It was Jack Singer who forced matters, insisting on a foreclosure auction, at which he bought the studio for himself for just $12.3 million. He renamed it Singer Studios, then sued Francis for repayment of his original $3 million loan, plus interest—a sum amounting to, Singer's filing said, another $8 million.

Francis came to feel this had been Singer's plan all along, and that the Canadian had loaned him the money as a way in to stealing his studio out from under him. But he was spent. Drained. He had put up his house and Napa Valley winery as collateral to his loans, and the banks were demanding repayment now, too.

He was left with no choice. He entered Zoetrope Studios into Chapter 11 proceedings and filed for personal bankruptcy.

Sometimes, near the end of cutting *One from the Heart*, when exhibitors were pulling out and the bills were piling up, Francis found shelter in the editing room, to sit with Kaja Fehr, who was on the picture as an assistant. Fehr's father, Rudi, had started working for Jack Warner in 1936, after fleeing Nazi Germany, and now ran Zoetrope's postproduction department, though Kaja got herself hired not just without his help, but against his wishes. Francis remembered Kaja from the late '60s, when she had occasionally tagged along with Missy on babysitting assignments. "I think he never really got over her, and wasn't at that time," Fehr says. "He still really cared about her."

He stood by Fehr's bench as she worked, and talked about Missy. One day, he told her that she was coming to visit the lot that day.

"How do you feel about seeing her?" Fehr asked.

"Well, you know," Francis said wistfully. "She's film royalty now." Fehr looked into his eyes and understood that he meant she was married to Harrison Ford; she was writing with Steven Spielberg; she had just had a huge hit of her own, entirely separate from him. Fehr sensed no bitterness, only acknowledgment of a truth and, perhaps, a cliché: With him, Missy had been only potential. Without him—entirely separate from him—she had become someone. It was only possible because she had left him behind.

Fehr thought of Francis's daughter, Sofia, who was eleven or twelve then. She thought of how close Francis was with her and Roman. How much he trusted Gio and Gio trusted him.

In the end, she thought, *everyone did the right thing.*

One from the Heart, though Francis never admitted it in the United States, had been about Missy. Nearly a year after the film's release, he confessed to the French film magazine *Positif* that he had made the movie out of pain—specifically, though he did not name her, the pain of leaving Missy. He had hated the Catholicism of his youth—"I thought the nuns were mean," he once explained—but the ritual of religion was important to him, present in all his films, from the blood-and-baptism ending of *The Godfather* to the guilt and desire for redemption that saturate *The Conversation* and *Apocalypse Now*. The songs that fill *One from the Heart*, the backlot replica of Las Vegas, even the film's unusual aspect ratio added up to another form of ritual, a way to process and express his own failed love story: the "inherent contradiction," he told his interviewer, the critic Michel Ciment, of something that is "as real as possible, even if you know if isn't real." The suspension of disbelief necessary to making a film—and to having an affair.

"Love can kill," Francis told Ciment. "I made the film in this particular way because I couldn't talk directly about a break-up, having lived through it myself. The days or nights of twelve hours of crying, the suicide attempts, were still present in my memory, and I wasn't interested in tackling them . . . There's no doubt I selected this type of distancing because the real story was still so fresh in my mind."

Francis had hoped the public would relate to the heartbreak in *One from the Heart*. Hadn't everyone gone through something like it at least once? He'd opened himself up for connection and—as happened time and time again—he'd been met with ridicule, strangers wanting to cut him down to size for the intense sincerity of his feeling.

"Anyhow," he told Ciment, recalling the pain of the film's disastrous release. "The experience killed me."

· 34 ·

THE WAY OF THE FORCE

His long, isolating tour around the galaxy far, far away burned George out. Shooting the final act of the trilogy, *Revenge of the Jedi*, over five months at the beginning of 1983 felt not like the culmination of over a decade of work, but more like a grueling ordeal. George and Lawrence Kasdan co-wrote a screenplay of three uneasy parts, in which, after rescuing Han from his carbonite prison inside Jabba the Hutt's Tatooine palace, Luke Skywalker finally confronts Darth Vader and Emperor Palpatine aboard a new Death Star; Lando Calrissian, redeeming himself, leads a fleet to destroy the space station before it becomes operational; and Han and Leia lead an expedition on the nearby moon of Endor to disable the power source to an energy shield that protects the Death Star from attack. They took pains to wrap up the trilogy's loose ends—most notably, Leia is revealed as Luke's twin sister, and in the final scenes, Darth Vader turns back to the light and sacrifices himself to save Luke from the Emperor—as well as balance the darker beats between Luke and his father with lighter fare on Endor, where C-3PO is joined as comic relief by a band of fuzzy, teddy-bear-like aliens with sweet squeaky voices, called Ewoks.

Expectations were unprecedented. George insisted on the purest possible experience for moviegoers, the same kind of surprise and anticipation you felt, as a kid, turning on a new episode of your favorite Saturday morning show. On set, the *Jedi* crew went around wearing baseball caps and T-shirts emblazoned with a fake title for a nonexistent horror film, *Blue Harvest*, and the call sheets were a roll call of pseudonyms: Mark Hamill was "Martin," Carrie Fisher was "Caroline," Harrison Ford just "Harry." They were all ready to move on, Hamill and Fisher to spread their careers beyond Luke and Leia, Ford to embrace his own stardom—Han Solo, he'd always felt, was a supporting character, not a lead. And while Lucasfilm might have been a family, crew members arriving at *Jedi*'s shooting locations were met every morning by signs reminding them the sets were more than closed; they were hermetically sealed: "No husbands, wives, children or friends . . ."

George had always been reluctant to take feedback, and now he was more closed off than ever. If a crew member volunteered an idea, he looked at them like he wanted to swat the offending words away with the back of his hand. The vision was in his head. It didn't need improving, as far as he was concerned. It just needed *out*.

"I'm not having fun," George told journalist Audie Bock when she visited the set for the *New York Times*. "I'm only doing this because I started it and now I have to finish it." He claimed he'd originally planned to direct just the first *Star Wars* film before turning it over to Fox, sitting back and watching the checks roll in, but had been surprised to find only he understood the world he had created. Only he could explain how it worked.

"I'd fallen in love with it. It's like marriage. You know what they say about women, 'You can't live with them and you can't live without them.' That's how this movie is."

The analogy wasn't entirely innocent. As he was finding it hard to live with *Star Wars* yet impossible to conceive of letting it go, George had lost something with Marcia.

The same scene played out almost every day. The heads of department on *Revenge of the Jedi* would gather together to screen the dailies, and as they watched take after take, a thick tension seemed to swell around the obscured room. After the last shot, the screen went dark, the house lights went up, and George and Marcia started arguing—loudly—while everyone else sat quietly glued to their seats, like kids lowering their heads around the dinner table while their unhappy parents went at it. "It was always about the picture," remembers sound editor Laurel Ladevich, "and it was almost always *good* for the picture. But it was fiery."

A stale stagnation had descended over all of Lucasfilm by that point. Everyone was tired after years on *Star Wars*, racing to make release dates, but a further heaviness came from the way George worked. Francis and Steven gave people opportunities, allowing collaborators to refresh the process by trying their hands at bigger and different things. George didn't. If someone was good at their role, and he knew to expect a performance from them, he kept them there. "No matter how much time passed, George never stopped thinking of me as a sound 'assistant,' and referring to me in that way," Ladevich says—even though, by *Jedi*, production had made her a full dialogue editor. It was one unexpected way Lucasfilm operated like a family: To the patriarch, one's place in the family unit always remains the same.

It was all *Star Wars*, all the time, for years on end, with little possibility for individual advancement or distinction. George had always been frugal, but he became, in the words of one ground staff employee at Skywalker Ranch, "a terrible cheapskate." He paid everyone the bare minimum wage and kept a close eye on expenses. Every new division or office Lucasfilm opened did so with the same directive: It had to at least break even, or it had to go. The staff at ILM made cracks about George's new mantra, with which he seemed to sign off on everything now: "It's good enough."

George had asked Kershner back to direct *Jedi*, but the older man disliked the script, which seemed to him a rehash of the first *Star Wars* movie, with a new breed of merchandisable cuddly aliens thrown in. (Kershner agreed to direct *Never Say Never Again*, the Bond film Francis had partly rewritten, instead.) George approached David Lynch, who was then working on a script of his own at Zoetrope, but Lynch told him he had "next door to zero interest" in directing someone else's movie. Lucasfilm placed a call to Canadian director David Cronenberg, who gave them the same answer. Eventually, George screened a spy film called *Eye of the Needle*, starring Donald Sutherland and directed by a little-known Welsh director, Richard Marquand, and liked Marquand's handling of the suspense and performances. He settled on Marquand as Kershner's replacement.

Marquand brought along his usual editor, Sean Barton, who had flown to California over the long Easter weekend in 1981 to interview with George. For Barton, who had toiled in commercials for a decade and only cut a handful of films, *Jedi* was a huge break. "Richard [Marquand] was quite laid-back," Barton says. "Richard was a pragmatist. He knew this was such a wonderful break, that if we completed it, if it went well and people liked it, it would turn into a wonderful break for everyone."

In the early weeks, George was on set every day, hanging over his new director. When he realized Marquand, a documentarian by trade, shot confidently with just one camera, George ordered the camera team to set up two additional cameras for backup coverage on every take. Marquand was put out but went along. Then George decided to dispense with the services of a full-time second unit director and oversee the blue-screen effect shots himself. When Marquand screened his rough cut of the film, George was disappointed—Marquand had "cut it too far," Barton admits. Marcia offered to take over.

"Marcia, you can make it different," George told her, "but you can't make it better."

He retained Barton as his own lead editor on the fine cut and assigned his wife, Barton remembers, to the "love scenes." In the cutting room next door to Barton's, George and his assistant Duwayne Dunham focused on the speeder bike chase through Endor. They all took turns on the sequence in which the Ewoks capture Luke, Han, and the droids. Every suite was set up with two KEM flatbeds, with a swivel chair in between: On the machine on the left, the editor could find and pick footage; they edited it on the machine on the right. George predicted that soon, when editing was done on video, all editors would work this way: with one screen on which to find footage, and another one on which to put it in sequence.

When they finally ran the whole cut, Barton turned to Lucas, excited. He had no doubt the film was going to be a hit.

"I don't know," George said. "The audience might have got tired of them by now."

He certainly had.

They finished early in the spring of 1983, just as the debt collectors put chains on the gate over at Hollywood General, and just in time for George to join Steven in Sri Lanka for the first weeks of filming *Indiana Jones and the Temple of Doom*, the second film in that series. There was no stopping.

In *Temple of Doom*, Indiana Jones, stranded in India with his sidekick Short Round and love interest Willie Scott, confronts a cult that has stolen a village's children—and its sacred fertility stones. When the movie came out, its darkness took critics and the public aback. There were those who claimed to see the difficulties in George's private life laid bare across the narrative: A father figure and his adopted child, encumbered by a nagging, shrieking romantic interest. The anxiety of having your children taken away from you. A man who has his still-beating heart ripped out of his chest. How was that for personal filmmaking?

"George was going through a dark period," Steven said. Lucas conceded he had not been "in a good mood . . . for a year or two." He thought too much was made of it, however. The second film in a trilogy was always darker—like *The Empire Strikes Back*. Lawrence Kasdan, who had written both *Raiders of the Lost Ark* and *Empire*, had wanted nothing to do with *Temple of Doom*. Its ugly mean-spiritedness, as he saw it, had repulsed him from the first moment it was pitched to him. Even Steven was uncomfortable. But he also felt jealous and possessive at the thought of anyone else directing an Indiana Jones adventure. Even when a film is mindless entertainment, the act of making it can turn it personal, too.

For the Lucases, *Star Wars* ending was like the kids moving out of the house: With the baby gone, George and Marcia looked at each other and wondered if they were still close enough as people—as close as they had been before. "He was burnt out," says Sid Ganis. "You know: Where do we go from here?"

And Marcia was—though it was painful to admit—bored of her life with him. She felt confined by George's unchanging personality. She wanted to travel; she wanted to have fun. He wanted to stay home, trust the same close circle of friends, and collect Norman Rockwell paintings. Though George had been relatively comfortable his whole life, a middle-class kid turned inconceivably wealthy in his early thirties, he lived in great fear of loss of money. Marcia, who had experienced hardship as a child, longed to be more carefree.

In May, as *Temple of Doom* was still filming, a new issue of *Esquire* hit newsstands. Among the stories within—previewed around the coyly smiling face of cover star Roy Scheider—was one about "Coppola and Lucas, an odd couple." The article, on the first page of the review section, was written by Dale Pollock, a film journalist who had been researching a biography of George for the previous two years. Its headline was nostalgic and titillating. It read, simply: "When George and Francis Were Friends."

In a preview of his biography, to be published later in the year, Pollock detailed the ups and downs of the two men's friendship, all the way to the present day, and Francis's upset that George, rich as Midas, had let him sink without extending a hand. Had watched

Zoetrope, their shared dream, end in bankruptcy for him and his family.

George and Francis had both openly spoken to Pollock, and now they regretted it. They rumbled that they might sue, but the journalist had recorded every conversation, kept extensive notes corroborating his work. Pollock's book was complimentary, yet George resented the mirror it held up to him: successful, visionary, but also awkward, arrogant, cheerless—and "extremely bitter," particularly over *Apocalypse Now*, which George still felt Francis had had no right to direct ("There was real anger over that on his part," Pollock says), and over the disrespect extended to *Star Wars*. It was around this time that George, who had often protested that the space opera was a kids' film and a fairy tale and nothing more, began insisting that the first film, in particular, had been a Vietnam allegory. He compared the Empire to imperialist America, the Emperor to Richard Nixon, the Rebel Alliance to the Vietcong. "He was very proud of *Star Wars* as a religion," too, Pollock says, "the impact of the Force—the potential for it as a positive force."

George took Pollock around Skywalker Ranch. He showed him binders full of treatments and story ideas for films he said he would make "when he was free of *Star Wars*," though even then, Pollock didn't believe him. "It was lip service from the start." Beverly Walker, who had worked on *American Graffiti*, agrees: "I'm not convinced George *ever* wanted to actually make arty films," she says. "Comic books and that sort of thing—that was his sensibility. He felt self-conscious about how successful his shallow popcorn film had become." (Said Milius: "George talks about [myth] all the time. He doesn't know how to use it . . . He doesn't understand myth at all.")

He bristled when people blamed him and Steven for Hollywood's obsession with blockbusters and high concepts. "George used to hate hearing that," Steven recalled. It made him sound Hollywood, and "he decried Hollywood."

He bristled, too, at Francis's reminders that he had followed in his footsteps—all the more so because it was indisputably true. "If you look at what George has built or done," says Anahid Nazarian, "it tends to follow what Francis has done, as the big brother." Francis's house in San Francisco was a white Victorian; the house George built at the Ranch was white mock-Victorian. Francis had sound editing facilities in a carriage house in Napa; the "Technical Building" that housed Skywalker Sound at the Ranch looked like a huge carriage house. Francis had vineyards; George got vineyards. Francis acquired the RKO research library for his private collection; George bought Paramount's and Universal's own research archives.

"There were a number of years where it got . . . anxious," Murch says of Francis and George's friendship. They were like brothers at a crossroads, so intertwined that any parting can only be painful. "When you're in a family," Ganis says, "I guess there are two ways of looking at it. Some people say: *Who cares about family?* And another kind of person says: *Oh my God. Why is he doing this to me? We're family.* Certainly there was a period in their relationship where George—I don't think Francis felt this way, I mean, I don't know how Francis felt—but George definitely felt . . . maligned by FFC."

George's dark period got darker. On May 25, *Return of the Jedi*—as George had renamed the film at the eleventh hour, having decided a true Jedi would never stoop to seeking revenge—hit American cinemas, to good reviews and great box office. It would end the year as the highest-grossing film of 1983, but the lowest-grossing installment of George's trilogy.

He could step off the treadmill; he was free of the galaxy far, far away. Many expected him to feel relief. Instead, on June 13, he called a meeting of the whole staff at Skywalker Ranch and announced, like a father speaking to his children, that he and Marcia were divorcing. Marcia moved down to Los Angeles and entered a new relationship with Tom Rodrigues, one of the production managers at Skywalker Ranch. It was unclear whether the two had begun seeing each other romantically before the divorce. When her and George's split was finalized, she walked away with a reported $50 million—a large, unplanned-for dent in George's wealth, so large it slowed down the expansion plans he had for Lucasfilm, for ILM, and for the Ranch. For years, he sold off assets piecemeal—including, in February 1986, the Lucasfilm Computer Division Graphics Group, to Apple co-founder Steve Jobs, who organized the group's forty employees and the technology rights that came with them into a new company he called Pixar.

Throughout the company's young history, George and Marcia had been parental figures. They hosted the annual Fourth of July barbecue. Every Christmas, they sent cards to the staff signed, "From the Lucasfilm family." Back when he'd made *THX 1138*, George had announced, with a young man's confidence, that his first film was about "people in cages with open doors . . . People would give anything to quit their jobs. All they have to do is do it. People would give anything for a divorce and there's nothing stopping them."

Marcia had walked out of her cage's open door. Word came down that Lucasfilm would go quiet for a little while. Many employees moved on, returned to Los Angeles, found staff jobs elsewhere. A few months after *Jedi*'s release, George called another company meeting for those who remained. While the tone at the divorce announcement had been somber, the mood now was stern, almost angry. Things, George told them, were going to change.

"This isn't a family," he said. "This is a business. You work for *me*. Sometimes, I feel like I'm working for *you*."

Every year, Lucasfilm had put out a yearbook, showcasing the staff and their achievements, along with developments at the Ranch. Marcia usually featured heavily. And then, Mike Kitchens says, "she disappeared from all the yearbooks. After she left . . . it was like she didn't exist anymore."

"She was excommunicated," De Palma says. "George sort of cut her off from any of the world that he was in because it was a very bitter divorce. And we never heard from Marcia again."

Kitchens remembers it upsetting Murch.

"It's revisionist history," Murch said. "She's been taken out of the story."

Unlike Francis, who had held onto Ellie but lost his studio, George retained Skywalker Ranch. The place sat quiet and beautiful in its idyllic valley. "There's nothing out there now that's necessarily producing films," Mike Kitchens says. "It's this sound and post facility. And just George, sitting in his Victorian building."

· 35 ·

THE EDGE OF THE FUTURE

Only Steven Spielberg knows what's popular today," Milius once joked. "Only Steven Spielberg will ever know what's popular. So leave it to him. He's the only one in the history of man who has ever figured that out."

Starting in the early '80s, critics filled column inches with attacks on Steven and George. They blamed the two friends for infantilizing American culture by making mawkish, simplistic films for and about children, and they blamed them for supercharging mainstream monoculture, as if the blockbuster successes of *Jaws*, then *Star Wars*—entertainments first and above all, unlike the two films to hold the top two spots in historical box-office charts before them, Francis's *The Godfather* and William Friedkin's *The Exorcist*, genre films made for adults—had single-handedly decimated the variety of the theatrical experience. Drive-in theaters across America closed. Double bills making space for low-budget and foreign films like the ones Roger Corman made and distributed, respectively, became a thing of the past. Aspiring film directors didn't just long to be as successful as Steven Spielberg—they aspired to look like him, in baseball caps and blue jeans and beards. It didn't matter that his films were more complex than they were given credit for, run through with a streak of mistrust for authority and a taste for cruelty; that, in the later words of scholar Phillip Maciak, they rewrote the idea of American fatherhood and masculinity, "haunted," as they were, "by absent fathers, dads abandoning their children for obsession, for pride, for madness, for infidelities large and small," or that his pictures were as literate about the history and uses of the film medium as any filmmaker's before or since. It didn't matter that *Star Wars*, at its core, told the story of guerrilla fighters standing up to a fascist empire, or that George's trilogy as a whole was an expression of his longstanding, deeply held beliefs in both freedom and fateful manifest destiny, the same paradox that animated the broader American psyche. Fundamentally, George's and Steven's films were about making the audience feel comfort, while filmmakers like Francis, Marty, and De Palma pursued *dis*comfort, for themselves and their viewers. Comfort sold tickets more reliably than unease. Familiarity, in the form of sequels and remakes, was a promise of comfort. Those were the films prioritized by Hollywood executives desperate to prove their worth and justify their pay packages to the conglomerates that had swallowed up the studios, whose shareholders understood success only as translated into profit margins and scrutinized box-office numbers as if they were stock prices. Steven Spielberg and George Lucas served up comfort better than anyone else, but successful as they were, they did not have the power to green-light a picture. The authority to make those choices rested with the suits in the C-suites, and American culture had moved, too, the way of Eisner, Diller, Katzenberg, and Simpson. Ronald Reagan, who liked to tell people "Jack Warner is why I became president," was in the White House. Sammy Glick—the backstabbing antihero of Budd Schulberg's 1941 novel, *What Makes Sammy Run?*, intended as an exposé and a cautionary tale and inspired by Jerry Wald, one of Jack Warner's favorite in-house writer-producers—had become an aspirational figure, so much so that when Schulberg received an honorary degree at Francis's alma mater, Hofstra, in 1985, a student enthusiastically shook his hand and earnestly told him he was modeling himself on the selfish wheeler-dealer, and hoped it would bring him success, a sentiment so widespread Schulberg wrote an afterword to a 1989 reissue of the book to condemn it.

"Back when Reagan was elected, the mood of the country changed, and the studios changed," says Walter Murch. "The successful films of the '70s taught the studios: Oh, this is the new template. *Jaws*, *Godfather*, *Star Wars*, *Apocalypse Now*, *Close Encounters*. Spielberg, Lucas, Scorsese, Coppola. *Okay, we could make this work*, the studio would say, *but we're going to do it our way*. Which immediately undercuts what made it successful. It's the trajectory of every revolution, you know. As Eric Hoffer said, every great idea starts as a movement, becomes a business, and winds up as a racket. That's just nature. That's what happens. It's like the life and death of any organism. All you can do is delay the curve."

Corporations were to be celebrated. Consolidation made wealth. Rich bottom lines made full pockets. Critics and columnists castigated Spielberg and Lucas for laying their golden eggs and, for the time being, turned their attention away from the executives who, like the countryman of Aesop's tale, were growing impatient, and cutting the goose open to get rich ever faster.

After the back-to-back successes of *Raiders of the Lost Ark* and *E.T.*, Sid Sheinberg resolved to tie Steven down—not with a contract, this time, but with thanks. Steven had finally founded his own production company, Amblin Entertainment, named after the short film that had caught Sheinberg's eye, and now Sheinberg, through the studio, offered to build Steven a physical place of his own. He had Universal build him a two-story Pueblo-style office building on a quiet road of the studio lot. The building was a movie-fantasy version of Steven's childhood Arizona, the Southwest by way of the backlot. The state-of-the-art television in the conference room hid inside an oak chest that opened up at the push of a button, like something out of a '50s fantasy of the future. Bruce, the great white from *Jaws*, emerged from the wishing well out front, under a gently swaying weeping willow. Eucalyptus planted outside filled the air around the building with a soothing, medicinal air.

Every film Steven had made revolved around a longing for home, from Clovis and Lou Jean's ill-conceived quest to be reunited with their children in *The Sugarland Express* to E.T.'s longing for his people. They were products of the boy who was driven back to his house afterward, to deal with a real world of loss, grief, and prejudice, a dark existential alienation he saw in the swaying shadows of trees at night, the numbers inked on neighbors' forearms, and, soon, the breakdown of his parents' love. Steven would speak over the years of the "estrangement" he had felt toward his father after the divorce. The same word applied to his experience of much of his life: estrangement from the gentile kids who strung their houses up with lights at the end of December, while his remained dark; estrangement from supposedly ideal '50s suburban American society, which made him feel his name, his nose, his history did not belong. Universal, like many families, had accepted him but also held him back. He stood somewhat on the fringes of Francis's crowd, the slightly older filmmakers who made darker movies and said provocative things and proclaimed a desire for independence and revolution.

Steven hired Kathy Kennedy and Frank Marshall to run the company for him. They didn't want to tell bleak films. They wanted to tell "hopeful stories," Kennedy said, "stories about triumph of the human spirit and the ability to rise above circumstance." Steven still didn't know about Kathy and Frank's relationship—"until one day, when I walked into my office, and saw the two of them making out on my couch."

Surrounded by reminders of how far he had come from crashing toy trains in Phoenix, everything, as it did then, revolved around Steven, and Kathy and Frank—the couple who found the money for his adult dreams, and the only two people Steven trusted to tell him no—stood in as metaphorical parents, like Leah and Arnold, who had stumped up the money for his childhood dreams, and never learned how to say no. Only here, at Amblin, couples in love got together instead of splitting up, movies cost millions instead of hundreds, and the kid who felt outside everyone else's hallucination was no longer an outsider, but in charge. Universal wanted him around so bad they paid, reports said, between $4 million and $6 million on the Amblin office.

Steven, Kathy, and Gary had Murphy beds built into the office. The way they figured it, if this was your job, why would anybody want to ever go home?

Sheinberg had one more gift for Steven. In October 1982, a few weeks into *E.T.*'s run in cinemas, he invited the younger man into his office at Universal, the same room in which they had first met when Steven was a young and green. Steven was in his mid-thirties now, bearded, a few weeks away from being the only person to have set the record for highest-grossing motion picture of all time twice. He was growing obscenely rich. His share of the profits for *E.T.*'s box-office receipts, but also sales of "*E.T.* posters, bed sheets, T-shirts, note pads, calendars, key chains, ice cream, and *E.T.* dolls," grew to half a million dollars every day.

"I want you to read a book called *Schindler's Ark*," Sheinberg said. "I'm sending the review to your house."

He sent Steven a clipping of a *New York Times* review of a novel by Thomas Keneally, fictionalizing the story of Oskar Schindler, a war profiteer bon vivant and member of the Nazi Party who eventually saved 1200 of his Jewish employees from the Holocaust.

"Universal just bought the book for you," Sheinberg told Steven. "Sir, this must be your next picture. This is a mission you must assign yourself."

Steven thought of the survivors in his mother's kitchen when he was a child. The thick accents and the tattooed forearms. His grandparents had come to America from Ukraine. Sheinberg's mother had fled from Ukraine, too, his father from Poland. Leopold Pfefferberg, one of the Polish Jews who credited his survival to Schindler, and who had inspired Keneally's book, wanted Steven to tell this story. He called Steven's office every day. He dropped in on his mother at the Milky Way.

But "I hadn't made what I'd call my first 'adult' film," Steven said, "and I was terrified of *Schindler's List* being my first, because what if I wasn't mature enough?" He didn't feel ready, "morally or cinematically." *E.T.* was a personal film, in its way. *Schindler's List* was an entirely different undertaking. Not gazing at the sky, but at the people around him, and the staggering shadow that had been cast over them—and himself.

Besides, Steven had *Indiana Jones and the Temple of Doom*, a sequel to *Raiders of the Lost Ark*, already lined up. The kind of thing he was much more comfortable with.

As the months and years passed, Steven sent the book to director Sydney Pollack and then to Barry Levinson, neither of whom felt up to it, either. He sent it to Marty.

"I'm not Jewish," Scorsese protested. On the other hand, he'd grown up surrounded by Jews, including Holocaust survivors. He had spent his life preoccupied with the nature of love and where grace comes from in complicated, flawed human beings—like Oskar Schindler.

"Marty was intrigued," Steven remembered. He said he would try it.

George shelved the nine remaining *Star Wars* films. Ganis announced no movies would ever be shot at Skywalker Ranch. George and Marcia had adopted a daughter, Amanda, two years before divorcing; he dedicated himself now to being a father. He worked only three days a week, and on those days he went in to Lucasfilm or ILM at eleven in the morning and made sure he was home by four. "Once I was a dad," he said, "it was like a bolt of lightning struck me."

He only waded back into the business to help friends or peers make films. He helped Akira Kurosawa finance *Kagemusha*. He produced Haskell Wexler's controversial war film *Latino*, uncredited, when no studio would touch it. When Paul Schrader, his brother Leonard, and his sister-in-law Chieko wrote a script about the life of the Japanese writer Yukio Mishima, an ambitious project told using flashback, fact, and dramatizations of some of Mishima's writings, he struggled to raise the budget he needed. Part of the money came from Japan, but many in the country of Mishima's birth resented the script openly portraying Mishima as homosexual. Eventually, Schrader convinced Tom Luddy to help, and Luddy brought in Francis, "who found some money," Schrader says, and then Luddy reached out to George, who surprised everyone by suggesting they go to Warner Bros.

George was acutely aware, after the success of *Star Wars* and the Indiana Jones films, of every studio wanting to be in the George Lucas business—and he was even more conscious, his friends knew, that the same studios had happily mistreated him on every film he had made before then. Over a decade later, Schrader says, "he was still pissed off at Warner Bros. for *THX*." The writer-director sat with Lucas as they met Terry Semel and John Calley, who ran Warner. It was a short meeting. George knew Warner Bros. wasn't interested in *Mishima*, Semel and Calley knew he knew, and they knew, too, that George felt they owed him for their earlier lack of faith.

"I want you to match the money we already raised in Tokyo," George told them.

"If we do," Semel answered cautiously, "we'd be doing you a favor."

"Yes," George agreed.

"It was like a meeting out of *The Godfather*," Schrader remembers. It wasn't about his film; it was a question of respect and an exercise in saving face. George wanted Warner Bros. to sign a check, for no reason other than his asking. Semel and Calley would sign the check, as long as it was agreed the "favor" expunged the offense they had committed.

They did George the favor and signed the check.

It never felt like business, with George; it was always personal.

Somehow, Francis kept it together throughout the '80s, continuing to make films even as banks and creditors pursued the debts he owed. After *One from the Heart*, he went straight into filming two loosely linked pictures—*The Outsiders* and *Rumble Fish*—back-to-back in semi-exile all the way in Tulsa, Oklahoma, the casts stocked with a new generation of young talented discovered by Fred Roos: fresh, almost adolescent faces named Tom Cruise, Patrick Swayze, Matt Dillon, Rob Lowe, Diane Lane, Emilio Estevez, Ralph Macchio, Mickey Rourke, and Francis's own nephew, Nicolas Cage. Instead of a studio, Francis set himself up in an abandoned school—production office at one end, construction shop at another. He had the young actors cook meals together in the house they used as their home on-screen, Swayze dancing to Springsteen songs, Francis sitting and laughing on the couch. Instead of Friday night parties, they had Friday night dinners, empty bottles of red wine collecting on the kitchen counter. He screened movies for them—not stuff they'd ever seen, but stuff like the 1933 Czech film *Ecstasy*, starring Hedy Lamarr, one of the first nonpornographic films to include a sex scene, though shot only on the actors' faces. He gave Mickey Rourke Herman Hesse's *Steppenwolf* to read. The author Dana Spiotta, daughter of Zoetrope president Robert Spiotta and then sixteen years old, followed Francis around as a "student observer." He wanted her to be ambitious, to read great books, to watch interesting movies. "I was just watching how he worked," Spiotta remembers. "He's willing to follow out something that's weirder, that other people don't get, and it doesn't particularly seem to bother him that other people don't understand what he's doing. It doesn't stop him from just doing what's beautiful or interesting to him." Francis, at times, bemoaned that young filmmakers in America aspired to be like George—in that they wanted to make millions of dollars. He wanted them to aspire to be artists. To know, as Spiotta puts it, "that it was okay to make being an artist your whole identity, that it was a way to live your life . . . a good life."

The Outsiders, a more commercial film, was a modest success; *Rumble Fish*, one of the weirder efforts that people might not get, tanked. Chris Lebenzon, who worked on *The Outsiders* as a first assistant editor, remembers mixing the picture's sound in a cellar room at the Napa vineyard in the winter, wearing gloves as protection against the cold, to save money on a facility rental. Francis had strung skulls and shrunken heads across the dirt driveway leading onto the property, as a deterrent against creditors and other plaintiffs looking to serve him legal documents. In '83, he reunited with Robert Evans and Mario Puzo when Evans hired him to rewrite and direct *The Cotton Club*, a drama about the 1930s heyday of the Harlem jazz club of the same name, but the magic was gone. Evans, reeling from a hurtful and unfair conviction for cocaine trafficking, had become persona non grata at Paramount after the dealing charge and the *Popeye* disaster. *The Cotton Club* was his attempt to follow in Francis's and George's footsteps, producing an ambitious, artistic event film he would own outright. He was millions in the hole before even hiring Francis, had mortgaged his house, had got in bed with shady investors, including Las Vegas casino owners Edward and Fred Doumani, Saudi arms dealer Adnan Khashoggi, and young theatrical promoter Roy Radin, who was killed in May 1983 by hit men hired by his girlfriend, cocaine dealer Karen Greenberger. On set, Evans and Francis clashed. The original $12 million budget ballooned to upwards of $50 million. The Doumani brothers hired a mobster to intimidate Evans and cut him out of the picture. Evans agreed, reneged, took them to court. Some members of the trade press gleefully painted the movie as another circus of Francis Ford Coppola's making.

Reversal after reversal. In February 1984, Jack Singer officially took ownership of the Zoetrope studio in Los Angeles. In the spring, as George and Steven knelt together outside Mann's Chinese Theatre and imprinted their hands into the concrete outside the historic cinema, and as *Indiana Jones and the Temple of Doom* was released to record-breaking first-week business, American Express cut off Francis's credit cards. In September, Michael Eisner—the architect of the kind of filmmaking Francis loathed above all—was announced as the new head of the Walt Disney Company, where he and Katzenberg, who followed him to become Walt Disney Studios chairman, would spend the next decade pulling the film industry further away from art and ever closer to fairground entertainment—prioritizing "franchiseable" intellectual property, acquiring production companies and television networks for vertical integration, green-lighting pictures as much for their merchandising implications and the potential of integrating them with theme park rides as anything else. In mid-December, as *The Cotton Club* came out and tanked, opening fifth and grossing under $3 million its opening weekend, Francis held on to the Sentinel Building by his fingernails, paying off an overdue $1.7 million loan just days before the Tower was to be auctioned off to the highest bidder. Zoetrope Studios was shuttered; the company was little more than a logo and an address on letterhead. Francis's dream of a "utopian society of filmmakers," in the words of his general counsel John Peters, was over. He had pursued it for seventeen years—since he and George, young and unknown, had spent the evenings sitting in Francis's poky Warner Bros. office after *Finian's Rainbow* wrapped for the day, entertaining their film school classmates, talking castles into the sky.

Francis missed those days, sometimes. Back when only people who really *loved* movies, like him and George, took a daily interest in them. Now, entering the second half of the 1980s, Jack Warner's favorite little informant, Ronald Reagan, was president of the United States, the most talked-about films of every year were financially supercharged versions of Corman's B-movies, made to sell toys and lunch boxes to twelve-year-olds, and anyone who picked up a newspaper anywhere in America scrutinized the weekend box-office numbers like they were stock market reports. "I liked it better when everyone wasn't so interested in movies," Francis lamented to Peter Cowie in the late-winter months of 1987. "I felt it was something that belonged to *me* a little bit. Now I even wonder if I'm part of it."

Francis, who made seven films in the fourteen years since meeting George, most of them masterpieces, directed seven more over the next seven years, most of them good but forgettable. He charged $2.5 million and 10 percent of the profits each time and funneled the money into paying off his debts. The winery in Napa—paid for with *Godfather* money—began to sustain itself in 1985, when the first bottles of wine labeled with the Coppola name appeared for sale. A modest but steady stream of income flowed into the family coffers from *The Conversation* and *Apocalypse Now*. Francis closed the restaurant on the ground level of the Sentinel, rented out every other floor of the building with the exception of his penthouse. He took uncredited script doctor gigs. He even directed a theme park ride for Eisner's Disney—the seventeen-minute 4D science-fiction film *Captain EO*, starring Michael Jackson. (George co-wrote and executive produced from an idea by Disney's Imagineers; Murch edited.) Francis, usually so unwavering, made compromise after compromise.

Ellie sometimes thought it would be a good thing if they stopped fighting and lost everything. They'd have each other, less public attention, fewer distractions. That fantasy remained just that—a fantasy. Francis wasn't capable of the "more quiet life" Ellie wondered about. He always found a chip and a chair somewhere.

In May 1986, Francis reunited with Jimmy Caan to shoot an adaptation of Nicholas Proffitt's novel *Gardens of Stone*. Caan had left

Hollywood for several years, lost in a cocaine addiction he used to cope, in part, with the sudden loss of his sister to leukemia. He'd got out of it, like Marty had, though others weren't so lucky. In '82, Steven's regular leading man, Richard Dreyfuss, had been arrested for crashing his Mercedes into a tree while high on cocaine; the same year, John Belushi, who had starred in *1941*, died of a cocaine and heroin overdose, alone in a bungalow at the Chateau Marmont. Two years later, ER doctors had to pump Carrie Fisher's stomach to save her life: She'd come to depend on booze, Percodan, and opioids to silence the demons rattling around her head. Film production companies insured themselves against losses caused by substance abuse. Costume designer Aggie Rodgers, who had worked on *American Graffiti*, *The Conversation*, and *Return of the Jedi*, learned which actors had to be dressed in long sleeves, because short would show the track marks.

Caan made it through. He told Francis how being a dad had saved his life; how coaching confidence into his son Scott in Little League baseball had saved his life. In *Gardens of Stone*, Caan played a hardened veteran assigned to Arlington National Cemetery, where he comes to terms with preparing young, naive men for their deaths before they are shipped out to Vietnam. Francis's own twenty-two-year-old son, Gio, was his right-hand man, as he'd been ever since *One from the Heart*. On May 26, Memorial Day, four days into principal photography, the cast and crew had the day off. Gio and his girlfriend, Jacqueline, several weeks pregnant with their daughter, went out on a speedboat off Annapolis with Griffin O'Neal, one of Caan's co-stars in *Gardens of Stone*. Jacqueline soon returned to land, "scared that we were all going to be killed," she remembered, by O'Neal's "wild" and "really crazy" piloting of the boat. Fifteen minutes after she'd left the two men, O'Neal, still at the wheel, tried to pass between two slower boats, not realizing the two were connected by a towline. He saw the line at the last instant and ducked. Gio didn't.

His death opened a pit of "pain and fury" in both Francis and

Ellie that neither could put into words. Francis blamed himself. Gio had asked him to come and he'd said no. "I should have been there," he said later. "Maybe, if I had been there . . . It's your job, as a parent, to be there to prevent the worst from happening to your children."

Years later, Ellie would try to make art about Gio's death. Francis finished *Gardens of Stone*. The film's funeral scenes were shot in the chapel where Gio's funeral had taken place.

The unimaginable loss brought something into focus for Francis. "Gio only lived 22 years, but he lived a very complete life," he told the *Los Angeles Times* a decade after the death of his son. "Life is short for everybody, whether it's 20 years for a person or 200 years for a tree. It's about how you live. As a kid, I was always fascinated by seeing a mosquito and thinking—does it know it only has a couple of days to live?"

Ellie described the loss as the most profound experience she had ever had. It was transformative for Francis, who spoke publicly of Gio's death only rarely. "I romanticized him . . . ," he said in 1988. "In order to hang on to him a little bit more, I have to be a little less interested in the real world because he's not in it anymore. But I do believe he's still out there, and somehow I'll find him again, because he's still one of the qualities of my existence. Anybody you love is like that."

Gio left Francis full of memories. Four-year-old Gio, his hair still nearly blond and yet to darken, goofing around on the set of *Finian's Rainbow*, wearing a stuck-on black beard and pretending to be his father. Ten-year-old Gio with his mother and siblings on location for *The Godfather Part II*, in costume as immigrants passing through Ellis Island. Teenage Gio and Roman taking over a little bungalow across from Francis's own writing cottage on the Napa vineyard grounds so they could write a script, too. How Francis would walk in there at the end of the workday and find the two of them together, surrounded by Coke bottles and beer cans strewn across the floor, movie posters pinned and hung on the walls.

Or the Fourth of July, a year before Gio's death, when the car-mad young man had dusted off his father's collectible 1948 Tucker Torpedo and driven it proudly in a local Independence Day parade.

Or the late Friday night, just two months before Gio's death, when he and Francis had sat together eating Chinese takeout in Studio 8H at Rockefeller Plaza, watching the NBC crews dress the sets for the following night's *Saturday Night Live*, which Francis was hosting.

Or the day, back in 1978, when Francis had found a letter from fourteen-year-old Gio, "in his terrible handwriting and with his little misspellings," pleading, "I don't want to go to school. I want to be with you, I want to learn everything there is to learn about films and entertainment, I want to study them and I want to be a director." Francis had pulled him out of school there and then. Worked alongside his "little fourteen-year-old son every day" thereafter, he thought of himself as Odysseus and Gio as Telemachus—a prince, his heir, "the president of Zoetrope." At the time of his death, Gio was about to fulfill the ambition he had put down on paper in that teenage letter and become a director. Steven was producing an anthology television series for NBC, *Amazing Stories*, partly as a way to give directing opportunities to people he liked—Matthew Robbins, Robert Zemeckis, Bob Balaban, Kersh, Marty. Steven liked Gio. He thought he should direct one of the episodes, too. Gio would become a director and a father in the same year—just like Francis had, back in '63, when Gio was born.

Now Gio was dead.

Francis had begun to think he could bounce back from anything. When Gio died, he thought, *It doesn't seem like I'm going to be able to undo this one.* The finality was devastating. He had always been ambivalent about the specifics of an afterlife, but Gian-Carlo had to still be somewhere, "somehow still there," Francis said about the loss two decades later. "I can't believe that something so specific is gone."

How important is anything? he asked himself. He stood outside the house in Napa and looked over the vineyards and the fields. He listened to the cows and the birds. San Francisco seemed to him, suddenly, silly and provincial, and the Hollywood game of reviews and box-office numbers even more otiose. He thought about being present—and no longer chasing, chasing. Chasing what? For what meaning? He had fortune and glory, every award available to win, each with his name engraved into the metal. His son was dead. *Perhaps*, he thought, *all you have to do to achieve is to be part of everything.*

It was around Gio's death, friends say, that Francis and George's rift began to heal. A year after the devastating loss, Francis rolled cameras on *Tucker: The Man and His Dream*, a biopic of the automobile entrepreneur he had admired his whole life. It was another film he had tried to make for years—once with Marlon Brando; once as a musical, with Leonard Bernstein writing the songs. Now he sought George out and admitted the "stinky kid" knew what audiences wanted better than he did. Maybe, for once, he could make something he loved into something accessible and commercial. Preston Tucker had had a way of bouncing back from disappointment, as Francis did, and Tucker's work and family lives had mixed—as the Coppolas' did. George, for all his love of cars, only knew about the automobile entrepreneur from the stories Francis told over the years. To him, Tucker's story was that of a visionary trying to innovate in a system designed to preserve the big-business status quo. It was his and Francis's story.

Francis directed, and George was the executive producer; Lucasfilm and Zoetrope would be credited side by side. The film was inspired by, and dedicated to, Gio. Francis rolled cameras for the first day of principal photography less than a year after his son's death, with Jeff Bridges as his Tucker. The crew shot all over Marin County for three months, with many of Francis's regular creative family around him: Vittorio Storaro behind the camera, Fred Roos co-producing, Dean Tavoularis designing the sets. Carmine composed some of the music. Anahid Nazarian covered the historical research. Shortly after filming wrapped without any complications, George went to Sid Ganis, who now ran Paramount, and made a deal for Paramount to cover the cost of making the film in exchange for distribution rights. The studio was already in business with George as the distributor of the Indiana Jones movies, the third installment of which was scheduled to start filming the following year, and it wanted Francis back into the fold to make a sequel of his own, *The Godfather Part III*—but Ganis was also a friend. Francis, meanwhile, drove out to Skywalker Ranch to work on the film's sound mix, the first time a movie's audio postproduction was done at George's newly completed facility. *Tucker*, in many ways, felt like a homecoming.

But, released in the summer of 1988 on the same day as Marty's *Last Temptation of Christ*, the film didn't do well at the box office. The reviews praised Francis for finally making a lighthearted, feel-good movie, but the filmmaker himself felt estranged from the final work. He had tried to be more like George, and flattened one of his lifelong labors of love into a whimsical, colorful crowd-pleaser. He had smoothed over Tucker's complexity and "stink," had foregone his usual process, in which he peeled himself open like a fruit and found seeds in himself to match those in the character. In personality, Bridges's Tucker is all Francis—charismatic, brash, daring. In meaning, though, he's all George: a dogged small-business entrepreneur with a visionary sense of the possibilities of technology, whose once derided innovations are finally embraced by the very same corporations who dismissed him.

The mishmash was a film that disappointed its director—and made him no money anyway. Francis blamed George. George, for whom *Tucker* existing and breaking even was enough, remained convinced the film would have been an even greater failure without him.

"Francis can get so esoteric it can be hard for an audience to relate to him," George lectured. "He needs someone to hold him back." Francis answered by comparing his friend to a marketing expert, rather than an artist. "He wanted to candy-apple it up a bit, make it like a Disney film. He was at the height of his success, and I was at the height of my failure, and I was a little insecure . . . I think it's a good movie . . . but it's not the movie I would have made at the height of my power."

They were the same barbs they'd aimed at one another for years, however, nowhere near sharp enough to draw blood. As the years passed, George grew more comfortable expressing his admiration for Francis. "Francis isn't just a filmmaker," he said. "He's an Italian opera. He's the kind of person who would've built the Vatican or, before that, the pyramids. He thrives on chaos and tumult. He was constantly jumping off cliffs, and I was the guy who kept running after him, saying, 'You can't do that!'"

By the time the 1980s came to a close, Francis had paid off his remaining debts to United Artists for going over budget on *Apocalypse Now.* He caved, accepted Paramount's pleas, and signed on to make *The Godfather Part III*—but only after extracting so much money from the studio he was able to settle what he still owed Jack Singer, even the last of the original "loan" Warner Bros.–Seven Arts had extended him, all those years ago, to set up American Zoetrope in the filthy old warehouse building on Folsom Street. In 1992, he, Ellie, and the Zoetrope Corporation filed for Chapter 11 bankruptcy protection. By then, Francis had paid off all his creditors—except Fred Roos, to whose production company he owed $71 million, wrote the *Los Angeles Times*, "through a series of complicated financial transactions." The reorganization plan submitted with the bankruptcy filing allowed Francis to avoid liquidation and keep his companies alive, as long as his sole creditor—Roos—approved of a new ownership structure in compensation. Francis "proposed" that Roos receive a 25 percent equity stake in Zoetrope Corp. and a 15 percent stake in Zoetrope Productions.

Roos, so often Francis's human chip and chair, accepted. And just like that, after a long, hardworking, painful decade, Francis and Zoetrope survived, free of encumbrances.

Francis reimagined the company as a family business. The company endures to this day, headquartered in the Tower on Kearny Street, a family business not dissimilar, though on a much smaller scale, to the nascent studios of Hollywood's early years. It has produced films by several Coppolas, including Francis's daughter, Sofia, and Gio's daughter, Gian-Carla, born on New Year's Day 1987. Ellie made sure to be in the delivery room. Everyone called the baby Gia.

Ellie had often compared herself to George. Both of them were quiet, steady introverts, appropriate counterpoints to Francis's grandiosity and recklessness. They had all had to learn to forgive and appreciate each other. They accepted things about each other that had once driven them mad.

"Oh, that's Francis," George would say.

"Well," went Francis's version, "you know what George is like."

They weren't going to change each other.

And to this day, says Anahid Nazarian, "George is probably his closest friend."

EPILOGUE

At lunch one day on the Sri Lanka set of *Indiana Jones and the Temple of Doom*—the first sequel of the second franchise George owned outright, because he had understood, nearly a decade earlier, that "those who control the means of production control the creative vision"—Steven stuck a straw into some chocolate milk and started slurping. George ate his lunch across from him. He looked up at his friend and watched him drink, and his eyes lit up. He pointed his fork at Steven's straw.

"You know," George said, "someday everything we learn, see, and hear will come from something that looks just like that."

Steven made a little noise and shrugged. That kind of odd comment wasn't unusual, coming from George. He was full of predictions about the future: about the video cameras everyone would one day use, the computers that would inevitably replace Moviolas and Steenbecks. They were interesting notions, but Steven had a movie to make and didn't think any more of it.

George, though, felt he had been hit by an electrical charge that had slowly been building up in the recesses of his brain. The crew on *Temple of Doom* were shipping the footage shot every day back to London, where the dailies were developed and reviewed; he and Steven wouldn't get to see them until they left Sri Lanka because they would take three days round trip to get back, by which time filming would have moved on anyway. What if a movie could be shot digitally and the rushes seen immediately, anywhere?

What if—instead of struggling against the way *Star Wars* came out of the camera every day, underwhelming, not *quite* like the world he had imagined in his mind—what if a filmmaker could pre-visualize a film digitally, show the crew exactly what needed achieving, and precisely lay out where and how special effects were required?

What if, down the line, you didn't need the studio system at all, because all it had was money and soundstages? What if digital pictures were cheap enough for anyone to make, and soundstages were obsolete because a digital world could create any location the mind could envision?

What if, instead of negotiating with Fox or Paramount to distribute his films, which then had to negotiate with distributors, which then had to make sure cinemas around the world received high-end identical prints and projected them with the right amount of light and played the sound on the right, expensive surround sound system—what if a film could be beamed everywhere, in a digital uniform—even, one day, to the public's own homes?

He had always felt safer with reliable machines than unpredictable humans, starting with the cars he had built and raced as a teenager, all the way to the heavy cameras he stood behind at USC and while shooting the making of *The Rain People*. They were tools to speed up life, give it the pace and harmony George wanted it to have, but they were also buffers between him and reality. They gave him control. As did his beloved editing tables, in the rooms he loved and enjoyed so much more than the chaotic set. On set, you always lost: You just made the best compromise you could. At the editing screen, you could win, turn something into more than it was before.

What if, George thought, technology could make the whole process that way? Streamline it, concentrate it, deliver your vision directly, with the ease of drawing chocolate milk through a straw?

When his filmmaker friends passed on the chance to come to Skywalker Ranch, George reimagined the retreat less as a campus and more as a facility dedicated to film technology. In 1996, a few years after producing *Indiana Jones and the Last Crusade*, the third film in the series—in which, finally, both he and Steven got to work with James Bond, casting Sean Connery as Indy's dad—George gave an interview to Randall Lane of *Forbes* magazine. The two men sat at Skywalker Ranch, by now a postproduction and service facility at which George himself only appeared once a week.

George told Lane his business was no longer filmmaking, but more "the business of using technology to advance the art of filmmaking and to liberate it from the constraints of time and place and costs." He predicted all-digital movies, directors who no longer needed to be on location, all-CGI sets, "digital images of actors" so producers, instead of hiring a full cast, could "download a bit character." He predicted "movies on the Internet" and a filmmaking ecosystem in which, in lieu of mainstream theatrical releases that would get the whole world talking and sharing an experience, each "product will have small market niches." His least favorite part of filmmaking had always been the people.

It was a strikingly prescient forewarning of the Hollywood of the twenty-first century, one in which, as these words are written, movies are made digitally and streamed to the audience's home on dozens of subscription services, and unions representing film crew members strike against studios for better pay and protection from "artificial intelligence" computer tools being developed to replace them. (As early as 2022, the company George had founded, Industrial Light & Magic, promoted its collaboration with Nvidia, a prominent maker of generative AI tools, to "showcase how they leverage their incomparable asset library . . . to provide filmmakers the ultimate flexibility when developing the right look and ideal lighting for a scene." Nvidia has since been sued for allegedly exploiting copyrighted works in the "training" of its AI tools.) Box-office charts are dominated by sequels and remakes, films for which, following the Diller Killer model, creative control rests with studio executives, not filmmakers. David Zaslav, the current president of the studio that bears Jack Warner's name, is familiar to audiences for the now routine practice of burying films before they are released, or disappearing them from distribution, if the studio estimates the tax write-off worth more than the potential revenue—an erasure of filmmakers' work more egregious than any "cutting off of the baby's fingers" that outraged George as a young man.

But George himself is out of the game. In 2012, he sold Lucasfilm, its holdings, and its intellectual property to the Walt Disney Company, in exchange for an estimated $4 billion. Bob Iger, Disney's chairman and CEO, celebrated the acquisition of "a world-class portfolio of content" the corporation could use to "drive significant long-term value." Over the next decade or so, Lucasfilm, owned by Disney and run by Kathleen Kennedy, produced five theatrical films and fifteen episodic series set in the universe George had created and once insisted only he understood. The studio, over the same period, was also behind the release of dozens of projects drawn from the Marvel comic book universe—though when audiences showed signs of tiredness at the repetition and similitude of these projects, Iger blamed filmmakers, and wished for more "executives really looking over what's being done day after day after day." It was the kind of statement that had made the George Lucas of 1972 disgusted with the studios, but it was also the same thinking that had motivated the same George Lucas, ten years later, to hang over Richard Marquand as he shot and cut *Return of the Jedi*. It was, after all—and as Bob Iger might have said himself—his money being spent.

Back in 1996, as George spoke to the reporter from *Forbes*, Steven was the chairman of his own studio, DreamWorks, founded in partnership with Jeffrey Katzenberg and former agent David Geffen, the latter of whom now owned and lived in Jack Warner's house, bought lock, stock, and barrel from the Warner family. Steven had matured, taken *Schindler's List* back from Marty in 1993, and directed a masterpiece out of it himself. Francis was filming an adaptation of John Grisham's legal thriller *The Rainmaker* for Paramount, the last work-for-hire film in a long list embarked upon to pay his debts. After its release, he "quit" mainstream filmmaking and went back to "try[ing] to understand what making movies is . . . by self-financing some very small, low-budget movies . . . [that] were not meant to be successful." Meanwhile, he produced and championed esoteric, risky pictures: Sofia's first film and Roman's first film; films directed by Duvall and De Niro; Thailand's most expensive and highest-grossing picture, Chatrichalerm Yukol's *The Legend of Suriyothai.*

But it was George who still thought of himself as the little guy—though he was a millionaire many times over, a Bay Area tech entrepreneur in his own right, and a film executive who no longer particularly cared to make films and produced almost exclusively franchise prequels and sequels. He had survived that car crash for a reason, and like many whose near-death experiences give them a sense of predestination or being part of a higher plan, and like many who are proven right time and again in the face of doubt and impediment, he felt himself to be righteous. What would be good for him, he figured, would be good for everyone.

Like many very wealthy people, the only people he felt comfortable building new bonds with were other very wealthy people. "Success ruined my father," Jack Warner Jr. had once said; because of it, "he had developed the attitude that everybody wanted something from him, which governed his life later."

George, too, had fought to get up the trail to the mountaintop. There he built a gated ranch as luxurious and opulent as any property Jack Warner had ever owned and—wittingly or not—rolled his own rock down the trail.

Before he let the journalist from *Forbes* go, George looked across Skywalker Ranch and made one final prediction.

"All studios are going to look like what we are," he said. "They're all going to be exactly like us."

ACKNOWLEDGMENTS

I am deeply indebted to:

Jenny Hewson at Lutyens & Rubinstein, for your taste, patience, honesty, and guidance.

Mackenzie Brady Watson, of the Stuart Krichevsky Literary Agency, for steering this book right, and Chandler Wickers, for your insight and enthusiasm early in the process.

Ryan Doherty, at Celadon Books, and Walter Donohue, at Faber & Faber, for believing in this book, bearing with me as I missed every deadline, and helping shape my mass of words until it was readable. If I was the director of this book—overwhelmed, easily distracted, complaining about cutting fingers off my baby—then you were the Walter Murches. The horse may talk.

Thank you to the team at Celadon for your work on this book, especially Faith Tomlin, Christine Mykityshyn, Jaime Noven, Alex Cruz-Jimenez, Emily Walters, Morgan Mitchell, Ryan T. Jenkins, Michelle McMillian, and Vincent Stanley.

The hundreds of people who took the time to speak to me and trusted me with their memories, insights, and experiences, including those who spoke to me on background or who are not directly quoted in the "final cut" of the book. Your generosity was invaluable, and I hope I have honored it.

The dozens of authors, journalists, documentary filmmakers, researchers, scholars, archivists, and others without whose earlier work on and around this subject I would have been lost.

Jason Sanders at the Berkeley Art Museum and Pacific Film Archive; Noela Hueso at the UCLA School of Theater, Film, and Television; Sandra Garcia-Myers, Billy Smith, and Stephen Hanson at the USC Cinematic Arts Library and Archives; Louise Hilton, Jeanie Braun, and Allison Francis at the Margaret Herrick Library at the Academy of Motion Picture Arts and Sciences; Emily Wittenberg at the Louis B. Mayer Library at the American Film Institute; Christian Hansen at the Danish Film Institute; Micaela Connolly at the University of Montana; Connie Wethington, Cynthia Young Russell, and Robyn Stanley at Skywalker Ranch; and Anahid Nazarian and Courtney Garcia at American Zoetrope, for your time, guidance, stewardship, and expertise.

Maureen Lambray, for taking the spectacular photograph on the cover.

Mardik Martin, for taking me seriously way back when.

Danit Brown, Doris Cheng, Ann Douglas, Kate Finlinson, Melissa Rivero, Ankur Thakkar, Arturo Vidich, Steve Wilson, and Hananah Zaheer, for the Slack blood pacts; and Rebecca Makkai, for teaching us how to think about writing.

Gary Forrester, Asta Jonasson, Mayura U, Jack Weatherley, and everyone else who showed patience over the years it took me to write this instead of the things I promised we would work on together.

Maven, for the coupons for free writing time. The only reason I haven't cashed them in is because I like them too much to give them up.

Kelty and Crosby, for everything.

Owen, for never going to bed until I do. I will miss you so much next time around.

Thank you, particularly, to everyone mentioned in the opening credits to this book, without whom it would not be a book, and whose work is vital to all books becoming books.

NOTES

Introduction

xiii **"manufacturing money":** Jack Warner, *My First Hundred Years in Hollywood* (Random House, 1965), 249.

xiv **"What's that saying?":** Jean Stein, *West of Eden* (Random House, 2017), 94.

xiv **who would be the last of the original moguls:** Foster Hirsch, *Hollywood and the Movies of the Fifties* (Alfred A. Knopf), 2023, 3.

xv **"An era ended":** Charles Champlin, "We No Longer Go to the Movies," program for the First Los Angeles International Film Exposition, 4–14 November 1971, Gary Kurtz Papers, Collection 2335, box 79, University of Southern California archives.

1: Twenty Years Later

3 **that's how George liked to tell it:** Historian Foster Hirsch dates October 31, 1969 as Warner's official last day at the studio that bears his family name (Hirsch, *Hollywood and the Movies of the Fifties*, 122). But Jack's resignation was announced in July 1967: see Vincent Canby, "Jack Warner, 75, Resigns Top Job," *New York Times*, 25 July 1967, 31.

4 **"the temperament of an artist who works alone in an attic":** Judy Stone, *Eye on the World: Conversations with International Filmmakers* (Silman-James Press, 1997), 715.

4 **"Look, one of us is going to get this":** Michael Ondaatje, *The Conversations: Walter Murch and the Art of Editing Film* (Vintage Canada, 2002), 13.

4 **"Traditionally, what a student did is go there":** Jeanine Basinger and Sam Wasson, *Hollywood: The Oral History* (Harper, 2022), 592.

4 **"completely empty":** Basinger and Wasson, *Hollywood*, 592.

5 **"my choices of what I was going to do were extremely limited":** Basinger and Wasson, *Hollywood*, 592.

5 **"They're the only people on the lot":** Basinger and Wasson, *Hollywood*, 592.

8 **"Maybe there's something else for me":** George Lucas, interview by Oprah Winfrey, *Oprah's Next Chapter*, Oprah Winfrey Network, 22 January 2012.

8 **"an extra day":** Lucas, interview by Winfrey, *Oprah's Next Chapter.*

9 ***Maybe everyone had been right:*** Basinger and Wasson, *Hollywood*, 528.

2: Beyond the Rainbow

11 **"In my family, that's what the issue was":** Michael Goodwin and Naomi Wise, *On the Edge: The Life and Times of Francis Coppola* (William Morrow and Company, 1989), 17.

12 **"Ever since I was a little kid":** Goodwin and Wise, *On the Edge*, 19.

12 **"I want to be rich and famous":** Goodwin and Wise, *On the Edge*, 19.

12 **"and then you can't move your legs":** Goodwin and Wise, *On the Edge*, 19.

13 **"a lot":** Lee Eisenberg, "The Conversation: Francis Coppola & Gay Talese," *Esquire*, July 1981, 84.

13 **"I had a little movie company there":** Joseph Gelmis, *The Film Director as Superstar* (Pelican Books, 1974), 241.

14 **"I want to conduct":** Roger Ebert, "'Napoleon' & Carmine Coppola," 19 April 1981. Accessed 1 June 2023 at https://www.rogerebert.com/interviews/and8220napoleonand8221-and-carmine-coppola.

14 **"let Daddy get his big break":** Goodwin and Wise, *On the Edge*, 18.

15 **"and I thought frankly that my father would be impressed":** Peter Biskind, *Easy Riders, Raging Bulls* (Bloomsbury, 1998), 36.

16 **"I was faking it":** Gelmis, *The Film Director as Superstar*, 247.

17 **"little pieces":** Gelmis, *The Film Director as Superstar*, 249–250.

17 **"a Titan crane":** J. W. Rinzler, *Howard Kazanjian: A Producer's Life* (Abrams Books, 2021), 79.

17 **you can't film a dance number:** Rinzler, *Howard Kazanjian*, 79.

17 **"set striking and construction":** *Finian's Rainbow* cost reports, Joel Freeman papers, f.82, Margaret Herrick Library, Academy of Motion Picture Arts and Sciences.

18 **"always looking at me":** Rinzler, *Howard Kazanjian*, 76.

18 **"Well, he's observing you":** Rinzler, *Howard Kazanjian*, 76.

18 **"Nothing much":** Rinzler, *Howard Kazanjian*, 75.

18 **"Can I hang around?":** Rinzler, *Howard Kazanjian*, 75.

19 **"I have no interest in Hollywood movies":** Basinger and Wasson, *Hollywood*, 592.

19 **"Why do you want to get off my movie?":** Basinger and Wasson, *Hollywood*, 593.

20 **"You're doing it all wrong":** Marcus Hearn, *The Cinema of George Lucas* (Abrams, 2005), 35.

20 **"That really was my strength":** Basinger and Wasson, *Hollywood*, 593.

20 **"more or less full-time":** Rinzler, *Howard Kazanjian*, 76.

22 **"Someday when they finally throw me out of here":** Hearn, *The Cinema of George Lucas*, 107.

22 **"Film is power":** Christopher Chang, ed., *Zoetrope at 50* (American Zoetrope, 2019), 30. Courtesy of Walter Murch.

22 ***I'm willing to die by his side:*** Chang, *Zoetrope at 50*, 30.

22 **For *Finian's Rainbow* budget and schedule:** *Finian's Rainbow* cost reports, Joel Freeman papers.

22 **"he was special":** Author interview with Robert Lovenheim, 17 May 2023.

22 ***Time* magazine ran a feature:** "Trends: The Student Movie Makers," *Time*, 2 February 1968.

23 **"and I went and asked my secretary":** Author interview with Mike Medavoy, 9 June 2022.

23 **"As a young agent":** Mike Medavoy, *You're Only as Good as Your Next One* (Pocket Books, 2002), 4–6.

23 **"Don't go over there and work for them":** George Lucas interview, oral history collection, American Film Institute.

23 **"You'll come along on *The Rain People*":** Lucas, oral history collection, American Film Institute.

24 **"I can't write" and following exchange:** Lucas, oral history collection, American Film Institute.

24 **"You have to learn":** Olivier Assayas, "Entretien avec George Lucas," *Cahiers du Cinéma* 677 (April 2012), 28. Translated by the author.

24 **"a great idea":** Lucas, oral history collection, American Film Institute.

24 **"Well, okay":** Lucas, oral history collection, American Film Institute.

3: Reality Ends Here

25 **"The editing rooms were literally stalls for horses" and other quotes from Bill Couturié in this chapter:** Author interview with Bill Couturié, 23 June 2023.

26 **"shut [him] out":** George Lucas, interview by Gene Youngblood, *George Lucas: Maker of Films*, KCET, 1971.

26 **On the spelling of Gene Peterson:** Spelled "Petersen" in several of his film credits, but "Peterson" by the university. See https://cinema.usc.edu/news/article.cfm?id=9831.

26 **"I don't know what you guys are doing here":** Author interview with Walter Murch, 8 October 2022.

26 **"All of those teachers" and other quotes from Walter Murch in this chapter:** Author interview with W. Murch.

27 **"available as consumer item[s]":** Ondaatje, *The Conversations*, 6.

27 **"sending our work":** Author interview with Matthew Robbins, 13 June 2022.

27 **"I came back to the United States":** Ondaatje, *The Conversations*, 11.

28 **"If you really want to go to film school":** Author interview with Robbins.

28 **"incredible, delicious, almost absurd":** Ondaatje, *The Conversations*, 11.

28 **"We arrived":** Author interview with Robbins.

29 **"You're doing it wrong":** *A Legacy of Filmmakers: The Early Years of American Zoetrope*, directed by Gary Leva, 2004.

29 **"Get out of here":** Dale Pollock, *Skywalking: The Life and Films of George Lucas* (Harmony Books, 1983), 51.

30 ***Where did this kid come from*:** Author interview with W. Murch.

30 **"Nobody there, including the teachers":** Pollock, *Skywalking*, 56.

30 **"If you went up":** Pollock, *Skywalking*, 49.

30 **"the most electrifying things you had ever seen":** Pollock, *Skywalking*, 55.

31 **"like Margaret Keane":** Rinzler, *Howard Kazanjian*, 17.

31 **"George made a few friends":** Brian Jay Jones, *George Lucas: A Life* (Back Bay Books, 2016), 47.

31 **"There was no going back after that":** Stephen Farber, "George Lucas: The Stinky Kid Hits the Big Time," *Film Quarterly* 27, no. 3 (Spring 1974). Reprinted in Sally Kline, ed., *George Lucas Interviews* (University Press of Mississippi, 1999), 35.

31 **"George was a quiet person":** "Howard Kazanjian: Master and Commander," *Star Wars Aficionado*, 2009. Accessed on 21 March 2023 at https://web.archive.org/web/20130603141659/http://www.starwarsaficionado.com/f/HOWARD_KAZANJIAN_INTERVIEW_2009.pdf.

31 **"Yeah, talented":** Author interview with W. Murch.

31 **"go prove [himself] in battle":** Lawrence Wechsler, "Valkyries Over Iraq," *Harper's Magazine*, November 2005, 66.

32 **"dumb things":** Pollock, *Skywalking*, 63.

32 **"motormouth":** Rinzler, *Howard Kazanjian*, 77.

32 **"It was like waving a red flag":** John Milius, interview by Francis Ford Coppola, 2010.
33 **"You give yourself to that anger":** Milius, interview by Coppola, 2010.
33 **"You should write this down":** Milius, interview by Coppola, 2010.
33 **"Put all the neat stuff in it":** Milius, interview by Coppola, 2010.
34 ***This is insane*:** Author interview with Michael Rachmil, 27 September 2022.

4: The Fear That Thrills

36 **"The only thing I want to do":** Joseph McBride, *Steven Spielberg: A Biography* (Faber & Faber, 2012), 36–37.
36 **"really original and terrific":** *Desert Island Discs*, BBC, 18 December 2022.
36 **"I realized that there was an entire generation":** Tom Shone, "Lucas vs. Spielberg," *Salon*, 14 June 2005. Accessed on 2 May 2024 at https://slate.com/news-and-politics/2005/06/lucas-vs-spielberg.html.
36 **"jealous to the marrow of my bones":** Shone, "Lucas vs. Spielberg."
37 **"We just became friends":** J. W. Rinzler, *The Complete Making of Indiana Jones* (Del Rey, 2008), Foreword.
37 **"You said you were taking me to a circus":** "Steven Spielberg Was a Fearful Kid Who Found Solace in Storytelling," *Fresh Air*, NPR, 9 November 2022.
38 **"It was a really terrifying, traumatic thing":** "Steven Spielberg Was a Fearful Kid," *Fresh Air*.
38 **"I was the one causing something":** "Steven Spielberg Was a Fearful Kid," *Fresh Air*.
38 **"The Spielbergs are dirty Jews":** Tom Tugend, "Leah Adler, Restaurateur and Mother of Steven Spielberg, Dies at 97," *Jewish Journal*, 22 February 2017. Accessed on 8 March 2025 at https://jewishjournal.com/judaism/obituaries/215427/leah-adler/.
39 **"gigantic fists, gigantic faces":** Jon Mooallem, "Inside the Mind of Steven Spielberg, Hollywood's Big, Friendly Giant," *Wired*, July 2016. Accessed on 02 March 2023 at https://www.wired.com/2016/06/steven-spielberg-the-bfg/.
40 **"I was not like everybody else":** McBride, *Steven Spielberg*, 54–55.
40 **"schnozz":** Diane K. Shah, "Steven Spielberg, Seriously: Hollywood's Perennial Wunderkind Confronts History, Sentiment and the Fine Art of Growing Up," *Los Angeles Times*, 19 December 1993. Accessed on 9 April 2023 at https://www.latimes.com/archives/la-xpm-1993–12–19-tm-3657-story.html.
41 **"Please don't tell your father":** Glenn Whipp, "Steven Spielberg Gave His Sisters Veto Power on 'The Fabelmans.' They Gave Him Their Trust," *Los Angeles Times*, 21 February 2023.
41 **"Come with me":** *James Cameron's Story of Science Fiction*, Episode 1, 2021.
44 **"hell on Earth":** McBride, *Steven Spielberg*, 115.
44 **"You want it, don't you?":** McBride, *Steven Spielberg*, 123.

5: I Lie to You All the Time

46 **"would be forever":** Peter Cowie, *Coppola* (Da Capo Press, 1994), 7.
47 **"bird-like and kind":** Email from Aggie Murch to the author, 19 July 2024.
47 **"an important director":** Cowie, *Coppola*, 7.
47 **"God, Bart, I envy you":** Author interview with Bart Patton, 23 June 2022.
47 **"drooling":** Interview with Patton, 23 June 2022.
48 **"Okay, I will":** Author interview with Melinda Johnson, 9 May 2023.
49 **"She was a sweet person":** Author interview with Kaja Fehr, 26 January 2024.
49 **"treated . . . like an intelligent, almost-adult":** "Judicial Profile: Hon. Melinda Ann Johnson, Private Judge," *Daily Journal*, 4 January 1993. Accessed on 17 March 2023 at http://

www.marchankin.com/PDF%20FILES/Judicial%20Profile/HON.%20MELINDA%20ANN%20JOHNSON.pdf.

50 **"I was the babysitter":** Author interview with Johnson.

50 **"Her senior year":** Author interview with Fehr.

50 **"I think she was eighteen":** On at least one occasion, it was reported Francis had met Missy when she was twelve, not eighteen. See Peter Biskind, "Raging Days, Boogie Nights," *Vanity Fair,* April 1998.

51 **"Francis had intended":** Author interview with Patton.

51 **"about things like respect and loyalty":** Stuart Husband, "James Caan: 'The Studio Thought The Godfather Was a Piece of Garbage,'" *The Guardian*, 22 August 1999.

51 **"a jungle":** Betsy Model, "The Ultimate Caan," *Cigar Aficionado*, January/February 2004. Accessed on 15 March 2023 at https://www.cigaraficionado.com/article/the-ultimate-caan-6167.

52 **"I wasn't going to be a butcher":** Husband, "James Caan."

52 **"girls, ball, beer":** Husband, "James Caan."

52 **"he was embroidered":** Clyde Haberman, "James Caan, Actor, Who Won Fame in 'The Godfather,' Dies at 82," *New York Times*, 7 July 2022. Accessed on 8 August 2022 at https://www.nytimes.com/2022/07/07/movies/james-caan-dead.html.

53 **"must get boring":** Laura Stevenson, "Robert Duvall, Hollywood's Number 1 Second Lead, Breaks for Starlight," *People*, 9 May 1977.

53 **"his little wife" and following conversation:** Author interview with Mona Skager, 11 June 2023.

54 **"We borrowed everything":** Author interview with Skager.

55 **"I had really no idea":** Leo Adam Biga, "Before *The Godfather*, Coppola Film Shot in Western Nebraska Played a Pivotal Role in Hollywood's Evolution," *Flatwater Free Press*, 21 August 2023. Accessed on 24 February 2024 at https://starherald.com/news/local/before-the-godfather-coppola-film-shot-in-western-nebraska-played-a-pivotal-role-in-hollywood/article_80488230–405e-11ee-992d-57a6260827ad.html.

55 **"If you're not willing":** *Filmmaker*, directed by George Lucas, 1968.

55 **"Francis will tell you":** Author interview with Robbins.

56 **"There were many good places":** Biga, "Before *The Godfather*."

56 **"Boy, you were right":** Chang, *Zoetrope at 50*, 32.

56 **"I'm writing this script":** Chang, *Zoetrope at 50*, 69

56 **"George was very slight":** Author interview with Skager.

58 **"If you kids stay here":** Zach Baron, "Francis Ford Coppola's $100 Million Bet," *GQ*, 17 February 2022. Accessed on 27 May 2023 at https://www.gq.com/story/francis-ford-coppola-50-years-after-the-godfather.

58 **"like Robin Hood and his band":** Cowie, *Coppola*, 54.

59 **"All you have to do today" and other quotes from this event:** Gerald Nachman, "Stage and Screen: The Most Pop Art of All," *Oakland Tribune*, 11 June 1968, 49.

6: Do You Wanna Be a Film Director?

61 **"I was on the outside of a wonderful hallucination":** Richard Corliss, "Show Business: I Dream for a Living," *Time*, 15 July 1985.

63 **"Jesus Christ" and following exchange:** McBride, *Steven Spielberg*, 164.

64 **"I think so, too":** McBride, *Steven Spielberg*, 165.

64 **"Hopefully you're going to have a lot of success":** Bill Higgins, "Steven Spielberg and Sidney Sheinberg," *Hollywood Reporter*, 16 December 2010. Accessed on 10 May 2023 at https://www.hollywoodreporter.com/news/general-news/steven-spielberg-sidney-sheinberg-59773/.

64 **"a lot of stuff that was very technical":** Higgins, "Steven Spielberg and Sidney Sheinberg."
64 **"Well, I haven't graduated yet" and response:** McBride, *Steven Spielberg*, 169.
64 **"I quit college so fast":** Corliss, "Show Business: I Dream for a Living."
65 **"Francis and George walked in":** Sam Wasson, "Book Excerpt: Emperor of the New Order," *Air Mail*, 25 November 2023. Accessed on 24 March 2025 at https://airmail.news/issues/2023-11-25/emperor-of-the-new-order.
65 **"This is what I want":** Wasson, "Book Excerpt: Emperor of the New Order."
65 **"If he'd gone to Vancouver":** Chang, *Zoetrope at 50*, 43.
65 **"You should move up here with the children":** Cowie, *Coppola*, 55.
65 **"Part of the bohemian idea":** Cowie, *Coppola*, 55.
66 **"It looked like a very consolidated film company":** Author interview with Dorte Skot-Hansen, 26 March 2024.
66 **"They clicked":** Author interview with Skot-Hansen.
67 **"He was easy to be with":** Author interview with Skot-Hansen.
67 **"I saw this mansion":** Cowie, *Coppola*, 55–56.
68 **"Skot lost a lot of money on that movie":** Author interview with Skot-Hansen.
68 **"nervous and under great emotional stress":** Gelmis, *The Film Director as Superstar*, 240.
69 **"a big fancy roadshow":** Gelmis, *The Film Director as Superstar*, 247.
69 **"abysmal":** Gelmis, *The Film Director as Superstar*, 247.
69 **"It's come to the point":** Gelmis, *The Film Director as Superstar*, 251.
69 **"lots of big pictures":** Gelmis, *The Film Director as Superstar*, 254.
69 **"half a million dollars":** Gelmis, *The Film Director as Superstar*, 253.
69 **"let's say *Finian's Rainbow* is a big flop":** Gelmis, *The Film Director as Superstar*, 253.
69 **"What I'm thinking of doing" and following exchange:** Gelmis, *The Film Director as Superstar*, 254–255.

7: Test-Tube Baby

71 **"joyless":** Renata Adler, "Screen: 'Finian's Rainbow' Back from Missitucky," *New York Times*, 10 October 1968, 59.
71 **"fake, its sentiments always bogus":** Joe Morgenstern, review of *Finian's Rainbow*, *Newsweek*, 21 October 1968.
71 **"pretty well":** Pauline Kael, review of *Finian's Rainbow*, *The New Yorker*, 19 October 1968.
71 **"the best-directed musical since *West Side Story*":** Roger Ebert, review of *Finian's Rainbow*, 14 October 1968. Accessed on 01 January 2023 at https://www.rogerebert.com/reviews/finians-rainbow-1968.
73 **"How much do you need to live on" and following exchange:** Erik Bauer, "I Was Never Conscious of My Screenplays Having Any Acts. It's All Bullshit," *Creative Screenwriting* 7, no. 2 (February 2015). Accessed on 24 March 2025 at https://www.creativescreenwriting.com/i-was-never-conscious-of-my-screenplays-having-any-acts-its-all-bullshit-john-milius/.
73 **"rewrite some piece of crap":** Bauer, "I Was Never Conscious of My Screenplays Having Any Acts."
73 **"I hear you might like to write screenplays" and following exchange:** Author interview with Robbins.
74 **"There is no way":** Cowie, *Coppola*, 56.
75 **"How would you like to move" and response:** Author interview with Skager.
76 **"Francis needs someone" and following exchange:** Author interview with W. Murch.
76 **"pied piper":** Author interview with Robbins.
76 **"I'm a young director working at Universal":** Rinzler, *The Complete Making of Indiana Jones*, 13.

77 **"this kid who was trying":** Rinzler, *The Complete Making of Indiana Jones*, 13.
77 **"I was a little bit in awe of him":** Rinzler, *The Complete Making of Indiana Jones*, 13.
77 **"That was the first time":** Rinzler, *The Complete Making of Indiana Jones*, 13.
78 **"seven guys":** McBride, *Steven Spielberg*, 177.
78 **"George was this kind of maverick":** Rinzler, *The Complete Making of Indiana Jones*, 13.

8: American Zoetrope

83 **"We were aware":** Author interview with W. Murch.
83 **"sexual centre":** Gayle Rubin, "The Miracle Mile: South of Market and Gay Male Leather, 1962–1997," *Reclaiming San Francisco: History, Politics, Culture* (City Lights, 1998), 272.
83 **"wine country":** Author interview with Skager.
83 **"What we're striving for":** Judy Stone, "A Turkey or a Triumph, THX 1138 Is Our World," *San Francisco Sunday Examiner & Chronicle*, 23 May 1971.
84 **"Literally my only experience in L.A.":** Peter Hartlaub, "George Lucas: *Star Wars* Creator in a Valley Not Far, Far Away," *SF Gate*, 27 April 2007. Accessed on 8 August 2022 at https://www.sfgate.com/entertainment/article/IN-A-VALLEY-NOT-FAR-FAR-AWAY-2599071.php#photo-2088224.
84 **"crowded garages":** Herb Caen, *Baghdad-by-the-Bay* (Comstock Editions, 1949), 5.
85 **"We didn't have a lot of takes":** Author interview with Maggie McOmie, 30 April 2023.
86 **"I do it with such an emotional charge":** Michel Ciment, "Entretien avec Francis Coppola," *Positif* 262 (December 1982), 30. Translated by the author.
86 **"How is it possible":** Chang, *Zoetrope at 50*, 47.
87 **George was given a camera:** Email from Walter Murch to the author, 26 January 2023.
87 **The music started:** Tom Sables, "Rock Nightmare Twenty Years Ago: Altamont Marked the End of an Era," *Chicago Tribune*, 5 November 1989.
88 **"Who's the most beautiful woman in San Francisco?" and following exchange:** John L. Wasserman, "A New, Unique Dream Studio," *San Francisco Chronicle*, 11 December 1969, 45.
88 **"and then against the wall":** Author interview with Richard Chew, 2 May 2024.
89 **"I don't want to be Louis B. Mayer":** John L. Wasserman, "A New, Unique Dream Studio," *San Francisco Chronicle*, 11 December 1969, 45.
89 **"the first sushi":** Chang, *Zoetrope at 50*, 49.
89 **"There was a lot of dope":** Chang, *Zoetrope at 50*, 58.
89 **"We have the means of production":** Chang, *Zoetrope at 50*, 53.
89 **"wanted to replicate the studio system":** Author interview with Medavoy.
90 **"It was never a cooperative venture":** Cowie, *Coppola*, 57.
90 **"Well, it's . . . my car" and following exchange:** Chang, *Zoetrope at 50*, 56.
90 **"Francis had no concept of failure":** Patrick Goldstein, "Francis Ford Coppola Rarely Met a Deal He Couldn't Refuse," *Los Angeles Times*, 4 August 1996. Accessed on 01 January 2024 at https://www.latimes.com/archives/la-xpm-1996–08–04-tm-31035-story.html.
91 **"Francis had this Mansonesque effect":** Biskind, *Easy Riders, Raging Bulls*, 97.
91 **"Francis always lived on the edge":** Author interview with Patton.
91 **"the Zoetrope thing":** Author interview with Chuck Braverman, 29 June 2022.
91 **"pretty damn cool":** Author interview with Drew Takahashi, 6 May 2023.
91 **"Three and a half feet high":** Author interview with Colin Michael Kitchens, 25 January 2024.
92 **"Francis wanted us to be artists":** Bauer, "I Was Never Conscious of My Screenplays Having Any Acts."
92 **"Sure, there was the giant cappuccino machine" and quotes in following meeting:** Stan

Adler, "Beginnings of the Coppola Brand," *Digiday*, 2 May 2013. Accessed on 17 April 2024 at https://digiday.com/marketing/beginnings-of-the-coppola-brand/.

94 **"Anything in there":** Author interview with Steve Kanaly, 22 January 2024.

95 **"all this macho stuff":** Author interview with Kanaly.

95 **"He was working":** Author interview with Kanaly.

95 **Studios were making fewer:** "Pic Prod'n Slump," *Daily Variety*, 30 November 1970, 1, and "Over One-Third of IA Is Jobless," *Daily Variety*, 20 November 1970, 1.

95 **"He and John Milius and the others":** Ken P., "An Interview with Gary Kurtz," *IGN*, 11 November 2002. Accessed on 20 April 2024 at https://www.ign.com/articles/2002/11/11/an-interview-with-gary-kurtz.

96 **"Just an evil dark screenplay":** Thomas Doherty, "For Francis Ford Coppola's Go-for-Broke Movies, All Roads Lead to Cannes," *Hollywood Reporter*, 22 April 2024.

96 **"Do you mind if I watch" and following exchange:** Author interview with W. Murch.

9: Black Thursday

97 **"The fact that the door had opened":** Peter Biskind, "Sherry Lansing, Dawn Steel and Sue Mengers: When the Broads Faced the Raging Bulls in '70s Hollywood," *Hollywood Reporter*, 9 December 2016. Accessed on 17 April 2024 at https://www.hollywoodreporter.com/news/general-news/sherry-lansing-dawn-steel-sue-mengers-broads-faced-raging-bulls-70s-hollywood-952235/.

98 **"This is your first film":** Jones, *George Lucas*, 118.

99 **"Wait a minute" and following exchange:** Jones, *George Lucas*, 118.

99 **"I'm here from the THX cutting room":** Author interview with W. Murch.

99 **"You gotta put them up front" and response:** Author interview with W. Murch.

100 **"When the studio didn't like it":** Biskind, *Easy Riders, Raging Bulls*, 100.

100 **"I would never have done that to a friend":** Jones, *George Lucas*, 124.

100 **"I always believe":** Jones, *George Lucas*, 124.

101 **"filled with sex and silliness":** Francis Coppola, introduction to *The Godfather: 50th Anniversary Edition*, by Mario Puzo (Penguin, 2002).

102 **"Just suck it up and do it":** Author interview with Matthew Robbins and Walter Murch, 15 February 2023.

102 **"Francis, just roll over":** Author interview with W. Murch.

102 **"What do you think I should do" and response:** Author interview with Robbins and Murch.

102 **"In my city":** Mario Puzo, *The Godfather* (G. P. Putnam's Sons), 2022, 272.

103 **"bought Paramount to get laid":** Nick Tosches, "The Man Who Kept the Secrets," *Vanity Fair*, April 1997. Accessed on 3 January 2023 at https://archive.vanityfair.com/article/1997/4/the-man-who-kept-the-secrets.

103 **"big-time" obsession with "pussy":** Robert Evans, *The Kid Stays in the Picture* (HarperCollins, 2013), 50.

103 **consigliere:** Tosches, "The Man Who Kept Secrets."

104 **"What's the bottom line?":** William G. Blair, "Charles G. Bluhdorn, the Head of Gulf and Western, Dies at 56," *New York Times*, 20 February 1983. Accessed on 1 March 2024 at https://www.nytimes.com/1983/02/20/obituaries/charles-g-bluhdorn-the-head-of-gulf-and-western-dies-at-56.html.

104 **"beat them at their own game":** Evans, *The Kid Stays in the Picture*, 117.

104 **"What did I have to lose?" and "I had plenty of green":** Evans, *The Kid Stays in the Picture*, 128.

104 **"The strongest period in Hollywood history":** Daniel Smith-Rowsey, *Star Actors in the Hollywood Renaissance: Representing Rough Rebels* (Palgrave Macmillan, 2013), 19.

105 **"If you're giving me the store" and response:** Evans, *The Kid Stays in the Picture*, 127.
105 **"Are you nuts" and following exchange:** Evans, *The Kid Stays in the Picture*, 239.
105 **"lurking within":** Coppola, introduction to *The Godfather*.
106 **"Coppola will make the picture" and following exchange:** Evans, *The Kid Stays in the Picture*, 239–240.
106 **"Don't use him, Bob":** Evans, *The Kid Stays in the Picture*, 240.
107 **"I'm used to being the youngest one":** Mary Pat Kelly, *Martin Scorsese: A Journey* (Hachette, 2022), 47.
107 **told her he was leaving her:** Author interview with Laraine Brennan, 9 March 2025.
108 **"Gee":** Jones, *George Lucas*, 121.
108 **"looking different":** Chang, *Zoetrope at 50*, 77.
108 **"I can't believe you made this film":** Chang, *Zoetrope at 50*, 78.
109 **"How could you let him":** Chang, *Zoetrope at 50*, 78.
109 **"Well," he asked, "what happened?" and response:** Chang, *Zoetrope at 50*, 78.
109 **"a going concern":** Author interview with Patton.
109 **"San Francisco wasn't much":** Author interview with Patton.
109 **"We were sort of like Wile E. Coyote":** Author interview with W. Murch.
110 **"It hasn't been released yet":** Author interview with W. Murch.
110 **"It was insane":** Judy Stone, "A Turkey or a Triumph, THX 113 Is Our World," *San Francisco Sunday Examiner & Chronicle*, 23 May 1971.
110 **"There was no point":** "THX 1138: The George Lucas Director's Cut, Media Information," *Cinéfantastique* magazine records—*THX 1138*, f.1783, Margaret Herrick Library, Academy of Motion Picture Arts and Sciences.
110 **"It's an injustice":** "THX 1138: The George Lucas Director's Cut, Media Information," *Cinéfantastique* magazine records—*THX 1138*.
110 **"reluctant to release":** Dan Madsen, "Irvin Kershner: Remembering *The Empire Strikes Back*," *Lucasfilm Fan Club Magazine* 11 (Spring 1990).
110 **"You're gonna let them cut it?":** Jones, *George Lucas*, 157.
110 **"Just cut these five minutes":** Chang, *Zoetrope at 50*, 82.
111 **"Francis was a good commander":** Chang, *Zoetrope at 50*, 83.
111 **"Everybody who knew Francis":** Chang, *Zoetrope at 50*, 84.
111 **"I had always regarded George":** Jones, *George Lucas*, 123.
111 **"Everybody utilized Zoetrope":** Pollock, *Skywalking*, 100.
111 **"You gotta make a movie that's about people":** Author interview with Brian De Palma, 26 January 2024.
111 **"Something funny":** Chang, *Zoetrope at 50*, 90.

10: I Believe in America

112 **"They showed us *THX*":** Author interview with Couturié.
112 **"He was just a bearded little guy":** Author interview with Couturié.
113 **"There is no audience tougher":** Author interview with Couturié.
113 **"I have two projects" and following exchange:** Author interview with Couturié.
114 **"Well, I'll just make up" and following exchange:** Chang, *Zoetrope at 50*, 94.
114 **"I did warn you" and following exchange:** Jones, *George Lucas*, 126.
114 **For Mario Puzo's brief biography:** Mel Gussow, "Mario Puzo, Author Who Made 'The Godfather' a World Addiction, Is Dead at 78," *New York Times*, 3 July 1999.
115 **"ruthless":** Gussow, "Mario Puzo."
115 **"Mario told me":** Coppola, introduction to *The Godfather*.
115 **"It was time":** Mario Puzo, *The Godfather: 50th Anniversary Edition* (Penguin, 2002).

116 **"entirely from research":** Gussow, "Mario Puzo."

116 **"so much fun to be with":** Coppola, introduction to *The Godfather.*

116 **"I had maybe 15 pages" and following exchange:** "To Make 'The Godfather' His Way, Francis Ford Coppola Waged A Studio Battle," *Fresh Air*, NPR, 16 November 2016. Transcript accessed on 10 November 2024 at https://www.npr.org/transcripts/502250244

118 **"Francis," Puzo wrote:** Mario Puzo, *The Godfather* (G.P. Putnam's Sons), 2022, 272.

118 **"though I don't recall any exercise":** Coppola, introduction to *The Godfather.*

118 **"a smile and a twinkling eye":** Coppola, introduction to *The Godfather.*

118 **"If you hit big losses":** Coppola, introduction to *The Godfather.*

119 **"What people don't understand":** Roger Ebert, *Scorsese by Ebert* (University of Chicago Press, 2008), 110–111.

120 **"a wonderful love story":** Al Pacino, *Sonny Boy* (Penguin Press, 2024), 105.

120 **"it really was special":** Dave Itzkoff, "Al Pacino on 'The Godfather': 'It's Taken Me a Lifetime to Accept It and Move On,'" *New York Times*, 9 March 2022. Accessed on 4 January 2023 at https://www.nytimes.com/2022/03/09/movies/al-pacino-the-godfather.html.

120 **"like a college professor himself":** Pacino, *Sonny Boy*, 105.

120 **"an energy within myself":** Pacino, *Sonny Boy*, 11.

120 **"My favorite quote of Michelangelo's":** David Marchese, "The Interview: Al Pacino Is Still Going Big," *New York Times*, 5 October 2024. Accessed on 13 October 2024 at https://www.nytimes.com/2024/10/05/magazine/al-pacino-interview.html.

120 **"I'm going to be directing** *The Godfather***":** Itzkoff, "Al Pacino on 'The Godfather.'"

120 ***How did they give him* The Godfather*?:*** Itzkoff, "Al Pacino on 'The Godfather.'"

121 **"handsome in a delicate way":** Puzo, *The Godfather*, 13.

121 **"I didn't have a choice":** Itzkoff, "Al Pacino on 'The Godfather.'"

121 **"there," Pacino thought, "but not quite showing up":** Itzkoff, "Al Pacino on 'The Godfather.'"

122 **"I understood immediately":** Pacino, *Sonny Boy*, 49–50.

122 **"Everybody tested for Michael":** Shawn Levy, *De Niro: A Life* (Crown Archetype, 2014), 124.

123 **"He's got something" and response:** Evans, *The Kid Stays in the Picture*, 234.

124 **"he['s] Cary Grant with a German accent":** Evans, *The Kid Stays in the Picture*, 228.

124 **"The iffy deal we had for Pacino":** Irvin Winkler, *A Life in Movies* (Abrams Press, 2019), 54.

124 **"You no-good motherfucker":** Evans, *The Kid Stays in the Picture*, 243.

125 **"I asked him":** Evans, *The Kid Stays in the Picture*, 244.

125 **"Don't quit":** Cowie, *Coppola*, 64.

11: The Family Business

126 **"I was 29":** "'The Godfather' at 50: The Making of a Classic," CBS News, 27 March 2022. Accessed on 1 April 2023 at https://wtop.com/entertainment/2022/03/the-godfather-at-50-the-making-of-a-classic/.

127 **"You know how much you mean to me":** Pacino, *Sonny Boy*, 119.

128 **"How are they going to fire you now?":** Mike Fleming Jr., "Francis Ford Coppola: How Winning Cannes 40 Years Ago Saved 'Apocalypse Now,' Making 'Megalopolis,' Why Scorsese Almost Helmed 'Godfather Part II' & Re-Cutting Three Past Films," *Deadline*, 13 May 2019. Accessed on 10 March 2025 at https://deadline.com/2019/05/francis-ford-coppola-apocalypse-now-cannes-40-anniversary-megalopolis-scorsese-godfather-part-ii-re-cutting-godfather-iii-cotton-club-interview-1202613659/.

128 **"film's a load of shit" and response:** Eleanor Coppola, *Notes on the Making of "Apocalypse Now"* (Limelight Editions, 1991), 63.

128 **"a nice, simple piece":** Alan R. Howard, "Graffiti Survived Studios' Rejection to Score at

B.O.," *Hollywood Reporter*, 24 August 1973. Accessed on 11 March 2024 at https://www.hollywoodreporter.com/movies/movie-news/american-graffiti-making-george-lucas-film-1130166/.

129 **"destitute":** Anthony Breznican, "Nobody Wanted *Star Wars*—But George Lucas Would Not Give Up," *Entertainment Weekly*, 25 May 2017. Accessed on 27 May 2023 at https://ew.com/movies/2017/05/25/star-wars-40th-anniversary-darth-vader/.

130 **"Well," he started, "in a week or so":** Breznican, "Nobody Wanted *Star Wars*."

130 **"I'm sure you understand" and following exchange:** Breznican, "Nobody Wanted *Star Wars*."

130 **"in severe trauma":** Jones, *George Lucas*, 133.

130 **"at all confident":** "Francis Ford Coppola," American Academy of Achievement, 17 June 1994. Accessed on 27 July 2023 at https://achievement.org/achiever/francis-ford-coppola/#interview.

132 **"the first and only person":** Francis Ford Coppola, Instagram caption, 3 July 2024.

133 **"weeping like a baby" and following exchange:** Itzkoff, "Al Pacino on 'The Godfather.'"

134 **"From what I hear":** Author interview with Medavoy.

134 **"nothing":** Breznican, "Nobody Wanted *Star Wars*."

134 ***Don't ever go into business with your hobby*:** Breznican, "Nobody Wanted *Star Wars*."

134 **"Okay, we'll do it" and following exchange:** Breznican, "Nobody Wanted *Star Wars*."

12: Unicorns

136 **"there was a big trough period":** Author interview with W. Murch.

136 **"If you boys don't fight for this music":** Author interview with Aggie Murch, 18 July 2024.

136 **"country mice":** "Cinema: The Movie Gang," *Time*, 30 May 1977. Accessed on 25 March 2025 at https://time.com/archive/6848712/cinema-the-movie-movie-gang/.

137 **"very social":** Author interview with Chew.

137 **"friendly homage":** Rinzler, *The Complete Making of Indiana Jones*, 14.

138 **"I remember very distinctly":** Rinzler, *The Complete Making of Indiana Jones*, 14.

138 **"Francis, you've got to come see this":** Rinzler, *The Complete Making of Indiana Jones*, 14.

138 **"very, very, very impressed":** Rinzler, *The Complete Making of Indiana Jones*, 14.

138 **"TV for me wasn't an art form":** *The American Cinema: Film School Generation*, directed by Alain Klarer, produced by the New York Center for Visual History in association with KCET/Los Angeles and the BBC, PBS, 1995.

139 **"excitement":** Kim Morgan, "Talking 40 Years of California Split," *Sunset Gun*, 17 December 2014. Accessed on 31 March 2024 at https://sunsetgun.typepad.com/sunsetgun/2014/12/weve-all-agreedto-meet-at-canters-deli-george-segal-joseph-walsh-and-elliott-gould-its-mid-september-one-of-tho-1.html.

139 **"You're better off" and following exchange:** Author interview with Medavoy.

140 **"Terry must have talked for about four hours":** Randall Lane, "I Want Gross," *Forbes*, 26 September 1994.

141 **"Francis and I had a perfect record":** Evans, *The Kid Stays in the Picture*, 247.

141 **"You don't know what you've got" and following exchange:** Evans, *The Kid Stays in the Picture*, 249–250.

142 **"the happiest days I can remember":** "Francis Ford Coppola," American Academy of Achievement.

142 **"I bought *The Great Gatsby*":** *People*, 18 November 1996.

142 **For the timeline of FFC's time writing *Gatsby*:** Evans, in his autobiography, remembered hiring Francis to write *Gatsby* after Francis had won Academy Awards for *The Godfather*, in March 1973. Francis, however, recalls it this way, and the *Hollywood Reporter* published a story on his hiring on 14 March 1972, the same day as the *Godfather* premiere. On the flip

side, Francis has, at least once, told the story of writing *Gatsby* so that he was still in Paris when the Corleone epic premiered—though photos show him present at the event in New York.

143 **he said he was still in Paris:** Francis Ford Coppola, "Gatsby and Me," *Town & Country*, 16 April 2013. Accessed on 29 March 2023 at https://www.townandcountrymag.com/leisure/reviews/a1042/francis-ford-coppola-gatsby-and-me/.

144 **"It's a big hit" and response:** Coppola, "Gatsby and Me."

144 **"trash," "unreadable":** Pauline Kael, "Alchemy: Francis Ford Coppola's 'The Godfather,'" *New Yorker*, 10 March 1972. Accessed on 20 December 2023 at https://www.newyorker.com/magazine/1972/03/18/alchemy-pauline-kael.

144 **"the *Gone with the Wind* of gangster movies":** Paul Zimmerman, "How Marlon Brando and Francis Ford Coppola Made 'The Godfather' an Instant Classic," *Newsweek*, 13 March 1972. Accessed on 20 December 2023 at https://www.newsweek.com/godfather-francis-ford-coppola-marlon-brando-534432.

146 **"a shy kid from Queens":** Coppola, introduction to *The Godfather*.

146 **"I just wanted to be his kid brother":** David Fear, "Francis Ford Coppola: 'I Have Nothing Left to Lose,'" *Rolling Stone*, September 2024, 44.

147 **"the girl who has a crush on her professor":** Michael Schumacher, *Francis Ford Coppola: A Filmmaker's Life* (Bloomsbury, 2000).

147 **"bearish looks":** Evans, *The Kid Stays in the Picture*, 249.

147 **"Till this day":** Evans, *The Kid Stays in the Picture*, 240.

148 **"My life before and after that film":** David Fear, "Francis Ford Coppola: 'I Have Nothing Left to Lose."

149 **"kind of scary that tickles":** McBride, Steven Spielberg, 64.

149 **"want[ed] ten or fifteen minutes":** "Mother Laments Death: Victim of Police Ambush is Buried in Lake Charles," *Alexandria Daily Town Talk*, 5 May 1969, 13.

150 **"First, there's a lot of money in features":** Steven Awalt, *Steven Spielberg and "Duel": The Making of a Film Career* (Roman & Littlefield, 2016), 193.

150 **"made in the South":** Gene Siskel, "Workaholic Burt Reynolds Sets Up His Next Task: Light Comedy," *Chicago Tribune*, 28 November 1976, E2.

150 **"I was pulverized":** *The Masterpiece That Almost Wasn't*, directed by Kim Aubry, 2008.

151 **"I've never made a movie anywhere near as good":** Stephen J. Dubner, "Inside the Dream Factory," *The Guardian*, 21 March 1999. Accessed on 26 July 2023 at https://www.theguardian.com/theobserver/1999/mar/21/life1.lifemagazine5.

152 **"What happened in the '70s":** Author interview with Paul Schrader, 27 January 2023.

152 **"Ten years ago":** Stephen Farber, "What's So Super About This Superdirector?" *New York Times*, 16 September 1973, 13.

152 **"once you have one unicorn":** Author interview with Schrader.

153 **"The thing that killed us":** Ruthe Stein, "Coppola: The Man and His Dreams," *San Francisco Sunday Examiner & Chronicle*, 22 October 1995, D26.

13: America's Fellini

155 **"I mean, we're constant complainers":** Rinzler, *The Complete Making of Indiana Jones*, 14.

156 **"a man born without enough skin":** Kelly, *Martin Scorsese*, 148.

157 **"at that time was the end of people's lives":** Kelly, *Martin Scorsese*, xxvi.

157 *If Jesus were here now:* Kelly, *Martin Scorsese*, xxiii–xxiv.

158 **"being disassembled":** Author interview with Brennan.

158 **"all the bloody parts":** Author interview with Brennan.

158 **"It really affected him":** Author interview with Brennan.

158 **"did not practice monogamy or sobriety":** Author interview with Brennan.
158 **"Marty grew up in the most loving family":** Author interview with Brennan.
159 **"I wanted more space":** Author interview with Brennan.
159 **"You know, I was a kid from the Lower East Side":** Ebert, *Scorsese by Ebert*, 172.
160 **"Everyone used to come to Trancas Beach":** Author interview with De Palma.
160 **a woman who then filled her uterus with Lysol:** Caitlin Flanagan, "The Sanguine Sex," *The Atlantic*, May 2007. Accessed on 20 March 2024 at https://www.theatlantic.com/magazine/archive/2007/05/the-sanguine-sex/305780/.
161 ***I Fucked Everybody*:** Nathan Rabin, "Remembering Margot Kidder," www.nathanrabin.com, 15 May 2018. Accessed on 20 March 2024 at https://www.nathanrabin.com/happy-place/2018/5/15/remembering-margot-kidder
161 **"When I party":** Judson Klinger, "The Education of Margot Kidder," *Rolling Stone*, May 2018.
161 **"I got fired":** Author interview with De Palma.
161 **"a truly amoral person":** Author interview with Beverly Walker, 7 February 2023.
161 **"artistically weak":** Zack Sharf, "Paul Schrader Criticizes Brian De Palma As 'Trite and Artistically Weak,'" *IndieWire*, 29 June 2019. Accessed on 20 April 2024 at https://www.indiewire.com/features/general/paul-shrader-brian-de-palma-trite-artistically-weak-1202154370/.
162 **"the Master of Flash":** Paul Schrader, *Los Angeles Weekly News*, 17 August 1973, 26.
162 **manic depressive:** David Smith, "Richard Dreyfuss: 'I Was a Bad Guy for a Number of Years,'" *The Guardian*, 24 June 2020. Accessed on 28 December 2025 at https://www.theguardian.com/film/2020/jun/24/richard-dreyfuss-bad-guy-hollywood-hellraising-metoo.
163 **"It was such a romantic time":** Nathan Rabin, "Random Roles: Margot Kidder," *The A.V. Club*, 3 March 2009. Accessed on 18 April 2024 at https://web.archive.org/web/20141213050305/http://www.avclub.com/article/random-roles-margot-kidder-24554.
164 **"We were just a bunch of kids":** Roel Haanen and Phil van Tongeren, "Margot Kidder," *Flashback Files*, October 2005. Accessed on 20 April 2024 at https://www.flashbackfiles.com/margot-kidder-interview.
164 **"At that time, movies were the center":** Author interview with Schrader.
164 **"they'll let you do it" and response:** Author interview with Schrader.
165 **"You had to go somewhere new every night":** Author interview with Schrader.
165 **"to keep the old Hollywood alive":** Richard Schickel, *Conversations with Scorsese* (Alfred A. Knopf, 2011), 23.
165 **"George wanted to create a studio":** Author interview with De Palma.
165 **"Marty and I went up together":** Author interview with De Palma.
166 **"Marty, you've just spent a whole year of your life":** Kelly, *Martin Scorsese*, 55.
166 **"To us, it was bullshit":** Kelly, *Martin Scorsese*, 59.
166 **"So do it":** Kelly, *Martin Scorsese*, 55.
166 **"Make films about what you know":** Ebert, *Scorsese by Ebert*, 13.
167 **"You used to hang out" and following exchange:** William Earl, "Martin Scorsese and Robert De Niro Go Deep: The Pair Reflect on Meeting Via Brian De Palma, How Their Partnership Thrives and Paying the Mob to Make 'Mean Streets,'" *Variety*, 16 June 2024. Accessed on 19 June 2024 at https://variety.com/2024/film/news/martin-scorsese-robert-de-niro-meeting-staying-friends-1236038954/.
167 **"That was a really terrific movie" and response:** Eric Andersson, "Robert De Niro and Martin Scorsese on Building 'Love' and 'Trust' During Their 50-Year Friendship," *People*, 10 February 2024. Accessed on 23 January 2025 at https://people.com/robert-de-niro-martin-scorsese-building-love-trust-50-year-friendship-exclusive-8575142.
167 **"Careerwise" and following exchange:** Ingrid Sischy, Colleen Kelsey, and Peter Brant,

"A Walk and a Talk with Robert De Niro," *Interview*, 21 March 2012. Accessed on 27 July 2024 at https://www.interviewmagazine.com/film/new-again-robert-de-niro.

168 **"When I first met Marty":** Alex Williams, "'Are We Ever Going To Make This Picture?'" *The Guardian*, 3 January 2003. Accessed on 22 January 2025 at https://www.theguardian.com/culture/2003/jan/03/artsfeatures.martinscorsese.

168 **"music I heard on the streets":** Kelly, *Martin Scorsese*, 84.

168 **"they had made a choice":** Author interview with Brennan.

169 **"Do you really think it's going to take ten years?":** Ebert, *Scorsese by Ebert*, 47.

14: Harrison Ford Is Not a Good Name for You

171 **"listening to the Doors":** *L'Univers de Jacques Demy*, directed by Agnès Varda, 1995.

171 **"Forget him":** *L'Univers de Jacques Demy*, directed by Varda.

171 **"The first time Tony Curtis ever appeared":** Virginia Luzón-Aguado, "It's the Years *and* the Mileage: Harrison Ford Grows Old Onscreen," in *Star Bodies and the Erotics of Suffering*, ed. Rebecca Bell-Metereau and Colleen Glenn (Wayne State University Press, 2015), 245.

172 **"Harrison Ford is not a good name for you":** Chris Heath, "Harrison Ford on *Star Wars*, *Blade Runner*, and Punching Ryan Gosling in the Face," *GQ*, 13 September 2017. Accessed on 1 December 2024 at https://www.gq.com/story/harrison-ford-gq-cover-story-2017.

172 **"the stupidest name I could think of":** Heath, "Harrison Ford on *Star Wars*."

172 **"out of my depth":** Robert Rorke, "Harrison Ford Was Joan Didion's Handyman Before He Hit It Big," *New York Post*, 26 October 2017. Accessed on 13 March 2023 at https://nypost.com/2017/10/26/harrison-ford-was-joan-didions-handyman-before-he-hit-it-big/.

172 **"I had a young family":** *Joan Didion: The Center Will Not Hold*, directed by Griffin Dunne, 2017.

172 **"an out-of-work actor":** Lili Anolik, *Hollywood's Eve: Eve Babitz and the Secret History of L.A.* (Scribner, 2019), 51.

173 **"He was the most charismatic guy":** Rorke, "Harrison Ford Was Joan Didion's Handyman."

173 **"from day one":** Ryan D'Agostino, "Harrison Ford Has Stories to Tell," *Esquire*, 31 May 2023. Accessed on 19 May 2025 at https://www.esquire.com/entertainment/movies/a43965150/harrison-ford-indiana-jones-interview/.

173 **He refused to trim his hair:** Author interview with Aggie Rodgers, 9 May 2023.

173 **"The movie's going to be a major hit":** Author interview with Suzanne Somers, 26 August 2023.

173 ***What a bunch of losers*:** Author interview with Somers.

173 **"trying to cash in":** Beverly Walker to Gary Kurtz, undated, Gary Kurtz Papers, collection 2335, box 80, folder 12, University of Southern California archives.

173 **"a ridiculous, dramatic intransigence":** Author interview with Walker.

174 **"George alienates everybody":** Author interview with Walker.

174 **"much about George Lucas":** *Tell Them Who You Are*, directed by Mark Wexler, 2004.

175 **"It was the ultimate magic trick":** Will Perkins and Ian Albinson, "David Fincher: A Film Title Respective," *Art of the Title*, 27 August 2012. Accessed on 16 April 2024 at https://www.artofthetitle.com/feature/david-fincher-a-film-title-retrospective/.

176 **"Hi" and response:** Sean Chavel, "David Fincher Interview," *Musiclog*. Accessed on 16 April 2024 at http://www.musicolog.com/fincher_interview.asp.

176 **"It was demystifying":** Paul Liberatore, "Director Fincher Got Taste For Film Growing Up in Marin," *Marin Independent Journal*, 12 December 2008. Accessed on 15 April

2024 at https://www.marinij.com/2008/12/12/liberatore-director-fincher-got-taste-for-film-growing-up-in-marin/.

176 **Because they could see it:** Mark Salisbury, "Guardian Interviews at the BFI: David Fincher," *The Guardian*, 18 January 2009. Accessed on 16 April 2023 at https://www.theguardian.com/film/2009/feb/03/david-fincher-interview-transcript.

15: Paranoia in North Beach

178 **"that facility was about Walter":** Author interview with Kitchens.

179 **"the ugliest decorated place":** Goldstein, "Francis Ford Coppola Rarely Met a Deal He Couldn't Refuse."

179 **"Francis liked to think of himself":** Author interview with Kitchens.

180 **"There's that lovely quote":** Author interview with W. Murch.

180 **"has always wanted to be":** E. Coppola, *Notes on the Making of "Apocalypse Now,"* 119–120.

180 **"I'm looking for a director who's new** Kelly, *Martin Scorsese*, 70.

181 **"That film is not ready to be released" and following exchange:** Author interview with Walker; Chang, *Zoetrope at 50*, 90.

182 **"I wish I'd been there":** Pollock, *Skywalking*, 119.

182 **"She was making those changes":** Author interview with Walker.

182 **"The critics will probably like it":** Ken P., "An Interview with Gary Kurtz."

183 **"I had the job in Hollywood":** Cowie, *Coppola*, 82.

183 **"Francis was questioning my honesty":** Pollock, *Skywalking*, 128.

184 **"I've got a chance to make this":** Pollock, *Skywalking*, 129.

185 **"he never got over it":** Pollock, *Skywalking*, 123.

16: From *Sugarland* to the Vineyard

186 **"She was only two years older":** Author interview with William Atherton, 25 April 2024.

187 **"He was six scenes ahead":** Author interview with Kanaly.

187 **"I never met anybody":** Author interview with Atherton.

187 **"Steven wanted to be a studio director":** Author interview with Atherton.

187 **"You have a choice of films" and following exchange:** Derek Taylor, *The Making of "Raiders of the Lost Ark"* (Ballantine Books, 1981), 13.

189 **"I don't understand this movie" and following exchange:** Tom Shone, *Blockbuster*, Kindle edition (Free Press, 2004).

190 **"You just have to be moderately intelligent":** Dennis McLellan, "Alan Ladd Jr. Dies; Oscar-Winning Producer and Studio Boss Greenlighted 'Star Wars,'" *Los Angeles Times*, 2 March 2022. Accessed on 1 May 2024 at https://www.latimes.com/obituaries/story/2022–03–02/alan-ladd-jr-dead.

190 **"Can you root for the hero":** Charles Higham, "What Makes Alan Ladd Jr. Hollywood's Hottest Producer?" *New York Times*, 17 July 1977, D9.

191 **"When I sit at a desk":** Rinzler, *The Complete Making of Indiana Jones*, 15.

193 **"a combination of *2001*":** Wayne Warga, "'American Graffiti's' George Lucas Sees the Handwriting on the Studio Wall," *Los Angeles Times*, 12 August 1973, 19.

193 **"like clockwork":** Author interview with Mike Medavoy. Medavoy's numbers were slightly off, but the spirit was right: The four Bond films UA released between 1969 and 1974 each cost $7 million to make, and each grossed over $65 million. *Live and Let Die* (1973), the first installment in the franchise to star Roger Moore, grossed $161 million worldwide.

193 **"Those movies always make $16 million":** Paul Hirsch, *A Long Time Ago in a Cutting Room Far, Far Away . . .* (Chicago Review Press, 2020), 91.

194 **"a third of the neurons":** Author interview with W. Murch.

194 **"The sound is interpreted as an internal state":** Author interview with W. Murch.

194 **"that was part of making a movie":** Author interview with Bloom.

195 **"Films mostly don't work":** Author interview with W. Murch.

195 **Dialogue from *The Six Wives of Henry VIII*:** *The Six Wives of Henry VIII*, developed by Maurice Cowan, produced by Ronald Travers and Mark Shivas for the BBC, 1970.

196 **"You have the formula":** Mike Fleming Jr., "Francis Coppola's New Cut of 'Godfather Part III' to Get Limited December Theatrical Release Before VOD," *Deadline*, 3 September 2020. Accessed on 15 July 2025 at https://deadline.com/2020/09/francis-coppola-godfather-part-iii-recut-limited-december-theatrical-release-1234570031/.

197 **"You're holding me up here" and response:** Pacino, *Sonny Boy*, 167.

197 **"He looked at it":** Schickel, *Conversations with Scorsese*, 55.

197 **"exuberant and full of fun":** Sarah Begley, "Steven Spielberg on Melissa Mathison: 'E.T.'s Glowing Heart' Was Hers," *Time*, 11 November 2015. Accessed on 12 March 2025 at https://time.com/4109365/melissa-mathison-steven-spielberg/.

198 **"When you get into a relationship like that":** Author interview with Fehr.

198 **"She's the greatest thing in bed":** Peter Biskind, "Raging Days, Boogie Nights," *Vanity Fair*, April 1998. Accessed on 20 May 2025 at https://archive.vanityfair.com/article/1998/4/raging-days-boogie-nights.

198 **"adoring young proteges":** Biskind, "Raging Days, Boogie Nights."

198 **"I just got coffee and Cokes":** Garry Jenkins, *Harrison Ford: Imperfect Hero* (Citadel Press, 1999), 142.

199 **"She loved writers and writing":** Begley, "Steven Spielberg on Melissa Mathison."

199 **"It was a terrible movie":** Author interview with Medavoy.

200 **"Look," Medavoy told Zanuck:** Author interview with Medavoy.

201 **"Go ahead":** Author interview with Medavoy.

201 ***Build the bridge in front of you*:** Carl Gottlieb, *The "Jaws" Log* (Newmarket Press, 2012), 31.

201 **"No long shots of a shark":** Gottlieb, *The "Jaws" Log*, 41.

17: You're Gonna Need a Bigger Boat

202 **a mechanical alternative:** A handful of shots were taken of a real shark by experts in Australia, to be spliced into the final cut of the film.

202 **"with new clubs on a strange course":** Gottlieb, *The "Jaws" Log*, 53.

203 **"creative compatriot":** Laurent Bouzereau, *Spielberg: The First Ten Years* (Insight Editions, 2024), 8.

203 **"It's not going very well":** Bouzereau, *Spielberg*, 8.

203 **"I'll be four or five days":** Gottlieb, *The "Jaws" Log*, 110.

203 **On Carl Gottlieb:** Gottlieb was also an actor, to whom Steven had already given the small part of an Amity Island newspaper editor. As screenwriter, Gottlieb saw the role was unnecessary to the plot, and conscientiously wrote himself nearly entirely out of the movie.

204 **"You look awfully depressed" and following exchange:** Bouzereau, *Spielberg*, 100.

205 **"Why don't you cast Ricky Dreyfuss?":** Bouzereau, *Spielberg*, 99.

205 **"I don't want to make a film" and following exchange:** Gottlieb, *The "Jaws" Log*, 66–67.

206 **"invaders":** Edith Blake, *On Location in Martha's Vineyard* (Bunch of Grapes Press, 1975), 10.

206 **"turned-up noses" and "turned-up palms":** Blake, *On Location in Martha's Vineyard*, 11.

207 **"Don't they see":** Blake, *On Location in Martha's Vineyard*, 22.

207 **"They just don't listen":** Blake, *On Location in Martha's Vineyard*, 33.

208 **"No wonder they all go nuts":** Blake, *On Location in Martha's Vineyard*, 27.

208 **"Waitresses arrived from the mainland":** Gottlieb, *The "Jaws" Log*, 107.

208 **"mother ship":** Blake, *On Location in Martha's Vineyard*, 103–104.

209 **"Fuck the actors!":** Bouzereau, *Spielberg*, 109.

210 **"We were shooting away":** Gottlieb, *The "Jaws" Log*, 94.

211 **"You're gonna need a bigger boat":** Mia Galuppo, "'You're Gonna Need a Bigger Boat': Jaws Writer Reveals Origins of Movie's Famous Line," *Hollywood Reporter*, 7 March 2016. Accessed on 1 December 2024 at https://www.hollywoodreporter.com/news/general-news/jaws-bigger-boat-quote-writer-872226/.

211 **"it's not the time it takes":** *Inside "Jaws": A Filmumentary*, directed by Jamie Benning, 2013.

212 **"Keep going" and following exchange:** Bouzereau, *Spielberg*, 111.

213 **"Steve is an opportunist":** Blake, *On Location in Martha's Vineyard*, 16.

213 **"While directing":** Blake, *On Location in Martha's Vineyard*, 123.

214 **"very spoiled":** Tere Tereba and Susan Pile, "New Again: Steven Spielberg," *Interview Magazine*, May 1977. Accessed on 18 November 2024 at https://www.interviewmagazine.com/film/new-again-steven-spielberg.

214 **"the director doesn't know what he's doing":** Blake, *On Location in Martha's Vineyard*, 58.

215 **"I had terrible, despairing days":** Bouzereau, *Spielberg*, 115.

215 **"as the last light":** Blake, *On Location in Martha's Vineyard*, 113.

216 **"Lord, this place will be a sea of blood":** Blake, *On Location in Martha's Vineyard*, 126.

216 **"Motherfucker, it's over!":** Gottlieb, *The "Jaws" Log*, 173.

18: Indiana Smith and Francis's Apocalypse

217 **"C'mon":** Rinzler, *The Complete Making of Indiana Jones*, 17.

218 **"The wives were very close":** Author interview with A. Murch.

218 **"Well, it's a better film":** Author interview with A. Murch.

220 **"It's your night" and response:** Evans, *The Kid Stays in the Picture*, 290.

220 **"Francis Ford Coppola" and FFC's speech:** Academy of Motion Pictures Arts and Sciences. Footage accessed on 19 April 2024 at https://www.facebook.com/watch/?v=849173239758486.

221 **fifteen hundred acres:** Nearly the entirety of the property. Ninety-three acres were sold off to a third party; Francis acquired them later.

222 **"tremendous":** Author interview with De Palma.

222 **the following January:** *Daily Variety*, 30 June 1975.

222 **"on any basis at all":** Cowie, *Coppola*, 121.

223 **"What the hell":** Pollock, *Skywalking*, 130.

223 ***It's my picture*:** Pollock, *Skywalking*, 130.

223 **"I didn't have any control":** Pollock, *Skywalking*, 130.

223 **"If you want to make it":** Pollock, *Skywalking*, 130.

223 **"I don't think I ever became conceited":** Robert Lindsey, "Coppola Returns to the Vietnam Era, Minus Apocalypse," *New York Times*, 3 May 1987, Section 2, page 19.

223 **"I had financed it":** Francis Ford Coppola, "Apocalypse Now: For the Record," *New York Times*, 27 May 2001, Section 2, page 4.

223 **"I had this idea":** Tony Chiu, "Francis Coppola's 'Apocalypse' Is Finally at Hand," *New York Times*, 12 August 1979, D17.

224 **"Francis," he said:** *Hearts of Darkness: A Filmmaker's Apocalypse*, directed by Fax Bahr and George Hickenlooper, produced by Zaloom Mayfield Productions and Zoetrope Studios, 1991.

19: We Could Get Another Scream Here

226 **"There are some really good scenes":** Kelly, *Martin Scorsese*, 110.
226 **"I didn't know anything about boxing":** Ebert, *Scorsese by Ebert*, 182.
226 **"I almost felt I wrote it myself":** Levy, *De Niro,* 160.
227 **"His problems aren't your problems":** Ebert, *Scorsese by Ebert*, 44.
227 **"lucid":** Elle Hunt, "'I Thought Drink and Drugs Enabled My Creativity': Julia Cameron on the Drama Behind The Artist's Way," *The Guardian*, 18 August 2022. Accessed on 15 May 2024 at https://www.theguardian.com/books/2022/aug/18/i-thought-drink-and-drugs-enabled-my-creativity-julia-cameron-on-the-drama-behind-the-artists-way.
228 ***My God, I've met the man*:** Jay MacDonald, "Julia Cameron: How the Artist Found Her Way," Bookpage.com, May 2006. Accessed on 19 April 2024 at https://www.bookpage.com/interviews/8351-julia-cameron-arts-culture/.
228 **"He was magical-seeming to me":** Penelope Green, "Julia Cameron Wants You to Do Your Morning Pages," *New York Times*, 2 February 2019. Accessed on 22 July 2024 at https://www.nytimes.com/2019/02/02/style/julia-cameron-the-artists-way.html.
228 **"use [her] talents":** Hunt, "'I Thought Drink and Drugs Enabled My Creativity.'"
229 **"*Jaws* just floored me":** Jon Burlingame, "John Williams Recalls *Jaws*," *Film Music Society*, 14 August 2012.
229 **"so simple":** Burlingame, "John Williams Recalls *Jaws*."
229 **"You can't be serious" and response:** Maddy Shaw Roberts, "'I Played the Shark Theme to Spielberg and He Said, "You Can't Be Serious!"'—John Williams on composing Jaws," *Classic FM*, 29 August 2022. Accessed on 20 Jan 2025 at https://www.classicfm.com/composers/williams/jaws-theme-spielberg-joke/.
229 **"Let's try it":** Burlingame, "John Williams Recalls *Jaws*."
230 **"You have to come down":** Bouzereau, *Spielberg*, 117.
230 *Oh my God, what have I done?*: Bouzereau, *Spielberg*, 117.
231 **"the largest expenditure":** John Charnay and Doug Mirrell, "Ripping Response to Jaws," *Hollywood Reporter*, 26 June 1975.
232 **"You know," Steven told Fields:** Bart Oosterhoorn, "Shot-for-Shot: Joe Alves," *Flashback Files*. Accessed on 1 April 2024 at https://www.flashbackfiles.com/joe-alves-interview.
233 **"On more than one occasion":** Gottlieb, *The "Jaws" Log,* 214.

20: Blockbuster

235 **"I remember when I met with Steven":** Simon Foster, "First Reformed: The Paul Schrader Interview," *Screen-Space*, 31 January 2018. Accessed on 25 August 2024 at http://screen-space.squarespace.com/features/2018/1/31/first-reformed-the-paul-schrader-interview.html.
235 **"superman":** Roger Ebert, "Starting Out at 2 a.m. with Paul Schrader after a Toronto Premiere," 14 December 2012. Accessed on 1 August 2024 at https://www.rogerebert.com/interviews/starting-out-at-2-am-with-paul-schrader-after-a-toronto-premiere.
235 **"embarrassing":** McBride, *Steven Spielberg*, 260.
235 **"I refuse to write" and response:** Foster, "First Reformed."
235 **"I figured," he said later:** Chris Nashawaty, *The Future Was Now: Madmen, Mavericks, and the Epic Sci-Fi Summer of 1982* (Flatiron, 2024), 14.
235 **"So I rented Francis Coppola's suite":** Nashawaty, *The Future Was Now*, 14.
236 **"I read everything on the market":** Richard Combs, "A Close Encounter with Steven Spielberg," *Sight & Sound*, Spring 1977. Reprinted 10 December 2021. Accessed on 19

March 2025 at https://www.bfi.org.uk/sight-and-sound/interviews/close-encounter-with-steven-spielberg.

236 **"wasn't interested in a film":** Clarke Taylor, "Isaac Asimov and Science Friction," *Los Angeles Times*, 7 February 1988. Accessed on 1 September 2024 at https://www.latimes.com/archives/la-xpm-1988–02–07-ca-41159-story.html.

237 **"a cokey movie":** Julia Phillips, *You'll Never Eat Lunch in This Town Again* (Random House, 1991), 212.

238 **"There's only one way":** Phillips, *You'll Never Eat Lunch in This Town Again*, 218.

238 **"The Lucas-Milius script":** Chiu, "Francis Coppola's 'Apocalypse' Is Finally at Hand."

239 **"He's not interested in a part":** E. Coppola, *Notes on the Making of "Apocalypse Now,"* 11.

239 **"The film will earn it back":** E. Coppola, *Notes on the Making of "Apocalypse Now,"* 12.

239 **"Two million":** E. Coppola, *Notes on the Making of "Apocalypse Now,"* 12.

241 **"whether they were in or not":** Garry Jenkins, *Empire Building* (Simon & Schuster, 1997), 76.

241 **"I'm a believer in this":** J. W. Rinzler, *The Making of "Star Wars"* (Del Rey, 2007), 93.

242 **"I'm not working a fucking door":** Jenkins, *Empire Building*, 84.

242 **Here's a possibility:** Rinzler, *The Making of "Star Wars,"* 102.

242 **"I wanted someone just like Harrison":** Rinzler, *The Making of "Star Wars,"* 102.

243 **he joked:** Michael Appler, "Al Pacino Recalls Turning Down 'Star Wars' Despite 'So Much Money,' Jokes: 'I Gave Harrison Ford a Career,'" *Variety*, 20 April 2023. Accessed 3 August 2024 at https://variety.com/2023/film/news/al-pacino-star-wars-1235589913/.

243 **"I always root for the losers":** Pacino, *Sonny Boy*, 24.

244 **"*Star Wars* was mine":** Louise Jury and Josh Pettitt, "'I Turned Down Star Wars Because I Didn't Understand the Script': Al Pacino Gets a Standing Ovation for His Ramblings and Reminiscences," *Evening Standard*, 3 June 2013. Accessed on 3 August 2024 at https://www.standard.co.uk/showbiz/celebrity-news/i-turned-down-star-wars-because-i-didn-t-understand-the-script-al-pacino-gets-a-standing-ovation-for-his-ramblings-and-reminiscences-8641804.html.

244 **"maniacal":** Rinzler, *The Making of "Star Wars,"* 124.

244 ***That's the best script*:** *Today Show*, NBC, 26 January 2016.

244 **"I think I had a problem with success":** *Today Show*, NBC, 26 January 2016.

245 **"I got pregnant":** Green, "Julia Cameron Wants You to Do Your Morning Pages."

245 **"the well-known tendency":** Ebert, *Scorsese by Ebert*, xiv.

245 **"You're raised to worship women":** Ebert, *Scorsese by Ebert*, 45.

246 **his biggest success yet:** *Taxi Driver* also won Scorsese the Cannes Film Festival's Palme d'Or, the most prestigious award in world cinema, later in the year. At the time of writing, Coppola is one of only nine directors, and the only American, to win it twice.

246 **"some bimbo whom he is fucking":** Phillips, *You'll Never Eat Lunch in This Town Again*, 224.

246 **"My name is, uh, Steve Spielberg" and rest of documentary scene:** "TVTV Looks at the Oscars," 1976, Media Burn Independent Video Archive. Accessed on 8 March 2025 at https://mediaburn.org/video/tvtv-looks-at-the-academy-awards-2/.

248 **after being turned down by Robert De Niro:** Marvin R. Shanken, "The Interview: Robert De Niro," *Cigar Aficionado*, September/October 2015.

249 **"Someday I won't just own this":** Sam Wasson, *The Path to Paradise: A Francis Ford Coppola Story* (Harper Perennial, 2023), 36.

21: Final-Cut Directors

250 **"You know," Mathison told Fehr:** Author interview with Fehr.

250 **"they were just compatible":** Author interview with Fehr.

250 **"I'm almost seven years in":** Author interview with Fehr.

251 **"The main female character":** Email from Laraine Brennan to the author, 23 February 2025.

251 **"a very personal movie for me":** Guy Flatley, "At the Movies," *New York Times*, 24 June 1977, C8.

251 **At film school:** De Palma studied theater at Sarah Lawrence, but film was his obsession, and he took film classes at NYU.

251 **"We were final-cut directors":** Author interview with De Palma.

252 **"gang was starting to break up":** Nathan Rabin, "Random Roles: Margot Kidder," *The A.V. Club*, 3 March 2009. Accessed on 18 April 2024 at https://web.archive.org/web/20141213050305/http://www.avclub.com/article/random-roles-margot-kidder-24554.

252 **"Suddenly," says De Palma:** Author interview with De Palma.

252 **They tore it down:** Brooks Barnes, "Scripting A Life Much Like Hers," *New York Times*, 21 July 2010. Accessed on 18 April 2024 at https://www.nytimes.com/2010/07/22/fashion/22salt.html.

22: Those Fuckers Are Crazy

256 **"Well," he said:** E. Coppola, *Notes on the Making of "Apocalypse Now,"* 34.

256 **"Ooooh, Daddy":** E. Coppola, *Notes on the Making of "Apocalypse Now,"* 34.

257 **"state of anxiety and fear":** E. Coppola, *Notes on the Making of "Apocalypse Now,"* 43.

257 **"He is really going through the most intense struggle":** E. Coppola, *Notes on the Making of "Apocalypse Now,"* 43–44.

258 **"The office called":** E. Coppola, *Notes on the Making of "Apocalypse Now,"* 77.

258 **"is so exhausted":** E. Coppola, *Notes on the Making of "Apocalypse Now,"* 80.

259 **"hopeless," "scared":** E. Coppola, *Notes on the Making of "Apocalypse Now,"* 88.

259 **"miserable":** E. Coppola, *Notes on the Making of "Apocalypse Now,"* 101.

259 **"angry," "trapped":** E. Coppola, *Notes on the Making of "Apocalypse Now,"* 122.

259 **"The film will not be good" and following exchange:** *Hearts of Darkness*, directed by Bahr and Hickenlooper.

260 **"Please," he slurred:** Ryan Parker, "Martin Sheen Begged Coppola to Film His Bloodied 'Apocalypse Now' Breakdown," *Hollywood Reporter*, 3 August 2020. Accessed on 1 December 2024 at https://www.hollywoodreporter.com/news/general-news/martin-sheen-begged-coppola-film-his-bloodied-demons-apocalypse-now-breakdown-1305611/.

261 **"I don't know if I am going to live through this":** Jean Vallely, "Martin Sheen: Heart of Darkness, Heart of Gold," *Rolling Stone*, 1 November 1979. Accessed on 4 January 2025 at https://www.rollingstone.com/tv-movies/tv-movie-news/martin-sheen-heart-of-darkness-heart-of-gold-80879/.

261 **"There was that emotional electricity":** E. Coppola, *Notes on the Making of "Apocalypse Now,"* 105.

23: A Walk in the Dark

262 **"When you're directing":** Pollock, *Skywalking*, 159.

262 **"embarrassing silence":** Pollock, *Skywalking*, 159.

263 **"I want you to tell me what you see":** Jenkins, *Empire Building*, 111.

263 **"They don't know what the fuck they're doing":** Jenkins, *Empire Building*, 110.
263 **"George! You can type this shit":** Chris Heath, "Harrison Ford on *Star Wars*."
264 **"was not well":** Author interview with De Palma.
264 **"but George was so depressed":** J. W. Rinzler, *The Making of "Star Wars": The Definitive Story Behind the Original Films* (Del Rey, 2007), 218.
265 **"That's when I really confirmed to myself":** Pollock, *Skywalking*, 173.
265 **"so staid and conventional":** Author interview with Chew.
265 **"George had to let go" and following exchange:** Author interview with Chew.
265 **"reassemble it into the dailies":** Author interview with Chew.
266 **"How come you didn't" and following exchange:** Author interview with Kitchens.
266 **"I loved Marcia":** Author interview with Kitchens.
266 **"When I showed them stuff":** Author interview with Chew.
267 **"Is the building talking?":** Hirsch, *A Long Time Ago in a Cutting Room Far, Far Away . . .*, xxi.
267 **"Marcia didn't want to do fantasy":** Author interview with Kitchens.
267 **"When I was assigned the gunport sequence":** Author interview with Chew.
268 **"was a walk in the dark":** Carolyn Giardina, "ACE Eddies Lifetime Achievement Honoree Richard Chew: 'We Are Essential, and What We Do Is Unique,'" *Hollywood Reporter*, 4 March 2022. Accessed on 28 May 2023 at https://www.hollywoodreporter.com/movies/movie-features/richard-chew-ace-eddies-lifetime-achievement-1235097465/.
268 **"crossing the screen":** Author interview with Chew.
268 **"Richard, don't fuck around":** Author interview with Chew.
269 **"Oh, don't worry about that":** Hirsch, *A Long Time Ago in a Cutting Room Far, Far Away . . .*, 14.
269 **"The fact that Marcia":** Hirsch, *A Long Time Ago in a Cutting Room Far, Far Away . . .*, 87.
269 **"You know, I thought of that" and following quote:** Author interview with Kitchens. In his 2020 memoir, Hirsch writes that he and De Palma had gone to see *Deliverance* together, and De Palma had commented that a similar shot in that film didn't quite land, which gave Hirsch the "inspiration" to try and better it.
270 **"distance between them" and following anecdote:** Author interview with Kitchens.
270 **"George, don't worry":** Author interview with Chew.
271 **"a buzz started to go around":** Hirsch, *A Long Time Ago in a Cutting Room Far, Far Away . . .*, 97.

24: This Is the Way the World Ends

272 **"the script says 'a pile of burning bodies'":** E. Coppola, *Notes on the Making of "Apocalypse Now,"* 126.
272 **"all familiar but different":** E. Coppola, *Notes on the Making of "Apocalypse Now,"* 168.
273 **"I was the wife":** E. Coppola, *Notes on the Making of "Apocalypse Now,"* 169.
273 **"magnificently":** E. Coppola, *Notes on the Making of "Apocalypse Now,"* 176.
273 **"so excited":** E. Coppola, *Notes on the Making of "Apocalypse Now,"* 173.
273 **"It's great":** E. Coppola, *Notes on the Making of "Apocalypse Now,"* 173.
274 **"My nose was off":** Jenkins, *Empire Building*, 145.
274 **"I was so upset":** Interview with Mark Hamill, *Gossip* magazine, June 1978.
275 **"I just wanted":** Jenkins, *Empire Building*, 146.
275 **"was the plushest I have ever seen":** Hirsch, *A Long Time Ago in a Cutting Room Far, Far Away . . .*, 108.
275 **"What was that stuff about a tractor beam":** Hirsch, *A Long Time Ago in a Cutting Room Far, Far Away . . .*, 108.

276 **"I made some cracks":** Author interview with De Palma.

276 **"I don't understand your story" and following exchange:** Ian Freer, Steve O'Hagan, Olly Richards, and William Thomas, "The Oral History of Star Wars," *Empire*, 28 November 2019. Accessed on 20 April 2024 at https://www.empireonline.com/movies/features/secret-history-star-wars/.

276 **"You're really hurting George's feelings":** Author interview with De Palma.

276 **"The trouble with the Hollywood system":** Author interview with De Palma.

277 **"George, it's great":** Biskind, *Easy Riders, Raging Bulls*, 335.

278 **"You're George Lucas, aren't you?" and response:** Hirsch, *A Long Time Ago in a Cutting Room Far, Far Away . . .*, 115.

278 **"now I just have to go through the birth canal":** Author interview with W. Murch.

278 **"negativity, disloyalty or jealousy":** E. Coppola, *Notes on the Making of "Apocalypse Now,"* 176.

25: Lucky Sandcastles

280 **"a hot poker on my chest":** Steven Travers, *Coppola's Monster Film: The Making of "Apocalypse Now"* (McFarland & Company, 2016), 124.

280 **"What happened?" and response:** Travers, *Coppola's Monster Film*, 125.

281 **"What the fuck is that?":** *Hearts of Darkness*, directed by Bahr and Hickenlooper.

281 **"He's not dead unless I *say* he's dead":** *Hearts of Darkness*, directed by Bahr and Hickenlooper.

281 **"I *chose* to have that heart attack":** *Hearts of Darkness*, directed by Bahr and Hickenlooper.

281 **"We were talking":** E. Coppola, *Notes on the Making of "Apocalypse Now,"* 180.

282 **"We're getting a divorce" and following exchange:** E. Coppola, *Notes on the Making of "Apocalypse Now,"* 193.

283 **"We wanted the last note to beg for a response":** Don Shay, "On the Dark Side of the Moon with Steven Spielberg" (draft), *Cinefantastique* magazine records—*Close Encounters of the Third Kind*, f.327. Margaret Herrick Library, Academy of Motion Picture Arts and Sciences.

283 **"things . . . beckoning me to leave the house":** Chris Hodenfield, "Science-Fiction in Steven Spielberg's Suburbia," *Rolling Stone*, 26 January 1978. Accessed on 20 March 2025 at https://www.rollingstone.com/tv-movies/tv-movie-features/science-fiction-in-steven-spielbergs-suburbia-44190/.

283 **"Nobody expects one mega-hit":** Shay, "On the Dark Side of the Moon with Steven Spielberg" (draft).

284 **"I got something very similar":** Steven Spielberg, "Of Narrow Misses and Close Calls: Raiders of the Lost Ark—Directing," *American Cinematographer*, 26 July 2017. Accessed on 24 March 2024 at https://theasc.com/articles/flashback-raiders-of-the-lost-ark-directing.

284 **"a series of *Raiders* sagas":** Taylor, *The Making of "Raiders of the Lost Ark,"* 13.

284 **"Look, this is a B-movie":** Taylor, *The Making of "Raiders of the Lost Ark,"* 13.

285 **"Hold your breath":** Spielberg, "Of Narrow Misses and Close Calls."

285 **"I broke up with my girlfriend":** J. W. Rinzler, *The Making of "The Empire Strikes Back"* (Del Rey, 2010), 2.

285 **"I couldn't get the movies":** Author interview with De Palma.

286 **"George had this whole plan":** Author interview with De Palma.

286 **"We are opposites":** "Cinema: The Movie Movie Gang," *Time*, 30 May 1977. Accessed on 1 March 2025 at https://time.com/archive/6848712/cinema-the-movie-movie-gang/.

286 **"Why should he":** Pollock, *Skywalking*, 197.

286 **"bad investment":** Pollock, *Skywalking*, 197.
286 **"too good for everyone":** Brian Jay Jones, *George Lucas: A Life* (Back Bay Books, 2016), 272.
287 **"Instead of showing their friendship":** "Cinema: The Movie Movie Gang," *Time*.
287 **"cocky":** Kelly, *Martin Scorsese*, 94.
287 **"the impossibility of two creative people":** Kelly, *Martin Scorsese*, 99.
287 **"without becoming part":** Ebert, *Scorsese by Ebert*, 176.
288 **"I was just too drugged out":** Biskind, *Easy Riders, Raging Bulls*, 339.
288 **"Marty had this feeling":** Kelly, *Martin Scorsese*, 98.
288 **"*Star Wars* was in":** Tom Shone, *Martin Scorsese: A Retrospective* (Abrams, 2014), 94.
288 **"Try and let the higher power":** Green, "Julia Cameron Wants You to Do Your Morning Pages."
288 ***Well,* she thought, *I can believe in that*:** Genevieve Fox, "'My Own Inner Critic Is a Bully': Julia Cameron on Creative Demons and Updating The Artist's Way," *The Guardian*, 12 May 2024. Accessed on 13 May 2024 at https://www.theguardian.com/lifeandstyle/article/2024/may/12/my-own-inner-critic-is-a-bully-julia-cameron-on-creative-demons-and-updating-the-artists-way.
289 **"What's the sense of hanging around":** Schickel, *Conversations with Scorsese*, 35.
289 **"I have very little time left":** Shone, *Martin Scorsese*, 94.
289 **"I took chances":** Stephen Galloway, "Martin Scorsese's Journey From Near-Death Drug Addict to 'Silence,'" *Hollywood Reporter*, 8 December 2016. Accessed on 1 January 2025 at https://www.hollywoodreporter.com/movies/movie-features/martin-scorsese-interview-death-drug-addict-silence-953300/.
289 **"Are you still interested" and response:** Spielberg, "Of Narrow Misses and Close Calls."

26: The Horse May Talk

291 **"Is this ever going to work?" and response:** Author interview with W. Murch.
291 **"What I'd really like to do":** Chiu, "Francis Coppola's 'Apocalypse' Is Finally at Hand."
292 **"They were thinking":** Author interview with Jeanne Rosenberg, 6 February 2024.
292 **"liked baseball too much":** Anolik, *Hollywood's Eve*, 149.
292 **"Meanwhile":** Author interview with Rosenberg.
292 **"everything open-ended":** Author interview with Rosenberg.
293 **"That's my pot dealer!":** Anolik, *Hollywood's Eve*, 51.
294 **"Francis promised me":** E. Coppola, *Notes on the Making of "Apocalypse Now,"* 214.
295 **"That was a difficult film to make":** "Harrison Ford: A Man of Few Words," *Ampersand* II, no. 9 (June 1979), 21.
295 **"One of the definitions":** E. Coppola, *Notes on the Making of "Apocalypse Now,"* 214.
295 **"naturally manic and stupid":** Author interview with Valerie O'Conor, 15 March 2024.
295 **"There are plenty of people":** Author interview with O'Conor.
296 **"heavy, pure Francis":** Author interview with O'Conor.
296 **"Almost none of it":** Author interview with O'Conor.
297 **"It was so unimportant":** Author interview with O'Conor.
297 **"He was a screaming, misogynistic":** Author interview with O'Conor.
297 **"Oh, it was his asthma":** Author interview with O'Conor.
298 **"very good":** Allen White, "Interview: Director John Milius," www.uncleanarts.com, 1999. Accessed on 13 April 2024 at https://uncleanarts.com/interview-john-milius/.
298 **"about filmmaking":** Author interview with Kitchens.
298 **"I was trying to say":** Chiu, "Francis Coppola's 'Apocalypse' Is Finally at Hand."

27: Do You Want to Live or Die?

299 **"Part of me has always believed":** E. Coppola, *Notes on the Making of "Apocalypse Now,"* 215.

299 **"the dynamic that has kept us together":** Cowie, *Coppola*, 224.

300 **"*Star Wars* will be number one" and following exchange:** E. Coppola, *Notes on the Making of "Apocalypse Now,"* 222.

301 **"pioneered the field":** Geoff Berkshire, "Box Office Pioneer Art Murphy Dies," *Variety*, 17 June 2003. Accessed on 3 March 2025 at https://variety.com/2003/film/news/i-variety-i-b-o-pioneer-art-murphy-dies-1117888073/.

301 **"misanthropic":** A. D. Murphy, "Film Review: 'Close Encounters of the Third Kind,'" *Variety*, 8 November 1977. Accessed on 3 March 2025 at https://variety.com/1977/film/reviews/close-encounters-of-the-third-kind-1200424081/.

302 **"heroic":** Francis Coppola and Ellie Coppola commentary track, *Hearts of Darkness: A Filmmaker's Apocalypse.*

302 **"Why was *Superman* a prudent film":** F. Coppola and E. Coppola commentary track, *Hearts of Darkness.*

303 **"No more coke":** Ed Power, "A Cocaine-Fuelled Folly: Why New York, New York Almost Killed Martin Scorsese," *The Telegraph*, 8 May 2023.

303 **"surprised that I was near death":** Galloway, "Martin Scorsese's Journey From Near-Death Drug Addict to 'Silence.'"

303 **"I almost died":** Ebert, *Scorsese by Ebert*, 61.

303 **"Do you want to live or die":** Mark Singer, "The Man Who Forgets Nothing," *New Yorker*, 19 March 2000.

303 **"What's the matter with you, Marty?":** Biskind, *Easy Riders, Raging Bulls*, 387.

304 **"Now, do you wanna shoot it?":** Ebert, *Scorsese by Ebert*, 61.

304 **"Let's get off the fence":** Kelly, *Martin Scorsese*, 106.

304 **"naivety and denial":** Galloway, "Martin Scorsese's Journey From Near-Death Drug Addict to 'Silence.'"

305 **"There is a great humanity in a pimp":** Kelly, *Martin Scorsese*, 80.

305 **"silent about where I came from":** Schickel, *Conversations with Scorsese*, 23.

305 **"Yes," he told Robertson:** Kelly, *Martin Scorsese*, 106.

28: Empire

306 **"If the second one works" and following exchange:** Madsen, "Irvin Kershner."

307 **"This is what this film will pay for":** Madsen, "Irvin Kershner."

307 **"It's not like saying":** Madsen, "Irvin Kershner."

307 **George had negotiated unprecedented terms:** Distribution agreement between Chapter II Company and 20th Century Fox, 21 September 1977, Gary Kurtz papers, Collection 2335, box 100, folder 15, University of Southern California archives.

309 **but Ford had only agreed to two:** "Howard Kazanjian: Master and Commander," *Star Wars Aficionado.*

309 **"Don't worry about the fact":** Michael Sragow, "Father Figure," *Salon*, 13 May 1999. Accessed on 2 May 2024 at https://www.salon.com/1999/05/13/kershner/.

310 **"What do I want to go up there for" and response:** Author interview with Bloom.

310 **"There was a communication problem":** Author interview with Bloom.

310 **"typical movie stuff":** Ken P., "An Interview with Gary Kurtz."

311 **"behind before we even started":** Madsen, "Irvin Kershner."

312 **"Okay, it's flash":** National Science and Media Museum, "Director Harley Cokeliss on The

Empire Strikes Back," 2012. Accessed on 3 May 2024 at https://www.youtube.com/watch?v=-5LrmMdrgtY.

312 **"the most difficult thing":** Madsen, "Irvin Kershner."

313 **"Sometimes he would want to control everything":** Ken P., "An Interview with Gary Kurtz."

313 **"George! Come over here!":** Madsen, "Irvin Kershner."

314 **"Don't change a thing":** Sragow, "Father Figure."

314 **"You tell him to get this done fast":** Hirsch, *A Long Time Ago in a Cutting Room Far, Far Away . . .*, 157.

314 **"humiliated":** Hirsch, *A Long Time Ago in a Cutting Room Far, Far Away . . .*, 152.

315 **"I've got you" and response:** Kim Masters, *The Keys to the Kingdom: The Rise of Michael Eisner and the Fall of Everybody Else* (HarperBusiness, 2001), 91.

315 **"It was excruciating":** Audie Bock, "Secrecy Shrouds a 'Star Wars' Sequel," *New York Times*, 11 July 1982.

316 **"He was very different":** Ken P., "An Interview with Gary Kurtz."

317 **"I think she ought to just say":** Rinzler, *The Making of "The Empire Strikes Back,"* 186.

317 **"Wait a minute" and following exchange:** Mike Ryan, "In Hindsight, *Empire Strikes Back* Director Irvin Kershner Would've Helmed One of the Prequels," *Vanity Fair*, 18 October 2010. Accessed on 23 July 2023 at https://www.vanityfair.com/hollywood/2010/10/irvin-kershner.

317 **"it would attempt":** Madsen, "Irvin Kershner."

318 **"sensible":** Pollock, *Skywalking*, 254.

318 **"The ranch is the only thing":** Pollock, *Skywalking*, 251.

319 **"He set Lucasfilm up":** Author interview with Bloom.

29: What If He Got the Dog?

321 **"She was terrible":** Mandalit Del Barco, "Kathleen Kennedy: From Standing in Line for 'Star Wars' to Producing It Herself," NPR, 17 December 2015. Accessed on 6 April 2024 at https://www.npr.org/2015/12/17/459976428/kathleen-kennedy-from-standing-in-line-to-see-star-wars-to-producing-it-herself.

322 **"It sounds made up":** Kim Masters, "Lucasfilm's Kathleen Kennedy on 'Star Wars,' 'Lincoln' and Secret J. J. Abrams Meetings," *Hollywood Reporter*, 8 February 2013.

322 ***Is this really what I want to do with my life?*:** Masters, "Lucasfilm's Kathleen Kennedy on 'Star Wars.'"

322 **"Kathy," says Casella:** Author interview with Martin Casella, 11 April 2024.

323 **"I thought that's what was expected":** Masters, "Lucasfilm's Kathleen Kennedy on 'Star Wars.'"

323 **"This is my next movie":** Del Barco, "Kathleen Kennedy: From Standing in Line for 'Star Wars.'"

324 **"a cockroach" and De Niro's response:** Shawn Levy, *De Niro*, 230.

324 **"Are you watching?":** Ebert, *Scorsese by Ebert*, 183.

325 **"I did it my way":** Kelly, *Martin Scorsese*, 120.

325 **"He's the most risk-taking director":** Author interview with Irwin Winkler, 12 June 2024.

325 **"This is going to be my last film":** Ebert, *Scorsese by Ebert*, 62.

325 **"without a net":** Ebert, *Scorsese by Ebert*, 164.

325 ***This is the last one*:** Ruth Kinane, "Robert De Niro and Martin Scorsese on Why Raging Bull Almost Didn't Happen," *Entertainment Weekly*, 21 June 2021. Accessed on 22 January 2025 at https://ew.com/movies/robert-de-niro-martin-scorsese-talk-raging-bull-at-tribeca-festival-2021l/.

325 **"Marty does [it] all on his own terms":** Kelly, *Martin Scorsese*, xv.

326 **"inch by inch" and following exchange:** Kelly, *Martin Scorsese*, 137.
327 **"I want to feel like Jake does":** Ebert, *Scorsese by Ebert*, 221.

30: The Dream

329 **"the most decadent":** Jeanne Miller, "Apocalypse Now," *San Francisco Examiner*, 16 August 1979, 25.
329 **"It was terrible":** Author interview with anonymous source, 7 February 2023.
330 **"I don't think politics":** Samuel Blumenfeld and Laurent Vachaud, *Brian De Palma: Entretiens avec Samuel Blumenfeld et Laurent Vachaud* (Calmann-Lévy, 2001), 141. Translated by the author.
330 **"I liked *Apocalypse Now*":** Author interview with Kanaly.
330 **"evidence of her superficiality":** Christopher Lehmann-Haupt, "Books of the Times," *New York Times*, 7 August 1979, C11.
330 **"bitter":** Harriet Van Horne, "Notes from a Candid Wife," *York Daily Record*, 29 August 1979, 14A.
331 **"Were you comfortable" and response:** Miller, "Apocalypse Now," 25.
331 **"He was saying":** Author interview with O'Conor.
331 **"how could she move through all that":** Author interview with Fehr.
331 **"I don't remember Francis talking much about Melissa":** Author interview with O'Conor.
332 **"I had no illusions":** Author interview with O'Conor.
332 **"very, very soft-spoken":** Author interview with O'Conor.
332 **"We watched the fog":** Author interview with O'Conor.
333 **"a whole studio in San Francisco":** Author interview with W. Murch.
333 **"And George thought about it":** Author interview with W. Murch.
333 **"I made you!" and response:** Author interview with W. Murch.
333 **"George was now bigger than Francis":** Author interview with W. Murch.
333 **"I dream of being part":** Chiu, "Francis Coppola's 'Apocalypse' Is Finally at Hand."
333 **"the full magic of technology":** Chiu, "Francis Coppola's 'Apocalypse' Is Finally at Hand."
334 **"Gee, George":** Author interview with Couturié.
335 **"Why would I want to go":** Author interview with Laurel Ladevich, 5 May 2023.
335 **"before the Ranch was the Ranch" and following exchange:** Author interview with De Palma.
335 **"It never really worked":** Author interview with Kitchens.
335 **"He based his operations":** Author interview with Chew.

31: High Concept

336 **"I'm gonna do a movie":** Willow Green, "Raiders of the Lost Ark: An Oral History," *Empire*, 11 June 2021. Accessed on 16 April 2024 at https://www.empireonline.com/movies/features/indiana-jones-making-raiders-lost-ark/.
337 **"I want to do this thing":** Green, "Raiders of the Lost Ark: An Oral History."
337 **"Indy drank and smoked":** "Howard Kazanjian: Master and Commander," *Star Wars Aficionado*.
338 **"I think I'm a *terrible* writer":** Kerry O'Quinn, "The George Lucas Saga," *Starlog*, 1981.
338 **"I've never really liked directing":** Rinzler, *The Making of "The Empire Strikes Back,"* 35.
339 **"done anything since *Star Wars*":** Taylor, *The Making of "Raiders of the Lost Ark,"* 80.
339 **"I can't get a job":** Author interview with Ladevich.
340 **the secretive script:** Selleck remembered reading the script in Spielberg's office.
340 **"Oh, shit":** Tom Selleck, *You Never Know* (Deyst, 2024), 162.

340 **"Let us worry about that":** Selleck, *You Never Know*, 162.
340 **"It was outrageous":** Masters, *The Keys to the Kingdom*, 91.
340 **"the deal was too rich":** Author interview with Medavoy.
341 **"Their attitude":** Author interview with Schrader.
341 **"the day Barry Diller came in":** Author interview with Schrader.
341 **"the annuity business" and "tent-pole assets":** Aljean Harmetz, "Who Makes Disney Run?" *New York Times*, 7 February 1988. Accessed on 10 April 2024 at https://www.nytimes.com/1988/02/07/magazine/who-makes-disney-run.html.
342 **"I have a cheeseburger heart":** Author interview with Craig Baumgarten, 30 April 2024.
342 **"peter-meter":** Biskind, "Sherry Lansing, Dawn Steel and Sue Mengers."
343 **"enormous amounts of business":** Dawn Steel, *They Can Kill You But They Can't Eat You* (Pocket Books, 1994), 139.
343 **"No girls":** Steel, *They Can Kill You But They Can't Eat You*, 139.
343 **"Katzenberg":** Harmetz, "Who Makes Disney Run?"
343 **ever since he'd dropped out:** Danielle Berrin, "Jeffrey Katzenberg: Mogul on a Mission," *Jewish Journal*, 17 July 2013. Accessed on 17 April 2024 at https://jewishjournal.com/culture/arts/119268/jeffrey-katzenberg-mogul-on-a-mission/.
344 **"This was a period":** Peter Biskind, "The Gambler," *Los Angeles Times*, 26 April 1998. Accessed on 16 April 2024 at https://www.latimes.com/archives/la-xpm-1998-apr-26-bk-43000-story.html.
346 **"Eisner, especially":** Steel, *They Can Kill You But They Can't Eat You*, 141–142.
346 **"critic-proof":** Justin Wyatt, *High Concept: Movies and Marketing in Hollywood* (University of Texas Press, 1994), 10.
346 **"Michael wanted to be in control":** Author interview with Baumgarten.
347 **"shape the movie":** Author interview with Baumgarten.
347 **"We have no obligation":** Masters, *The Keys to the Kingdom*, 103.
348 **"He was a heat-seeking missile":** Author interview with Baumgarten.
348 **"I broke a lot of precedents":** Green, "Raiders of the Lost Ark: An Oral History."
348 **"the first ten pages":** Masters, *The Keys to the Kingdom*, 93.
349 **"Eisner would just go crazy":** Author interview with Baumgarten.
349 **"dispatch[ing] Martin Sheen":** Green, "Raiders of the Lost Ark: An Oral History."
350 **"a chaperone":** Masters, *The Keys to the Kingdom*, 107.
351 **"You sure you want to make this deal":** Masters, *The Keys to the Kingdom*, 92.
351 **"everybody thought Michael had lost his mind":** Author interview with Baumgarten.
351 **Up to 77 percent:** Randall Lane, "The Magician," *Forbes*, 1 March 1996. Accessed on 27 March 2025 at https://www.forbes.com/2002/05/15/0516lucasinterview.html.

32: Like the Old Serials

352 **"We need a guy" and response:** Gregg Goldstein, "What It's Really Like to Work for Kathleen Kennedy and Frank Marshall," *Variety*, 16 November 2018. Accessed on 5 April 2024 at https://variety.com/2018/film/awards/what-its-really-like-to-work-for-kathleen-kennedy-and-frank-marshall-1203028020/.
353 **"I don't know":** Goldstein, "What It's Really Like to Work for Kathleen Kennedy and Frank Marshall."
353 **"Would you be interested" and following exchange:** Frank Marshall acceptance speech, 2018 Academy Governors Award, 18 November 2018.
353 **"Call the producer":** Kathleen Kennedy acceptance speech, 2018 Academy Governors Award, 18 November 2018.
354 **"Could you please stop":** Masters, "Lucasfilm's Kathleen Kennedy on 'Star Wars.'"

354 **"this really cute guy":** Masters, "Lucasfilm's Kathleen Kennedy on 'Star Wars.'"
354 **"I haven't done much model-building":** Kathleen Kennedy acceptance speech, 2018 Academy Governors Award, 18 November 2018.
354 ***Huh,* Kennedy thought:** Sarah Ellison, "Meet the Most Powerful Woman in Hollywood," *Vanity Fair*, 8 February 2016. Accessed on 27 July 2023 at https://www.vanityfair.com/hollywood/2016/02/kathleen-kennedy-hollywood-producer.
355 **"It was the early '80s":** Hollywood's Power Couple," *Time*, 2 November 2007. Accessed on 5 April 2024 at https://content.time.com/time/subscriber/article/0,33009,1680131,00.html.
355 **"a new face":** Selleck, *You Never Know*, 161.
355 **"It was hometown":** Author interview with Ganis.
355 **"What about that guy":** "Steven Spielberg," *SmartLess* podcast, 16 January 2023.
355 **"she came in and she was Marion":** Author interview with Casella.
356 **"It's stuff I don't want to wear":** Author interview with Casella.
357 **"What is it?" and following exchange:** Author interview with Ladevich.
357 **"They were, they are":** Author interview with Ganis.
358 **"A friend of mine":** Author interview with Casella.
358 **"—new idea" and response:** Author interview with Casella.
358 **"*That,*" said Steven:** Marco R. Della Cava, "Lucasfilm's Kathleen Kennedy Has Produced Quite a Career," *USA Today*, 5 June 2013.
358 **"the responsibility to bring other women along":** Del Barco, "Kathleen Kennedy: From Standing in Line for 'Star Wars.'"
359 **"failed screenwriter":** Mooallem, "Inside the Mind of Steven Spielberg."
359 **"I have an idea" and following exchange:** Jim Wright, "Her Pen Kept 'E.T.' Down to Earth," *The Record*, 11 June 1982, B1.
359 **"I don't like science fiction" and response:** Bouzereau, *Spielberg*, 236.
360 **"Thank you very much":** Jenkins, *Harrison Ford: Imperfect Hero*, 175.
360 **"That's who we babysat":** Author interview with Johnson.
361 **"Steven, stop looking at the whole storyboard":** Author interview with Johnson.
361 **"I was just knocked out":** Bouzereau, *Spielberg*, 237.
361 **"You're not crazy":** Bouzereau, *Spielberg*, 237.
361 **"You know what?":** Ellison, "Meet the Most Powerful Woman in Hollywood."
361 **"Don't tell anyone":** Ellison, "Meet the Most Powerful Woman in Hollywood."
362 **"anti-stars":** "Cinema: The Moonchild and the Fifth Beatle," *Time*, 7 February 1969. Accessed on 6 May 2025 at https://time.com/archive/6633029/cinema-the-moonchild-and-the-fifth-beatle/.
362 **"a real movie star":** Jenkins, *Harrison Ford: Imperfect Hero*, 206.
362 **"we all wanted to make sequels":** Author interview with Baumgarten.
363 **"In order for you to know where you are":** Ellise Shafer, "Zoe Saldaña Says Working With Steven Spielberg on 'The Terminal' 'Restored My Faith' in Big Hollywood Productions After Bad 'Pirates of the Caribbean' Experience," *Variety*, 12 October 2024. Accessed on 8 March 2025 at https://variety.com/2024/film/festivals/zoe-saldana-steven-spielberg-the-terminal-restored-faith-hollywood-pirates-of-the-caribbean-1236175530/.
363 **"Why did you use Reese's" and following exchange:** Author interview with Fehr.
364 **"I know just how far back":** Jenkins, *Harrison Ford: Imperfect Hero*, 186.
364 **"my mom would have Wagner on":** Allyson Shiffman, "The Dough Rollers' Massacre," *Interview*, 24 July 2013. Accessed on 26 December 2023 at https://www.interviewmagazine.com/music/the-dough-rollers-the-slipper-room.

33: Shangri-Coppola

365 **"I had no idea":** Author interview with Rebecca De Mornay, 14 June 2024.

365 **"new in town":** Author interview with De Mornay.

366 **"How can you be an understudy?" and response:** Author interview with De Mornay.

366 **"to see if it works":** Author interview with De Mornay.

366 **"You're here":** Author interview with De Mornay.

366 **"That was my film school":** Author interview with De Mornay.

367 **"a company along studio lines":** Cowie, *Coppola*, 237.

368 **"the Golden Age of Hollywood":** Jon Lewis, *Whom God Wishes to Destroy: Francis Coppola and the New Hollywood* (Duke University Press, 1995), 9.

368 **"I thought it was a terrific idea":** Author interview with Schrader.

368 **"I disagreed with Francis":** Mitch Tuchman and Ann Thompson, "I'm the Boss," *Film Comment* 17, no. 4 (July/August 1981), 50–51.

368 **"Lookit":** Lewis, *Whom God Wishes to Destroy*, 57.

369 **"to flush out the pipes":** Author interview with W. Murch.

369 **"Get rid of Chicago":** Author interview with W. Murch.

370 **"Francis's problem":** Serge Daney and Jonathan Rosenbaum, "Entretien avec Brian de Palma," *Cahiers du Cinéma* 677 (April 2012), 15. Translated by the author.

370 **"by any means necessary":** Olivier Assayas and Serge Toubiana, "Zoetrope Studios: Entretien avec Francis F. Coppola," *Cahiers du Cinéma* 677 (April 2012), 47. Translated by the author.

370 **"He had a wrap party":** Author interview with De Mornay.

370 **"I want everyone to come see this":** Author interview with Cindy Kania, 26 November 2024.

370 **"It was very lavish":** Author interview with De Mornay.

370 **"It was the most wonderful place on Earth":** Author interview with Lainie Kazan, 27 February 2023.

371 **"dream the impossible dream":** Author interview with Kazan.

371 **"It went wrong straight off the bat":** Author interview with Walker.

371 **"I don't like the wall":** Author interview with Kania.

371 **"do I *have* to do it *like that?*":** Author interview with Kania.

371 **"writ in skywriting":** Author interview with W. Murch.

372 **"Parts of the studio":** Author interview with Anahid Nazarian, 3 May 2023.

372 **"He doesn't think in the order other people think":** Author interview with Nazarian.

372 **"Everybody loved him":** Author interview with Fehr.

372 **"just ambitious kids":** Author interview with Walker.

373 **"a very male-centric":** Author interview with Walker.

373 **"really gross and forward":** Author interview with Kania.

373 **"looking up in the air":** Author interview with De Mornay.

373 **"It was atrocious":** Author interview with Walker.

373 **"didn't want to follow the screenplay":** Assayas and Toubiana, "Zoetrope Studios," 47. Translated by the author.

374 **"more intrusive in the creative process":** Lewis, *Whom God Wishes to Destroy*, 9.

374 **"It was very, very stressful":** Author interview with Kazan.

376 **"I think he never really got over her" and following exchange:** Author interview with Fehr.

376 **"I thought the nuns were mean":** Deborah Solomon, "Independent Streak: Questions for Francis Ford Coppola," *New York Times*, 16 December 2007. Accessed on 2 October 2024 at https://www.nytimes.com/2007/12/16/magazine/16wwln-Q4-t.html.

376 **“inherent contradiction”:** Ciment, “Entretien avec Francis Coppola.”
377 **“Love can kill”:** Ciment, “Entretien avec Francis Coppola.”
377 **“The experience killed me”:** Ciment, “Entretien avec Francis Coppola.”

34: The Way of the Force

379 **“No husbands, wives”:** Bock, “Secrecy Shrouds a ‘Star Wars’ Sequel.”
379 **“I’m not having fun”:** Bock, “Secrecy Shrouds a ‘Star Wars’ Sequel.”
379 **“I’d fallen in love with it”:** Bock, “Secrecy Shrouds a ‘Star Wars’ Sequel.”
380 **“It was always about the picture”:** Author interview with Ladevich.
380 **“No matter how much time”:** Author interview with Ladevich.
380 **“a terrible cheapskate”:** Email from Doug Korty to the author, 2 April 2023.
380 **“It’s good enough”:** Ken P., “An Interview with Gary Kurtz.”
381 **“Richard was quite laid-back”:** Author interview with Sean Barton, 25 April 2024.
381 **“Marcia, you can make it different”:** Author interview with Barton.
382 **“The audience might have got tired”:** Author interview with Barton.
382 **“George was going through a dark period”:** “Temple of Doom: An Oral History,” *Empire*, May 2008.
382 **“in a good mood”:** “Temple of Doom: An Oral History,” *Empire*.
383 **“He was burnt out”:** Author interview with Ganis.
384 **“extremely bitter”:** Author interview with Dale Pollock, 27 February 2023.
384 **“He was very proud”:** Author interview with Pollock.
384 **“when he was free”:** Author interview with Pollock.
384 **“It was lip service”:** Author interview with Pollock.
384 **“I’m not convinced”:** Author interview with Walker.
384 **“He doesn’t understand myth at all”:** Bauer, “I Was Never Conscious of My Screenplays Having Any Acts.”
384 **“George used to hate hearing that”:** Bouzereau, *Spielberg*, 202.
385 **“it tends to follow what Francis has done”:** Author interview with Nazarian.
385 **Francis acquired the RKO research library:** Coppola eventually added MGM’s and Warner’s libraries to his holdings.
385 **“There were a number of years”:** Author interview with W. Murch.
385 **“When you’re in a family”:** Author interview with Ganis.
386 **“people in cages”:** Stone, “A Turkey or a Triumph, THX 113 Is Our World.”
386 **“This isn’t a family”:** Author interview with Ladevich.
386 **“she disappeared from all the yearbooks”:** Author interview with Kitchens.
386 **“She was excommunicated”:** Author interview with De Palma.
387 **“It’s revisionist history”:** Author interview with Kitchens.
387 **“There’s nothing out there now”:** Author interview with Kitchens.

35: The Edge of the Future

388 **“Only Steven Spielberg knows”:** Bauer, “I Was Never Conscious of My Screenplays Having Any Acts.”
389 **“absent fathers”:** Phillip Maciak, “The Auteur of Fatherhood: How Steven Spielberg Recast American Masculinity,” *Yale Review*, 4 March 2024. Accessed on 10 April 2024 at https://yalereview.org/article/phillip-maciak-steven-spielberg.
390 **“Back when Reagan was elected”:** Author interview with W. Murch.
391 **“estrangement”:** *Spielberg*, directed by Susan Lacy, 2017.

391 **"hopeful stories":** Kathleen Kennedy acceptance speech, 2018 Academy Governors Awards, 18 November 2018.

391 **"making out on my couch":** Steven Spielberg speech in honor of Frank Marshall and Kathleen Kennedy, 2018 Academy Governors Awards, 18 November 2018.

392 **a few weeks into *E.T.*'s run:** Spielberg remembered this meeting happening "two weeks" into *E.T.*'s run in theatres, but the review of *Schindler's Ark* he remembered Sheinberg showing him appeared in the October 18 edition of the *New York Times*.

392 **"*E.T.* posters, bed sheets":** "Spielberg's Creativity," *New York Times*, 25 December 1982, 30.

392 **"I want you to read a book":** Scott Feinberg, "'Schindler's List': An Oral History of a Masterpiece," *Hollywood Reporter*, 21 February 2024. Accessed on 8 March 2025 at https://www.hollywoodreporter.com/movies/movie-features/schindlers-list-oral-history-steven-spielberg-liam-neeson-1235830436/.

392 **"Universal just bought the book":** Feinberg, "'Schindler's List': An Oral History of a Masterpiece."

393 **"my first 'adult' film":** Feinberg, "'Schindler's List': An Oral History of a Masterpiece."

393 **"I'm not Jewish":** Mike Fleming Jr., "Martin Scorsese, Leonardo DiCaprio & Robert De Niro on How They Found the Emotional Handle for Their Cannes Epic 'Killers Of The Flower Moon': The Deadline Q&A," *Deadline*, 20 October 2023. Accessed on 8 March 2025 at https://deadline.com/2023/10/martin-scorsese-interview-killers-of-the-flower-moon-leonardo-dicaprio-robert-de-niro-1235359006/.

393 **"Marty was intrigued":** Feinberg, "'Schindler's List': An Oral History of a Masterpiece."

393 **Ganis announced no movies:** Ivan Sharpe, "George Lucas' Secret Empire in Mill Valley," *San Francisco Examiner*, 5 June 1983, B1.

394 **"Once I was a dad":** "George Lucas Reveals What He Hopes His Obituary Says," *CBS News*, 15 December 2015. Accessed on 5 March 2025 at https://www.cbsnews.com/news/star-wars-creator-george-lucas-kennedy-center-honors-directing-career/.

394 **"who found some money":** Author interview with Schrader.

394 **"he was still pissed off" and account of meeting at WB:** Author interview with Schrader.

395 **"I was just watching how he worked":** Author interview with Dana Spiotta, 27 November 2024.

396 **"a way to live your life":** Author interview with Spiotta.

397 **"utopian society for filmmakers":** Cowie, *Coppola*, 193.

398 **"I liked it better":** Cowie, *Coppola*, 228.

398 **"more quiet life":** Goldstein, "Francis Ford Coppola Rarely Met a Deal He Couldn't Refuse."

399 **Film production companies insured themselves:** Robert Lindsey, "Pervasive Use of Cocaine Is Reported in Hollywood," *New York Times*, 31 October 1982, 1.

399 **"scared that we were all going to be killed":** *London Evening Standard*, 16 December 1986.

399 **"pain and fury":** E. Coppola, *Notes on the Making of "Apocalypse Now,"* 289.

400 **"I should have been there":** S.D., "'Il Faut Donner Tout Ce Qu'On A': Entretien avec Francis Ford Coppola," *Cahiers du Cinéma*, April 2012, 12. Translated by the author.

400 **"Gio only lived 22 years":** Goldstein, "Francis Ford Coppola Rarely Met a Deal He Couldn't Refuse."

400 **"I romanticized him":** Jill Kearney, "Francis Ford Coppola," *Mother Jones*, September 1988.

401 **"in his terrible handwriting":** Cowie, *Coppola*, 208.

401 ***It doesn't seem like I'm going to be able to undo this one*:** Cowie, *Coppola*, 231.

401 **"somehow still there":** Deborah Solomon, "Independent Streak: Questions for Francis Ford Coppola," *New York Times*, 16 December 2007. Accessed on 9 October 2024 at https://www.nytimes.com/2007/12/16/magazine/16wwln-Q4-t.html.

401 ***How important is anything*:** Cowie, *Coppola*, 3.
402 ***be part of everything*:** Cowie, *Coppola*, 3.
403 **"stink":** Susan Braudy, "Francis Ford Coppola," *The Atlantic*, August 1976. Accessed on 10 October 2024 at https://www.theatlantic.com/magazine/archive/1976/08/francis-ford-coppola/662909/.
403 **"Francis can get so esoteric" and FFC response:** Robert Lindsey, "Francis Ford Coppola: Promises to Keep," *New York Times*, 24 July 1988, Section 6, page 22.
404 **"Francis isn't just a filmmaker":** Goldstein, "Francis Ford Coppola Rarely Met a Deal He Couldn't Refuse."
404 **"a series of complicated financial transactions":** John Lippman, "Coppola Files for Bankruptcy a Third Time," *Los Angeles Times*, 1 July 1992. Accessed on 10 September 2024 at https://www.latimes.com/archives/la-xpm-1992–07–01-fi-1253-story.html.
405 **"Oh, that's Francis" and FFC equivalent:** Chang, *Zoetrope at 50*, 27.
405 **"George is probably his closest friend":** Author interview with Nazarian.

Epilogue

407 **"something that looks just like that":** Lane, "The Magician."
409 **"showcase how they leverage":** NVIDIA press release, September 2022. Accessed on 27 January 2025 at https://www.nvidia.com/en-us/on-demand/session/gtcfall22-a41351/.
410 **"drive significant long-term value":** Walt Disney Company press release, 30 October 2012. Accessed on 27 January 2025 at https://thewaltdisneycompany.com/disney-to-acquire-lucasfilm-ltd/.
410 **"executives really looking over":** Bruce Haring, "'The Marvels' Lacked On-Set Supervision, Bob Iger Admits in Analysis of Its Dismal Box Office," *Deadline*, 2 December 2023. Accessed on 27 January 2025 at https://deadline.com/2023/12/the-marvels-lacked-on-set-supervision-bob-iger-admits-1235649619/.
411 **"not meant to be successful":** David Fear, "Francis Ford Coppola: I Have Nothing Left to Lose," *Rolling Stone*, September 2024, 44.
411 **"Success ruined my father":** Stein, *West of Eden*, 52.
412 **"They're all going to be exactly like us":** Lane, "The Magician."

INDEX

About the Author

Paul Fischer is the author of *A Kim Jong-Il Production*—chosen as a best book of the year by *Kirkus Reviews*, NPR, Amazon, and *Library Journal*—and *The Man Who Invented Motion Pictures*, a *New York Times* Editors' Choice. His writing has appeared in the *New York Times*, the *Los Angeles Times*, the *Independent*, *Bright Wall/Dark Room*, and the *Narwhal.*

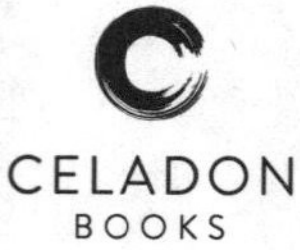

Founded in 2017, Celadon Books, a division of Macmillan Publishers, publishes a highly curated list of twenty to twenty-five new titles a year. The list of both fiction and nonfiction is eclectic and focuses on publishing commercial and literary books and discovering and nurturing talent.